Black, White & Olive Drab

The American South Series

EDWARD L. AYERS, EDITOR

Black, White & Olive Drab

Racial Integration at Fort Jackson, South Carolina,
and the Civil Rights Movement

ANDREW H. MYERS

UNIVERSITY OF VIRGINIA PRESS
CHARLOTTESVILLE AND LONDON

355.7
M996

University of Virginia Press
© 2006 by the Rector and Visitors of the University of Virginia
All rights reserved
Printed in the United States of America on acid-free paper

First published 2006

9 8 7 6 5 4 3 2 1

Library of Congress Cataloging-in-Publication Data

Myers, Andrew H., 1964–
    Black, white, and olive drab : racial integration at Fort Jackson, South Carolina, and the civil rights movement / Andrew H. Myers.
        p.   cm. — (American South series)
    Includes bibliographical references and index.
    ISBN-13: 978-0-8139-2575-2 (cloth : alk. paper)
    1. Fort Jackson (S.C.)—History—20th century. 2. United States. Army—African Americans—History—20th century. 3. African American soldiers—Civil rights—South Carolina—History—20th century. 4. South Carolina—Race relations—History—20th century. 5. Civil rights movements—South Carolina—History—20th century. 6. South Carolina—Politics and government—1865–1950. 7. South Carolina—Politics and government—1951– I. Title. II. Series.
    UA26.F664M94 2006
    355.7089'96073075771—dc22

2005037587

Contents

Acknowledgments | vii

Introduction: A Visit to Fort Jackson | 1

1. Organizational Racism at Fort Jackson during the Second World War | 5

2. Alienating Black Civilians: Columbia and Fort Jackson during the Second World War | 27

3. Tangled Connections and Lost Opportunities: Fort Jackson at the End of World War II | 54

4. The Open Secret of 1950: Army Integration at Fort Jackson | 74

5. Turning Out Soldiers: Fort Jackson after Integration | 92

6. Getting Them "Off Our Neck": Military Bureaucracy and Bus Desegregation | 105

7. School Desegregation on and around Fort Jackson: The Unintended Consequences of Federal Power | 123

8. Fort Jackson and the Desegregation of Public Facilities: Military-Social Relations at the Local, State, and National Levels | 136

9. Staying Out of Trouble: Fort Jackson Soldiers and Columbia Sit-ins | 160

vi | Contents

10. Counting Bodies in Columbia: Fort Jackson and
Equal Housing | 174

11. Fighting at Home and in Vietnam: Howard Levy,
the UFO Coffeehouse, and the Fort Jackson Eight | 189

12. The Forgotten Decade of the Civil Rights Movement:
The Seventies | 206

Notes | 221

Sources Consulted | 253

Index | 267

Acknowledgments

I have incurred many debts since beginning work on this project twelve years ago. Though retired, Paul Gaston continued serving as advisor for the dissertation that became the basis for this book. He has been a good mentor and friend. Walter Edgar welcomed me to Columbia, introduced me to key people, and infected me with his love for the history of South Carolina. Fred DeMag, Judy Matteson, and Bessie Williams of the Fort Jackson Museum gave invaluable assistance.

I was honored to have Vernon Burton and Bernard Nalty as outside readers. The detailed and thoughtful comments of these distinguished scholars have made this a much better work than it otherwise would be. I am also thankful to Susan Brady, Richard Holway, Angie Hogan, and Mark Mones at the University of Virginia Press for shepherding the manuscript through the publication process, and to Galen Schroeder for creating the index. All errors, of course, remain my own.

In addition to my colleagues at the Upstate campus of the University of South Carolina, I owe much to the following individuals: Debbie Avery, Ed Ayers, Brian Balogh, Ed Barber, Keller Barron, Julian Bond, Tom Brown, Catherine Flemming Bruce, Thorne Compton, Ted Dow, Bonnie Driggers, Gerald Driggers, Bob Ellis, Fritz Hamer, John Harden, Charles Hendricks, Tom Johnson, Fred Kameny, Clayton Kleckley, Cash Koeniger, Nelson Lichtenstein, Jim Loewen, John Hammond Moore, Margaret Myers, Steve O'Neill, Bill Parks, Charles Perdue, David Perry, Miles Richards, Wim Roefs, Hillyer Rudisill III, John Sproat, Homer Steedly, and Tibby Steedly.

My gratitude goes as well to the staffs at the following research facilities: Alderman Library, University of Virginia, Charlottesville; the Combined Arms Research Library, U.S. Army Command and General Staff College, Fort Leavenworth, Kansas; the Dwight D. Eisenhower Library,

viii | Acknowledgments

Abilene, Kansas; the Lyndon B. Johnson Library, Austin, Texas; the Harry Truman Library, Independence, Missouri; the Library of Congress, Washington, D.C.; the United States Army Center for Military History, Washington, D.C.; the Pentagon Library, Arlington, Virginia; the United States Army Infantry School Technical Library, Fort Benning, Georgia; the Richland County Public Library, Columbia, S.C.; the South Carolina Department of Archives and History, Columbia, South Carolina; the South Carolina State Library, Columbia, South Carolina; the Clemson University Special Collections, Clemson, South Carolina; the South Caroliniana and Thomas Cooper Libraries of the University of South Carolina, Columbia; and the National Archives and Records Administration in Washington, D.C., College Park, Maryland, and Suitland, Maryland.

Parts of chapter 3 were published in the *Proceedings of the South Carolina Historical Society.* Thanks go to Steve Lowe, Tracy Power, and Rodger Stroup for arranging for those portions to appear here.

The U.S. Army has affected this work in a number of positive ways that merit mention. I spent much of my childhood as an Army brat, attended college on an ROTC scholarship, and served more than four years on active duty in the Regular Army. Continuing my career as a Reserve officer kept me out of debt while going to graduate school, gave me the privilege of meeting many people of fine character, and provided me with a wealth of enriching experiences. In fact, the genesis for this book came after I had the opportunity to command basic training companies at Fort Jackson for two weeks at a time in 1993 and 1995. I must emphasize that my experiences, and the Army's agreement to release photographs and maps for this book, do not constitute Army endorsement.

I am grateful to the former Susan Rudisill, who while working at USC's South Caroliniana Library, brought me an obscure document pertaining to a 1967 court-martial at Fort Jackson. After striking up a conversation about my strange request and accepting my invitation to lunch, she critiqued drafts and has been my constant companion and friend. I thank her not only for her assistance but for becoming my wife and the mother of our son, Thomas.

My parents, Jesse and Chloe Myers, demonstrated extraordinary patience as I left a relatively secure career in the Regular Army to pursue my dream of becoming an historian. They were instrumental in helping me to accomplish the additional research and writing necessary to transform my dissertation into a book manuscript. For their love and encouragement, I dedicate this work to them.

Black, White & Olive Drab

Introduction

A Visit to Fort Jackson

In 1952, journalist Lee Nichols began researching race relations in the armed forces. Four years had passed since President Truman directed the services to integrate, and the newsman felt an article updating the situation would interest readers. Nichols worked for United Press International (UPI) in Washington, D.C. Through his contacts at the Pentagon, he met an Army major from the personnel section who advised him to go to Fort Jackson, South Carolina.

Nichols was puzzled that anyone would recommend going to a state where segregation remained the norm, but the major said that he was not authorized to say anything more.

"He refused to tell me why I should visit Fort Jackson or what I would find there," the reporter remembered.

Nichols obtained a week's leave of absence from UPI and drove to South Carolina. What he saw came as a pleasant surprise. As he remembered almost forty years later: "Here, adjacent to a major Southern city in full view of anybody who looked, was a fully integrated training base."[1]

Interviews reinforced this favorable first impression. He learned that the commanding general had, at his own initiative, mixed blacks and whites together during the summer of 1950. The decision made the post one of the first in the Army to implement the president's executive order on a large scale. The commander prevented possible unrest in the neighboring city of Columbia by persuading local editors to suppress the news. Nichols found the experiment had worked well. Civilians stayed calm, and soldiers of both races had positive things to say about integration.

The reporter used these recollections in his 1954 book *Breakthrough on the Color Front.* His account of Fort Jackson became part of the Defense Department's official history of armed forces integration, and the story has been repeated numerous times elsewhere.[2] In the introduction

2 | BLACK, WHITE & OLIVE DRAB

to the 1993 reprint of *Breakthrough,* Nichols claims on good authority that two Supreme Court justices read a copy of the manuscript as they pondered the *Brown* decision.[3]

Although the book remains one of the best works available on the subject of armed forces integration, it does not tell the complete story about Fort Jackson. Nichols was given the incorrect month during which the change occurred at the post. As a result, he oversimplifies the coordination that occurred between military authorities and local civilians. Additionally, he was not told about the surveys of racial attitudes conducted there the previous summer by social scientists, whose findings were classified until the mid-sixties. Furthermore, Nichols had no knowledge of the secret domestic intelligence and inspector general reports detailing the wave of violence involving blacks that surged on and around the post during the forties. These incidents, ironically, hastened the end of military segregation there and elsewhere.

Declassified documents and other sources have since emerged, revealing a more complex picture of events than anyone could have painted at that time Nichols wrote his book. They arouse curiosity as to how and why integration took place as early as it did at Fort Jackson. The passage of time gives rise to another intriguing question: What effect, if any, did armed forces integration have in the area around the South Carolina post during the civil rights movement that followed in the fifties and sixties?[4]

This is the kind of query that falls between the cracks of the categories by which the past has customarily been divided. Military historians devote most of their attention to periods of war and actual fighting.[5] Those who write about African American soldiers, sailors, airmen, or marines concentrate along similar lines.[6] Those who address desegregation of the services almost always trace the evolution of policy at the federal level.[7] Chroniclers of the civil rights movement have done local studies, but they usually emphasize lawsuits, legislation, and protest marches by civilians.[8] Exceptions to this compartmentalization exist, but they hardly abound.[9] Historians have largely left the field to social scientists.[10]

This book therefore has modest goals. first, it will determine how and why integration took place at a single post. Second, it will assess the impact of that change on the desegregation nearby of civilian buses, schools, houses, and public facilities. Throughout, it will examine ways in which commanders and staff at the installation level navigated challenges arising over racial issues in their workings with municipal authorities, state

Introduction | 3

politicians, federal legislators, and the upper echelons of the military bureaucracy and executive branch. It will also address how post leaders dealt with the potential for participation in civil rights demonstrations by soldiers under their command.

A regional study or comparison between different installations or services would be interesting as well, but those will require later volumes built upon works like this one. Fort Jackson is a good place to start for many reasons besides its location in the South and its being among the first to integrate. It belonged to the Army, which had more African Americans in terms of proportion or number than did the other services. National Guard and Army Reserve units also trained there. The desegregation of these components is an important, but neglected story. In addition, government-contracted scientists frequently visited Fort Jackson to conduct tests involving soldiers. Many of the experiments resulted in significant improvements to Army training techniques, which is ironic given that critics of racial integration in the ranks often voiced concerns about using the armed forces as a social laboratory.

The civilian environs of Fort Jackson have qualities that make the post an even more attractive candidate for a case study. The adjacent city of Columbia is the capital of a state in which one party, the Democrats, controlled a majority of offices from mayor to governor to senator during the period in question. As a consequence, the dynamics of local, state, and national power reveal themselves very clearly here. South Carolina's congressional delegation was notable for its involvement with military affairs. L. Mendel Rivers, who served as chairman of the House Armed Services Committee for much of the Vietnam War, took great interest in Fort Jackson even though he represented the Charleston district. J. Strom Thurmond, who held a Senate seat for almost half a century, was a two-star general in the Army Reserve. His office had a strong reputation for assisting uniformed constituents.

Columbia's unusually close relationship with Fort Jackson makes finding a link between military and civilian racial practices more likely than elsewhere. The post boosted a civilian economy otherwise dependent on the presence of the state government and the University of South Carolina. The mayor and other civic leaders regularly exchanged friendly visits with the commanding general and his staff. The local chamber of commerce had an active armed services committee. With the help of Chairman Rivers and the blessings of the post commander, Columbia actually annexed Fort Jackson into the city limits in 1968. No American municipality had ever done anything like this before.

4 | Black, White & Olive Drab

Finally, many nearby blacks had ties to the military that gave them an understanding of the post's potential for influencing civilian segregation. James Hinton, the leader of the state conference of the National Association for the Advancement of Colored People (NAACP), held a commission as an Army officer during World War I. The president of the Columbia chapter, E. A. Adams, was father of the highest-ranking African American to serve in the Women's Army Corps during World War II. Ethel Bolden, a pioneer in the desegregation of Columbia schools, was the wife of an Army veteran and a mother whose son became a space shuttle pilot and Marine Corps general. Before coming to South Carolina, journalist Osceola McKaine saw combat in Mexico with the "Buffalo Soldiers" of the Tenth Cavalry. Civil rights attorney and federal judge Matthew Perry helped construct barracks on Fort Jackson in 1941. Both he and his law partner Lincoln Jenkins later went through the induction center there as soldiers. Milton Kimpson, who directed the Greater Columbia Human Relations Council, underwent his basic training at the post. So, too, did James Felder, who served as the chief pallbearer at the funeral of President Kennedy and who subsequently led statewide efforts to register voters.

These personal connections are perhaps the most important legacies of black participation in the armed forces. As this study will reveal, the services had a limited ability to influence the civil rights movement. Genuine change came about as individuals, often shaped by contact with the military, became more active in their communities and began to influence legislators by expressing themselves at the ballot box. Installations like Fort Jackson helped to provide stability throughout this process by serving as models of successful integration. As the Pentagon major suggested to Lee Nichols in 1952, the post is worth a visit.

1
★☆

Organizational Racism at Fort Jackson during the Second World War

Because they were persuaded that what had happened was just a minor incident, and because they wanted to protect the "good name" of Fort Jackson, white newspapers of nearby Columbia never published the full story of the outbreak which happened at Fort Jackson on Sunday, April 20.

—PITTSBURGH COURIER, 14 June 1941

African Americans who joined the Army in 1941 knew they might have to dodge bullets at some point during their service, but none expected baptism by fire at Fort Jackson. That terrifying moment arrived for many on the night of 20 April in the barracks of the post "colored area." Black soldiers had brawled earlier in the day with white Civilian Conservation Corps (CCC) workers over use of a diving platform at a nearby lake. During the afternoon the unrest had festered, spreading through the segregated compound, the adjoining CCC tents, and a mile west to the encampment of the 121st Regiment of the Thirtieth Infantry Division. When these Georgia National Guardsmen learned that a Negro had dared to strike a white man, they grabbed their rifles. Some were in civilian clothes; others wore the uniform of the country whose constitution they had sworn to defend. Weapons in hand, about seventy of them started marching eastward.

The drama ended quickly, but the tension lingered. African American servicemen comprised a tiny minority at Fort Jackson. They lived in geographic and social isolation when not on duty. In their assigned jobs, Army policy and command structures excluded them from the infantry divisions that were the post's primary reason for being. Blacks toiled instead as "boys" alongside women, prisoners, and the physically impaired as part of the stage crew who supplied labor while the more capable white "men" acted out the drama of war. These conditions were hardly

6 | BLACK, WHITE & OLIVE DRAB

unusual for the time. Nevertheless, they are significant because the unfavorable reputation Fort Jackson acquired during the forties helped to lay the foundation for the post's integration a decade later.

★☆

Some readers might be surprised to learn that African Americans stationed at the installation during the first World War received far more respect than those stationed there for the Second. The year 1917 marked the creation of Camp Jackson and the assignment to it not only of the all-white Eighty-first Infantry Division but also the all-black 371st Infantry Regiment. After undergoing training in South Carolina, the latter unit fought in Europe as part of the French army. Its doughboys contributed to victories in several battles and won multiple decorations for valor. One of its soldiers, Cpl. Freddie Stowers, became the only African American of World War I to be awarded the Medal of Honor. After the armistice, the surviving members of the 371st marched in a victory parade down the streets of Columbia to the cheers of both blacks and whites.[1]

Much had changed by the time Camp Jackson reopened in 1939 as part of the American response to the German invasion of Poland. Although most senior leaders of the Army had served during the first World War, few of them knew about the effectiveness of African Americans who had fought with the French. Relying on controversial stories about "colored" units assigned to U.S. forces, they believed instead that blacks did not perform well under fire. They also feared a recurrence of a 1917 riot where soldiers had attacked white civilians in Houston, Texas.

As a consequence, War Department planners operated under the paradoxical assumption that African Americans made poor fighters who, when given arms and grouped in large numbers, created a violent, organized menace. Federal laws dating back to the Reconstruction era required the Regular Army to maintain four Negro combat arms regiments, but neither these nor any of the other black units raised during the early days of World War II were selected for frontline duty.[2]

Whereas Camp Jackson had hosted both a white division and a black regiment in 1917, only the former was assigned in 1939. The Sixth Infantry Division began training there that October. Those whites departed for corps-level maneuvers in April 1940 and did not return to South Carolina. Camp Jackson stood empty for several months.[3]

The tempo of operations picked up after the French surrendered to the Nazis two months later. Congress passed the first peacetime conscription act in American history. The War Department rechristened Camp Jackson as a "fort" and assigned to it the Eighth Infantry Division.

This all-white organization had the mission of training incoming draftees. No black units came with it.

Congress also mobilized eighteen divisions of the National Guard. One of them, the Thirtieth Infantry, was sent to Fort Jackson. It consisted of regiments from South Carolina, North Carolina, Tennessee, and Georgia. Although a few states at the time had units within their Guards set aside for blacks, these four did not.

The first African Americans to come to Fort Jackson were not soldiers, but civilians who helped with the enormous expansion of infrastructure that began in August 1940. Workers both black and white erected three thousand wooden buildings. They paved over a hundred miles of roads, improved railroad connections, laid sewage lines, constructed a water-filtration plant, strung wires for telephones and electricity, and built one of the most modern rifle ranges in the Army. Completed at the end of 1941, the $22-million project gave Fort Jackson the ability to house and train forty-three thousand soldiers.

The first African Americans to come to Fort Jackson for explicitly military purposes arrived in December 1940.[4] They were draftees reporting to the Post Induction Station. Here they underwent medical examinations to determine their fitness for duty. Those who met the standards took the oath of office and then went home briefly before returning for processing at the Fort Jackson Reception Station. There, they received items of personal equipment, filled out various forms for things like pay, and took aptitude tests to determine their occupational specialty.

The induction and reception stations handled blacks and whites on alternating days to avoid mixing the races.[5] All African Americans then went to other posts for basic training. The expense and time taken to transfer blacks elsewhere highlighted the illogic of segregation because, throughout its history, Fort Jackson's existence has revolved around the training of new soldiers.

There and elsewhere in the United States, the first eight weeks of initial indoctrination stayed remarkably simple and consistent over the course of the twentieth century. Common activities included marching, improving physical fitness, administering first aid, firing weapons, and learning the customs and courtesies of the Army.[6]

Blacks could easily have accomplished these tasks at Fort Jackson as they did during earlier and later decades; however, the program for World War II differed in one key respect. Rather than becoming generic fillers for units across the Army, soldiers who went through Fort Jackson during the first part of the forties eventually fought overseas under the

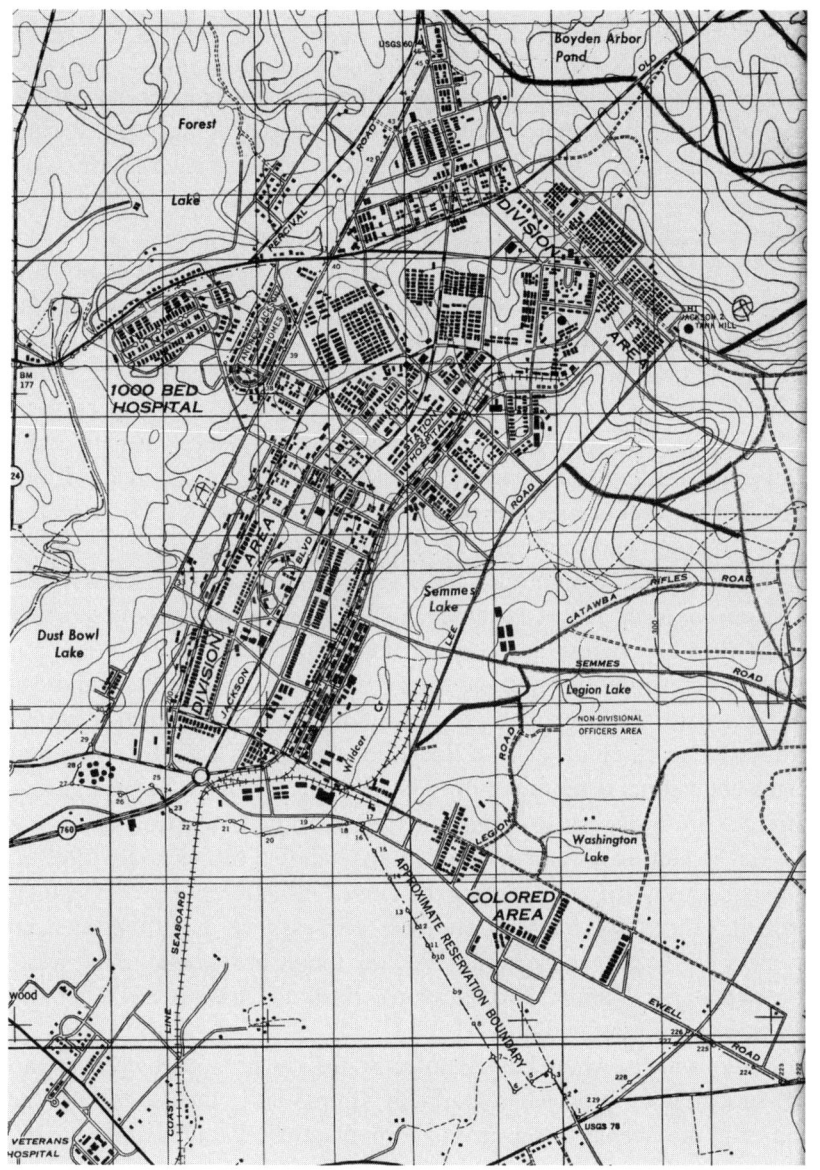

Fort Jackson, 1949. This map depicts the post much as it looked during the Second World War. (U.S. Army photograph, courtesy of the Fort Jackson Museum)

Organizational Racism at Fort Jackson | 9

command of the same men who first trained them. The Sixth, Eighth, and Thirtieth Divisions were all-white. African Americans had no corresponding organizations at the post to which they could be assigned.

The Japanese attack on Pearl Harbor created pressure to constitute forces where none had existed previously. In early 1942, the War Department developed what amounted to a military assembly-line. The Army selected groups of approximately 1,300 officers and sergeants to serve as the nuclei of new, 15,000-man divisions. These cadres initially worked as basic training instructors. Once this individual phase was complete, they joined their former pupils to practice operating together as squads, platoons, companies, battalions, regiments, and finally as whole divisions. After participating in corps-level maneuvers, they were considered ready for combat.

The War Department selected Fort Jackson to test the new concept when it activated the Seventy-seventh Infantry in March 1942. Over the next two years, the post also witnessed the births of the One Hundredth and 106th. These three consisted entirely of white men. Although the Army did raise two Negro infantry divisions, the Ninety-second and the Ninety-third, neither was created using this method, and neither was stationed in South Carolina.

Of course, not every soldier assigned to Fort Jackson belonged to a combat unit. Some drove trucks that hauled food, fuel, and ammunition for the people undergoing training. Others did paperwork at the post headquarters or worked in warehouses as part of what was called the "station complement." Still others staffed the hospital, served as police, or accomplished the various day-to-day maintenance vital to keep the place functioning.

These activities fell under the control of the Fourth Service Command, which had authority over posts across the South. The Fourth was part of the Army Service Forces, or ASF. Tactical units like the Seventy-seventh, One Hundredth, and 106th Divisions answered to the Army Ground Forces, or AGF. (The third major command within the United States was the Army Air Forces, or AAF, which eventually became a separate service after the war.)[7]

Many of the people who performed support tasks at Fort Jackson were South Carolinians whom doctors had classified as unfit for combat. S.Sgt. Ernest M. Lander Jr., for example, suffered poor eyesight. He taught classes at the post's Special Training Unit. There, he used his civilian experience as a college professor to give remedial instruction to

draftees who had failed to meet minimum standards on the entrance examination.[8]

German prisoners of war provided another important manpower source. Fort Jackson was the central headquarters for the twenty-eight POW camps in South Carolina. One of the compounds stood on the western edge of the reservation, and it housed two thousand prisoners. Besides assisting local farmers, these Germans repaired roads and performed similar tasks for the Army. They earned eighty cents per day. They could not contribute much, however, because the Geneva Convention forbade using prisoners directly in the war effort.[9]

Civilians comprised a large part of the labor force. In 1942, Fort Jackson employed over four thousand of them. Many were women. The first female employees arrived in February 1941, when six were hired as switchboard operators. Soon more came as exchange clerks, service club hostesses, secretaries, Red Cross workers, and laundresses.[10]

Female nurses played a vital role. The post eventually had over two hundred. Although the hospital hired some civilian professionals, the majority were commissioned officers belonging to the Army Nursing Corps.[11] In early 1943, Fort Jackson became the home for the 130 members of Detachment Number 1 of the Women's Army Auxiliary Corps (WAAC). Living in a specially constructed barracks with a laundry, ironing boards, and beauty shop, they performed clerical duties. The WAAC ceased being an auxiliary in July 1943 and became a full-fledged Women's Army Corps (WAC).

Fort Jackson's support personnel included almost all of the African Americans stationed there during World War II. Their numbers never exceeded five thousand people, but they performed a host of functions that made training of the infantry divisions possible.[12]

The first permanently assigned blacks came to Fort Jackson in December 1940. They were career noncommissioned officers from the four segregated regiments of the Regular Army (the Ninth and Tenth Cavalry and the Twenty-fourth and Twenty-fifth Infantry). Like their counterparts in the infantry divisions, these NCOs became a nucleus around which new units would form.[13]

Approximately five hundred privates came a month later. Most of them entered service from homes in Louisiana. Unlike most of the incoming whites of this rank, they had already completed basic training. A quarter of these soldiers were assigned to the station complement, where they worked at Fort Jackson's warehouses and supply facilities.

Organizational Racism at Fort Jackson | 11

The rest became truck drivers in a "colored" quartermaster battalion. Organizations like this one expanded and diversified as more soldiers arrived that spring. Gas supply companies carried fuel. Railhead companies loaded and unloaded train cars. Pack troops moved equipment with mules and horses. By June 1941, the post had over 1,200 African Americans assigned to organizations like these.[14]

In October, the War Department directed post commanders to include blacks as military policemen (MPs). The policy came in the wake of a series of racial incidents that occurred across the United States, including the April one at Fort Jackson.[15] African American soldiers were selected that fall for police duty. Training took place during the winter, and the Colored MP Detachment was activated in April 1942.[16] By June, it had reached its full strength of sixteen men.[17]

The MPs initially worked only at the segregated facilities for off-duty soldiers. They were not allowed to carry weapons until local black civilians mounted a protest.[18] They eventually were issued firearms. Their duties expanded to keeping order on local buses and patrolling black civilian neighborhoods in Columbia that soldiers frequented. Later, they helped to guard German prisoners of war.

Early 1942 also witnessed the activation of the first medical sanitation companies at Fort Jackson. The surgeon general had devised this type of unit a year earlier in an effort to find a place for the Medical Corps' share of black draftees. Soldiers in Fort Jackson's three companies provided unskilled labor at the hospital.[19]

African American women worked at the same facility. They belonged to WAC Detachment Number 2, which was activated at the post in 1943. "The women in the outfit, which was attached to the regional hospital, were doing the most menial work," one veteran remembered. "They were washing walls and carrying bed pans, and not much of anything else."[20]

The Army Nursing Corps remained all-white until 1944, but female black civilians like Georgia Davenport of Columbia were hired to tend patients at the Fort Jackson Hospital. African American women also worked at the segregated service club and PX. Three hundred and seventy-five had jobs at the post laundry. They comprised three-quarters of the work force there. None held supervisory positions. According to a 1944 report: "White foreladies are used because experience has shown that this class of colored people particularly prefer to work under a white person."[21]

All of these support organizations—civilian and military—fell un-

der the purview of the Fourth Service Command of the ASF. So, too, did a twenty-three-piece drum and bugle corps and a forty-voice chorus consisting of African American musicians that arrived in November 1943.[22]

Only a few black units stationed at Fort Jackson belonged to the combat-oriented AGF, and none stayed for long. The first was the 367th Infantry Battalion, which had orders to deploy to Liberia. Its 1,500 men moved to the post in October 1942 to await transit from an east coast port. Although local blacks welcomed them, the battalion's arrival sparked fears among whites that the Army was planning to station a division of such soldiers at Fort Jackson. Post spokesmen quelled these rumors. Delays caused the 367th to remain in South Carolina for over three months.[23]

In March 1944, the post received its first contingent of African American engineers, the 1700th Combat Engineer Battalion. Although it belonged to the AGF and was supposed to have prepared for war by training to clear mines and obstacles, complaints from soldiers indicate that they performed considerable unskilled labor. The battalion left for overseas duty after nine months.[24]

The AAF had blacks stationed nearby at Columbia Air Base. They belonged to the three chemical maintenance companies and comprised parts of two aviation squadrons. They apparently used the Fort Jackson Hospital and the segregated post facilities. Available sources provide few details about these men other than their participation on sports teams, but records of their existence appear as early as 1943. References to a motor pool and drivers suggest that many of these airmen performed similar work to that of a quartermaster truck company.[25]

Although duty in support units like these was an important, honorable way to serve, exclusion from the infantry divisions contributed to the prejudice, common among whites at the time, that African Americans had neither the courage nor ability to fight. The national command structure within the United States helped to perpetuate this belief by relegating most of them to duty with physically disabled white men, prisoners of war, civilians, and women. Perceptions of inferiority were magnified all the more at places like Fort Jackson, which had no black combat units assigned for any significant length of time.

President Franklin D. Roosevelt himself helped to drive this point home during March 1941, when he and the Army chief of staff toured the post. They spent all of their time observing the Eighth and Thirtieth Infantry Divisions. British prime minister Winston Churchill and Lord Mountbatten similarly ignored African Americans when they came to

Organizational Racism at Fort Jackson | 13

Fort Jackson in June 1942. Churchill later recalled: "I . . . visited . . . an Army Corps trained in South Carolina and we saw there the spectacle of what you may call the mass production of divisions. . . . This is an achievement which the soldiers of every other country will always study with admiration and envy."[26] Mountbatten also wrote about his visit: "Of the many remarkable and inspiring sights I saw on the tour the one that made the greatest impression was the sight of the 77th Division marching by in review order like veterans."[27] None of these leaders had anything to say about the quartermaster battalions or station complement.

Other factors as well helped to make African American soldiers in South Carolina feel alienated. When not on duty, they lived in what maps and aerial photographs of the times labeled the "colored area." It sat on low ground near Wildcat Creek. Mirroring many civilian communities, a set of railroad tracks divided this part of the post from the main cantonment. Parallel rows of warehouses heightened the sense of separation.[28]

The white Eighth Infantry Division had set up tents on this land in 1940, but it moved after completion of the new barracks. Blacks began occupying the site in January 1941. They shared it with three companies of CCC workers, who lived nearby until another camp for whites was built on higher ground. African Americans passing through the induction and reception stations on their way to other posts were also billeted in the "colored area." Construction started in February on twenty barracks to augment the tent city.[29]

Building began at the same time on recreational facilities for black servicemen. Soon, they had a separate PX, guesthouse, and theater.[30] The service club for African Americans held its debut in October 1941. Officially designated Club Number 3, it had a ballroom, lounge chairs, writing desks, and a 500-volume library. Fifty women from Columbia and 150 soldiers attended the opening.[31]

Dances like this one marked a high point of social life. Lonely young men had the opportunity to socialize with the opposite sex in a wholesome environment. Black female students came from two nearby institutions, Allen University and Benedict College. Some women traveled from as far away as Claflin College in Orangeburg. Local bands like June's Swingmasters provided the music.[32]

Distinguished African Americans visited the post occasionally. For example, heavyweight boxing champion Joe Louis came to Fort Jackson in January 1944 as part of a national tour. He served during World War II as a sergeant, and the Army used him to build morale. Sergeant Louis shook hands with patients at the station hospital and gave a demonstration of

14 | BLACK, WHITE & OLIVE DRAB

his skills by sparring a few rounds at the post gymnasium with a member of his entourage. His visit excited not just blacks but also whites and the local press. Despite his fame, he ate in the colored-area mess hall.[33]

Benjamin O. Davis Sr., the first African American brigadier general in the Regular Army, toured the post on a couple of occasions. Army leaders avoided placing black officers in positions where they would supervise white officers, so they made General Davis an inspector for the War Department. He came to Fort Jackson in 1942 and 1944. In a question that revealed the aspirations of many black soldiers at the post, one of the men asked the general if he could join the prestigious Tuskegee Airmen. General Davis answered that the chances were slim, diplomatically adding that the Army had a long "reserve" list for fliers.[34]

African American soldiers had other ways to spend their off-duty time when not welcoming special guests like Louis and Davis. The service club held talent shows and drama readings. Occasionally the Army sponsored special shows for blacks at the theater. A glee club sang spirituals at the station hospital, and a quartet from that group performed over the radio. Post authorities also used the theater to show training films, particularly every April during Negro Health Week. This campaign was part of an effort to reduce the high venereal disease rate that plagued black soldiers in disproportionate numbers.[35]

Negro Health Week activities also took place in Chapel Number 18, which, when not hosting lectures on venereal disease, served the religious needs of African American soldiers. Chaplain Feltham S. James, a white minister, coordinated most of the activities during the early years of the war. A few black chaplains stayed briefly, but none was assigned permanently until late 1943.[36]

The hot, sticky South Carolina weather made swimming a popular pastime for soldiers of all races. African Americans had two bodies of water available: the Washington Lake (also known as YMCA Lake) and the Legion Lake, both located just north of the "colored area." The Red Cross offered a special class for blacks to receive training as lifeguards.[37]

Besides swimming, blacks engaged in a variety of sports. Cpl. George R. Ledbetter won the Negro Tennis Championship in August 1943. That summer, the 274th Quartermaster Battalion hosted a track meet. Its four companies fielded teams for assorted sprints, vaults, and throws. The Post Colored Service Detachment sponsored a highly regarded basketball team, the Fort Jackson Rams. It earned an enviable record over several seasons and attracted attention from the white press. The team was not allowed to compete against whites, however. The Rams instead

Organizational Racism at Fort Jackson | 15

played other black squads like the one at Allen University. The Army even provided vehicles to travel to games hundreds of miles away.[38]

Ironically, local transportation posed a greater challenge. The Army operated a separate bus for African Americans and went so far as to build a segregated shelter in which they could wait.[39] Off-post, city ordinances required blacks to sit in the rear of buses. Trains had segregated passenger cars. Soldiers from Fort Jackson sometimes became embroiled in disputes over seating.[40]

Blatant segregation on-post supposedly ended in March 1943 when—as a result of pressure from civil rights groups and a number of racial incidents involving both civilians and soldiers—the War Department issued a directive forbidding racial discrimination at federal facilities.[41] The policy covered exchanges, theaters, service clubs, and any government-owned or -operated transportation. It had one loophole, however. Local commanders could assign facilities and buses on a unit-by-unit basis. The distance of the "colored area" from the rest of Fort Jackson meant that segregation could continue. The accidental drowning in September 1943 of a black private at a previously all-white lake suggests that some integration may have taken place, but complaints to the War Department about "colored" and "white" signs at the post persisted as late as 1947.[42]

Black soldiers had several sources of news besides the local, white-controlled *Columbia Record* and the *State* papers. The biweekly *Army Times* provided one alternative. Almost every issue featured a positive story about African American servicepeople. In addition, the *Army Times* published a four-page supplement produced by the Fort Jackson Information Office. This section regularly contained stories about black activities on-post.

Occasionally, the editors of the *Army Times* included items that African Americans would have found offensive. One issue of the national edition contained a carton from Camp Van Dorn, Mississippi, in which a white private attempts to catch the eye of a pretty WAC at a train station. Desperate for female attention, he dons blackface and dresses as a porter to carry her bags. Not surprisingly, Camp Van Dorn experienced serious racial disturbances during the war.[43] Another cartoon depicted a minstrel-like soldier at an induction station who quipped, "Can I phone my folks I'm abducted now, suh?"[44]

The information office at Fort Jackson added similar items. The following anecdote that appeared in the November 1941 supplement reveals much about white perceptions of black soldiers:

16 | BLACK, WHITE & OLIVE DRAB

> First Lieutenant Frederic W. Symmes of Company D, 240th Quartermaster was checking outposts one night this week when he came upon one of his colored sentries unarmed.
>
> "Soldier," he demanded, "if you're not armed, how would you expect to repell [sic] any intruder on your post here?"
>
> "Ah'd knock'em down with one of these, suh," replied the colored boy, revealing a huge rock concealed in each pocket.
>
> "You wouldn't really throw one of those at anybody, would you?" the amazed OD [Officer of the Day] questioned.
>
> "Yessuh," the sentry assured him. "But Ah'd throw'em easy, suh."[45]

Black soldiers certainly did not want to be insulted. Instead of the *Army Times,* many of them subscribed by mail to newspapers like the *Atlanta Daily World,* the *Baltimore Afro-American,* and the *Chicago Defender.* In addition, they had access to the local *Palmetto Leader* and the *Lighthouse & Informer.*

The *Palmetto Leader* was the more conservative of the latter two. Its editors often reprinted Fort Jackson press releases verbatim. Consequently, articles often put a positive spin on the worst of circumstances. For example, one story featured a black military police sergeant who had just escorted a batch of German prisoners back to South Carolina. He described the African American troops he had seen overseas: "Those boys didn't know the meaning of the word rest—they labored 24 hrs. a day, seven days a week! If we had more Negro Quartermaster outfits in North Africa, loading and unloading and other supply problems that now plague the American Army just wouldn't be known."[46]

The *Lighthouse & Informer* had a more skeptical outlook. As the next chapter of this book will detail, its editor, John McCray, did not hesitate to expose the racism of white Fort Jackson officials. Post intelligence agents considered the paper subversive enough to monitor regularly.[47]

The newspaper that caused the most concern among whites at Fort Jackson was the *Pittsburgh Courier.* One of its writers, P. L. Prattis, who had little favorable to say about the treatment of blacks anywhere in the Army, wrote an especially scathing article about the post in 1941. Among other things, he described how authorities there misassigned well-educated African Americans and denied them adequate recreational facilities. He also painted two high-ranking officers as insensitive racists. Rather than take these criticisms to heart, Fort Jackson officials dismissed the story as propaganda. Indeed, the intelligence officer used that word explicitly in his monthly reports to the Fourth Service Command.[48]

Organizational Racism at Fort Jackson | 17

In 1943, two black soldiers accused a white lieutenant at Fort Jackson of confiscating and burning their stack of the *Courier*. The national editor informed the War Department that he might attempt to sue the officer. Officials in Washington demanded a quick reply from Fort Jackson. In the resulting letter, the post commander said that he had not banned the *Courier*. He nevertheless justified the confiscation by asserting that the soldiers did not have a permit to sell anything on-post.[49]

Even if black soldiers at Fort Jackson did read the *Courier*, they remained relatively uninformed. Ultimately, they had to rely on word of mouth, which led to exaggerations. No doubt rumors contributed to a general sense of alienation and insecurity. Moreover, the black national press may even have served to demoralize them further. Stories about the exploits of the Tuskegee Airmen may have reminded them that African Americans in other places did more than unskilled labor. In South Carolina, they could only watch the white infantry divisions from the sidelines.

Black soldiers wrestled with a tangle of emotions. The Army offered many of them opportunities for employment unmatched in the civilian world, yet some felt stifled by unchallenging assignments and lack of advancement opportunity. The military provided food, clothing, and medical care, yet it denied African Americans their human dignity. Success as a soldier meant following the rules, yet obedience implied acquiescence to an unjust system. How an individual reconciled these contradictions depended largely on education, social origin, and rank.

Most black servicemen at Fort Jackson came from the South. They had endured the poverty, hunger, disease, and violence that came with life at the bottom of the social order in the nation's poorest region. Unless they migrated to the North, most had few civilian alternatives to a life of hard labor on the margins of subsistence. Consequently, even before the war, the Army had little difficulty recruiting or keeping blacks.

The *Pittsburgh Courier* featured an African American who typified the average black soldier. Angus Williams went through the Fort Jackson Induction Station in June 1941. Prior to volunteering, he worked as a farm laborer in Bamberg, South Carolina. His photograph indicates that he was a brawny, strong young man. As a civilian, he earned sixty cents per day plus room and board in a wretchedly poor part of the state. By joining the Army, he increased his monthly salary by more than two dollars and received the additional bonuses of clothing and medical care. The doctor who examined Williams commented that eagerness to join and anxiety over possibly failing the medical screening had caused an ele-

vated heart rate. The inductee also struggled with the eye test because could not read well enough to name the letters on the chart. Even so, he passed the physical and eventually went to Fort Bragg for basic training.[50]

Many black soldiers had difficulty with the entrance examination. The Inspector General's Office at Fort Jackson studied the problem in 1943 after the induction station rejected 2,360 out of 4,756 African Americans (49.6 percent) for substandard scores during a single month. The investigating officer concluded that many of the questions on the test bore no relation to the life experiences of poor, rural blacks.[51] As a consequence, thousands of African Americans who might have contributed to the war did not. Low scores also limited those who met the minimum requirements. Lists in the *Army Times* of Fort Jackson soldiers selected for technical training and officer candidate school make no mention of anybody going from the black units.

Not all southern blacks fit this mold. Cpl. George C. McDemmond, for example, had a college education, and he had worked as an assistant supervisor in the Work Projects Administration (WPA) before the war. According to one colonel, he also had experience working in hospitals. Regardless, he remained a junior NCO in the medical section of the station complement. Corporal McDemmond showed his dissatisfaction by requesting additional training and a new assignment. Although his request was not granted, he later received promotion to sergeant.[52]

The African American women in WAC Detachment Number 2 were on average better schooled and came from a more refined social background than did their male counterparts. Two of them tried to do something about the menial labor that the detachment performed in the station hospital. They wrote a letter to the commander and worked out an agreement for the women who did not have skills to receive additional training. One of the two, Dorothy Daily Jones, said, "We convinced them that it was a waste to use expensive WACs for jobs that comparatively inexpensive civilians could do."[53]

Not always, however, did the chain of command at Fort Jackson respond favorably. A black military policeman said in a 1944 letter that he was threatened with a court-martial for complaining about racial discrimination and requesting a transfer away from the Fourth Service Command. He said: "It has been my duty to serve at several 'German Prison Camps' as Provost Sgt. throughout South Carolina and Georgia. On my oath German prisoners are treated better than the Colored Soldiers are treated in the South under Southern White Army Officers."

The sergeant added that commanders also discouraged African Amer-

Organizational Racism at Fort Jackson | 19

icans from seeking help from outside authorities, even ones within the Army. "I know of one Commanding Officer who threatened his entire Battalion with violence if they went to Gen. Davis with a complaint while he was visiting Ft. Jackson, S.C.," he said.[54]

African American MPs like this sergeant labored under a double burden. They endured all the humiliation suffered by blacks, but they also were the means by which Fort Jackson authorities enforced the prevailing social order. Besides guarding German prisoners, they patrolled segregated buses and civilian black neighborhoods. At what point did controlling unruly soldiers become accommodation to a racist system? At what point did black military policemen become latter-day house slaves and "Uncle Toms"?

Black servicemen occasionally engaged in mass protest. On 22 October 1943, the entire 702nd Maintenance Company at Columbia Air Base refused to attend a formation. Five privates had organized their comrades the previous night. The commander issued a direct order for all soldiers to assemble, and the rebellion ended.[55] Unfortunately, no other information about these events is extant.

Post intelligence reports during the war often described racial conflicts at the Columbia Air Base. At least four disturbances occurred on local buses in which black servicemen sat in front, talked back, or assaulted the driver.[56] In November, a black airman told a white dispatcher at the motor pool that he would "break his G — D — head with a stick."[57] During the summer of 1944, an altercation between a black airman and white civilian nearly resulted in a lynching. In this incident, the serviceman had fought with a white teenager who had passed him at high speed in a car. The youth's friends became involved and gave chase to the soldier. MPs took the African American into custody before the group could harm him. Air base authorities described the man as "race conscious and hard to handle." They transferred him immediately to Kentucky. A few days later, three white men with blackjacks and pistols accosted three black soldiers who had just stepped off a bus. According to civilian eyewitnesses, one of the men was the father of the boy involved in the previous fight. "This isn't the one we want," said the man, who released the African Americans unharmed.[58]

Tensions at Fort Jackson remained high, too. A soldier from the all-black 1700th Engineer Battalion sent two letters to the *Pittsburgh Courier* in 1944. In the first, he said that he was being forced to work eighteen to twenty hours a day. He also complained about enforcement of a midnight curfew by the military police and subsequent fines levied by the

officers in his command. He did not give his name because he feared retribution.[59] A day later, he sent a second letter in which he claimed that post authorities were allowing the military police to beat and even shoot soldiers from his unit. Revealingly, he said that members of his unit were doing the same kind of work as prisoners and that the prisoners were allowed greater freedom than they were. "We are being taught to be cowards here at Fort Jackson in the largest respect," he said. "Reference is again made especially to the 1700th Combat Engineer Battalion where men are treated worse than dogs."[60]

The *Pittsburgh Courier* did not cover the story or even print the letters, probably because some of the charges were unfounded. No evidence exists to substantiate the claim of murder. People in the Army often worked eighteen- to twenty-hour days regardless of race. Everybody, not just blacks, had to obey a midnight curfew when off-duty.

Evidence does support the complaint that the justice system treated African Americans more harshly than whites. The Army did not preserve records of low-level courts-martial, but a domestic intelligence report for October 1945 mentions that the Fort Jackson stockade held 250 whites and 45 blacks, a highly disproportionate number given that African Americans never comprised more than 8.3 percent of the post population.[61]

Regardless of its accuracy, the soldier's plea shows how segregation encouraged blacks to view their world in racial terms. It demonstrates how marginalized they felt at Fort Jackson. A poem written by Cpl. Lonnie Boykin of the post MP detachment and published in the *Army Times* hints at the despondency African Americans there must have felt:

> Our Victory lies over the Ocean
> Our Freedom lies over the Sea
> So I think I'll go over the ocean
> And bring back that Victory with me. . . .[62]

The newspaper editors cut short the poem, leaving readers to wonder if Corporal Boykin intended to bring back his freedom with him as well.

African American senior NCOs faced even greater challenges. Like military policemen, they inhabited the twilight between two worlds. Among the first black sergeants to arrive at Fort Jackson was 1st Sgt. Bennie Perry. A native of Albany, Georgia, he belonged to the Regular Army and served previously at Fort Benning, Georgia. He came to South Carolina as part of the cadre sent in December 1940. He became the senior sergeant of Company G, Twenty-eighth Quartermaster Truck Regiment.

First Sergeant Perry testified in a 1941 investigation concerning sev-

Organizational Racism at Fort Jackson | 21

eral incidents that occurred between white military policemen and black civilians from Columbia. Apparently he had been at a town brothel retrieving two of his soldiers when one of the altercations happened. During testimony, Perry demonstrated the kind of diplomacy his position required. "If I ask you some questions that will make your friends and associates think less of you as a man, you do not have to answer it," the interrogator told him. The obliqueness of the responses belies the NCO's attempt to uphold his manhood. When asked if he knew anything about MP treatment of civilians, he did not answer, "I don't know." Instead, he said, "I really couldn't answer that truthfully." When asked if the black madam was operating a brothel or liquor store, he said, "I wouldn't say what kind of place she was running but it didn't look suitable to me." When pressed for details about a rumor concerning MP brutality, he said: "I'd rather not say anything about it." When asked if white MPs verbally abused black soldiers, he said: "Not in my presence."

"I makes it my business" to check on soldiers in Columbia, first Sergeant Perry said, but he displayed an incredible ignorance and lack of observation—at least in his testimony. In return for such deference, first Sergeant Perry received a certain amount of respect. The white MPs "treats me swell," he said. "[I] always go there to the Desk Sergeant and he immediately gives me all the assistance I want." They were "always very gentlemanly about it."[63]

Not all black sergeants exercised such restraint. M.Sgt. Linwood Beverly of the station complement lodged a complaint in Washington when the Seaboard Railroad refused to serve him a meal.[64] This NCO differed from first Sergeant Perry in a substantial way, however. Although he held higher rank than most of his comrades, he did not have nearly as much responsibility. First Sergeant Perry had to choose his words and actions more carefully.

The example of another African American sergeant underscores the precariousness of Perry's position. In 1943, several white soldiers at the Fort Jackson Reception Station were placed on a barracks cleaning detail under the supervision of a black NCO. They later complained to the leaders of their hometown American Legion, who wrote to South Carolina senator Ellison "Cotton Ed" Smith. "Both races have a place in the war," the letter said, but "the colored man's place is not in charge of any Southern white man."

Rather than defend the authority of black sergeants, the post executive officer answered the inquiry by denying the accusation. "All fatigue details of white soldiers are supervised by white men or white non-

22 | BLACK, WHITE & OLIVE DRAB

commissioned officers," he said. "The only contact by these details with a colored man is when the colored janitor . . . hands out brooms, mops, buckets, etc., to be used by the details." The executive officer added: "the colored janitor has no control or direction over the fatigue details."[65]

First Sergeant Perry appeared to reconcile himself to the situation at Fort Jackson by trying to keep his soldiers out of trouble and establishing a rapport with the military police. "I am always down to the headquarters building looking out for the colored soldiers," he said. "I promised to help Colonel Page [the provost marshal] all I could." Perry made certain that his subordinates behaved. "When we were taking Privates Pompey and Stoval back to the Camp I made them stop talking back to the MPs," he said. "I made them shut up, and reported it back to the company commander."[66]

The first sergeant's relationship with the company commander was a main point of racial interaction. Almost all of the officers who led African American troops at Fort Jackson were white. Details about the few black lieutenants who served there are sketchy. This situation existed for three reasons. First, most African American officers were assigned elsewhere to black infantry regiments. Second, Army policy did not permit black officers to supervise white ones, which prevented most African Americans from rising above the rank of lieutenant or captain. Third, having significant numbers of black officers would have required additional accommodations for meals and quarters. The lack of quality white officers compounded the problems. African American units often had inept, unmotivated leaders who lacked the ability or drive to find a position elsewhere. Moreover, the Army often assigned southern whites to lead black units on the grounds that they had more experience dealing with African Americans.

Fort Jackson had more than its share of southern officers, and true to stereotype, many of them held condescending, insensitive, and racist views. The attitude pervaded the upper echelons. In an attempt to show his empathy with blacks during an interview with a *Pittsburgh Courier* reporter, the chief personnel officer for the post boasted that his grandfather had been the second largest slaveholder in South Carolina.[67]

Not all white officers shared these views, and even if they did, not all of them permitted their prejudices to disrupt duty performance. Lt. Gene Kaiser of the 274th Quartermaster Battalion received the Soldier's Medal for rescuing one of his subordinates from drowning.[68] Capt. W. E. Wilson, who commanded the 274th, made the effort to train his men on the firing range and personally awarded them their marksmanship

Organizational Racism at Fort Jackson | 23

badges.[69] While returning from leave, a white lieutenant and private from Fort Jackson worked hand-in-hand with a black corporal to save the lives of thirteen people after their bus plunged into a river.[70] Another white lieutenant asked a black soldier to sit down next to him on a Columbia bus only to have a white man threaten them with a revolver.[71]

At the highest levels, white officers preferred to steer clear of controversy. The post commander, Brig. Gen. Royden Beebe, tried to minimize racial problems and suppress complaints. When the glare of publicity struck him, however, he deftly tried to court black favor. After the negative stories appeared in the *Pittsburgh Courier* in 1941, he held a review parade for his African American troops. In June 1943, when racial incidents peaked at Columbia Air Base and elsewhere, he threw out the first ball at a game played by the 723rd Medical Sanitation Company "Red Caps."

Beebe's successor, Duncan Richart, was just as careful. Previously, he had been assigned to the Ninth Cavalry Regiment and was one of the few white officers to have worked for Brigadier General Davis. Richart welcomed his former supervisor warmly during inspection visits to Fort Jackson. Like Beebe, Richart held review parades for his black troops, and he even awarded a Good Conduct Medal to Master Sergeant Beverly, who had earlier complained to the War Department about railroad segregation. Conditions under Richart's tenure, however, were not much better than they had been under Beebe's.

Although many African American officers served as doctors and chaplains, few, if any, came to Fort Jackson. Available records make no mention of black doctors, and the post's first permanent black chaplain did not arrive until 1943. He was 1st Lt. Llewellyn T. Thornhill, and he served in the 274th Quartermaster Battalion. He had been a pastor in West Virginia prior to entering the Army. Before him, the only black chaplains had belonged to the 367th Infantry. Capt. George W. Williams arrived soon thereafter. He had preached as a Methodist minister in nearby Sumter, South Carolina, prior to joining the Army.[72]

Like military policemen and sergeants, black chaplains were torn between conflicting forces. On one hand, tending to the spiritual needs of soldiers helped the war effort. A person at peace with his soul made a better fighter. On the other hand, a good chaplain was supposed to serve as an advocate for the troops. All military ministers faced this conundrum, but the racial factor created an additional burden. Moreover, white authorities sometimes suspected African American chaplains of subversion. A local domestic intelligence report for June 1943 claimed that black religious leaders had hatched a nationwide plot to undermine the

24 | BLACK, WHITE & OLIVE DRAB

United States. It said: "Negro chaplains are believed to be the chief perpetrators of this plan within the Army because of their superior rank and education."[73]

An Armywide shortage better explains the lack of African American chaplains at Fort Jackson than any white fears of insurrection. Blacks simply did not have sufficient numbers to pose a threat to the large, well-armed population of white infantrymen. Indeed, the only major racial incident at the post involved trying to control the latter, not the former.

The violence began on the afternoon of 20 April 1941. It involved black soldiers from Company G of the Twenty-eighth Quartermaster Truck Regiment, where first Sergeant Perry was the ranking NCO and where CCC workers were living nearby in tents next to the "colored area."[74] Both the soldiers and the civilians had been swimming at nearby Washington Lake because the post engineers had cut off running water. Apparently, the white men "ducked" one of the black soldiers underwater after he attempted to use a diving platform occupied by the whites.

The CCC workers were natives of South Carolina and Georgia. They probably resented having to share with the black troops. According to the subsequent investigation, the African American soldier was known as a "troublemaker." The incident escalated into rock throwing and the brandishing of sticks. Several truckloads of blacks reinforced their comrades, and a general melee ensued. Two white lieutenants broke up the fight and sent both groups back to their quarters.

The sergeant in charge of the blacks—presumably first Sergeant Perry—issued instructions to keep all white people out of the area. Later in the afternoon, according to unconfirmed reports from the time, African American soldiers may also have assaulted a white from the Thirtieth Infantry Division who entered the compound.

Tensions spread to the all-white 121st Regiment of the Thirtieth, which was then located in the part of the main cantonment closest to the "colored area." Rumors flew that eight white men had been killed. Approximately sixty-five to seventy-five of the Georgia National Guardsmen grabbed rifles and ammunition before heading off in a group toward the "colored area." Two sources claim they had machine guns, too.[75] That they were able to obtain bullets, which are normally locked away separately, suggests that some officers and sergeants were involved. Before they could reach the black compound, however, the military police arrived and sent them back to their barracks.

The white soldiers made another attempt to exact revenge two hours later. This time their numbers swelled to over four hundred people. The

Organizational Racism at Fort Jackson | 25

African American troops knew what was coming. Approximately 350 of them stood guard in a perimeter as the infantrymen shot into the barracks. Sources differ as to whether the blacks fired back or fled into the woods. The MPs arrived once more to send the whites back. This time the authorities maintained a continual presence along Washington Road, which connected the "colored area" to the billets of the 121st.

Royden Beebe had not yet been assigned to Fort Jackson, and the commanding general of the Thirtieth Division was technically in charge. The post executive officer, Lt. Col. Frank Whittaker, handled most of the day-to-day business. He attempted to minimize the incident by calling it a "comedy of errors." He told reporters that "it didn't look like a race matter or anything like that." He persuaded them that the altercation had been minor and that any negative articles they published would sully the good name of Fort Jackson. He spoke only of the fight at the lake with the CCC, however, and ignored the more serious shooting by the 121st. The white reporters went along with the charade. Nobody questioned why post authorities had sent trucks into Columbia to bring back all black soldiers on the night of the incident or why the military had requested riot guns from the civilian police.

Thanks to Lieutenant Colonel Whittaker's efforts, both the *Columbia Record* and the *State* relegated the story to the inner pages. The *Pittsburgh Courier* carried a brief headline, too. The *Militant* printed an account by a Fort Jackson soldier, but that journal had a limited circulation. The gravity of the incident did not come to light on a large scale until *Pittsburgh Courier* reporter P. L. Prattis visited the post two months later. He interviewed eyewitnesses and saw the bullet holes in the barracks.[76]

The violence was part of a nationwide series of incidents.[77] The unrest started earlier in April when a black soldier at Fort Benning, Georgia, was found hanging by his neck from a tree, hands tied behind his back. Later, a black NCO was beaten in Louisiana; white MPs at Fort Bragg shot to death an African American soldier; and a race riot took place at Camp Robinson, Arkansas. All of these incidents caused grave concern at the War Department.

Back at Fort Jackson, the commander of the Thirtieth Division convened an investigating board and then acted on its recommendations. He issued an order designating Washington and Legion lakes exclusively for black use. He then directed the Thirtieth Division to conduct classes in race relations, establish tighter control over its ammunition supply, and remind its officers of the sections in the military regulations governing "rioting."[78] Because he acted so swiftly, the *Pittsburgh Courier's*

26 | BLACK, WHITE & OLIVE DRAB

exposure of the truth had few repercussions for him. This general was re-lieved of command in 1942, but that decision likely had more to do with negative reports from maneuvers that had taken place earlier that spring.[79] No racial incidents as serious as the ones of 20 April 1941 would again occur on-post.

Although the sources of unhappiness for black soldiers during World War II were legion, the one that most stood out within the Army was the command structure itself. In no other part of American society did racism permeate so deeply into the organizational fabric or with such a bold stamp of federal government approval. The military is an institu-tion, but the term "institutional racism" does not apply in this case. Those words were taken and defined during the 1960s to mean the subtle discrimination within a society resulting from unequal power relation-ships or unspoken assumptions.[80] "Organizational racism" or "structural racism" might be more appropriate labels for the Jim Crow military.

This system became unwieldy on a national scale as available Amer-ican manpower dwindled toward the end of the war. In fact, the Army began to integrate some infantry companies in Europe by early 1945. The old arrangement continued to work with considerable efficiency, how-ever, at places like Fort Jackson. As P. L. Prattis wrote in his 1941 article about conditions at the South Carolina post: "The end result is to create the impression among whites that the Negroes are not quite up to them and to cause the Negro soldier's heart to burn with envy, because he can't, without a lot of explaining, say to a white soldier, 'I'm a soldier just like you.'"[81]

2

★☆

Alienating Black Civilians

Columbia and Fort Jackson during the Second World War

There were either two or three, I believe three, niggers who distinguished them-
selves from the rest of the crowd. They were evidently preachers or ministers. . . .
I thought they didn't belong in with the crowd because the rest of the niggers in
there were seemingly a working class of people and these niggers had their Sun-
day clothes on. . . . One of these nigger men dressed up said, "We are a commit-
tee, and we are here to prevent the officers and the military policemen from
beating up our people. . . ." I replied to him that the military police did not beat
up niggers or any other civilians.

—Pfc. John Calhoun, Fort Jackson Military Police, 1941

Fort Jackson had a limited effect on the civil rights movement in the surrounding area partly because of the discord that existed between local
black leaders and post authorities. During the early days of World War II,
the latter turned a blind eye to the blatant and clearly unconstitutional
beatings of African American civilians on the streets of Columbia by military policemen. Later in the war, the Fort Jackson commander used fear
of offending white elites as an excuse not to take action over the un-
justified killing of a black soldier by a city policeman. The general demonstrated no such reluctance, however, when he wanted to eliminate
unsightly billboards along a civilian highway. People like the South Carolina NAACP's James Hinton eventually lost faith in the ability or willingness of Army officials at the installation level to take action against
racism. For the next twenty years, Hinton would appeal directly to the
Pentagon when racial incidents involving soldiers took place in Columbia. This bypassing of the chain of command won him few friends at Fort
Jackson. Lingering bitterness and distrust on both sides would resonate
into the sixties.

28 | BLACK, WHITE & OLIVE DRAB

★☆

The reopening of Camp Jackson in 1939 came as a welcome boost to Columbia. The post generated a monthly payroll of $2 million by 1941, and the city grew from 62,000 people in 1940 to over 75,000 by 1943. Nevertheless, Fort Jackson did not overwhelm what was a diversified local economy. Columbia sat astride many of the area's most important road and rail networks. It had several large textile mills and was the home of the South Carolina government as well as the state's flagship university, penitentiary, and mental hospital.[1]

Whites retained a tight grip on the reins of power there. They comprised a majority in the city and ruled through a mayor and council elected by at-large elections. Mayor Lawrence B. Owens entered office in 1926 and stayed there until his death in 1941. Longtime city councilman Fred Marshall replaced him for five years until Owens's son Frank won election in 1946. The government of Richland County, to which Columbia belonged, was also majority white. It had limited influence because the South Carolina constitution relegated most of the important county-level decisions to the legislature. To a greater extent than the county, the chamber of commerce was the city's most valuable ally. Like the council, it was all-white. This organization served to unify political and economic interests, particularly in regard to the military. Boosters from the chamber led the rally for the building of Camp Jackson in 1917, and the interwar years did little to dampen the enthusiasm of their descendents.

No person better typified the tightly knit local power structure and its close relationship with Fort Jackson than did *Columbia Record* editor George A. Buchanan. A native of Darlington, he had first come to the capital city during the the second decade of the twentieth century to study at the University of South Carolina. His education came to an abrupt halt, however, when he criticized the USC president in an article for the school newspaper. Buchanan remained in Columbia following his expulsion. He took a job as a reporter for the *State* in 1918, soon after Camp Jackson was built. He became editor of the *Record* and president of the chamber of commerce by the time the installation reopened. He was a leading figure on the liaison committee that helped to find housing for wives and off-duty entertainment for troops. So intertwined was he with the fort that when Royden Beebe received his promotion to brigadier general in 1942, Buchanan attended the ceremony and presented him with new stars on behalf of the chamber.[2]

Besides Buchanan, a large proportion of Columbians engaged in what historian John Hammond Moore has called a "head-over-heels love

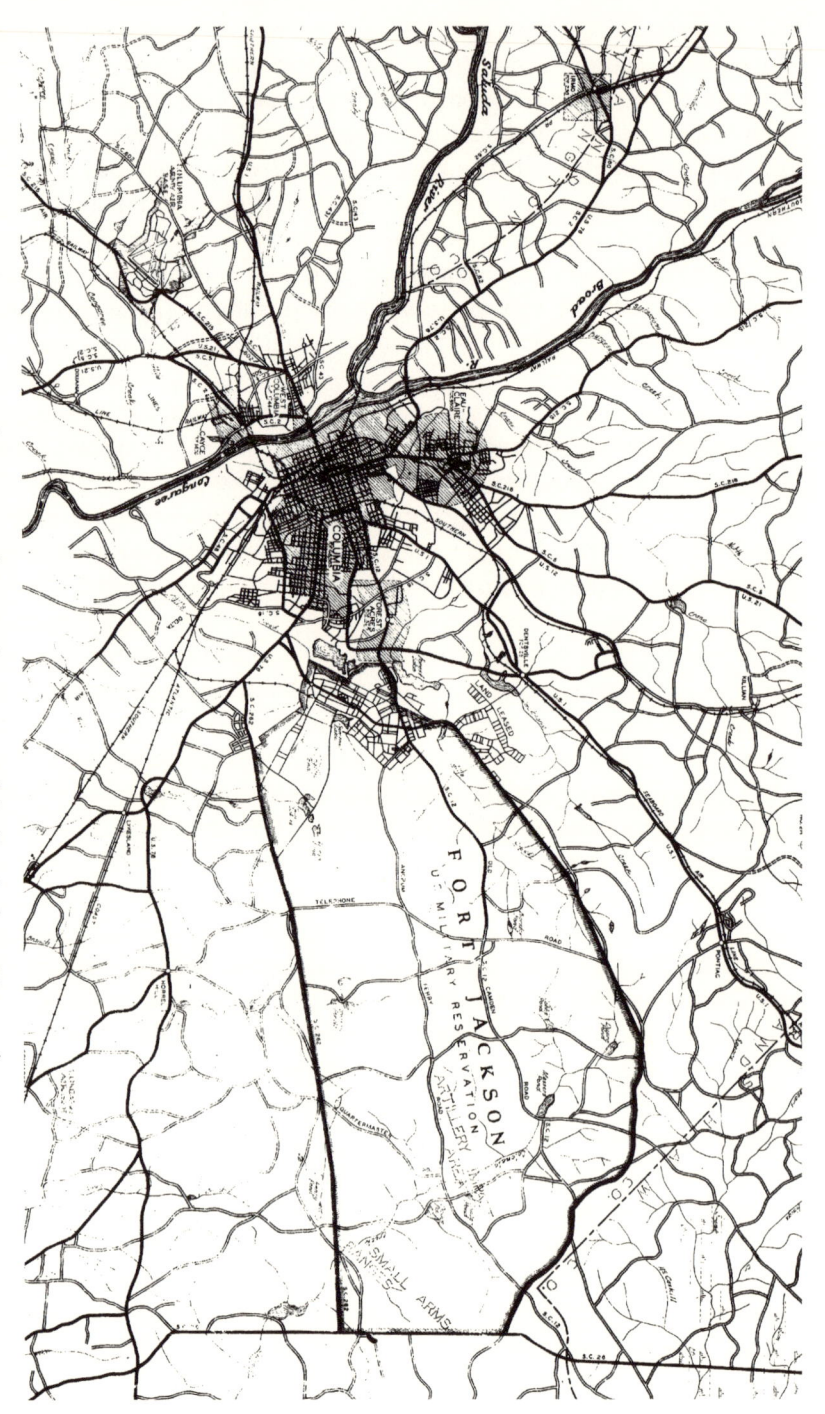

Fort Jackson and Columbia area, 1942. (U.S. Army photograph, courtesy of the Fort Jackson Museum)

affair with the GI.''[3] Citizens embraced soldiers at a personal level, welcoming them into churches and inviting them home to Sunday dinner. Officers and wives who did not have places to live on-post could often rent a spare room with a local family. An "SOS," or "Soldiers Offered Seats," program encouraged people to share rides. Civic organizations like the Elks and YMCA sponsored checkers tournaments and singing nights. The WPA Defense Recreation Committee helped to coordinate these efforts. It also arranged for the donation of books and furnishings by civilians for company day rooms.

Although a few stores in town posted signs forbidding soldiers, most merchants welcomed the increased business. The newly built four-lane boulevard that stretched outside the main gate of Fort Jackson toward Columbia soon had an embryonic sprawl of pubs and stores. The corner where this road connected to Garners Ferry Road became the location for a new drive-in theater in 1941. Soldiers could take a bus from post to the central shopping district located near the statehouse and the intersection of Gervais and Main Streets. They crowded the restaurants, drugstores, and theaters there. Some rented rooms at the Wade Hampton or Jefferson Hotels to be with wives or catch up on lost sleep. On the corner of Laurel and Assembly Streets, a $300,000 United Services Organization (USO) building opened in 1942. By the end of the war, five such facilities—three for whites and two for blacks—drew servicemen into the city's heart.

The presence of thousands of troops attracted its share of "camp followers" as well. Gates Street, also known as Park Street, had long been notorious for brothels. During the First World War, the commander at Camp Jackson had lodged complaints with the city council about the area. Local laws nevertheless permitted prostitution there until the mid-thirties. This red-light district existed within a predominantly African American neighborhood.

Black Columbia extended far beyond Park Street. In fact, three large neighborhoods bracketed the downtown. African Americans comprised one-third of the population but had no black representatives on the city council or any South Carolina governing body. Few could even vote. They rode in the backs of buses and in separate railroad cars. Their children played in one of two segregated public parks while whites enjoyed the use of twelve. Those youngsters who did attend schools went to inferior facilities with shorter terms. Lack of education combined with prejudice to create economic disparity as well. At one Columbia store, for example, three black men earned a combined total of $8 per week while a

Alienating Black Civilians | 31

single white employee received $11.00. Many African American women worked as domestic servants, earning $1.50 to $3.50 per week.[4] The average black male in Columbia earned $6.00. This amount did not rival the average amount earned by whites, but it did exceed the pay received by a new soldier at Fort Jackson, and it certainly was more than an African American made as a field hand.

Besides pay, blacks in Columbia enjoyed other benefits that their counterparts in the countryside did not share. The city had the only accredited, nonwhite public high school in South Carolina—Booker T. Washington. It also had two of the state's premier black institutions for higher learning—Allen University and Benedict College.[5] People in town had access to several physicians and two hospitals. They worshipped together and supported one another in the scores of churches that dotted the neighborhoods. African American businesses had tripled during the first four decades of the twentieth century and provided an abundance of goods and services. Victory Savings Bank, the state's only black-owned financial institution, financed the capital for much of this growth.

Over time, this urban concentration had given rise to a middle class of lawyers, preachers, educators, doctors, morticians, insurance agents, and merchants. They tended toward conservatism in their social outlook. Many of them took their cue from the Reverend Richard Carroll, a local orator known as Columbia's "Booker T. Washington," by tacitly accepting social segregation and striving for self-improvement. Although Carroll had died in 1930, his legacy lived on through his son Seymour, who was a leading citizen. Richard Carroll, incidentally, had held an officer's commission as an Army chaplain during the Spanish-American War. During World War I, he was the sole African American to serve on Columbia's Central Committee on Civic Preparedness. His son spent the Great War as an enlisted man working at the Camp Jackson hospital.[6]

Columbia's black middle class banded together in a variety of organizations: the Negro Business League, a veterans' club, social fraternities, a chapter of the NAACP, the Palmetto Teachers' Association, and several short-lived ministerial alliances. The agendas of these groups—if they had any—were for equal treatment under the law, not integration.

The *Palmetto Leader* underscored this conservatism. N. J. Frederick founded the paper in 1925. A crusader against lynching, he used it to challenge white power. During the twenties, he served as the defense attorney in the sensational trial and subsequent lynching of a black man accused of raping a white girl. When Frederick died in 1938, however, publisher George H. Hampton softened the paper's edge. For example,

when A. Philip Randolph made his famous nationwide call in 1941 for a march on Washington, the *Leader* said: "A demonstration like the one planned is entirely out of order. . . . It certainly will not do the Negro race the desired good which it hopes to accomplish." According to a *Pittsburgh Courier* poll taken near the time, this editorial reflected the majority opinion of South Carolina blacks.[7]

The state's NAACP was in its infancy. Chapters from eight cities met in 1939 to form a state conference, but leadership remained fragmented and feeble.[8] Ending segregation would require stronger leadership, better organization, and a unifying issue around which to rally. The Second World War made all three possible.

Like Columbia whites, local blacks welcomed the opening of Fort Jackson. Contractors hired laborers of all races to build barracks and roads. Elsewhere on-post, a new laundry employed a large force of African American women. Black elites organized a committee to sell war bonds and stamps. Many of them saw the conflict as an opportunity to advance freedom at home. Almost all enjoyed the respite from the hard times of the Depression.

When the first African American soldiers began arriving at Fort Jackson in December 1940, the black community rolled out a red carpet. Prominent citizens such as Seymour Carroll joined the Colored Committee of the WPA Defense Recreation Committee. In January, the Reverend J. Clarence Colclough set up a forum at the Sidney Park Colored Methodist Episcopal Church. The Kappa Alpha Psi fraternity established a recreation center. Allen University hosted a dance.

Life on-post was difficult enough for black soldiers, but they faced a minefield of uncertainty once they left the main gate of Fort Jackson on pass. Most of them came from the South and were familiar with Jim Crow, but they still had to learn the arbitrary nuances of local customs, where to go and where to stay away, whom they could trust and whom to avoid. A misstep could have as fatal a consequence for them as if they were on a foreign battlefield. They came quickly to know that the service stations and pubs along Jackson Boulevard did not welcome their business and that they were not allowed at the new drive-in theater at the intersection of Garners Ferry Road.

African American soldiers often went to the Waverly District. Here resided the black elite of Columbia. The neighborhood encompassed Allen University and Benedict College plus a host of businesses. Gervais Street in this part of town became such a boisterous gathering place that local whites dubbed it "Burma Road." Nearby on Taylor Street, blacks

Alienating Black Civilians | 33

could attend dances at the Township Auditorium or at one of the two nonwhite USOs. On Harden Street, they could watch movies at the Carver Theatre or go to the other USO. The latter had an active program for spouses.

Black soldiers who did not want to go to the USO or to Waverly could take a slightly longer bus trip to Columbia's black downtown, which was located on Washington Street. Here, Durham Counts operated a drugstore, where he filled prescriptions written by Doctors Robert Mance and Frank Johnson. Hemphill Pride Sr. practiced dentistry nearby, and Willis Johnson operated a funeral home. This place had the densest concentration of black-owned businesses in the city. Many of the proprietors lived at their shops or in adjacent houses, so the area had a mixture of residences and stores.

Further west along Washington Street, between Assembly and Park Streets, the neighborhood grew considerably rougher. At this point, the central black business area blended into Columbia's red-light district. Perhaps the best-known place here was the Big Apple dance hall. In 1937, white visitors to the nightclub began mimicking the movements of the African Americans who danced there. The steps caught on and spread up the East Coast in a fad called the "Big Apple." The craze inspired a big band recording of the same name by Tommy Dorsey. For authorities, however, the Big Apple was a "notorious dive."[9]

Whites called this section "Congo Square." Besides the Big Apple, it contained the Capitol Theater, owned by Sidney Friedman, a Jewish man. His son Ralph ran the adjacent Dew Drop Inn. Nearby was Mose's Café. On one corner of Washington and Park, Willis Johnson had his funeral home. On the other side, Charlie and George Williams ran the Blue Palace Café. Fort Jackson's assistant provost marshal described the latter in 1941: "After having walked through this section and inspecting it, it is a place of filth and is a menace to the welfare of Military personnel. . . . This place called the Blue Palace . . . is a den in which any crime is liable to occur." Another Army officer added: "It is apparent from the numerous times in which the name Charles Williams and references to the Blue Palace Café appear . . . that it must be, as stated by witnesses, a hang-out for persons of the criminal element."[10]

Although servicemen had numerous entertainment options, many gravitated toward the Blue Palace. They came in search of prostitutes and cheap liquor. The supply for both grew rapidly, and Fort Jackson authorities responded by placing Columbia's black neighborhoods off-limits to white soldiers. The policy helped, as Provost Marshal Lt. Col.

34 | BLACK, WHITE & OLIVE DRAB

Lewis Page said, "to keep white soldiers away from the negro prostitutes."[11]

Enforcing the restrictions required that military policemen walk the streets of the city because civilian lawmen had no jurisdiction in such matters. The mission stretched available manpower. Originally, the provost marshal had only twenty to thirty MPs under his command. At his request, the infantry regiments of the Eighth Division detailed soldiers to him for temporary duty. The Thirtieth did the same. By December 1940, the then all-white force had 145 MPs. Sixty of these walked the civilian beat.

Lieutenant Colonel Page established an auxiliary police station next to the Township Auditorium on Taylor Street. The MPs patrolled in pairs and often teamed up with city patrolmen. In theory, the former handled the situation when the teams encountered soldiers, and the latter took care of civilians. In practice, the teams often dealt with soldiers dressed in civilian clothes or faced emergencies in which everyone felt compelled to participate.

"What civilians do *off* the post is *no concern* of the individual Military Policeman," the Fort Jackson handbook said in October 1940.[12] Indeed, federal law prohibited military forces from making arrests or performing domestic police duties without explicit authorization. How vigorously Lieutenant Colonel Page emphasized this point, or whether he thought that the stipulation applied to blacks, remains unknown. Page came from North Carolina. "He has a Southerner's viewpoint and understanding of our people," said Seymour Carroll, implying that Page condoned racism.[13] Southern-bred, too, was the MP company commander, Capt. Carey Robinson, who came from Alabama. The day-to-day supervisor, Desk Sergeant Carl Stone, laced the epithet "nigger" into his speech, even under oath, as did many of the enlisted men under his charge.

Few of the MPs had formal training. Most had received hasty instructions after having been yanked from an infantry squad. The power to arrest people, use a club, and shoot a pistol dazzled some of the young men. Within two months, commanders on-post began to complain about bullying and excessive force used on white soldiers. Besides overzealousness, many of the MPs held prejudiced ideas about blacks. Like their chain of command, the majority came from the South. "I didn't bother negroes as long as they kept their places," said one.[14]

The civilian police made poor mentors for their inexperienced military counterparts. Several patrolmen admitted they habitually made illegal searches and used excessive force. "It has been our custom," said

Alienating Black Civilians | 35

Officer Isaac F. Gardner, "to search houses for liquor and when anybody becomes involved on the street to search them for weapons." He added: "We had more trouble among the niggers in that section before the military police came than we are having now."[15] Lack of regard for constitutional safeguards—combined with racism, poor training, and overlapping jurisdictions—boded ill for local black civilians.

The first reported incident of brutality took place in October 1940. Henry Dore lived next to the Blue Palace and washed cars for a living. One night he was having an argument with his wife on the 1300 block of Assembly Street. Several MPs noticed the commotion and intervened. "He hit me with his hand," Dore recounted. "He knocked me down. I got up. I didn't say anything. I saw the MP on the sleeve. Another walked up, came from around the corner and said, 'Let's beat the hell out of the black son-of-a-bitch.'" Dore lost several teeth and was arrested by civilian authorities for disorderly conduct.[16]

That same month, a second incident took place at the home of Nezzie Young, who operated a brothel across from the Big Apple. The police claimed somebody from within her house fired a shot at them. Officer Isaac Gardner and Pfc. John Bassett charged onto the porch where Young sat. "He started to beat and slap me and jerked me out of the chair a couple of times and beat me with his hand and struck me a couple of times, and said I was a liar," the woman testified.[17]

The violence, however, had only begun. In November, an unidentified MP assaulted Hardy Hopkins, a laborer at the farmers' market on Assembly Street. "Me and a boy was standing on the corner arguing, and up come two MPs and the boy tried to run and started to cross the street, said Hopkins. "One was holding me and one caught him and kicked him, and the one who was holding him come back and said to me, 'Feel that and see if it would knock a nigger's brains out.'" The MPs then broke Hopkins's jaw with a club.[18]

Granted, the credibility of these witnesses falls somewhat short. Only one could identify the MP in question. All three had participated in some kind of disturbance prior to the arrival of the police. Two had criminal records. Regardless, the MPs had no legal grounds to intervene, much less use force. As Robert Mance, a black doctor who lived in the neighborhood at the time, pointed out: "Most of them are poor negroes in this area, but even among them are some respectable people. You can't determine a negro's morals on the basis of his dress or personal appearance or economic situation."[19]

Word of these incidents must have reached Lieutenant Colonel Page

36 | BLACK, WHITE & OLIVE DRAB

because on 8 January 1941 he issued a letter that said: "no distinction should be made between race, color, or creed." The memorandum also reiterated that MPs should not molest civilians. The provost marshal took no action to punish any of the soldiers involved.[20]

In fact, circumstances conspired to make the situation worse. In January, Lieutenant Colonel Page and Mayor Owens announced a plan to rid Columbia of vice. Given the strapped resources of the police department, the mayor embraced the program enthusiastically. He went so far as to suggest during a city council meeting that the military be granted authority over local civilians. "As much as I should like to see this done," the provost marshal responded, "because of the fact that the civil and military authorities cooperate so well . . . it is impossible to go beyond the army regulations, which do not permit it." In a letter reprinted in the *State*, he recommended that all prostitutes be locked up for being public health nuisances, treated for disease, and not released until they learned another trade. The city did not act upon this suggestion, but the joint campaign against vice coincided with an increase in law enforcement violence.[21]

In late January, Patrolmen Isaac Gardner and Ernest D. Harrell along with an unidentified MP went into the Blue Palace Café. They found thirty-one-year-old Mabel Jackson, a well-known prostitute. "I just walked in and was just about to pull up a chair when two MPs ran in and grabbed me and threw me against the door," she said. "Before I had time to straighten myself up . . . they threw me out in the street and I fell on my knees." Willis Johnson witnessed the assault from the door of his funeral home across the street. He continued the story: "While she was on the ground one of the military police kicked her, and she was pulled up and headed toward police headquarters." Jackson was jailed overnight and charged with being drunk and disorderly.[22]

On another evening that January, restaurant worker Raymond White had just finished watching a movie at the Capitol Theater. He called for a cab and then went out onto Washington Street to wait. "As I came out of the taxi office I started home and there was a crowd running up on the sidewalk," White remembered. "I wanted to get out of the way so I stood in the middle of the street, and an MP walked from between two parked cars. First he struck me in the face. . . . He struck me again on top of my head." White tried to escape the blows. "I rolled back under a parked automobile. I went out of my senses for a minute. He said, 'Come out or I'll shoot.'"[23]

Willis Johnson saw this incident, too. "I saw the boy run from that

Alienating Black Civilians | 37

automobile and as he ran across the street I heard the report of a pistol." The bullet missed White. One of the MPs, Cpl. William Musselwhite, later admitted to his role. "I didn't do any shooting but I did chase the nigger," he said.[24]

Capitol Theater owner Sidney Friedman learned about the incident and complained to the provost marshal by phone. Page referred him to Captain Robinson, and the two apparently discussed the situation. Willis Johnson also decided to take action. He contacted J. Andrew Simmons, the principal of Booker T. Washington High School, who organized a committee consisting of Johnson, Dr. Mance, and D. A. Jenkins. Simmons then contacted Lieutenant Colonel Page. The provost marshal greeted them cordially. He asked them first if they had any connection with a "Jew" he had talked to over the phone recently. When they answered in the negative, he said: "Well, I'll talk to you all but I won't talk to a Jew." Page later denied making this statement.[25]

Meanwhile, the mistreatment on Washington Street continued. On 30 January, MPs clubbed a deaf-mute woman named Geneva Wallace for no apparent reason as she walked to the drugstore to get medicine for her husband. On 1 February, MPs searched and assaulted David Hall, admittedly drunk, as he helped a companion get into a taxi. He had allegedly called one of the MPs a "son-of-a-bitch." On 1 March, Henry Arthur received a blow to the head for not getting out of the way of an MP on the sidewalk.

Mabel Jackson was accosted again on 10 March in a revealing episode. The prostitute had very light skin, so the MPs mistook her for a white woman. She said: "We had half a pint of old Dover and two MPs walked up—we was in the 1000 block of Lady Street. . . . They flashed the light in my face and said, 'Aren't you white,' and I said, 'No sir, I am colored,' and he said, 'You are a damned liar, you is a white bitch going for negro,' and the stout one looked at the slim one and said, 'What should we do, lock them up or take the liquor off them,' and the little one said he didn't know. So it was left with him, and they told us to beat it on down the street. 'We should either lock both of you up or beat you up.'"[26]

That MPs would treat people this way came as no surprise to the Williams brothers, who ran the Blue Palace Café. "They come in and just walk up and down and search the customers," said George Williams.[27] Businessmen and professionals witnessed this kind of behavior throughout the black community. Dr. Mance complained that MPs had searched the house of one of his bedridden patients. Dr. Frank Johnson overheard an MP on the telephone at Count's Drug Store talking about how much

38 | BLACK, WHITE & OLIVE DRAB

he regretted not having killed a certain Will Geiger. MPs would arbitrarily shove black civilians, force them off the sidewalks, and berate them with crude language. Wealth and position did not seem to matter. Nobody was safe.

NAACP secretary James M. Hinton became involved at this point. Born in North Carolina in 1891, he grew up in New York City after his parents died. He attended public high school and the Bible Teachers Training School in the Bronx. He worked briefly for the post office when World War I began. Hinton joined the Army but did not go overseas. Commissioned as a second lieutenant of infantry, he spent most of the war at Camp Hancock, Georgia, where he was a machine gun officer. He returned to Georgia after the war to work for an insurance agency in Augusta and transferred to the company's Columbia office in 1938. Hinton's part-time work as a minister and Army experience made him an excellent candidate for the top job when a state conference of the NAACP was formed in 1939. Despite this high position, he remained a relative outsider within Columbia's tightly knit black elite.[28]

Hinton took pride in his military service. As a former infantry officer, he expressed disappointment that none of the African American soldiers at Fort Jackson were allowed to serve in the combat arms. He took offense not only at the racism of the MPs but at their unsoldierliness and the failure of post leaders to control them.

At first, Hinton tried to work with Fort Jackson authorities. He wrote a letter to Major General Russell during the second week of March telling him about the abuses that had taken place. Russell sent the Thirtieth Division inspector general to the Hinton home. A few days later, Lieutenant Colonel Page invited the NAACP leader to the post. Hinton brought with him several local ministers: E. A. Adams, J. Clarence Colclough, and James Reeder. He also sought the assistance of J. Andrew Simmons and Willis Johnson.

The meeting did not go well. According to the ministers in attendance, Page asserted bluntly that MPs were not to strike civilians, but then put his finger to his lips in a gesture that meant the reality of the situation differed somewhat from official policy. Page also allegedly said the mayor had told him to "give 'em hell."[29] The provost marshal later denied making any gestures or statements to the mayor.

Hinton and Page developed a mutual dislike for each other. Said Hinton, "I do not feel that Colonel Page's attitude toward the matter from the beginning nor since has been one of cooperation nor sympathetic toward our racial group." Page later said: "The agitation in this particular

Alienating Black Civilians | 39

case is headed by the negro representative, Hinton, who is using the criminal colored element involved and has the support of the property owners of the places of business or habits of the criminal elements involved."[30]

Problems continued after the visit to Fort Jackson. On 15 March, an unidentified MP assaulted Sam Williams at the Blue Palace. The next day, two MPs accosted sixteen-year-old Robert Pearson and his friend Matthew Ethridge. "They pushed us back and slapped me and began to search us," Pearson said. "Went through all our pockets." Pfc. John Bassett paid Nezzie Young another visit on 16 March. "Slapped her down[,] too," he told an investigator. "In fact, I knocked her down three times." When asked why he behaved so violently, Bassett answered: "Officer Gause and myself had had trouble with her before."[31]

Hinton and the other ministers organized a mass meeting on 23 March at the Zion Baptist Church. A large crowd attended. Participants discussed the brutality of the Fort Jackson MPs as well as other issues such as the unequal park facilities in Columbia and discrepancies between pension checks received by blacks and whites. The assembly resolved to take their grievances before the city council. The Colored Citizens' Committee was created in the wake of the meeting.[32] Though dominated by clergy, it contained representatives from all of the major black groups in Columbia, including the NAACP, the Ministers Interdenominational Alliance, and the Negro Business League. The committee selected three ministers to represent them on the MP issue: Colclough, Reeder, and Adams.

The three ministers decided to see conditions on Washington Street for themselves before going to the city council meeting. On the night of 25 March, they went on foot into the red-light district. They held an impromptu meeting with patrons at Mose's Café. Two MPs—Pvt. David Nichols and Pfc. John Calhoun—and a plainclothes police officer noticed the assembly. Private First Class Calhoun described what happened:

> Well, we were coming up Washington Street, and there is a little place called Mose's Café, a nigger place. . . . We noticed a lot of loud talking, seemingly a disturbance in this place. It is a small café and I imagine there were approximately anywhere from 35 to 40 nigger men and women in there. . . . I don't recall any in uniform. . . . The second we got inside the door there were either two or three, I believe three, niggers who distinguished themselves from the rest of the crowd. They were evidently preachers or ministers. . . . I thought

they didn't belong in with the crowd because the rest of the niggers in there were seemingly a working class of people and these niggers had their Sunday clothes on. . . . One of these nigger men dressed up said, "We are a committee, and we are here to prevent the officers and the military policemen from beating up our people. . . ." I replied to him that the military police did not beat up niggers or any other civilians."[33]

The Reverend James Reeder said that Calhoun had replied, "I'll beat any God-damn stinking nigger" and ordered everybody to get out. Calhoun denied the accusation and said that café patrons had cleared of their own volition. The ministers described the incident at a city council meeting the next day and presented a petition. The mayor said that he would set up an appointment with Army officials about the matter but apparently never did. The news appeared in the *State*, complete with details about the 14 March visit to Fort Jackson and a rebuttal from Lieutenant Colonel Page.[34]

James Hinton lost faith in the ability or willingness of local whites—military or civilian—to act justly. On 25 March, the day of the city council meeting, he sent a letter to Army Chief of Staff Gen. George Marshall. In it, he said that post MPs had exceeded their authority and acted illegally and that the provost marshal had done nothing to stop the violations. He also sent letters to Secretary of War Henry Stimson and National NAACP director Walter White. The latter then notified William Hastie, who was the civilian aide to the secretary of war for racial matters. Either Hinton or White must have contacted the National Negro Congress and the Associated Negro Press, too, because both organizations sent inquiries to the War Department. As a result of this letter-writing campaign, the Army inspector general's office in Washington ordered its Fort Jackson branch to investigate.[35]

Colonel Tallant of the Eighth Division and Colonel Dempsey of the Thirtieth collected affidavits from civilians who claimed to have been mistreated and questioned the MPs involved. They sent their report to the Fourth Service Command on 18 April. The two colonels recommended that MPs no longer patrol with civilian officers and that all soldiers receive a reminder not to molest civilians. The problems, they said, resulted not from a faulty system, but from the behavior of an errant few.[36]

Hinton was initially impressed by the swiftness of action, but he understood the workings of military bureaucracy and followed up by checking on the disposition of the report. His pleasure with the Army

turned to renewed outrage when he learned that the Fourth Service Command had buried the investigation results in its filing system and never forwarded it higher up the chain of command. That knowledge—combined with the 20 April attack on black soldiers by troops of the Thirtieth Division—moved him to send another barrage of letters.

This time, the First Corps office of the inspector general received the order to investigate.[37] The task fell upon Col. Andrew Krieger, who interviewed witnesses and collected evidence. Allegations of Lieutenant Colonel Page's anti-Semitism appear to have motivated him to thoroughness. He produced a notably lengthy and devastating report.

"Private Bassett is an excitable, hot-tempered man," he said. "He has no consideration for colored people. . . . He likewise is entirely mistaken as to the scope of the duties of military police with regard to civilians with whom they come in contact. . . . His relief should have a salutary effect."[38]

The Columbia police fared no better in Krieger's estimation. "Sergeant Ernest D. Harrell apparently has the idea of some old policemen that the civil rights of persons suspected of wrong doing are of no importance."[39]

The colonel expressed frustration with the lack of help he received from the city's top lawman. "The investigating officer called on Chief Campbell before taking any testimony, and requested and was assured of his cooperation. Thereafter it was a game of tag." He eventually settled for using an affidavit the chief had given earlier to Colonels Tallant and Dempsey.[40]

Krieger damned the provost marshal with faint praise. "It is apparent that Colonel Page at least listened to the complaints made. . . . His attitude on the stand seemed to be that of a person who is justifying rather than excusing his actions."[41]

As a result, the post commander received a letter notifying him of the War Department's displeasure. The general had already been relieved of command as a result of training deficiencies, but the decision nevertheless was a moral victory. Nobody in Columbia learned about it, however, because the Army classified the report.[42]

The investigation was nevertheless significant because it elevated James Hinton to prominence as a community leader. Hinton had been a newcomer on the fringes of the black elite prior to the MP incidents. In 1941, Seymour Carroll had omitted him when listing the influential African Americans of Columbia. "There are two groups of thought," Carroll had said. "Among the more conservative, I would name C. A. John-

42 | BLACK, WHITE & OLIVE DRAB

son. Mr. Johnson is Supervisor of Schools. J. J. Starks, President of Benedict College; Dr. Robert W. Mance, physician; W. C. Johnson, Funeral Director; Mr. A. B. [Frank] Johnson, physician." Among the more radical, Carroll listed "J. Andrew Simmons, Principal; Mrs. M. M. Simkins, Field Representative, South Carolina Tuberculosis Association; Reverend J. P. Reeder . . . Reverend J. Clarence Colclough." Carroll made no mention of Hinton.[43]

The investigation also helped to unify the local black community. The Colored Citizens' Committee served as the means. Through it, conservatives like Mance and Willis and Frank Johnson found common cause with liberals like Simmons, Reeder, and Colclough.

Fort Jackson authorities themselves thwarted people who might have dissuaded Hinton from going to the War Department. Seymour Carroll, for example, had the potential to rival Hinton and defend the Army. He bore the military legacy of his prominent father, served himself as a soldier at Camp Jackson during World War I, belonged to the WPA Defense Recreation Committee, and maintained close relations with a brigadier general in the South Carolina National Guard. Unfortunately for him, none of these credentials mattered to the Fort Jackson MPs.

On 6 April, Carroll took his wife and some friends to the post for a parade. "I was going to Fort Jackson on Army Day and we had some girls in the car and Mr. Madden, his wife and my wife," he said. As they passed through the main gate, "an MP said, 'look at the high yellows.'" Such blatant, public humiliation served to silence conservative voices like Carroll's and bound the Colored Citizens' Committee closer together.[44]

Hinton unified the group further by developing fresh tactics. While others had groveled ineffectively before the city council, he took decisive action by writing to Washington. He brought pressure on the Fort Jackson command by involving national civil rights groups and the War Department. He achieved concrete results by forcing the Army to appoint an external investigator. As a result, he established himself as a leader. This victory was partial, however. The war continued both abroad and at home.

On 5 June, Ike Jeeter backed his car out of a parking space on Washington Street. He almost hit a military police vehicle that had come up behind him. The MPs exited their car. One of them pointed a gun at Jeeter and ordered him out. The MP then slapped him while the other one threatened the gathering crowd.

Sidney Friedman watched these events unfold from inside the Capitol Theater. A Jewish man of European origins, he often tried to help his

Alienating Black Civilians | 43

customers who ran into trouble with the police and even bailed some of them out of jail. When Friedman came outside, one of the MPs told him to mind his own business. Jeeter meanwhile agreed to accompany the soldiers in their car to the station headquarters rather than summon a civilian law officer. Friedman followed.

The Jewish theater owner was a profane man by all accounts, and when the group entered Army annex at the Township Auditorium, he uttered something about "MP sons of bitches." The desk sergeant, T.Sgt. Carl Stone, responded by punching Friedman. Clearly, the Krieger investigation had done little to alter the behavior of military police toward civilians.

Lieutenant Colonel Page had learned a lesson, but not the one intended by local blacks. After Hinton sent a letter of complaint, the provost marshal appointed an investigating officer, a field artillery major on temporary duty. The proceedings took place in the offices of the chamber of commerce. Besides gathering the basic facts on the case, the investigator received an earful from Columbia businessmen about the degraded character of Sidney Friedman. The Jew drank, they said. He swore profusely but lacked the physical courage to back up his words with deeds. Worse, he slept with Negro women.

The investigating officer absolved Technical Sergeant Stone from all wrongdoing. He said that the striking of Friedman "was justified under a code of conduct respected in the opinion of Americans in general." One of the MPs, however, was charged with hitting Jeeter and found guilty. The soldier received an unspecified punishment.[45]

The conviction had little deterrent effect. On 27 July, a civilian policeman attempted to arrest Herbert Myers. The man resisted the officer, so Cpl. William Musselwhite went to assist. This soldier was the same one who had chased Raymond White from underneath a parked automobile six months earlier. "He is not of large stature, but is powerfully built," Colonel Krieger had described him. He "impressed the investigating officer as being the type of individual, who, placed in a position like that of a policeman, might not be too careful of the civil rights of persons with whom he came in contact."[46] True to form, Corporal Musselwhite struck Myers several times, at least once while the man was handcuffed.

James Hinton continued working within the system and gave authorities at Fort Jackson every chance to act without pressure from higher headquarters, but his good faith in the Army continued to crumble. He called Technical Sergeant Stone to inquire about Myers's arrest. "Upon

finding that I was colored," Hinton said, "[he] immediately changed from courtesy to noncourtesy in his conversation over the telephone."[47]

Despite the rudeness of the desk sergeant, post officials knew the influence that Hinton wielded and sought to appease him. Assistant Provost Marshal Capt. John McVoy said in a 31 July memorandum that "from the factual standpoint, Musselwhite can be tried for assault and battery and because of this colored Committee influence [sic] with Washington and to avoid any contention that we are not carrying out orders, I recommend that Musselwhite be tried for violation of AW [Article of War] 96."[48] Musselwhite was tried and acquitted on 19 August.

Hinton vented his rage in a letter to post executive officer Col. Frank Whittaker. He said: "Our Committee cannot expect anything in the future from reporting such cases to proper authorities in Fort Jackson, and we regret this, as we had hoped, that we would not again have to resort to Washington to get relief from such occurrences, but there is no other course open to us, even though we were assured by Washington that we would receive adjustments in the future. It appears that facts mean nothing in an apparent white-washed case."[49]

Still another incident took place on 15 September. The Columbia police responded to a call about a domestic disturbance on Gates Street. Hearing that a black soldier in civilian attire was involved, an MP came along with the officers. When they arrived at the scene, they found a civilian named John Hampton arguing with five women. He fled, and all three of the police gave chase. Hampton ended up with his leg broken in five places. The police claimed he fell in a ditch, which was an odd story given that the ditch in question measured only three feet wide by three feet deep.

This time the committee complained to Fort Jackson and Washington simultaneously. Hinton wrote to Colonel Whittaker on 23 September: "We are bringing this matter to the proper authorities in Washington also, as we felt that something must be done to stop such unwarranted actions, and in light of our last case, where nothing was done to punish the member of Military Police, even though facts showed that another citizen was struck."[50] On the same day, Hinton sent a letter to William Hastie. The message reminded the civilian aide about the riots that had torn Fort Bragg during July after MPs had killed several black soldiers and implied that the potential for the same existed at Fort Jackson. "We are asking that your department bring every pressure to bear, that a repetition of Fayetteville will not be duplicated."[51]

Hastie, however, had several more pressing matters. Besides the vio-

lence in Fort Bragg, a black soldier had been found dead in Fort Benning hanging from a tree with his hands bound. Civilian police in Louisiana had seriously beaten an African American staff sergeant. A. Philip Randolph had just called off his march on Washington. Consequently, the situation in Columbia drew far less attention than it did previously.[52]

After the complaints to Washington brought little immediate result, Hinton tried the new post commander, Col. Royden Beebe. He wrote in a letter dated 27 September: "We have tried to work with your department . . . if you do not feel you care to work with us, you may so state this." The NAACP leader had almost given up hope in the Army.[53]

In the fall, Hinton acquired two new allies when the *Lighthouse & Informer* newspaper moved from Charleston to an office on Washington Street. The paper's editor, John H. McCray, would become a pivotal figure in South Carolina's civil rights movement. Educated at Charleston's Avery Institute and Talladega College in Alabama, he had edited the *Lighthouse & Informer* since 1938.[54] McCray believed not in charity, but in self-improvement and hard work. He had no sympathy for self-pitying people, black or white. Nevertheless, he was strident in his demands for equal, fair treatment for African Americans. His periodic allusions to black self-defense shocked many white people and made them wary.

Despite the suspicion the *Lighthouse & Informer* would eventually generate within Army circles, McCray supported the military wholeheartedly. By November 1942, he had become chairman of the drive to get blacks to purchase war bonds. His paper kept up with news about African American servicemen.[55]

He found a partner with equal fire in Osceola McKaine. Over ten years older than McCray, McKaine had enlisted in the Army early in the second decade of the twentieth century. He rose to the rank of second lieutenant and became a staff officer in the Tenth Cavalry Regiment. His combat experience included the Mexican Punitive Expedition and World War I. McKaine left the Army and organized veterans in New York City during the height of the Harlem Renaissance. He then moved to Europe, where for fifteen years he operated a nightclub in Belgium. He fled the German invasion and came to Columbia, where he became a correspondent for the *Palmetto Leader*. He took pride in his military service and went by the title of "Lieutenant" in his byline.[56]

McKaine was concerned about the effect that Army treatment of African American troops had upon race relations in the South. In a September 1941 letter to President Roosevelt, he wrote, "In view of the constant friction caused by the presence of Negro troops in the South and

46 | BLACK, WHITE & OLIVE DRAB

the pernicious effect upon our morale resulting therefrom, we, in the desire to promote *National Unity,* recommend their removal to other sections."[57] As his later actions would prove, McKaine was willing to go to greater extremes in his choice of solutions than were McCray, Hinton, or other local leaders. Certainly he must have chafed at the conservatism of the *Palmetto Leader.* By September 1941, he had quit to become associate editor of the *Lighthouse & Informer.*

This weekly journal would figure significantly in the next wave of MP incidents. On 22 December, two white military policemen were walking their beat down Park Street. When they came to the corner of Washington Street, they encountered four or five young black men blocking the sidewalk. As the MPs shoved their way through, one of the men said that he was a citizen and that the MPs had no right to push him. An argument ensued, and fisticuffs followed. The MPs quickly resorted to their billy clubs while a crowd of fifty to seventy-five people gathered. As they withdrew from the scene, they met Willis Johnson, who from inside his funeral home had heard the commotion and had come to investigate. The MPs called him a "nigger" and a "son-of-a-bitch" and told him to get off the street.

The next issue of the *Lighthouse & Informer* treated the black men involved as heroes and the MPs as cowards. Part of the article read: "Using only his fists the civilian sent the MP sprawling on the sidewalks with a right hook, delivered in Joe Louis style. Lifting himself and drawing his service revolver, the MP hunted in vain for the man who had quickly fled the scene. A few minutes later when about fifty colored men suddenly appeared from nowhere to settle the matter the MP sized the situation up and made a hasty retreat."[58]

This time, the authorities at Fort Jackson tried to preempt Hinton by notifying William Hastie of the altercation themselves. They also attempted to discredit black civilians in that area of Columbia who might complain by persuading an African American soldier to submit an affidavit describing how the Williams brothers, who owned the Blue Palace, had mistreated him and his wife.[59] To their credit, the post officials did conduct an investigation. The officers appointed made conclusions that reflected the experience of the previous months. They recommended that the privates involved receive reprimands. Additionally, they suggested that black MPs be trained to replace the white ones.[60]

The matter might have ended amicably, but McCray's depiction of the incident had offended the honor of MP noncommissioned officers like T.Sgt. Carl Stone, who had earlier punched Sidney Friedman. On

Alienating Black Civilians | 47

16 January 1942, local blacks and a white civilian patrolman became in-volved in a scuffle. Cpl. Kie Haithcock and Pvt. Peter McCarthy decided to help. They subdued two black men with clubs and dragged them to the police station. When the prisoners appeared before city recorder Richard Broome (who functioned as a magistrate), Sergeant Stone re-marked that a "nigger newspaper" had threatened to give "Joe Louis uppercuts" to the MPs and that his men had taken care of the situation. Although Stone and Broome later denied that this was ever said, Hinton stood in the court as an eyewitness.

Hinton became enraged when the post commander declined to be-lieve his side of the story. Colonel Beebe made matters worse by tartly concluding a letter to him by saying, "May I suggest that in your work of improving conditions that you constantly give your support to the of-ficers of the law and discourage lawbreakers and disorderly elements."[61]

The Colored Citizens' Committee leader wrote a reply castigating Colonel Beebe for allowing the MPs to get away with their behavior. He concluded with a scathing attack on the post commander as a military leader. "Being an Officer in the last war," he said, "it is hard to believe that men in high commands would condone such treatment to citi-zens."[62] Having burned the last bridge with Fort Jackson, Hinton sent yet another round of letters to Washington and various national civil rights groups. The War Department responded by sending Lt. Col. Charles Richtel of the Fourth Service Command to investigate.

Not only did Lieutenant Colonel Richtel interview MPs and ag-grieved civilians, he called the post commander, the mayor, and the chief of police to the stand. In addition, he acquired as evidence a very candid letter the city recorder had written to the post commander. Colonel Beebe spoke the most diplomatically of the four men. He stated em-phatically that he had done everything possible to remedy the situation and offered no opinion on Hinton. Mayor Fred Marshall, who had re-cently succeeded Lawrence Owens, said of the MP situation, "I don't think it is a complaint to be disturbed over." Of Hinton, he said: "I do not like his attitude. I think he is too aggressive."[63]

Police Chief Campbell said: "I consider that most of this trouble is caused by agitators among the negro population."[64] City recorder Richard Broome weighed in the most stridently with a letter written to the post commander on 14 February. He said: "I wish to state that Hin-ton is apparently trying to take over the control of the Military Police de-partment . . . and is always intermeddling where he has absolutely no right. The type of negroes that the Military Police are called upon to

48 | BLACK, WHITE & OLIVE DRAB

arrest are a type that is continually giving trouble." Broome held the black preachers responsible for the unrest in the community and suggested that they "instill some decency in this tribe."[65]

Lieutenant Colonel Richtel disagreed. In a final report, he said: "Mr. Hinton and the Colored Citizens' Committee are correct in their remonstrations." The MPs "were seeking trouble. . . . There is no question that the action of these soldiers was due to the fact that the individuals in question were negroes and they took advantage of their position as military policemen. . . . It is probable that some of the members of the detachment . . . have not only *not* avoided trouble with citizens but . . . either sought it or deliberately mistreated and insulted negro citizens."[66]

Apparently expecting that the investigator would side with Hinton, Colonel Beebe took steps to minimize the fallout. He placed the area around Washington Street off-limits to all personnel and instructed the MPs to use automobiles instead of walking. Lieutenant Colonel Richtel praised the post commander for these policies, but he additionally suggested "ordering the members of the military police detachment to stop calling the negro citizens or soldiers 'nigger' and in no case to address or strike a negro unless it is in self-protection." He recommended that the War Department take "no further action."[67]

The furor subsided after this episode for several reasons. First, Colonel Beebe's new policies worked. Second, the escalation of American involvement in the war overseas distracted attention from domestic conflict. Third, and most important, African American military policemen began patrolling the Washington Street beat. Both Beebe and Hinton tried to claim credit for the black MPs, but this program was actually part of a nationwide effort directed by the War Department.[68]

Although Washington Street remained relatively calm, racial problems in Columbia involving soldiers from Fort Jackson persisted throughout the war. The Colored Citizens' Committee lent its support to any situation concerning African American soldiers or civilians. The shooting of Pvt. Larry Stroud was the most serious of the later incidents. On 4 November 1942, city patrolmen H. W. Steinhart killed Stroud with a pistol at a residence on Harden Street. Apparently the serviceman had slapped a civilian girl, which resulted in a brawl between soldiers and local blacks. The policeman claimed he shot Stroud in self-defense, a suspicious story given that the bullet had struck the private in the back of the head from a distance of twenty feet. Despite this evidence, the Richland County coroner declined to press charges.[69]

The Citizens Committee became involved as well with numerous

minor incidents. It assisted the master sergeant who had suffered discrimination on a railroad dining car in 1943. That same year the group intervened after the white lieutenant confiscated and burned a stack of *Pittsburgh Courier* newspapers at the station hospital. In 1944, the committee advised civilian black laundry workers at Fort Jackson who had complaints about their supervisor.[70]

Hinton continued as the committee's leader, and in every instance, he directed his grievances to the federal government or to national-level organizations. He had lost faith in the ability or willingness of the local chain of command to render justice. By 1942, Hinton had become the director of the state conference of the NAACP, and he remained a leader in the South Carolina civil rights movement until the sixties. Available records suggest strongly that he never had direct dealings with Fort Jackson again.

Many military men had no great love for Hinton or his colleagues. The Fort Jackson G2 intelligence officer began to keep records on him and forwarded the information to the Fourth Service Command. The *Lighthouse & Informer* was classified as propaganda. Domestic intelligence reports for subsequent years contained frequent references to James Hinton, John McCray, and Osceola McKaine as their activism broadened across the state.

Clearly, authorities at the post had cast their lot with the white elite of Columbia. The resolution of the investigation into the death of Private Stroud makes this point explicitly. The Fort Jackson officer assigned to investigate the case concluded that "even though I am not satisfied that Patrolman Steinhart was compelled to shoot Private Stroud . . . there is nothing further that can be accomplished by this investigation." After noting the policeman was a civilian, he said: "The only recourse of the military authorities would be the lodging of a protest with the City of Columbia. Such protest would accomplish no tangible benefits but would perhaps cause friction, antagonism and prevent future cooperation, which in the main has been excellent in the past."[71]

Although the morality of this decision was questionable, the understanding of the area's civilian power structure was flawless. Local whites controlled nearby resources, and they had connections to powerful congressmen such as Senators Ellison D. Smith and Burnet Maybank. South Carolinian James Byrnes functioned as the president's right-hand man in managing the domestic wartime economy. The members of the Colored Citizens' Committee were barely able to vote, let alone wield influence with such people.

50 | BLACK, WHITE & OLIVE DRAB

The post commander nevertheless had a choice. Furthermore, he displayed a willingness to offend local whites and shape state laws when the occasion suited him. Colonel Beebe originally came from Vermont, and he had a New Englander's abhorrence for roadside signs and billboards. In fact, he had once ordered the removal of all stop signs on-post—with disastrous results.

Perhaps self-impressed by his new stars, Brigadier General Beebe in the summer of 1942 decided he did not like the sprawl that had begun to line the sides of Jackson Boulevard as it left the main gate toward Garner's Ferry Road. "We had a rather shabby looking entrance," he said. "I wrote letters to the Chamber of Commerce and the Merchants' Association of the City of Columbia asking for their cooperation."[72]

The billboards posed a difficult problem because they stood on private property. The Warner Poster Advertising Company coordinated with local landowners and rented out space to businesses. Beebe contacted the advertising manager and practically ordered him to remove the signs. The civilian responded that he could not do so because he would have to break contracts and incur severe financial losses.

The post commander persisted. He contacted the businesses that rented billboard space and requested that they cease advertising. Most of them complied. For those who did not, Beebe ordered his post exchange officer not to pay outstanding bills. The latter knew that the Army could not legally renege on a debt, so he tried to accomplish the general's intent instead by threatening to deny the businesses access to customers on-post. At this point, the Warner Advertising Company filed a complaint with the War Department. Lieutenant Colonel Richtel returned to Fort Jackson, conducted another investigation, and put a stop to Beebe's interference with civilians.

The testimony of local businessmen in this matter reveals that Brigadier General Beebe possessed influence far beyond his legal mandate and suggests that he could have done more to seek justice for black troops like Private Stroud. Said one Columbia merchant, "I did not care to strain our relations out there." Said another, "I just wanted to work in harmony with the U.S. Army." Although he lost in the billboard case, the post commander displayed a willingness to upset powerful local businessmen in the furtherance of goals he truly desired.

The brutality of the military police, the mistreatment of black soldiers, and the insensitivity of the chain of command soured the attitude of many local African Americans toward the Army. "I'll be God Damn if they will draft me and send me to Fort Jackson," one black civilian at

Alienating Black Civilians | 51

the Columbia Air Base reportedly said. "They won't put me in any God Damn Army!"[73]

Most people supported the war, however. In fact, the Williams brothers at the Blue Palace Café became leading contributors to the 1943 war bond drive. That same year, John McCray earned praise from Mayor Marshall for writing editorials in the Lighthouse & Informer pleading with the blacks of Columbia not to emulate the race riots that were then taking place in Detroit, Harlem, and elsewhere. In 1943, the War Industrial Commission rated Columbia as a "C" in regard to racial tensions, with "A" the worst and "D" the best. Nevertheless, several factors exacerbated the division between the post and the local black community.[74]

First, the units stationed at Fort Jackson had almost no African American officers. Whereas white Columbia leaders made social contacts with the white officer corps, the equally class-conscious black elites had few, if any, such counterparts. These civilians took great pride in the career of E. A. Adams's daughter Charity, who graduated from the first-ever class of WAAC officers, rose to the rank of lieutenant colonel, and commanded the only battalion of black female soldiers to go overseas during the war. She was never stationed at Fort Jackson, however. No doubt African Americans in Columbia would have welcomed minority officers closer to home. Better relations with the post might have resulted.

Second, the mistreatment of black laundry workers on-post generated hard feelings toward the post. Some sent a letter to the civil service commissioner in 1944. They wrote: "We love our job, and is willing to work, but we are being treated so mean and unfair until some times we dont much care if we work or not please sir dont think we want to be equal with the white people. We dont want that. We are colored and if we mind our own business and stay in our places we will get along alright. But Mr. Commission you know yourself if you are treated as if you was some wild beast in a forest and every one was afraid of you, you would resent it to."[75]

They said that their supervisor used the epithet "nigger" and did not follow the procedures outlined in the handbook for civilian employees. They requested "some northern person to work us." They signed the letter as "Just a bunch of hard working colored women." Though anonymous, the complaint apparently stemmed from the firing of another African American woman who had sought help from the Colored Citizens' Committee. The inspector general responded by questioning nine women at random. Fearing for their jobs, the workers kept their mouths shut or answered obliquely. Nothing came of the complaint.

52 | BLACK, WHITE & OLIVE DRAB

The third reason many blacks felt alienated from Fort Jackson was that the issues primarily concerned men. With the exception of the laundry workers, some PX employees, a hundred or so WACs, and a few dozen prostitutes, the problems did not cross gender lines. The soldiers stationed on-post were overwhelmingly men, and the MPs usually beat up males. If indeed "men led and women organized," as historian Charles Payne posits, then any movement regarding Fort Jackson had a key element missing.[76]

The behavior of Modjeska Simkins suggests that such may have been the case regarding military-social relations in Columbia. She had campaigned for better black health care prior to World War II and had already displayed the aggressive spirit that would make her a leading figure. Seymour Carroll identified her as one of the town's more radical voices for civil rights. She took an interest in soldiers by giving lectures at the Harden Street USO during Negro Health Week in 1943 and later became affiliated with the United Negro Veterans. Simkins remained conspicuously absent during the MP brutality episodes, however, even though her husband owned a liquor store located directly across the street from the Blue Palace. Given this vested interest, her silence suggests that women had few opportunities to lead or organize over military issues.[77]

Fourth, and most important, African American troops from Fort Jackson sometimes did make nuisances of themselves. They brought in much-appreciated business, but they also drank, fought, spread venereal diseases, and drove up prices. Prior to being shot by a policeman, Private Stroud had slapped a civilian girl and was fighting with local blacks. Only the tragic outcome of this incident made it unusual. As the assistant provost marshal pointed out in 1942: "The feeling was very bad between the colored citizens and the negro soldiers. The reason for this is that the colored soldier is more profitable than citizens. The colored soldiers take the girls away from the colored citizens." The writer of a 1944 letter to the *State* agreed. "Even the colored people are divided into two classes: those in uniform and those not."[78]

Although the poor relationship between Columbia blacks and the authorities at Fort Jackson would harm the post's long-run potential for affecting civil rights change in South Carolina, events leading up to the rift benefited African Americans by generating a powerful local movement that would eventually influence events elsewhere. The MP brutality incidents galvanized support by presenting a common danger that roused not only the lower classes but also Columbia's rising black middle

Alienating Black Civilians | 53

class. The Colored Citizens' Committee brought them together. In addition, the tumult gave rise to such leaders as James Hinton, John McCray, and Osceola McKaine, newcomers who under ordinary circumstances would have had greater difficulty breaking into the tightly knit community. Together, they adopted new tactics. Instead of appealing to the city council and post officials, they directed complaints to the federal government and national civil rights organizations.

The movement formed over issues generated by Fort Jackson, but its ultimate direction took an unusual twist away from the military. Before the war ended, movement leaders would become involved in a statewide effort to equalize pay for teachers, gain the right to vote, and begin the long road to public school desegregation. The Colored Citizens' Committee would give rise to the Negro Citizens' Committee and the Progressive Democratic Party. In the ensuing struggle, Fort Jackson and the Army would continue to play a part.

3
★☆

Tangled Connections and Lost Opportunities
Fort Jackson at the End of World War II

There is a persistent story at Jackson that President Truman actually closed the post in 1948, partly for reasons of economy and partly to strike back at Dixiecrat defectors from the Democratic party.

— Tom Scanlan, ARMY TIMES GUIDE TO ARMY POSTS, 1963

One of the more enduring local legends surrounding Fort Jackson is that Harry Truman ordered it shut down because Strom Thurmond had run for president against him in 1948. The simplicity of this myth has over-shadowed the complexity and larger significance of the actual story. People and events connected to Fort Jackson and South Carolina were important strands in the web of circumstances that led the president to issue his executive order ending segregation of the armed forces. Iron-ically, they contributed as well to a subsequent decision to close the post, which in turn set the stage for Fort Jackson to be among the first to integrate.

★☆

The mid- to late 1940s witnessed an intensified struggle for civil rights. Availability of jobs during the war had fueled the economic well-being, political power, and social activism of African Americans. Meanwhile, many black veterans returned from overseas demanding full citizenship. Ability to participate fully in the electoral process was a major issue. In many states, African Americans could not vote in party primaries. The restriction especially harmed blacks in the South, where single-party rule rendered general elections irrelevant. The U.S. Supreme Court struck down this practice by the Texas Democratic Party in the 1944 case *Smith v. Allright*. The decision had national implications.

In South Carolina, the all-white legislature passed over a hundred bills designed to circumvent the ruling.[1] State blacks were divided. Some

Tangled Connections and Lost Opportunities | 55

thought that strengthening the Republican Party was the best course of action. Prominent among these people was Isaac Samuel Leevy, a Columbia mortician who had founded the city's chapter of the NAACP during the twenties. In 1944, he ran as the district's Republican candidate for state legislature. Although he lost, the notoriety he gained enabled him to found Lincoln Emancipation Clubs across the state. These groups encouraged voter registration and pushed for various civil rights initiatives.[2]

Other African Americans disagreed with Leevy's approach. They thought that voting as a Republican meant little in terms of real power when the Democrats controlled every state office. *Lighthouse & Informer* editor John McCray led their effort to gain a foothold in the party of Franklin Roosevelt. He founded the Progressive Democrats. Foreshadowing tactics that the more famous Mississippi Freedom Democratic Party would use two decades later, McCray and his supporters tried unsuccessfully to unseat the white South Carolina delegation at the 1944 convention.

After a second attempt failed in 1946, the Progressive Democrats took a different tack. They began to challenge the constitutionality of the laws passed in 1944 that kept African Americans from voting in the primaries. In 1947, a Columbia businessman named George Elmore filed a lawsuit against the leader of the state Democratic organization, John I. Rice, in the case *Elmore v. Rice*. This case would become a turning point in South Carolina history.

Throughout this period, the Negro Citizens' Committee served as a unifying force among competing factions of South Carolina blacks. Available evidence suggests it evolved out of the Colored Citizens' Committee that arose in response to the 1941 Columbia MP incidents.[3] The group organized bases of support in each of the state's congressional districts. It also raised funds for lawsuits against the Democratic Party's all-white primary.[4] Although most of its leaders supported the Progressive Democrats—James Hinton delivered the keynote address at the party's first convention—the committee remained politically neutral. This policy sometimes caused friction. Osceola McKaine, for example, charged the committee with inactivity and failure to use effectively the three to four thousand dollars of donations it had collected. "The Negro citizens committee should be dissolved immediately and its funds should be turned over either to the NAACP State Conference or to the Progressive Democratic Party," he said. "Either of these organizations would get us some action."[5]

56 | BLACK, WHITE & OLIVE DRAB

Hinton's committee was involved with other activities besides voting. The drive to get black policemen and equal playground facilities in Columbia remained perennial issues.[6] The committee also continued to assist African American troops from Fort Jackson. Interestingly, the state-level organization still served as the primary source of contact for GI complaints from the post even after a Richland County chapter of the committee was formed in 1944.

In November 1946, the state committee intervened on behalf of a black soldier named Charley Jackson. Columbia police had arrested him after he had come to the assistance of a comrade who had sat down next to a white girl on a city bus. A lawman also slapped Jackson for not addressing him as "sir." The local judge added insult to the injury by setting the serviceman's bail higher than the one who had violated the segregation law in the first place. "We are not condoning the wrong of the soldiers nor the fine assessed against them," Hinton said in a letter to the mayor, "but we are asking for an investigation of the slapping of the 'Jackson' soldier in jail after he had been arrested, taken to jail, and searched."[7]

Rarely, if at all, did Hinton or his colleagues seek assistance from the Fort Jackson post headquarters. The MP incidents of World War II had destroyed any hope that local military authorities would act justly. Letters written by Hinton on behalf of soldiers were addressed to city officials, as happened in the Jackson case, or to the Army in Washington, as would happen over the next few years.

One possible exception to this rule was John McCray. The editor held staunchly anti-Communist views, which placed him increasingly at odds with Osceola McKaine, whose political orientation leaned more to the left. Eventually, the rift would drive the two apart. FBI files reveal that a confidential source at the *Lighthouse & Informer* had reported information about McKaine to the Fort Jackson provost marshal in 1946. Evidence suggests that McCray might have been the informant.[8]

Regardless of any such behind-the-scene activities, public involvement with Fort Jackson by Columbia blacks clearly dropped by the close of World War II. Frustration with post officials, growing disenchantment with rowdy soldiers on pass, and the paucity of black officers with whom the local elite could interact contributed to the lack of interest.

The closing of the Harden Street USO cut an especially vital link. Of the two wartime clubs for African Americans, this one had been the most active. The other one, on Taylor Street, was less a part of the community because its Catholic director upset the conservative Protestants who ran

Tangled Connections and Lost Opportunities | 57

Allen University and Benedict College. By 1947, neither of the schools would allow their female students to attend USO dances, although, as John McCray acidly noted in a column, they did invite soldiers to fund-raising block parties. An Army officer appointed to examine community relations commented that February, "The attitude of both white and colored citizens toward the colored soldiers of Fort Jackson is that of indifference."[9]

The reduction of personnel at the post also loosened military-social connections between Columbia and the post. After the all-white 106th Infantry Division and the all-black 1700th Engineer Battalion departed in 1944, no new units replaced them. Soldiers began streaming back to South Carolina in the middle of 1945, when the War Department opened an out-processing station for them at Fort Jackson. The often-boisterous behavior of these transients served to unravel community ties further.

Civil rights activists in Columbia nevertheless tried to assist returning soldiers. In 1945, I. S. Leevy's Lincoln Emancipation Clubs made acquisition of black nurses in Veterans Administration hospitals a top priority. Osceola McKaine wrote articles for the *Lighthouse & Informer* telling servicemen about their rights under federal law. In 1949, the state NAACP intervened after a school in West Columbia was discovered to have been taking GI bill funds while "teaching" their black "students" how to do menial construction work on a new building. Those who failed this contrived course of study lost any further benefits.[10]

Local leaders recognized that veterans had the moral authority and organizational experience to become a potent force for change. In 1946, Modjeska Simkins and John McCray helped to found a national group called the United Negro and Allied Veterans Association (UNAVA). They brought activist-entertainer Paul Robeson to Columbia in 1947, where he performed a benefit at the Township Auditorium. Only twenty-five people attended as momentum for the UNAVA dwindled to nothingness.[11]

James Hinton tried to involve black veterans with elections. One of his recruits was Matthew Perry, a South Carolinian who was discharged from the Army in 1946 after serving overseas in Europe. Perry entered college at South Carolina State that fall but took time from his studies to rally voters. Although he belonged to the Republican Party at the time, he went from house to house encouraging blacks to register as Democrats. Perry did not remember anything about the UNAVA, and despite his work, he and his former comrades-in-arms were never a major factor in

58 | BLACK, WHITE & OLIVE DRAB

state politics. Black ex-servicemen did join segregated chapters of the state's American Legion, but these groups did not have much influence either.[12]

Unorganized soldiers caused more of a stir in South Carolina than did ones in formal groups. African American veterans awaiting discharge at Fort Jackson started several near-riots in late 1945 and early 1946. The exact causes are unknown, but Army intelligence agents considered their origins to be racial. In November 1945, black soldiers brawled at the colored-area PX, assaulted the black female civilian clerks, and looted the store. In December, two white peanut vendors claimed to have been attacked on three separate occasions by three different pairs of black soldiers. In February 1946, according to a domestic intelligence report, "a riot of small proportions occurred . . . when a crowd of Negro soldiers returning from a theater created a disturbance by throwing bottles at a service club building." In March, a riot involving almost four hundred African American troops took place at the post theater. Although none of these incidents made headlines in the local papers, they clearly increased racial tensions. One white commander grew so fearful and suspicious that he ordered blacks on guard duty to carry broomsticks instead of weapons.[13]

Unrest among African American troops extended beyond Fort Jackson into Columbia.[14] In December 1945, a group of soldiers threatened to shoot up a civilian bus. In January 1946, three soldiers from Fort Jackson stabbed two white Columbians, injuring both but killing neither. The police caught only one of the assailants, who received six months in the stockade after a court-martial.[15] In March, a white Columbia woman accused a black soldier from Fort Jackson of throwing her to the ground and attacking her. A bystander heard screams and came to her aid. The city police arrested the soldier but released him after the woman admitted some days later that he had done nothing more than speak to her. The serviceman said later that the woman had become unduly frightened after he had asked her the whereabouts of his girlfriend.[16]

Conflicts between black soldiers and civilians occurred across the state. In April 1945, police in Florence arrested an airman from the nearby base for sitting next to a white girl. In May, two soldiers scuffled with a Greenville taxi driver. During the same month, two airmen from Myrtle Beach Army Airfield got into a fight at a filling station.[17] In December 1945, police in Darlington arrested two soldiers for being drunk and disorderly on a civilian bus. The judge there gave the pair the choice

Tangled Connections and Lost Opportunities | 59

of paying a $12 fine or spending twenty days on the chain gang. Neither soldier had enough money. After a few days of hard labor, however, one of them sold his watch. He then paid his fine and notified Army authorities, who had erroneously believed them to have been AWOL.[18]

Some of the encounters resulted in death. In August 1945, a white civilian from Elko shot a recently discharged veteran in what *Lighthouse & Informer* editor John McCray termed a lynching.[19] In November, a Johnsonville police officer killed another veteran with a pistol for undetermined reasons.[20] Fatal or otherwise, all of these events provided the context for South Carolina's most notorious racial incident involving a veteran, the blinding of Isaac Woodard.[21]

Woodard was a native of Winnsboro, located twenty-five miles to the north of Columbia. He went through the induction station at Fort Jackson in 1942 before spending most of the war in the Pacific theater as a military longshoreman. He received his discharge at Camp Gordon, Georgia, on 12 February 1946. That evening, he boarded a bus for Columbia and his hometown.

Exactly what happened remains unclear. Nighttime had fallen, and the bus contained a mixture of civilian travelers and soldiers. Some of the latter raised eyebrows by talking together in integrated groups. A bottle of whiskey apparently passed hands, but nobody knows exactly who imbibed. The driver, A. C. Blackwell of Columbia, claimed that he had seen Woodard drinking, that he had heard him swearing, and that the disruption had offended a white female passenger. Woodard denied consuming any alcohol, and several witnesses testified to his sobriety. All agreed, however, that he attracted the driver's ire after he had asked if there was time for him to empty his bladder during a stop. The driver said Woodard made the request in a vulgar manner by asking to "take a piss."[22]

"Boy, go on back and sit down and keep quiet and don't be talking out so loud," Blackwell told the soldier.[23]

"God damn it, talk to me like I'm talking to you. I'm a man just like you," Woodard replied.[24]

When the bus stopped at Batesburg, the driver asked the soldier to step off and talk with two lawmen he had summoned, Chief Lynwood Shull and Officer Elliot Long. Woodard testified that one of the policemen struck him when he tried to tell his side. A soldier sitting on the bus supported this account. Shull said he had only shaken a blackjack at Woodard because he would not be quiet, used profanity, and reeked of alcohol. According to the chief, the soldier had created enough of a dis-

turbance outside of the bus to warrant arrest regardless of what had occurred inside. Shull led Woodard away by the arm. Long stayed behind to question a white soldier.

All parties agreed that the blinding occurred after the pair rounded a corner out of sight of the bus. Whether by accident or intent, Shull twisted his prisoner's arm. The chief said his attention was diverted when he looked back to see if Long was following. Woodard said he had angered Shull by answering "Yes" instead of "Yes, sir" to a question. He also admitted that he "lit into" the chief and tried to take away the blackjack.[25] In fact, he claimed to have successfully removed it only to have Long arrive with a gun. Shull was equally candid. "I hit him across the front of the head," he later said. "He attempted to take away my blackjack. I grabbed it away from him and cracked him across the head."[26] Exactly how many blows were struck is unknown, but the force of one or more of them ruptured both eyeballs. After gaining the upper hand, Shull took the soldier to jail.

Woodard had difficulty seeing when he awoke the next morning. Rather than taking him for treatment, they hauled him before the magistrate, who charged him with drunk and disorderly conduct. The soldier pled guilty and was fined $50. He had only $44 in cash, so the judge took the available money and suspended the remainder. The police escorted Woodard back to his cell, where they attempted first aid with a hot towel and nonprescription eye drops. Later during the day, the police drove him to the veterans' hospital in Columbia. Woodard underwent treatment for two months. He emerged completely sightless in April.

The incident would have gone unnoticed except that Woodard moved to New York City, where his parents lived and where the national office of the NAACP was headquartered. Executive secretary Walter White intervened personally on his behalf. A group of celebrities including boxer Joe Louis and actor Paul Robeson arranged a benefit for Woodard. Folk singer Woody Guthrie composed a song for the occasion, "The Blinding of Isaac Woodard," and performed it for the twenty thousand people who attended the show that August. The case became a national and international sensation after Orson Welles reported the story on his American Broadcasting Company radio news broadcast.

The story attracted attention in South Carolina not out of concern about Woodard, but because Orson Welles misidentified the site of the blinding as the town of Aiken. Municipal leaders there were furious. They banned from their theaters all films directed by Welles, who by this time was already famous for *Citizen Kane*. James Hinton and John

Tangled Connections and Lost Opportunities | 61

McCray helped Walter White to pinpoint Batesburg as the location. Woodard, understandably, had been uncertain about the exact place.

In September, the NAACP began making plans for the veteran to speak before audiences across the country. The national tour would raise money for a trust fund and increase awareness of the dangers facing black veterans. The Batesburg incident was one of many to occur in 1946. During late February, armed African Americans in Tennessee fought off a lynch mob of whites who wanted to kill a former navy sailor. In July, a group of whites in Georgia shot to death an Army veteran and three members of his family. In August, a former soldier was released by the Louisiana police into the hands of men who tortured him to death slowly with a blow torch and meat cleaver.[27] News of these atrocities circled the globe to France and the Soviet Union.[28] The revelations were a source of tremendous embarrassment to the United States, which at the time was involved with prosecuting prominent Nazis at Nuremberg for war crimes.

Not by coincidence, September marked the beginning of greater involvement in these cases by the federal government. Part of the impetus came from the upcoming congressional elections that November, but part came from the very genuine outrage of President Truman. On 20 September, after a meeting the day prior with Walter White, the president wrote a letter to his attorney general, Tom Clark: "I had as callers yesterday some members of the National Association for the Advancement of Colored People and they told me about an incident which happened in South Carolina where a negro [sic] Sergeant who had been discharged from the Army just three hours, was taken off the bus and not only seriously beaten but his eyes deliberately put out."[29] Truman asked what could be done.

As a result, the federal government prosecuted Chief Shull for violating Woodard's rights under the Constitution.[30] The charges were filed at the federal district court in Columbia, which had jurisdiction over the Batesburg area. The judge who normally would have presided, George Bell Timmerman Sr., was a local native and knew Shull personally, so the case went to J. Waties Waring of Charleston.

The trial began that November. U.S. Attorney Claude Sapp had spent so little time preparing that he did not even know how to pronounce Woodard's name correctly in front of the jury. The defense attorneys meanwhile pointed out the veteran's earlier guilty plea to drunk and disorderly conduct as well as his admission that he had attempted to disarm a police officer. They built a persuasive case that Shull had not violated

62 | BLACK, WHITE & OLIVE DRAB

Woodard's constitutional rights. The lawyers were not content to rest on reason or the evidence, however. They laced their closing statement with raw appeals to racism. Woodard belonged to the "inferior race." Worse, he lived in New York. "That's not the talk of a sober nigger from South Carolina," one of them said. If the all-white jury convicted Shull, they warned, the police would no longer be able to protect wives and children. If siding against the federal government prosecutors meant the state should secede from the Union as it did in 1860, then it should do so again.[31]

The jury took twenty-five minutes to deliver a verdict of "not guilty" to the cheers of spectators. The twelve would have returned sooner, but Judge Waring, sensing the outcome, decided to take a twenty-minute walk.[32] Woodard wept with what remained of his eyes. The case remained in the public eye for another year. The NAACP continued with Woodard's national tour and raised enough money to establish an annuity for him. He attended the Avon School for the Blind in Connecticut where he learned basic survival skills like reading Braille. He also filed a civil lawsuit against the corporation that owned and operated the bus on which everything started.[33] That case was decided against him in November 1947. Woodard then disappeared into obscurity, living forty-six years in darkness before passing away in 1992.

White people in Columbia did not ponder long over the injustice done to Woodard or over the similar mistreatment of Fort Jackson soldiers or even over the racial disturbances on-post. The military story that garnered the biggest local headlines during this period involved a white Army doctor from the post who had allegedly poisoned his wife with sleeping pills and buried her in a shallow grave.[34] Although the Woodard case had little direct bearing upon Fort Jackson, it would have long-term consequences for the area. The blinding of the soldier made a lasting impression on the consciences of two influential people—President Truman and Judge Waring—who in turn would set into motion a long chain of events that would reverberate nationally and back to the post.

The judge was an unlikely crusader. A Charleston native, he had an ancestry that stretched back to the seventeenth century in a city where such distinctions mattered. He attended the College of Charleston, married a woman of prestigious lineage, established a law practice, and took his place among in the local elite. As a lawyer during World War I, Waring defended the leasing of a recreation area to the Army on the condition that only whites could use it.

His racial views became more moderate by the 1940s, however. He

Tangled Connections and Lost Opportunities | 63

shocked Thurgood Marshall in 1943 by giving equitable treatment to black public school teachers from Charleston who had sued for equal pay in the case *Duval v. Seignous*.[35] Nevertheless, the judge believed that integration should not take place abruptly. He said in a 1945 letter: "I really believe that we liberal minded southerners may be able to eventually cure this situation . . . by moderate, gradual[,] and understanding action."[36]

Waring's advocacy of civil rights became much more strident after the Woodard case. He ended the segregation of spectators and unequal treatment of black jurors in his courtroom. He began reading books like Gunnar Myrdal's *An American Dilemma*. Some critics claim that Waring's later rulings stemmed from a desire to punish white elites for snubbing his second wife. The judge in 1944 had callously divorced his first spouse, ejected her from her ancestral home, and hastily remarried a northerner with liberal political views. The new couple withdrew from Charleston society. Regardless of whether or not she was ostracized, Mrs. Waring did play a part in her husband's transformation. She attended the Woodard trial and wept at the verdict. She grew more interested in civil rights and read Myrdal aloud at nights.

The change in Waring became apparent six months later when he presided over the *Elmore v. Rice* lawsuit filed by blacks wanting to participate in the primary. He based his decision for the plaintiffs on constitutional grounds, but the language of his ruling had clear connections to Woodard. His written opinion concluded with a direct rebuttal to the closing argument of Lynwood Shull's lawyer: "It is time for South Carolina to rejoin the Union."[37] The choice of words, as much as the substance, made *Elmore v. Rice* a milestone in state history.

Waring would later make a contribution of national significance. In 1948, parents in Clarendon County, South Carolina, petitioned for their district to provide buses for black children. Although African Americans made up 75 percent of this county's population, only the whites had transportation. With the help of Thurgood Marshall and James Hinton, the parents sued for equal facilities. Waring rejected the initial plea and advised them to argue directly against the idea of segregation. The lawsuit, *Briggs v. Elliot*, went before a panel of three judges, who decided against the plaintiffs in 1951 by a vote of 2–1. Waring cast the opposing vote. In his dissent, he became the first federal jurist to argue explicitly against the "separate but equal" doctrine set forth in *Plessy v. Ferguson*. The Clarendon lawsuit eventually became one of the cases subsumed under *Brown*.

The Woodard case had similar reverberations at the White House.

64 | BLACK, WHITE & OLIVE DRAB

President Truman retained the prejudices of a Missouri upbringing and was known to make occasional racist remarks. The mistreatment of veterans like Woodard violated his sense of justice, however. The president said in a letter to an old friend: "When a Mayor and a City Marshal can take a negro Sergeant off a bus in South Carolina, beat him up and put out one of his eyes, and nothing is done about it by the State Authorities, something is radically wrong with the system."[38] In December 1946, Truman appointed a commission to investigate. The group submitted its findings the next year in a report called *To Secure These Rights*. Its recommendation that armed forces segregation end would become the foundation for a subsequent executive order.

The president's decision to integrate the armed forces came within the context of his 1948 campaign for reelection. He faced a strong challenge from the Republicans, who had taken control of Congress in 1946. Worse, his party suffered from deep divisions. Many left-leaning Democrats favored replacing Truman with Henry Wallace, who had served as Roosevelt's vice president during a previous term.

Truman sought to co-opt this challenge by adopting a more liberal stance while staying to the political right of Wallace. Crucial to this strategy was winning the votes of urban blacks, and from this effort arose many of his civil rights initiatives. As for the South, the president followed the advice of his aide Clark Clifford and made a conscious decision to ignore any protests regarding race that might come from the region. They reasoned that southerners would have no alternative but to vote for the Democrats.

Southern Democrats answered by launching a third-party movement of their own that journalists quickly dubbed the "Dixiecrats." Their candidate was J. Strom Thurmond of South Carolina. This Edgefield County native, whose political career would span the twentieth century, had a lifelong thirst for office. He entered his first election in 1928 as a candidate for school superintendent. He was a judge by 1941. He resigned this office and volunteered for the Army when the country entered the Second World War. His combat experience included riding a glider into Normandy on D-Day. After the war, he parlayed his veteran's status into the governor's mansion. Thurmond became the nominee of the States Rights Party at a July 1948 convention in Birmingham. He would win electoral votes in four states.[39]

The defection of Thurmond and his followers further emboldened Truman to adopt many of the recommendations put forth by the Commission on Civil Rights. Two weeks after the Dixiecrat convention, on

Tangled Connections and Lost Opportunities | 65

26 July 1948, he issued Executive Order 9981. It stated that "there shall be equality of treatment and opportunity for all persons in the armed services without regard to race, color, religion, or national origin." The order did not call for an immediate end, but "as rapidly as possible, having due regard to the time required to effectuate any necessary changes without impairing efficiency or morale." The order also established an advisory committee to oversee the process. Within a few months, Alabaman Charles Fahy would receive the appointment of chairman.[40]

Truman's order received relatively little attention in South Carolina because people there were preoccupied that same month with a major court ruling over the right to vote in primary elections. During the 1947 *Elmore v. Rice* case, Judge Waring had ordered the Democrats to stop excluding blacks. Instead of obeying the spirit of the ruling, party leaders changed the rules for registration. African Americans could participate, but only if they swore an oath to uphold segregation. The state NAACP sued to end this requirement the following year in *Brown v. Baskin.* Judge Waring again presided, and he agreed that the Democrats had gone too far. He overturned the oath requirement, calling it a "flagrant disregard of the rights of American citizens to exercise their own views and opinions."[41]

Reactions to this ruling dominated the headlines and editorials in South Carolina's major newspapers that July. By contrast, Truman's order to desegregate the armed forces did not seem as consequential. In the *Columbia Record,* for example, George Buchanan placed the article that announced it below the fold of the front page and titled it "Race Clauses Subdued in Truman's Message." He did not write an editorial about the new policy until two days later, when he said that the order would "accomplish very little of either good or evil, except to serve to make the Southern Democrats still madder."[42]

South Carolina politicians remained relatively quiet. Senator Maybank, who had worked to maintain a segregated draft and who stridently condemned the rulings of Judge Waring, declined to speak out directly against the executive order. Instead, he commended Chief of Staff Gen. Omar Bradley for his assurance that the Army would continue to "put men of different races in different companies." Bradley, who had spoken before actually reading the president's words, was forced to recant his statement a few days later. No doubt some people in South Carolina failed, like the general, to pay sufficiently close attention to the order.

Another reason Truman's directive had little effect on Fort Jackson, however, was that virtually no African Americans were stationed there

66 | Black, White & Olive Drab

in 1948. Oddly, this had been the case for only a short while. The post nearly had a preponderance of blacks only eighteen months earlier. The War Department had designated the post as one of the nation's six replacement training centers. Given the high percentage of African Americans in the Columbia area, Pentagon planners decided to make Fort Jackson the central location for the basic training of black soldiers.[43]

To that end, Army Ground Forces attached the Fifth Composite Training Regiment to the post in October 1946. The Army Ground Forces no longer trained divisions as a whole as had been the practice during World War II. Rather, individuals went to basic training prior to their permanent assignment. The Fifth Regiment joined at least two white regiments in fulfilling this mission at Fort Jackson. The Fifth consisted of two training battalions, the 101st and the 102nd. The total number of African Americans in these units would swell to almost one thousand people. Whites commanded the battalions, but a considerable number of black officers did work in the companies. Sources remain sketchy, but apparently the regiment occupied buildings on the northern part of post. This area had more space than did the old "colored area."[44]

In November 1946, the same month Lynwood Shull went on trial in Columbia for blinding Isaac Woodard, the War Department began solidifying plans for sending all of the Army's black trainees to South Carolina. Civilian Aide for Negro Affairs Marcus Ray disagreed strongly with this decision. He sent a letter to War Secretary Robert Patterson in which he noted the racial problems that the Army had experienced in this region during World War II. When his warnings went unheeded, Ray leaked the news to the press.[45]

National black newspapers such as the *Pittsburgh Courier* predictably recoiled at the idea of stationing black troops in the South. In its 25 January 1947 issue, it said that Fort Jackson "was considered one of the worst posts at which colored troops were stationed during the war. Colored soldiers stationed there complained of race discrimination and segregation, both on the post and in the adjacent civilian communities."[46]

By early 1947, almost a thousand black troops were assigned to Fort Jackson. Complaints began almost immediately. "Colored" and "white" signs still marked some facilities on-post even though a 1943 War Department directive had forbidden such practices. This same policy had forbidden discrimination by race in post exchanges, theaters, and service clubs. On 23 January 1947, however, the hostess at Fort Jackson's Service Club Number 1 had asked four black soldiers to leave and use the club in their own area.[47]

Tangled Connections and Lost Opportunities | 67

The newcomers fared little better off-post. Not only did they face Jim Crow laws, they received little support from the civilian black community. The leaders of Allen University and Benedict College, for example, did not allow their coeds to frequent the Taylor Street USO. Most of the support for dances and recreational activities came from South Carolina State University in Orangeburg. Besides these infrequent occasions, the soldiers had only the segregated bars of "Burma Road" for entertainment.[48]

Additionally, personnel managers had difficulties finding units to which blacks could be assigned permanently once they had completed basic training. During the Second World War, the Army could expand its number of engineer and quartermaster labor battalions. Postwar budget constraints had ended this practice. Furthermore, the Army had explicit guidelines as to where black soldiers could be assigned and in what numbers. Matching racially driven manpower requirements to the incoming flow of draftees and volunteers was a virtually impossible task given the available information technology of the time. Fort Jackson began to experience a backlog of unhappy basic training graduates.

The presence of black officers complicated the situation further. The establishment of an officers club in the Fifth Regimental area kept the races apart socially. Unlike most enlisted soldiers, however, the duties of officers varied much more from day-to-day and ranged across the post. Interracial conflict erupted unexpectedly and in uncontrolled milieus where tempers could easily flare.

On 17 January 1947, for example, 1st Lt. Ronald Mordecai of the 102nd Training Battalion attended a briefing on how to process military claims. Major William T. Lane served as the class instructor. When he described a recent car accident involving soldiers, he noted that the crash had taken place in Columbia's "niggertown." Mordecai complained during the next break period. The major told the young black officer, "Take your seat and don't try to ruin my lecture." He then grabbed Mordecai by the arm and attempted to escort him to a seat. When the class resumed, Lane explained his remarks concerning "negrapeople."

"I am a Southerner and I meant no disrespect speaking as I did," he said. The lieutenant "is not due an apology from me."[49]

Lieutenant Mordecai took his complaint first to his battalion operations officer, who had witnessed the incident. At his suggestion, Mordecai went to the division operations officer. Within three weeks, his complaint reached Marcus Ray at the War Department. The quick elevation of the case came mainly because of the media attention that was drawn

68 | BLACK, WHITE & OLIVE DRAB

to the post during this time by papers like the *Pittsburgh Courier*. In fact, the War Department had already dispatched an officer from the inspector general's office to determine the overall suitability of Fort Jackson.

Lt. Col. Sam Elliot spent several days in South Carolina during early February. He interviewed the Fifth Regimental commander, the chaplain, and fifty African American soldiers chosen at random. He found that most of the blacks had concerns about their being stationed at Fort Jackson. He uncovered several incidents of discrimination on-post. He found that few of the people interviewed had ever ventured off the military reservation more than once or twice.

Nevertheless, the inspector went off-post to interview George Buchanan, John McCray, Chief of Police Campbell, the secretary of the chamber of commerce, the presidents of Allen and Benedict, and numerous other civic leaders. Lieutenant Colonel Elliot determined that the racial climate of Columbia was not unduly hostile to African American soldiers. The white citizens preferred no blacks, but they wanted to keep Fort Jackson open and did not mind having soldiers of color so long as their numbers did not create a majority of African Americans in the area.

In his 14 February report, Elliot recommended that the number of blacks at Fort Jackson not exceed the number of whites. He added that the Army should ensure that African American soldiers who finished basic training receive their permanent assignments promptly.[50]

Pressure from the black press had already forced the War Department to act without regard to Elliot's conclusions. In early February, AGF issued an order rescinding the policy of sending all black troops to Fort Jackson. Instead, it mandated that none should be sent to the post for basic training. Draftees and volunteers from the Third Army Area (formerly the Fourth Service Command) would go to Fort Dix, New Jersey, or Fort Knox, Kentucky. In order to balance this influx of people northward, an equivalent number of whites that ordinarily would have gone to Dix or Knox would go to South Carolina.[51]

The headquarters at Fort Jackson quickly expanded its out-processing capacity and began transferring African American troops. The soldiers trickled to other assignments over the next two to three months. As Lieutenant Mordecai wrote to Marcus Ray that March: "By the time you receive this letter, only two colored officers will be left at Fort Jackson. The last large group will be leaving for Fort Knox, Kentucky and Fort Dix, New Jersey tomorrow. There are still approximately eight hundred colored enlisted men here, but they are being shipped out

Tangled Connections and Lost Opportunities | 69

gradually." Mordecai did not go, however. He resigned his commission and left the Army.[52]

Racial tensions did not end until the last of the Fifth Training Regiment had departed. Apparently somebody at Fort Jackson thought that the out-processing soldiers would make handy sources of labor and began to use them for work details. Some African American corporals and sergeants received orders that April to clean barracks, a duty that offended them both as noncommissioned officers and as blacks. They complained to the Negro Citizens' Committee, and James Hinton promptly wrote a letter to Marcus Ray. "We have not seen or heard of any White NonComs cleaning up any quarters of Negro Soldiers," Hinton wrote. Ray gave the Columbia leader a polite reply and let the problem solve itself by attrition.[53] By July, even the Taylor Street USO had closed.

Virtually no black soldiers remained when the Fifth Infantry Division was activated at Fort Jackson during the summer of 1947. Commanded by Maj. Gen. George Decker, the Fifth differed from the infantry divisions that had trained at the post during World War II in that it was intended explicitly for training and would not deploy to a combat area. Army planners used the designation only to give basic trainees a sense of belonging to a famous division. The soldiers would cycle through basic and move to a permanent assignment with another unit. Captain Roy Hogan came to the post as a company commander in the Fifth Division during late 1947 and did not remember seeing any African American servicemen.[54]

Indeed, only 289 of them were assigned by the time President Truman issued his 1948 executive order. The Fahy Committee nevertheless took a look at Fort Jackson when it surveyed racial conditions at various installations. A staff member named Joseph Evans conducted the visit to South Carolina. Unfortunately, he died suddenly and never gave formal testimony. He did leave the questionnaires he had collected, and these provide a valuable snapshot of the post in early 1949.[55]

All of the remaining black soldiers belonged to Section 2 of the 3431st Area Service Unit. This section had descended from the Colored Detachment of the station complement that had existed during the war.[56] In fact, its members performed essentially the same tasks. Most of the personnel belonged to the supply and engineer sections. Eighty-nine soldiers were classified as drivers while the others worked as mechanics, cooks, clerks, and medical technicians. Sixteen men served as military policemen, and like their predecessors, they patrolled the black sections

70 | BLACK, WHITE & OLIVE DRAB

of Columbia as well as the service club and theater in the "colored area" of Fort Jackson.

The 3431st had only one African American officer, 1st Lt. Joseph H. Green, who served as a dentist. Finding social accommodations for this lone black officer posed a problem after the Fifth Regiment Officers Club closed. According to the Fort Jackson representative who filled out the questionnaire, the lieutenant had been extended membership in the main officers club, but he had voluntarily declined to join. "As only members are allowed to use club facilities, he does not use them." Army custom made joining the club virtually mandatory for officers, so Lieutenant Green's behavior was highly unusual.

The black dentist did not supervise any white soldiers, nor did any of the African American sergeants. The Fort Jackson headquarters had little direct responsibility for this arrangement. Rather, a Table of Distribution and Allowances (TDA) established the positions and coded them explicitly by race and gender. The TDA specified no black females for Fort Jackson although it did call for thirty white enlisted women and two white female officers. The post also had 243 African American civilian workers, most of whom held positions in the laundry.[57]

Although little appeared to have changed at Fort Jackson since World War II, one thing had: African Americans competed with whites in sports competition.[58] This integration did not extend beyond post boundaries, but it marked a step toward changing attitudes and reflected the recent breaking of the color barrier by Jackie Robinson in major league baseball. The growing inefficiency of segregated units, however, did more toward ending division of the races in the ranks than did athletics. As the Army became increasingly bureaucratized, TDAs such as the one that governed the 3431st Army Service Unit became widespread. Trying to fill slots on the basis of race caused an administrative nightmare, created extra work, and undermined the logic of segregation.

People at and around Fort Jackson had little opportunity to grapple with these kinds of issues or Truman's order because they soon became embroiled in a struggle for survival. On 23 August 1949, Secretary of Defense Louis Johnson announced a series of nationwide military cutbacks that included installation closures. The post was tentatively selected as one of several to become National Guard encampments. In effect, it would revert to the status it had held between the two world wars.[59]

This change would have a tremendous impact on Columbia. Fort Jackson would lose 11,275 troops and 1,185 civilian jobs. These people earned a combined total of $1.21 million, most of which they spent in

Tangled Connections and Lost Opportunities | 71

nearby businesses. Over two thousand military-related families rented or purchased homes in the surrounding community. Local construction contractors received a large share of the $1 million spent on improvements during the previous year. The post further stimulated the economy by spending an average of $237,915 monthly on contracted services and purchases.[60]

The move to close Fort Jackson came as a shock to city leaders, but they regrouped quickly. Mayor Frank Owens worked closely with the president of the chamber of commerce as well as the chairman of the chamber's Armed Services Committee, editor George Buchanan. The Columbians asked the South Carolina congressional delegation to intervene and sent telegrams directly to the Department of Defense. Mayor Owens went to Washington and, with Senator Maybank, made a personal appeal to Secretary of the Army Gordon Gray on 26 August. These efforts failed. By the end of the month, the Department of Defense decided that the post would be reduced to a "standby" status effective 1 July 1950. A second delegation from Columbia visited Washington in September, but the Pentagon's decision stood firm.[61]

The formal announcement added insult to injury by noting that the choice had been between Fort Jackson and Camp Gordon. Installations designated as "Fort" were supposedly more permanent than those called "Camp." People such as George Buchanan interpreted this slight as an indication of Washington's failure to assess the situation correctly. The editor sought without success to comprehend the closure in a 31 August editorial. "Apparently the voluminous file in the war department relating to Fort Jackson wasn't even consulted," Buchanan griped. He implied that the Dixiecrat rebellion had something to do with the decision by concluding: "President Truman announced that the cuts in the armed services were made on his order."

The *Columbia Record* ran an article a few days later in which the Second District congressman insisted that Fort Jackson's closing was not politically motivated, but few people in Columbia agreed. A soon-to-be-unemployed civilian worker wrote to President Truman: "We know that Secretary Johnson made the statement that the closing of these projects was an 'economy move', [sic] but we also know that it isn't true and is only meant to spite the Governor." Another correspondent wrote to Senator Olin Johnston: "It looks more like a case of to get even with the Dixiecrats than to economize." Even the congressman from the district surrounding Fort Jackson believed that revenge was a motive. In 1955, Representative John Riley wrote to Senator Thurmond: "I am inclined to

72 | BLACK, WHITE & OLIVE DRAB

think that Jackson was dropped from the list during the regime of Louis Johnson after Truman was elected in 1948, but, of course, I cannot give any publicity to this."[62]

Although this belief lasted even through the 1990s, now-declassified Department of Defense documents refute it. According to a memorandum dated 29 August 1949, Secretary of the Army Gray held a meeting to discuss the situation with the Army chief of staff, General Lawton Collins, and several Pentagon colonels. All present wanted to shut down both Fort Jackson and Camp Gordon, but relocating all the soldiers and equipment would cost too much. Given a choice between the two, they agreed that Camp Gordon should remain open for another year because this installation had several technical schools that would be more expensive to close. Fort Jackson, by comparison, had only a training division that required minimal infrastructure. By the end of the meeting, the group decided that Fort Jackson would be inactivated in 1950 and that Camp Gordon would follow in 1951 when the Army presumably would have more money.[63]

Secretary Gray had the memorandum classified "Secret," most likely to avoid giving the community surrounding Camp Gordon sufficient time to mobilize lobbying forces. After all, Senate Armed Services Committee chairman Richard Russell represented the State of Georgia. Chief of Staff Collins did worry about the "adverse political reactions" that the closing of Fort Jackson might have, but nothing came of these concerns. Unfortunately, classification of these facts permitted rumor and eventually myth to fill the vacuum.

Nothing in the available record would indicate that the president sought to punish South Carolinians for their support of Thurmond in 1948. In fact, Truman was attempting to bring the States Rights Democrats back into the fold during the same month that Secretary Gray was holding his secret meeting. Correspondence between the president and Burnet Maybank suggests how far removed the president stayed from the base-closure process. The Missourian had known the South Carolina senator from their earlier days on Capitol Hill and stayed on good terms through the Dixiecrat crisis. In letters, he addressed Maybank as "Burnet." The two communicated on a variety of issues, including cutbacks of federal employees at the Charleston Naval Yard. Nevertheless, no letters exist regarding the shutdown of Fort Jackson, even through Maybank played a central part in lobbying other officials in 1949. The senator understood clearly that the decision lay not with Truman, but within the Department of Defense.[64]

Tangled Connections and Lost Opportunities | 73

In retrospect, Strom Thurmond did not believe that Truman sought revenge either. "The 1948 Presidential election was a very exciting and controversial event," he said in a 1997 letter. "Frankly, Harry Truman never forgave me for running against him. There was some talk, in 1949, that President Truman was trying to embarrass me by closing Fort Jackson, but it seems hard to believe that the Department of Defense would have gone along with such a political vendetta."[65]

Throughout their attempts to fathom the catastrophe that had befallen them, Columbia leaders never realized they had squandered their most valuable resource, the African Americans who made up a third of the city's populace. Army officials had wanted to station black troops at Fort Jackson because the area had a favorable ratio of whites to blacks. Indeed, they had tried in 1946 to send all new ones there. The post and its surroundings had acquired such a negative reputation, however, that African Americans were assigned elsewhere. Although poor race relations were apparently not a factor in reaching a final decision to close the post, the resulting inefficiency had without question made Fort Jackson less attractive. By comparison, Forts Dix and Knox were not considered for shutdown during this time. Had Columbians created a more hospitable climate for blacks, Fort Jackson could have been as indispensable an asset as were the other two posts in 1949. They almost paid a dear price for their lack of vision.

4
★☆

The Open Secret of 1950
Army Integration at Fort Jackson

The military establishment had wrapped a tight curtain of secrecy around its program of racial integration. Why was such a bold human rights initiative hidden from public view?
—Lee Nichols, THE FREEMAN, 1990

Integration took place at Fort Jackson during September 1950. The timing made it one of the first in the Army to comply with President Truman's order. Ironically, the very problems that had given the post a poor reputation among African Americans helped to bring about this surprising turn of events. The 1947 decision by the Army to assign blacks outside the region meant the installation did not have a segregated infrastructure to dismantle. In addition, South Carolina's single-party political system undercut armed forces desegregation as an issue for the fall elections. Local blacks meanwhile were concerned with other events taking place in the state's civil rights movement.

★☆

Fort Jackson resembled a ghost town by June 1950. Basic training had ground to a halt earlier in the spring, and the Fifth Division had retired its colors in a sad farewell parade that April. Only a few Regular units stayed to help with the summer training of three National Guard divisions. The remnants included sections of the 3431st Area Service Unit, a medical dispensary, and a small headquarters commanded by Brig. Gen. Frank C. McConnell. They were scheduled to leave the post on 1 September after the last of the Guardsmen had departed.[1]

Events half a world away changed this picture. On 26 June 1950, the Korean War began. Communist-led North Korea won quick victories over the capitalist-supported South and threatened to overrun the entire peninsula. A week later, with the approval of the United Nations, Presi-

dent Truman dispatched U.S. Army and Marine infantry divisions that had been stationed in Japan. Back in the United States, the Defense Department canceled its austerity program and began rushing reinforcements across the Pacific. Congress reinstated the draft. The president ordered mobilization of the National Guard and Reserves.

The hasty expansion brought Fort Jackson back to life. On 17 July, the Department of Defense reactivated the post and made plans to begin training troops there within a month. Civilians who had faced loss of their jobs were reinstated. Two hundred officers and one thousand enlisted cadre members arrived throughout late July and early August. Many had only transferred away from the post during the previous months.[2]

On 17 August, Fort Jackson was designated as headquarters for the Eighth Infantry Training Division. Brigadier General McConnell would command the new organization, which had the capability of training up to fifteen thousand replacement soldiers at a time.[3] Unlike the Eighth Division that had been stationed at Fort Jackson during the Second World War, the new one was never intended to go into combat. Once the cadre finished with one group of trainees, it started with another. In this regard, the division more closely resembled its recent predecessor, the Fifth Infantry. The Eighth retained its three traditional regiments and supporting units, but these designations did not always follow function. The Sixty-first Infantry Regiment, for example, operated as an induction center for draftees while the Division Artillery Regiment ran the reception station. Only the Thirteenth and Twenty-eighth Infantry Regiments actually conducted basic training.[4]

The program of instruction for the new soldiers remained virtually unchanged from the Second World War. After going through induction and receiving, a trainee started with six to eight weeks of physical conditioning, rifle marksmanship, marching, and other fundamentals. Afterwards, he took eight or more weeks of advanced individual schooling in various specialties to become an infantryman, cook, mechanic, or clerk. Units from the Eighth Division sponsored most of the requisite courses. In addition, those young men who scored high enough on the Army General Classification Test could qualify for the leadership academy run at Fort Jackson by the Forty-first Heavy Tank Battalion. Here, recent graduates of basic training prepared for accelerated promotions to sergeant.

As preparations for war accelerated, the Army continued to lag behind the Navy and Air Force in following President Truman's order to integrate.[5] The relative slowness stemmed in part from the comparatively larger numbers of people involved. It also came about because many sen-

76 | BLACK, WHITE & OLIVE DRAB

ior leaders believed the Army had already accomplished the president's intent by implementing reforms set forth earlier by the Gillem Board.

In October 1945, Chief of Staff Gen. George C. Marshall had appointed a board of officers led by Lt. Gen. Alvan C. Gillem Jr., to study Army racial problems during World War II and recommend possible solutions. Their report, published as War Department Circular 124, *Utilization of Negro Manpower in the Postwar Army*, became the foundation for personnel policy. It called for African Americans to serve in numbers proportionate to their representation in the civilian population, approximately 10 percent. Segregated units would be limited in size to no larger than a regiment.[6] The Gillem Board resulted in integration to a point. For example, the all-black Twenty-fourth Infantry Regiment became an organic part of the Twenty-fifth Infantry Division in Japan.[7]

The first Army division to undergo complete desegregation was the Fourth Infantry Training Division at Fort Ord, California. In late 1949, the commander there decided that his division trained too few African Americans to justify the cost of maintaining separate facilities. His cadre of seven black officers and 165 enlisted men sometimes supervised only twenty trainees. The disparity came about because Fort Ord drew most of its soldiers from the West Coast, which had a smaller civilian population of African Americans than elsewhere. Although the experiment involved a limited number of people, it proved successful by all accounts.[8]

Nevertheless, Secretary of the Army Gordon Gray agreed with many of his senior generals that the main issue regarding African Americans was equality of opportunity, not integration, and that the Army could provide it within the context of segregation. He released a plan during the fall of 1949 that opened Army schools and promotions regardless of color but kept intact racially based enlistment quotas and segregated units. Although Secretary of Defense Louis Johnson accepted this policy, the Fahy Committee did not, and neither did many blacks.[9] In Congress, Representative Jacob K. Javits of New York called for legislation to end the Army's stalling.[10] President Truman treaded these treacherous political waters carefully, but he indicated to Gray that he sided with Fahy as well.[11]

In January 1950, Gray issued Special Regulation 600–629–1, *Utilization of Negro Manpower in the Army*, which stated, "the policy of the Department of the Army is that there shall be equality of treatment and opportunity for all persons in the Army without regard to race, color, religion, or national origin." SR 600-629-1 neither mandated continued segregation nor called for an end to it, but it laid the groundwork for

The Open Secret of 1950 | 77

integration by holding division- and installation-level commanders responsible for execution.[12]

The Army secretary chose to interpret the new regulation narrowly. He refused to lift the 10 percent cap on enlistments because he feared African Americans would overwhelm the Army if allowed to enlist indiscriminately. Under pressure, he struck a bargain with President Truman in March 1950. Gray would lift the quota, but the president agreed to allow him to revert to the old policy if the new one did not work.[13] The quota was removed in April, and black enlistments shot up from 8.2 percent in March to 25.2 percent in August.[14] Gray no longer had the option of turning back, however. The Korean War had broken the latches of this Pandora's Box.

The end of racial enlistment quotas and the wartime surge of trainees

This photograph was taken on 23 August 1950 during a visit to South Carolina by Lt. Gen. Alvan C. Gillem Jr. (*center*), commander of Third Army and immediate supervisor of Brig. Gen. Frank C. McConnell (*second from the left*), who integrated the post. Gillem headed a 1946 board that recommended that the Army continue segregating blacks and limit their proportion to 10 percent of the service. He retired eight days after this trip. The post was integrated during the next month. (U.S. Army photograph, courtesy of the Fort Jackson Museum)

78 | BLACK, WHITE & OLIVE DRAB

had an especially disruptive effect on Fort Jackson. The Pentagon had designated the post as the central processing point for soldiers from eleven mostly southern states.[15] Unlike Fort Ord's source of troops, this region had the nation's highest concentration of African Americans. In addition, the Selective Service no longer issued draft calls by race. Nobody knew how many blacks or whites to expect in each new busload of conscripts. This uncertainty posed a problem at Fort Jackson because the post had neither sufficient facilities to segregate large numbers of trainees nor the cadre to train them separately. A small contingent of black officers and sergeants had transferred southward from the Ninth Infantry Training Division at Fort Dix, New Jersey, but they could handle only a few thousand people at most.[16]

According to Lt. Col. Franklin W. Patton, the Eighth Division personnel officer (G1) who spoke with journalist Lee Nichols in 1952, the cadre from Fort Dix never trained anybody at Fort Jackson on a segregated basis. Brigadier General McConnell decided to integrate almost immediately in August after Patton had shown him a newspaper clipping describing what had happened at Fort Ord the previous year. The general discussed the ramifications with his staff and decided that SR 600-629-1 allowed him to act on his own. "It was all the authority I needed," he said. "If we didn't ask permission, they couldn't stop us."[17]

McConnell waited until the last minute to inform his boss at Third Army, Lt. Gen. John R. Hodge. Fortunately for the post commander's career, Hodge agreed with the decision. McConnell also contacted *Columbia Record* editor George Buchanan and asked him not to publish the story. Buchanan in turn persuaded his fellow editor Samuel Latimer to keep it out of the *State*. McConnell then ordered that the next fifty-five soldiers to arrive, regardless of race, would go into the next platoon. Segregation thus ended at Fort Jackson.[18]

This story first appeared in Lee Nichols's 1954 *Breakthrough on the Color Front* and has become the standard account of how segregation ended at Fort Jackson. It does not bear close scrutiny, however. Patton spoke with Nichols two years later and long after McConnell left for another assignment. According to Nichols's own notes, the quotes attributed to the post commander are hearsay. Additionally, McConnell could not have officially informed Hodge about the decision in August because the latter did not take over Third Army until 1 September. Furthermore, the *Columbia Record* published an article on 11 September that described six all-black companies.[19] Buchanan might have withheld information, but printing deliberate falsehoods would have been out of character for

The Open Secret of 1950 | 79

the veteran newsman. More likely, Patton's version of how integration happened collapses a more complex chain of events. The available evidence is more suggestive than conclusive, but it indicates that the integration at the post took place in mid-September and involved considerable preparation.

If people at the Pentagon did not realize the practical consequences of sending large numbers of African Americans to Fort Jackson, then Brigadier General McConnell did. According to a 21 August newspaper report, he clearly anticipated a flood of people in September. Other ar-

This photograph of Lt. Gen. John R. Hodge (*left*) and Brig. Gen. Frank C. McConnell (*right*) was taken on 5 September 1950. Hodge assumed command of the Third Army five days earlier and was making his first trip to Fort Jackson. The post was integrated a few weeks later. He returned on 6 November to present the Distinguished Service Cross to the family of Cpl. Levi Jackson Jr., an African American soldier from the nearby town of Cayce who had died heroically in Korea. "I knew your son," Hodge told Jackson's parents. "I knew him well and I talked with him many times when he was a boxer at Fort Bragg [N.C.] and I was commander there. . . . He was a brave man" (quotation from the *State*, 7 November 1950). (U.S. Army photograph, courtesy of the Fort Jackson Museum)

80 | BLACK, WHITE & OLIVE DRAB

ticles from that week prove that he took steps to prepare the surrounding civilian area for the changes to come, racial and otherwise. On 24 August, for example, he conferred with the Columbia city manager. He met with Governor Thurmond and South Carolina Adjutant General James Dozier at a National Guard parade the next day.[20]

Articles favorable to the idea of black troops began to appear in the local papers. On 20 August, the *State* featured the successful integration of Fort Ord. The *Columbia Record* ran this story again four days later under the headline "Korean War May Help Solve Race Problem." The *Record* also printed a photograph on 12 September that showed black and white inductees standing together at a recruiting station.

The articles in themselves, however, do not prove any collusion with military authorities. The editors of both newspapers had already begun to recognize the accomplishments of African American soldiers. The *Record*, for example, had noted in July the victory of the all-black Twenty-fourth Infantry Regiment at Yechon.[21] Still, the articles of late August seemed unusually explicit and seemed designed to sway opinion. That they coincided with the arrival of a new Eighth Division public information officer is probably more than happenstance.[22]

The most solid evidence that Fort Jackson authorities made advance plans to integrate comes not from newspapers but from the files of Secretary of Defense Louis Johnson. A South Carolina judge named A. G. Kennedy apparently learned about plans for integration at the post weeks before it happened. He likely received this information from Major General Dozier, with whom he served as a National Guard officer in World War I. Kennedy recoiled at the idea of allowing blacks in the ranks. He wrote a scathing letter of protest to Johnson in which he castigated President Truman and made dire predictions.

"I would not blame any white man forced to train, eat, sleep, and be mixed with negroes while sick to burn the cantonment buildings, [and] shoot the insolent negro officers and non-commissioned officers," he said. "You know General James C. Dozier, Adjt. Gen. of S.C. Ask him for his opinion of non-segregation of the negroes and whites at Fort Jackson." The letter was dated 21 August.[23]

Why did Brigadier General McConnell not integrate Fort Jackson immediately? Judge Kennedy had little or no influence in this situation, but the post commander did have a formidable obstacle in the person of his immediate supervisor, Lt. Gen. Alvan C. Gillem Jr., who was not replaced by John Hodge until that September. Gillem, of course, had served as chairman of the 1945 board whose recommendations had

The Open Secret of 1950 | 81

formed the foundation of Army segregation policy throughout the late forties. Complete integration of a post under his command might have caused personal embarrassment, created a public relations dilemma, and undermined Secretary of the Army Gray's delaying actions in Washington. Lt. Gen. Gillem visited Fort Jackson in late August. McConnell's most prudent course of action, given the background of his supervisor, was to wait until after the Third Army commander retired as scheduled on 31 August.[24]

New soldiers had already come to Fort Jackson by this time. The first arrived on 21 August, and approximately two hundred per day followed throughout the rest of the month. About a fifth of this number had served in the military previously and did not require basic training. They went directly to tactical units after processing at the reception station. The others underwent four days of testing, counseling, and assignment to training companies.

On 1 September, the first six hundred white soldiers received a beginning-of-cycle briefing as new members of the Thirteenth Infantry Regiment. The first African Americans began training soon afterwards in the Twenty-eighth Infantry Regiment, nicknamed the "Black Lions." The special cadre sent from Fort Dix staffed this unit. By 11 September, the Thirteenth had twelve white companies and the Twenty-eighth had six black ones for a total of 3,400 trainees.[25]

The mass of incoming people quickly exceeded the ability of the system to train them on a segregated basis. During the second week of September, 3,680 men came through the reception station with a record of 1,821 arriving within a single twenty-four-hour period. A total of 20,000 had passed through the gates by 2 October. That number rose to 37,160 by 15 November. Twenty-six percent were African Americans. The inability to provide basic training for these nearly ten thousand black soldiers was the crucial factor in deciding to mix the races.[26]

Integration of the Eighth Division most likely took place sometime between 12 and 16 September, when the surge began. In comments written on 22 November 1950, an officer who conducted an inspection of the Fort Jackson G1 Personnel Section provides additional evidence for this period: "For over four weeks there have been no all white or all Negro training companies starting training, only mixed companies."[27]

The policy generated great savings in facilities, resources, and personnel. Assigning bunks alphabetically by last name allowed commanders to fill limited barracks space to maximum capacity during every training cycle. Eliminating separate mess halls helped to minimize food

82 | BLACK, WHITE & OLIVE DRAB

wastage during a time when many soldiers complained to their congressmen about going hungry. Moreover, having an integrated division permitted leaders to adopt a "committee" approach to training.

Under this concept, cadre from each of the regiments specialized in various parts of basic training. Lieutenants and sergeants from one regiment, for example, became instructors of bayonet fighting, squad tactics, first aid, and other subjects mandated by the Army Training Plan. They set up classes at specified locations, and companies from the entire division rotated through the stations over a period of weeks. This system allowed a relatively small number of cadre members to handle thousands of trainees within a tight schedule. Desegregation thus helped to maximize trainers and time.[28]

A 1951 yearbook for the Thirteenth Infantry Regiment provides vivid photographic evidence that integration worked. African Americans comprised approximately a third of the basic training companies. Black and white soldiers lived in the same barracks and ate in the same mess halls. They played sports and spent their off-duty hours together.[29]

The cadre led by example. Photographs from the time depict black sergeants teaching classes in rifle marksmanship, hand grenades, and machine guns before a racially mixed audience. In another, white soldiers stand at rigid attention while an African American sergeant assists the inspecting officer. Black commissioned officers remained in short supply, however. The Thirteenth Infantry yearbook shows a total of only seven in that regiment.[30]

Despite demonstrable proof that blacks and whites could coexist, integration at Fort Jackson did not extend outside the Eighth Division. The 3431st Area Service Unit kept its segregated Section 2 until at least the summer of 1952. The National Guard, however, accounted for the largest number of segregated soldiers. From January 1951 until April 1952, the Eighth Division shared the post with the Thirty-first Infantry Division. President Truman activated it and other National Guard units after the Communist Chinese entered the Korean War during the winter of 1950.[31]

The Thirty-first consisted of 350 officers and 7,000 men from Alabama and Mississippi under the command of Maj. Gen. Alexander G. Paxton.[32] Nicknamed the "Dixie Division," the organization had deep roots in the Confederacy. Jefferson Davis himself had commanded one of its regiments during the Mexican War. The rebel flag hung in the headquarters areas and was painted on the bumpers of military vehicles. The band paraded at official functions in Confederate gray uniforms.[33]

Although the Dixie Division excluded African Americans, its soldiers

The Open Secret of 1950 | 83

encamped in tents set up on the south end of Fort Jackson near the old "colored area." Several writers at the time pointed out the irony of whites segregating themselves in inferior facilities just to avoid mixing with blacks, but a shortage of barracks is more likely the reason for the Thirty-first's location.[34] Fort Jackson had a building capacity of 25,262 that could barely house the Eighth Division and reception station. The tent area, which the World War II Eighth used in 1940, could accommodate 21,024 soldiers. It had a long history as a location for temporary division encampments.[35]

A different mission and source of recruits also contributed to the Thirty-first's isolation. The division prepared for combat as a team. Officers and sergeants trained the same privates whom they would presumably lead into battle. Entire families moved to Columbia from Alabama and Mississippi in order to stay close to loved ones in service. This process naturally created greater internal cohesion than in a replacement training outfit like the Eighth, where privates rotated every eight to sixteen weeks.

Additionally, the Thirty-first did not draw personnel from the Fort Jackson Reception Station. National Guardsmen were state soldiers on federal duty, not draftees. To mix the two groups would have caused numerous administrative headaches. Instead, the Thirty-first received 11,000 fillers who had belonged to National Guard units in New England. Ironically, many of the newcomers came from the Twenty-sixth Infantry Division, which was nicknamed the "Yankee Division."[36]

The National Guard remained largely white almost everywhere in the United States, not just the South. The surge of blacks that had occurred in the Regular Army did not take place within this institution. Additionally, nobody at the Pentagon wanted to tangle with the National Guard Bureau or Congress over racial policy. This reluctance cut both ways. When the integrated Forty-seventh Infantry Division from the Minnesota National Guard arrived at segregated Camp Rucker in 1951, post officials there left the organization alone because Minnesota Senator Hubert Humphrey promised dire consequences for anybody who tried to resegregate the division.[37]

Similarly, nobody pressured the Thirty-first to integrate at Fort Jackson. Several visitors from Washington came to discuss various issues with Major General Paxton, but nothing in the record indicates that they ever mentioned black soldiers.[38] When a New Yorker complained to his congressman about continued segregation there in 1952, the legislative liaison responded that integration "has not been extended to include Na-

tional Guard units because they are completely organized before entering active service."[39]

Even though SR 600-629-1 gave Major General Paxton the authority to integrate his division, he made a decision different from General McConnell's. That he would deviate from his active counterpart is ironic. A few years earlier, when the New Jersey National Guard had attempted to desegregate, Paxton had argued that it should follow the same policies as the Regular Army. "National Security is an obligation of all the states, and its necessity in time of emergency transcends all local issues."[40] The Thirty-first Division stayed completely white until it left Fort Jackson in 1952. Unwillingness to face the problem of racism in the National Guard would have unfortunate consequences during the decades to follow.

Indecision over the National Guard mirrored the Army's larger lack of direction regarding integration. Pentagon statements and actions during this time were marked by surprise over what had happened, inconsistent policies, and secrecy. The following excerpt from a December 1950 document titled "Policy Regarding Negro Separation" reflects the sense of astonishment: "In many training divisions, including that at Fort Jackson, South Carolina, Negroes and whites are integrated in the same companies during the training cycle, eating, sleeping, and training together, so far without friction."[41]

Inconsistency gave rise to irony at places such as Fort Dix. Whereas the lack of facilities and training cadre hastened integration at Fort Jackson, the presence of a segregated infrastructure served to hinder it at the New Jersey basic training post. The Ninth Infantry Training Division had trained African Americans at Fort Dix for several years. Consequently, the division had the internal resources to handle increased numbers of blacks on a separate basis. Desegregation of the Ninth began to occur during late September 1950 only after Congressman Javits drew attention to the situation.[42]

The pressures of war drove change in Korea. Units there suffered tremendous losses during the first months of war. Battlefield commanders became so desperate for men that they began using South Koreans as fillers in American units. Meanwhile, surging black enlistments resulted in a backlog of replacements in Japan. The final impetus for desegregation in Korea came as a result of the poor performance of the Twenty-fourth Infantry Regiment. This venerable regiment of African Americans had won one of the first U.S. victories at Yechon, and its members performed many acts of individual valor. Nevertheless, the Twenty-

The Open Secret of 1950 | 85

fourth established an indisputable reputation for unreliability. Maj. Gen. William Kean, who commanded the division to which the Twenty-fourth belonged, asked for permission to disband it in September 1950. Although official approval would not come for another year, de facto integration began to take place there and across the Korean peninsula.[43]

Pentagon officials had no overarching policy for implementing integration, but whether in South Korea or South Carolina, they went to considerable lengths to keep quiet about what had happened. They could not afford to offend powerful southern congressmen such as Mississippi's Carl Vinson, who led the House Armed Services Committee, or Georgia's Richard Russell, who led the Senate Armed Services Committee. "We agreed there would be no publicity," a senior Army officer told Lee Nichols in 1952. "We were afraid that if there were a lot of stories in the papers, southern congressmen would get up on their hind legs and oppose it. We wanted to get it done without fanfare—then tell about it."[44]

They also sought to avoid criticism from the black press, which had repeatedly published embarrassing stories about Army racial practices during World War II. The attempt to control information flow is apparent in a March 1950 Department of Defense memorandum regarding the lifting of enlistment quotas. The change "will be handled in a routine manner," the letter said. "It is probable, following the receipt by Army field agencies of these instructions, that press inquiries will be stimulated. If so the Secretary will merely acknowledge [it] after the fact."[45]

These and other contingencies proved to be unnecessary because the black press became sidetracked over the issue of the performance of the Twenty-fourth Infantry Regiment in Korea and the subsequent courts-martial given to black soldiers for cowardice. Throughout the fall of 1950, articles about the military appearing in the *Pittsburgh Courier* concentrated primarily on an alleged smear campaign against the Twenty-fourth and a death sentence given to an African American lieutenant. Later that winter, emphasis shifted to a trip by Thurgood Marshall to Korea. Only in the spring of 1951 did the *Courier* and other black papers begin to report on the racial situation among soldiers stationed within the continental United States.[46]

The Army's policy of open secrecy succeeded partly because southern congressmen behaved with restraint and partly because the black press became more interested in the Twenty-fourth Infantry than in the broader triumph of desegregation. Secrecy could not have worked, however, without the cooperation of people in South Carolina. Integration at

86 | BLACK, WHITE & OLIVE DRAB

Fort Jackson could easily have became a political flashpoint had black or white leaders at the state and local level decided to make integration an issue. Why did they choose to remain silent?

The timing of integration at Fort Jackson made the event politically irrelevant for white leaders. The dire nature of the Korean emergency, of course, made civilian office seekers reluctant to question military decisions, but an additional factor was at work in South Carolina. In many states, the desegregation of a major southern installation during September of an election year would have generated considerable grandstanding. In South Carolina, however, the Democratic Party had established almost total control. The crucial elections for the state took place not in November, but during the primaries in July.

Governor Thurmond had in fact attempted to score political points with white voters in June 1950 by raising the specter of armed forces integration when he ran for the U.S. Senate against incumbent Olin Johnston. At a campaign rally in Newberry, Thurmond accused Johnston of doing nothing to stop Truman's 1948 executive order. Johnston called Thurmond a liar. The governor, ever eager to prove his physical prowess, challenged the senator to step outside. Even though Johnston declined to fight, he won the primary.[47]

As Thurmond served out the remainder of his term as governor, he kept quiet while black troops entered the ranks at Fort Jackson. Besides the obvious failure of his election bid, he had a practical, personal reason to keep his mouth shut. The genuine possibility existed he could have been activated for military duty. A veteran of World War II, Thurmond still held a commission as a colonel in the Army Reserve.[48]

Nor did Congressman Hugo Sims Jr. have much to say about Fort Jackson during the summer and fall of 1950. He, too, was a lame duck who had lost in the primaries.[49] The victor, John Riley, would represent the district containing Fort Jackson until dying in 1962. Riley also maintained a neutral stance on armed forces integration, and his position underscores an important converse of the "states rights" defense of segregation: local laws do not apply to federal property. Riley's wife later wrote in a letter to Olin Johnston, "It was never John's policy to interfere with the military conduct of a base."[50]

Governor-elect James F. Byrnes made this same point in a 1953 letter to President Eisenhower. He said: "The exclusive Federal jurisdiction, both civil and criminal, over Federal installations . . . is generally recognized. It can be disputed by no one."[51] Byrnes had already served a distinguished career as a U.S. senator, Supreme Court justice, and secretary

The Open Secret of 1950 | 87

of state before winning the governorship in 1950. His views on segregation—both at military posts and in the schools—would affect race relations in South Carolina long after his term of office expired.

Congressman William Jennings Bryan Dorn represented a district adjacent to Fort Jackson. He apparently did not agree with the decision to integrate. Judge A. G. Kennedy, the same man who wrote the letter of protest about Fort Jackson to the secretary of defense in August 1950, wrote a letter to Dorn during the spring of 1951 in which he again complained. Dorn responded, "I can see from reading your card that we both agree on almost everything along these lines."[52] Nevertheless, he maintained a public silence.

National-level pressure helped to keep South Carolina politicians quiet about Fort Jackson. District 1 representative L. Mendel Rivers provides a revealing example. The Charleston congressman had a deep interest in military affairs, including Fort Jackson, and would eventually become chairman of the House Armed Services Committee. No available record exists of Rivers's opinion about the integration of Fort Jackson, but his reaction to a 1952 letter from a female soldier stationed at Fort Lewis gives a good indication of where he stood. In her letter, the young servicewoman complained about blacks at the post asking her for dates. Rivers forwarded her request for assistance to then-chairman Carl Vinson. "I do not propose to let this thing go idly by," Rivers scribbled on an attached note. "Please let's do something about it."[53] Vinson took no further public action, which suggests that he did the same regarding integration at Fort Jackson. Rivers did nothing either.

Although nobody publicly connected military integration with economics, Fort Jackson's close brush with extinction earlier in 1950 certainly played a part in the silence over integration. However erroneously, many people believed that Truman had ordered the closing of Fort Jackson because of the Dixiecrat rebellion. No politician wanted to shoulder the blame for losing federal money and jobs. Thurmond's defeat in the recent primary drove this lesson solidly home.

Senator Johnston and his counterpart, Burnet Maybank, devoted considerable effort to having Fort Jackson designated as a permanent installation after it reopened.[54] Fighting over racial integration at the post had the potential to hurt their cause with the Pentagon. Furthermore, it brought virtually no political advantage at home and carried great potential risk. Maybank had even more reason to avoid taking such a divisive stand because he was the acting Senate majority leader during the fall of 1950.[55]

88 | BLACK, WHITE & OLIVE DRAB

State leaders, too, had little to gain and much to lose. At the very time Fort Jackson was integrating, Edgar A. Brown of the South Carolina Senate was conducting secret negotiations with the federal government to build a massive plutonium-processing facility. Located along the Savannah River in Brown's home county, the plant would employ several thousand people. Brown would not have wanted these jobs lost on account of Fort Jackson.[56]

Municipal authorities in Columbia had the most at stake, and they did much to prevent conflict from arising over the post's integration. The city had converted to a managerial form of government in July 1950. The new city manager attended numerous meetings at Fort Jackson throughout the summer.[57]

Quick reaction by Columbians to a congressional investigation reflected their desire to accommodate to the wishes, racial or otherwise, of the Army. During the spring of 1951, the Senate Preparedness Committee conducted a three-day inspection of Fort Jackson. The report, published several weeks later, received wide publicity and generated considerable alarm. Chief among its findings, the committee noted that servicemen had limited recreation facilities in the surrounding community. Within months, local civilians opened two new USO facilities—one for whites and the other for blacks. Even with integration, white people in Columbia clearly wanted the post to stay open.[58]

City councilman Lester Bates began his long association with Fort Jackson about this time. The Columbia businessman had run unsuccessfully against Strom Thurmond and Olin Johnston in the 1950 senate race, and he had campaigned on a platform of white supremacy. Eventually, however, he would help to bring about the remarkably peaceful desegregation of Columbia during his later tenure as mayor. He began this transition from racist demagogue to integration champion through his work with Fort Jackson.

Representing the city Optimist Club, Bates coordinated with the Army to hold the "Optimist Service Bowl" in December 1951.[59] This football game pitted the Fort Jackson "Golden Arrow Dixies" against a team from Carswell Air Force Base in Texas. The players consisted of draftees, most of whom had previous collegiate experience.[60] Announcements for the event encouraged African Americans to attend and mentioned that a special seating section for blacks would be provided. The "Golden Arrow Dixies," incidentally, received a drubbing in this first and only bowl game.

Few people in Columbia had invested as much time and effort in promoting Fort Jackson as *Record* editor George Buchanan, and few did as

The Open Secret of 1950 | 89

much to prevent conflict over integration at the post as he. Buchanan believed that "segregation in the South must end gradually, yet gradualness is often the quickest way." He thought that the Army had implemented its policy at Fort Jackson in an "offensive way." Nevertheless, he agreed to keep stories about black soldiers at Fort Jackson out of his paper.[61]

Buchanan also persuaded his fellow editor Samuel Latimer to withhold news from the *State*. As a longtime spokesman for business development, Latimer understood the economic realities of the situation. As a World War I veteran and active member of the American Legion, he eventually came to support segregated chapters of African American veterans. By 1951, twelve such groups existed in South Carolina.[62]

Although the two editors refused to print anything that dealt directly with integration at the post, they did feature one African American hero from the Columbia area. In November 1950, both papers covered a ceremony at Fort Jackson for Corporal Levi Jackson Jr. The Cayce native was posthumously awarded the Distinguished Service Cross for actions while serving as a medic with the Twenty-fourth Infantry Regiment. On 13 August 1950, Corporal Jackson had gone forward of friendly lines to aid two comrades. He refused to leave when an artillery barrage began. Instead, he covered the injured men with his own body and was killed. Jackson's father received the award on his behalf.[63]

Whether George Buchanan coordinated with *Lighthouse & Informer* editor John McCray to keep quiet about Fort Jackson's integration is unknown. No record of any such agreement exists in McCray's papers, and no copies of his newspaper from the summer of 1950 have survived. Military intelligence analysts kept track of the *Informer*, however, and they often quoted it in their biweekly reports. They make no mention of anything unusual regarding Fort Jackson during this time.

McCray's likely willingness to have gone along with Buchanan's conspiracy of silence is not surprising. He received income from the Army by running recruiting advertisement, and, as previously detailed, he might have been secretly reporting information about Osceola McKaine to the Fort Jackson provost marshal's office.[64] Furthermore, he had another problem that commanded much of his attention. On 5 January 1950, McCray had been indicted for libel for writing about the execution of Willie Junior Tolbert, who had assaulted a sixteen-year-old girl. The victim's father, a prominent businessman from Greenwood, accused McCray of defaming his daughter. McCray pleaded guilty on the advice of his lawyer and was sentenced to three years' probation and a $3,000 fine. The editor was later fined $5,000 and sentenced to sixty days on the

chain gang because he twice failed to report to his probation officer before leaving the state to make speeches. McCray served his time. Soon thereafter, he closed the *Lighthouse & Informer* and became a columnist for the *Pittsburgh Courier*.[65]

No other blacks in South Carolina took McCray's place. James Hinton, still the leader of the state NAACP, did nothing to capitalize upon the opportunity presented by Fort Jackson, nor did he press the Army very hard to correct remaining grievances on the part of African American servicemen. In January 1951, for example, a nineteen-year-old black soldier stationed at Fort Jackson was beaten by police in Saluda County. The young private survived, but he suffered a fractured skull and partial paralysis that warranted transport to Walter Reed Army Hospital in Washington, D.C. Although the South Carolina State Conference of the NAACP issued a public statement demanding action, Hinton stayed in the background to a much greater extent than he had done previously with military affairs.[66]

The NAACP leader had many other issues with which to contend. At the same time as Fort Jackson's integration, he and his organization were deeply involved with the federal lawsuit filed by parents in Clarendon County against the local school board. Hinton also became embroiled in a battle with state education officials over the decertification of several hundred black teachers as a result of an alleged examination cheating scandal.[67] Given this situation, and given Hinton's previous disillusionment over Fort Jackson, he probably chose not to waste precious time and energy over military affairs.

Whatever their motivation, local and state leaders of both races behaved with remarkable restraint in the wake of integration at Fort Jackson. They consequently reaped the benefits. By comparison, the city of Columbus, Georgia, suffered turmoil that climaxed in 1951 when black soldiers from nearby Fort Benning threw hand grenades at civilian police during a riot.[68]

According to George Buchanan, there were "no protests" and "none from [the] uneducated group" in South Carolina.[69] Two social clubs at Fort Jackson burned during the winter of 1951, but investigators found no evidence of arson. More likely, the highly flammable pine wood buildings caught on fire by accident.[70]

When a few white people did complain about the presence of African Americans at Fort Jackson, civilian leaders worked to soothe fears rather than stoke them. For example, a woman from Chester wrote to Senator Maybank in 1952. She did not like the idea of black and white soldiers liv-

The Open Secret of 1950 | 91

ing together in the same tents. Maybank's staff responded with a polite reply explaining to her that battlefield experience in Korea had shown integration to be the best policy.[71]

South Carolina leaders hesitated to make an issue over the post's integration because they wanted the installation to remain open. They had little to gain politically from racial demagoguery because of the way the primary election system worked. They were accustomed to arranging deals behind closed doors and suppressing news. Unfortunately, this secrecy meant the complete story of Fort Jackson's integration would remain in twilight for many years.

5
★☆

Turning Out Soldiers
Fort Jackson after Integration

None of you are black S.O.B.'s, none of you are white S.O.B.'s; you're going over there to fight together and you're going to get along!

—Anonymous Fort Jackson lieutenant, 1952

The secrecy in which the integration of Fort Jackson took place helped to mask the day-to-day problems that emerged in the aftermath. Details can be found, however, in the records of inspectors, journalists, social scientists, and others who either visited or were assigned there during the early 1950s. Some of the challenges were bureaucratic. Others arose from the legacy of racism. Still others were the result of personal prejudice. As with the initial integration of the post, individual leadership made a difference.

★☆

Some of the first outsiders to see Fort Jackson after integration were Army inspectors. These men had the task of determining how well the post commander ran his organization and then reporting that information back to a higher headquarters. Inspections of training took place on a semi-annual basis while evaluations of administrative and logistic facilities happened every year. The first one of each occurred from 20 to 22 November 1950. Later inspections for which records survive include those from May 1951, November 1951, January 1952, and March 1954. A statistical report for 1952 provides supplemental data. So, too, does a Senate Preparedness Committee investigation of early 1951.[1]

These reports have at least two limitations. First, the inspectors did not seek primarily to evaluate anything racial. Second, they looked only at Regular Army units such as the Eighth Division while ignoring National Guard divisions like the Thirty-first. Nevertheless, the inspections reveal much about several issues concerning African Americans: com-

pliance with the president's executive order; court-martial rates; venereal disease rates; classification test scores; and race-based assignments.

By 1950, obeying Truman's integration directive in the Army meant following SR 600-629-1. The inspection for November of that year noted that this regulation was "being complied with in the utilization of Negro troops. The enlisted men in the training companies are assigned bunks alphabetically, not by race." The report added: "for over four weeks there have been no all white or all Negro training companies starting training, only mixed companies."[2]

The inspectors of November also looked at the 3431st Area Service Unit, which remained segregated. They noted some indiscipline in the ranks, but they did not specify whether the soldiers concerned were black or white. The laxity observed probably transcended race. Headquarters units such as the 3431st typically were less strict than a training company.

In February 1951, the Senate Preparedness Committee inspected Fort Jackson. Although the investigators wanted to know mainly about facilities, they were impressed by the extent of integration. "No attempt is made to regulate the number of white or colored troops within the individual company," the report said. "The result is that some units are almost all white, while others are as much as 75 percent colored, depending entirely upon the order of processing."[3] The training report for May 1951 rated the utilization of black personnel as "excellent." It said that "a nonsegregation policy is in effect, all personnel occupy barracks and utilize mess and divisional recreational activities regardless of race. Incidents and complaints are practically nonexistent."[4]

Rates of courts-martial at Fort Jackson were not broken down by race, but overall, the Eighth Division had a lower than average number of prosecutions. In cases where trends did manifest themselves along racial lines, the Army normally kept statistics. For example, African American soldiers had disproportionately high levels of venereal disease. Syphilis and gonorrhea created special difficulties in a military environment because of crowded barracks and lack of sanitation during field exercises. From August 1953 to December 1953, 90 percent of all reported cases of venereal disease at Fort Jackson came from blacks.[5] The post commander worked to solve this problem by expanding off-limits areas in Columbia, encouraging the use of prophylactics, and emphasizing the subject in character-guidance classes.[6]

Fort Jackson officials also kept racial statistics concerning intelligence test scores. The reception station administered the Army General

94 | BLACK, WHITE & OLIVE DRAB

Classification Test to 79,696 people during calendar year 1952. Over one-third of this group was African American, and they averaged 72.7 points in the area of reading and vocabulary. This score relegated most of them to Category IV, which was the lowest classification one could have to remain in the Army. White soldiers averaged 91.2, which placed them in Category III.[7]

About one-third of all basic trainees at the post during the early fifties were black. Consequently, the G1 Personnel Office at the Pentagon regularly reassigned African Americans from Fort Jackson to other installations. A 1953 memorandum said: "At the end of basic combat training there will be inter-change of Negroes and whites with other training centers to bring Jackson's Negro population down to approximately 13% in advanced individual training."[8]

Officials in Washington attempted to keep similar ratios of whites to blacks in Korea, which meant that fresh soldiers coming from training centers like that of Fort Jackson had to be assigned on the basis of race. This policy created unhappiness among all involved. If the levy for Korea called for whites and no blacks, some of the whites would invariably complain. The opposite occurred when the levy called for blacks. Often the soldiers or their families appealed to their congressmen.[9] Maj. Gen. Harry Collins, who replaced Brigadier General McConnell in January 1951, became caught between these opposing forces. On at least one occasion, he sought to have the quotas ended.[10]

While inspection reports provide hard statistical data, accounts by visiting journalists such as *Pittsburgh Courier* reporter Collins George put a human face on integration at Fort Jackson. Himself an African American, George had covered racial conditions in the military for years. He embarked on a tour of thirty installations belonging to all four armed forces during March 1951. He wanted to assess personally the progress of integration not just within the South but also throughout the continental United States.[11]

George visited Fort Jackson that April. A black chaplain named Captain Albert J. Tibbs met him at the Columbia Airport and served as his escort. Chaplain Tibbs provided many positive stories relating to his ministry. Chapel services on-post were integrated. African American chaplains had white assistants and officiated over the marriages of white couples. During the course of George's visit, a white soldier who had recently finished basic training came into Tibbs's office to thank the chaplain and tell him good-bye.[12]

The *Courier* reporter found a less positive situation in Section 2 of the

Turning Out Soldiers | 95

3431st Area Service Unit. Post officials had told him that the unit remained all-black because the men wanted to stay together. Out of white earshot, the soldiers said they had no desire to maintain segregation and complained about discrimination. George concluded that continued segregation in this organization contributed to low morale and caused those affected to define all of their problems in terms of race.

He also noticed a lack of African American officers. No blacks at Fort Jackson held the rank of major, which was understandable given that the entire Army had about two hundred. Still, the journalist found only five officers of color on-post. Two were chaplains, and two were lieutenants belonging to the 3431st Area Service Unit. What happened to the black officers pictured in the January 1951 yearbook is unknown. George could have missed them, or they could have been transferred to Korea.

George's observations contradicted inspection reports that said segregation no longer existed in recreational facilities. He found that most black soldiers gravitated to Service Club Number 3, which was operated by two African American women. Additionally, he learned that the post commander had issued an order forbidding interracial dancing. The reporter viewed everything he learned—including allegations of racism—with a skeptical eye. When told that the regimental clubs of the Thirteenth and Twenty-eighth Infantry did not welcome blacks, he tested the claims. He visited both places and found that African American soldiers used them without incident.

Conditions in Columbia disappointed George the most. He felt that the requirement for soldiers to ride into town using segregated taxicabs hindered good race relations because the policy discouraged off-duty socializing between blacks and whites. Like the congressional inspectors, he pointed out the lack of a USO. In addition, he noticed the class distinctions that marked the city's African American community. "The soldiers feel that even the colored civilians in Columbia do not make them welcome," he wrote. "One hears that a soldier in uniform is not wanted at affairs at one of the two Negro colleges in Columbia—Benedict College and Allen University."[13]

Overall, though, George was pleasantly surprised by what he saw at Fort Jackson and wrote a glowing report for the *Courier*. Later, in an article for the *Detroit Free Press*, he wrote, "I was particularly struck by the training division at Fort Jackson in Columbia, S.C., where race relations never have been noted to be particularly advanced."[14]

George did not give such praise lightly, nor did he hesitate to criticize sharply. He wrote scathing descriptions about other places such as Fort

96 | BLACK, WHITE & OLIVE DRAB

Bragg and Camp Lejeune, North Carolina. He found the worst situation not in the South, but at Camp McCoy, Wisconsin.[15]

In fact, conditions at Fort Jackson so impressed George that he used it in subsequent reports as a benchmark for Army success. "Dix is like Fort Jackson, S.C.," he said of the New Jersey post. After he discovered poor conditions at Camp Edwards, Massachusetts, he noted that such things "did not occur at Fort Jackson, S.C." When he found that racial conditions at Fort Lewis had deteriorated since a previous 1950 visit, he explained that the "post commander at its finest period was Gen. Harry Collins, now at Fort Jackson, S.C., the man who has made Fort Jackson one of the most beautiful examples in the country of compliance with the President's order on racial integration, in spite of the bigoted area in which the fort lies."[16]

Despite his thoroughness and fairness, the reporter did propagate the myth that the Thirty-first Infantry Division chose to live in Fort Jackson's old Jim Crow area in order to avoid integrating. George did not even take a firsthand look at these Alabama and Mississippi National Guardsmen. "It would have been pointless to have visited the 'Dixie Division' where the policy of white degeneracy runs full blast," he said.[17]

Three months after George left, a team of social scientists arrived at Fort Jackson. They belonged to Project Clear. On 29 March 1951, the Army had contracted with the Operations Research Organization (ORO) at the Johns Hopkins University to investigate the effects of integration in Korea and at posts within the United States. ORO gathered together a group of sociologists to perform the fieldwork.

Their leader was Leo Bogart, a Brooklyn native with a doctorate from the University of Chicago. He had served as a staff sergeant during World War II and had experience doing studies of racial attitudes, so he was well-qualified for the job. "Our assignment was to investigate how the Army could best use its black troops," Bogart remembered. "If I or my colleagues on the research team had been segregationists, or perhaps simply unimaginative, we might have defined the task as one of measuring the degree to which white soldiers accepted racial integration." Had they done that, "the findings would have put a brake on changes to the status quo."[18] Bogart and his staff did not want this result. "We all shared an utter abhorrence of segregation," he said.[19]

The research consisted of analyzing statistical data taken from unit reports, written surveys, and personal interviews. Bogart selected two African American sociologists, John Morsell and Tilman C. Cothren, to interview black soldiers. The team went to Korea during the spring of

Turning Out Soldiers | 97

1951 and found integration there to have been successful. "The results demonstrated that integration imposed from above led to acceptance," Bogart said.[20]

The social scientists then turned to the home front. Although the shock of integration had receded somewhat by this time, the domestic study had two advantages. First, the team had more time to plan. Second, the continental United States was a less turbulent setting than the battlefields of Asia. Both factors allowed for more systematic analysis. They chose Fort Jackson partly because of the contrast that existed between the integrated Eighth Division and the segregated Thirty-first. They also were interested in the surrounding civilian area. As team member Robert Haberstein remembered: "One of my first assignments at Columbia, South Carolina, was to interview the chief of police, city manager (I think) and some other community officials."[21]

Unfortunately, little remains of Project Clear. Seventy-five cubic feet of questionnaires, surveys, and other raw data used to compile the report were sent to ORO in 1953 and subsequently destroyed. The Army meanwhile classified everything "secret" until 1966. Leo Bogart published two of the three studies in 1968 and again in 1990. The third involved community relations, but Fort Jackson and Columbia were not among the nine bases selected.

Only the second contained data collected from South Carolina, and this information has some serious limitations. Even though these scientists had more time to prepare than they had in Korea, they still worked in haste. They did not take statistically significant samples, and their findings reflect the situation at Fort Jackson almost a year after integration had taken place. The work of Bogart's team nevertheless provides important knowledge about the post.

Although the final report gave a glowing assessment of Army integration as a whole, the findings at Fort Jackson revealed the negative effects of segregation in Columbia and in the National Guard. The sociologists reached this conclusion by dividing their sample of soldiers stationed at the post into two categories: those from the North and those from the South. They questioned some who had just started basic training and others who had several more weeks of experience in the military.

Sixty-nine percent of the new trainees from the North (out of a sample of ninety-eight) said "I like it" to the question about racial integration. Only 37 percent of the more experienced northern trainees (out of 224) said the same. Twenty-seven percent of the new southerners (out of ninety-two) had favorable comments while only 11 percent of the

experienced ones (out of thirty-eight) said the same. This drop in support indicated that the experience of integration had actually made the idea less palatable. This result contradicted what the sociologists had found at three other training posts located in the North and West.[22]

Strongly negative attitudes increased correspondingly. Seven percent of northerners objected to integration at the beginning of basic training. That rose to 14 percent out of the 224 who had several more weeks of experience. Thirty-nine percent of the southern trainees objected to integration during the early weeks. Fifty-five percent of the later ones said the same.

The scientists blamed this situation in part on segregation in the civilian community. In other places, off-duty interracial comradeship had helped to further integration. Jim Crow laws in Columbia thwarted that process at Fort Jackson. Here, 65 percent of early trainees (out of a sample of 194) had interracial friends, and 51 percent had gone to town with a member of another race. After eight weeks, 66 percent of them (out of a sample of 262) had interracial friends, and 36 percent had gone to town with a member of another race. These findings, too, differed from ones at northern and western posts. "Where local practices support an originally favorable disposition, opinions became more favorable," the report concluded. "Where these practices are unfavorable, opinion is influenced accordingly."[23]

The team also attributed the higher level of negative attitudes about racial relations at Fort Jackson to the presence of the segregated Thirty-first Infantry Division. The sociologists found that even the northern National Guardsmen absorbed racist sentiments.[24] Bogart said that they "became a source of resistance to desegregation."[25]

The Dixie Division had left South Carolina by the time Lee Nichols arrived at Fort Jackson during the summer of 1952. The reporter came across the story almost by accident. Having grown up in the Quaker faith, he did not participate in World War II and had no military experience. "I thought that there was racial progress in the U.S. in general that had not been fully reported and that might make a magazine article," he wrote later in his unpublished memoirs.[26] He arranged with the editor of Collier's magazine to write an article about integration in the armed forces.

Pentagon officials cooperated fully and encouraged him to write the story. Besides Fort Jackson, they gave the reporter access to servicemen and facilities at Fort Bragg, North Carolina; the marine base at Quantico, Virginia; and the Norfolk Naval Shipyard. They promised to exercise no control over the contents of any subsequent writings, but they did re-

quest to read any advance copies in the interest of accuracy. They also leaked classified information from Project Clear. They did not appear, however, to have provided Nichols the less favorable sociological findings that had come from Fort Jackson.

Some things at the post in 1952 remained the same since Collins George and Leo Bogart had visited. The military population was still approximately one-third African American. Of 2,500 cadre at the post, approximately 500 were black. Most African Americans continued to congregate at Service Club Number 3. Moreover, Section 2 of the 3431st had yet to desegregate. Fort Jackson authorities told Nichols that the mission required this arrangement.

Much had improved despite these lingering vestiges of segregation. Fort Jackson had many more African American officers. Fifteen of them worked at the company level in the integrated training regiments. They belonged to the officers club and brought their wives to dances and social events there.

The new post commander, Maj. Gen. Whitfield P. Shepard, had also taken steps to alleviate the lack of entertainment for black troops. He authorized the use of government buses to transport soldiers to the Air Force base at Myrtle Beach. There they could stay at an old base hospital for one dollar per night and eat in the mess hall. Programs such as the beach trips did wonders for morale. Nichols questioned soldiers from various units across the post. The African American troops said that they liked integration and got along fine with whites.

White soldiers shared the positive outlook of their comrades. A letter sent to the Defense Department a few months before Nichols's visit provides a good example. The writer's brother had recently completed basic training at Fort Jackson and had come home for a visit. "He told me that the non-segregation policy in the enlisted barracks worked perfectly as far as he could see. The colored boys were accepted by the Southern boys without resentment, reservation, informal segregation, overdone politeness, or any other sign that non-segregation was not working."[27]

Some of the whites did express misgivings. One told Nichols that he thought African Americans stunk. He did say, though, that he liked the two who lived in his barracks. A white Columbia businessman went so far as to say that his son shared a bunk with a black soldier who came from the same city. The two got along so well that the African American offered to shine the white's shoes.

Nichols's observations provided added evidence that leadership made a difference. One lieutenant fostered better race relations in his

platoon by focusing their minds on the war in Korea: "I tell them, none of you are black S.O.B.'s, none of you are white S.O.B.'s; you're going over there to fight together and you're going to get along!"

The timing of Nichols's visit provided him the opportunity to explore an additional dimension of armed forces integration: the significance of combat. A large number of Korean War veterans, black and white, had returned to the United States by 1952. Apparently battlefield experience made some African Americans more willing to assert their rights. The special services officer at Fort Jackson told Nichols that several such blacks had caused a stir by attempting to dance with white girls at the service club. The war in Korea had a mixed effect on white veterans. Some of the ones interviewed by Nichols spoke favorably of blacks as fighters; others called them slackers and cowards. Clearly the war did not necessarily bring the races together. Reminiscences of two leaders—one white and the other black—make this point clear.

Captain R. Smith (not his real name) arrived at Fort Jackson in August 1951. A native of Mount Airy, North Carolina, he had enlisted in 1940 after graduating from high school. He fought as an infantryman in Europe during World War II and rose to the position of first sergeant before being wounded. Afterwards, he received a direct commission as an officer. He participated as a company commander in some of the fiercest battles of the Korean War.[28]

He admittedly disliked African Americans. "That color," he said. "I can't stand them." Nevertheless, his experience in Korea with black soldiers led him to support the president's decision to integrate the armed forces. "I hate to say it, but he was right. . . . As long as they were together, they didn't want to do nothing, but if you put them every other one they actually would go."

Smith said that his unit at Fort Jackson was about 30 percent African American when he took charge of Company D of the Sixty-first Regiment during the summer of 1951. He remembered: "I'd call the blacks together, and I'd say . . . look, as long as you're on Fort Jackson I can handle it . . . but you're in South Carolina and if you go out off of that post . . . ain't no telling what you're going to run into." He also warned whites to obey the orders of superior-ranking blacks. "I'd call the whites together, and I'd say you do as they say, like it or not."

Such situations arose regularly because Smith was not averse to placing African Americans in positions of authority. "I had one big black," he said. "He was six foot three. . . . I made him the acting NCO. I'd just tell

Turning Out Soldiers | 101

him what I wanted done, and, boy, you'd be surprised at the results I got. He was a man!"

Smith's white soldiers also had to obey the African American officer who served as second-in-command of the company. Lieutenant Porcher L. Taylor Jr. had been assigned since the spring of 1951. The son of a newspaper editor in Jacksonville, Florida, he had forsaken a college football scholarship to volunteer for duty in World War II. "I know that blacks are treated like dogs in a lot of places," he remembered, "but I needed to get out there." He enlisted in the navy and served as a signalman on a submarine chaser in the South Pacific. Later, he attended Tuskegee Institute, where he earned a commission as an Army Reserve officer. He was called to active duty in early 1951 as one of thirty-four black officers sent to Fort Jackson. "All of these officers came basically out of ROTC programs at black universities across the country," he said.[29]

He knew nothing about the Fort Jackson, positive or negative, prior to receiving orders, but he was aware of the problems that African Americans faced elsewhere during World War II. "A number of black soldiers were habitually killed by white MPs at Fort Bragg and other southern Army posts," he said. "[I] used to read about it in my daddy's paper all the time." Despite his family's connection to journalism, Taylor never met John McCray or James Hinton and did not read the *Lighthouse & Informer*. He had no knowledge of the secret arrangements made with George Buchanan during the previous year.

Taylor said that integration "definitely started to grab hold" at Fort Jackson. He recalled seeing only one fight involving two soldiers of different colors, and he did not think the cause was racial. He said that black and white officers went to the same regimental club and that at least one African American commanded a company. He had no memory of ever coming into contact with Collins George, Lee Nichols, or Leo Bogart's team of social scientists.

He had especially high praise for Maj. Gen. Harry Collins. "He made it comfortable for blacks," Taylor said. "As a matter of fact, I had a chauffeur as a second lieutenant, who took me downtown to orient me to the area. . . . If he [Collins] had not done that, I would not be in the Army today, because I would not have stayed, because there were many negative things out there. Collins demonstrated that he didn't care what color you were. He wanted integration to work."

The soldiers of the Dixie Division stood out particularly among his unpleasant experiences. Although the soldiers of the Thirty-first

102 | BLACK, WHITE & OLIVE DRAB

bivouacked in a separate part of the post, the Alabama and Mississippi National Guardsmen often encountered integrated soldiers from the Eighth Division at various training ranges. "They treated us like dirt," Taylor said. "They didn't respect black officers." Similar problems arose occasionally within his company. "Sometimes, some of the white trainees would do . . . like they were going to go up to salute, and put their hand down and keep on walking and laugh about it."

Captain Smith made a positive first impression on Taylor. "I thought my first company commander was an outstanding soldier, full of discipline and that type of thing," the latter said. Any amity that existed quickly evaporated. The white company commander had a low overall opinion of black officers. He thought that many of them did not have sufficient intelligence to merit having a college degree, which apparently irked him because he did not have one. He also felt that senior commanders like Major General Collins, whom he contemptuously referred to as "Hollywood Harry," held African Americans to a lower standard in an effort to court Pentagon favor. Smith quickly took a dislike to his subordinate. "I had a lieutenant I ran off by the name of Porcher Taylor, *dark-skinned*," he said, emphasizing the adjective with contempt.

"He was racist through his entire body, *every bone in his body*," Taylor said of Smith with equal vehemence. "I kept that unit together. I kept that unit together by being even-handed. I didn't play no black mess. I didn't play no white mess either. . . . He should have appreciated that."

Smith did not. Instead, he gave the lieutenant an extremely negative officer efficiency report (OER). "He would have given me a "2" or a "1" if he could have," said Taylor, who received consistently high marks throughout his career. "I guess he caught himself and compromised by giving me a "3," which is horrible for an OER." He added that "the battalion commander backed him up," but that the regimental commander "jumped sky-high."

Taylor was transferred out of the company to serve as the assistant personnel officer in the regimental headquarters. There he took part in numerous courts-martial, sometimes as the defense counsel, other times as the prosecutor. He also had the opportunity to attend the physical fitness school at Fort Bragg, where he helped to develop the Army's primary field manual for calisthenics. Later at Fort Jackson, he worked on the committee that tested the conditioning of trainees. He gave great credit to David Powell, an African American officer who worked in the Eighth Division G3, for helping his career. "He was only a first lieu-

Turning Out Soldiers | 103

tenant, but he was very powerful," Taylor said. "He guided a lot of blacks on-post. He made sure that you got the right schooling and so forth."

Smith meanwhile took an extended leave after his father passed away in late 1951. He took over a company of the Twenty-eighth Regiment upon returning. There he developed a brutal way to enforce discipline among African Americans. "A couple of those blacks started getting smart, and we had two other blacks kick their ass," he said. The practice got out of hand when the two soldiers went too far and used an entrenching tool on their victim. "Oh, they worked him over," said Smith. The Criminal Investigative Division became involved. Both trainees and the company executive officer were court-martialed. Their commander narrowly avoided a similar fate.

He also continued to come into conflict with black officers. On one occasion at a training range, he embarrassed an African American lieutenant who was having difficulty zeroing the sights of his weapon. "He was from South Carolina State. Worthless. We had a unit fund. . . . He couldn't even add two and two." Smith, who was a very capable marksman, had little patience. He snatched the rifle away from the lieutenant, placed several shots into the target, and told him there was nothing wrong mechanically. The battalion commander later criticized the white captain for his handling of the situation.

Smith had another altercation that arose over a basketball player who later became famous playing for the Harlem Globetrotters. "I had Meadowlark Lemon in my company," he remembered. "I got into trouble over that. . . . Had a lieutenant named Larkin, a colored fellow, from South Carolina State, come walking into my company. 'I'm here to get Private Lemon to practice basketball,' [he said.] I said: 'He's here' for basic training, and that's where he's going to stay." He looked at me and said 'Captain.' And I said, 'Lieutenant, I'm going to give you about thirty seconds to clear this room or I'm going to knock your ass plumb out of that door. And there ain't no rank involved.' I said: 'You're a little bit bigger than me, but you ain't got the beer hall and the whorehouse experience that I've got.' And he took off. Next thing I know, I'm called up to the regiment."[30]

Porcher Taylor knew nothing about Meadowlark Lemon even being at Fort Jackson, but he was acquainted with Lieutenant Larkin. "Tall, bronze-skin guy, played basketball," he said immediately upon hearing the officer's name during an interview almost half a century later. Interestingly, though, he agreed with Smith that training should have come before basketball practice. "I don't blame him," Taylor said. "We were

concerned about turning out soldiers. That was our primary mission. Our soldiers were dying in Korea."

Both Smith and Taylor highlight the importance of the Korean War in fostering integration. Preparing young men for combat took precedence over prejudice and left little time for nursing grievances. The suddenness of the Asian crisis within the larger context of the Cold War forced Americans to work together. They did not arrive at any perfect solutions to racial problems, but they came up with many good ones.

The Korean emergency aside, personal leadership at the installation level made a clear difference at Fort Jackson. Post commanders such as Frank McConnell and Harry Collins took responsibility for integration upon themselves. They had little besides SR 600–629–1 to protect them from the ire of local civilians and the shifting political winds that gusted through the Pentagon. They handled persisting segregation on-post in the National Guard and 3431st Area Service Unit. They dealt with visiting inspectors, reporters, and social scientists. They managed the daily problems of integration that ranged from test scores and venereal disease to advanced training assignments and levies to Korea. They encouraged their subordinates to act justly and mentor young black officers. This window of opportunity for generals like McConnell and Collins to shape race relations, however, was a small one.

6
★☆

Getting Them "Off Our Neck"
Military Bureaucracy and Bus Desegregation

Even though we were on our way to fight (and possibly give our lives) for our country, white folks treated us like dirt.

—Nathaniel Abraham Sr., former
Fort Jackson trainee; editor, Carolina Panorama

Leadership of the sort exercised at Fort Jackson in 1950 had its limitations, especially later in the decade when Army authorities at the highest echelons began trying to distance themselves from civil rights issues. In this environment, bureaucratic inertia often trumped individual initiative. The restraints became apparent in the ways commanders and staff reacted to the 1953 arrests of fifty soldiers from Fort Jackson on a Columbia city bus after one of the men sat down next to a white woman. The incident, which drew national attention and came at a time of heightened racial tensions in South Carolina, had the potential to spark a local movement in the state capital against segregated transportation. From Fort Jackson to the Pentagon to the White House, people at all levels worked diligently to prevent the armed forces from becoming embroiled in the controversy.

★☆

Desegregation of the Army had succeeded remarkably by the time the Korean armistice was signed in July 1953. African American soldiers enjoyed greater freedom and had more opportunities than did many black civilians. Fort Jackson served as a model for the magnitude of this change. An October 1953 Department of Defense report said: "Integration of whites with Negroes is 100% complete at Fort Jackson. Negro enlisted personnel represent about 25% of the total enlisted population of the post. Columbia has about 35% Negro in it's [*sic*] population. There are no known racial problems either on-post or in Columbia."[1]

106 | BLACK, WHITE & OLIVE DRAB

These figures were in compliance with the Army's policy at the time of keeping the proportion of African Americans assigned to any given installation lower than that of the surrounding civilian community. Fort Jackson drew trainees from as far west as Mississippi and as far north as the District of Columbia. Blacks coming from this region comprised about 24 percent of arrivals at the reception station.

The statistics did pose a problem with the Army goal of limiting the number of African Americans in a unit to 10 percent, which reflected their proportion of the civilian populace. Personnel administrators redistributed soldiers to other posts after they completed the first eight weeks of basic training. The percentage of blacks attending advanced individual training at Fort Jackson dropped to 13 as a result.

One of the African American soldiers who came to the post during late 1953 was Milton Kimpson. The son of a sharecropper, he had grown

This January 1952 photograph shows soldiers battling in the "struggle pit." Divided into two teams, they attempt to eject their opponents from the hole. The training was part of the leaders' course, which prepared selected soldiers for accelerated promotion. (U.S. Army photograph, courtesy of the Fort Jackson Museum)

up near the Calhoun County town of St. Matthews, South Carolina. His family moved to Columbia in 1949 after he finished high school. He began taking classes at Benedict College, paying his tuition by working at a local grocery store. He graduated in the spring of 1953. Kimpson had just begun teaching at Columbia's Booker T. Washington High School in September when his induction notice arrived in the mail.

Prior to joining the Army, Kimpson shared the mixed feelings that some Columbians had toward soldiers from Fort Jackson. While a student a Benedict College, he never interacted with the soldiers who congregated on the other side of Taylor Street at the USO for blacks. "Some people would not let a soldier come to their houses to see their daughter," he said. "They felt soldiers were there to exploit them."

Kimpson's sister nevertheless had a boyfriend from Fort Jackson. The family accepted him in part because she had met him several years earlier while attending South Carolina State. The young man's status as an Army lieutenant impressed Kimpson. "One day we were downtown," he remembered. "The [white] soldiers came up, and they had to salute him."

Despite this encounter, Kimpson remained unaware that Fort Jackson had integrated. "My impression of Fort Jackson from just a long time was, segregated base," he said. "You never saw white and black soldiers downtown together."

Kimpson's first experiences in the military did little to change this opinion. He and his fellow inductees took their physical examinations at Columbia's Laurel Street USO. Although the entertainment facilities there were reserved for white soldiers, people of all races came there for inductions.

At lunchtime, one of the sergeants marched the group a block down the street to the Elite Epicurean Restaurant. The NCO ordered the black men to enter through the back door into the kitchen, where the manager had set up a makeshift table of carpenter's horses and boards. The African Americans ate lunch sitting on old chairs and nail kegs while waitresses served the white inductees in the main dining room. After the meal, everybody marched back to the USO in an integrated formation.

Familiar as he was with the ways of his hometown, Kimpson was still shocked. "How in the world could a democracy be so unfair, treating me like an animal, and still expect me to go to Korea and fight?" he asked himself. When the time came that afternoon to take his oath and indicate his willingness to serve by stepping forward, he hesitated. "I started not to take that step. And I tell you the truth, if I had not been afraid not to, I wouldn't. But I knew if I hadn't, I would have been put in jail."

The situation improved markedly as soon as Kimpson and his fellow inductees arrived at the Fort Jackson Reception Station. Everybody was treated equally from that point onward. At first, Kimpson could not believe that what he saw was true: "I started believing it in my basic training when I found out that some of our squad leaders were black . . . many of our instructors were black, some of our superior officers were black, and I saw whites treat those officers with respect. I saw in the classroom . . . how sharp these people were. . . . I saw that . . . I could be accorded the same respect as anybody else."

Kimpson had an African American company commander and first sergeant. They gave the entire company briefings about equal opportunity within the Army, but they warned the trainees that they should obey the laws of the community once they left the installations. Off-post activities did not particularly concern Kimpson because he spent most of his free time with his family. Unlike most other soldiers, he did not have to ride Jim Crow buses into town.

Race relations within Kimpson's platoon were strained, but pleasant. He sang in a quartet with another black soldier and two whites. He noted, however, that some whites became angry when African Americans spoke to white women. He also remembered that he never took one of his white comrades home to Columbia with him to visit with his parents although he did invite several black soldiers.

Overall, Kimpson had a positive experience at Fort Jackson. He stayed at the post from September 1953 until March 1954, completing both basic training and advanced individual training. He said: "That's the first time as a black person I had the opportunity to realize that I was as smart as some white people, smarter than others, and not quite as smart as some of them, but race had nothing to do with it."[2]

Segregated public transportation became a major bone of contention during the early 1950s in Columbia just as it did in Montgomery and other cities throughout the South. It was also the civil rights issue that had the largest and most immediate effect upon soldiers from Fort Jackson. Here lay a common interest that had the potential to unite the civilian black community and African American soldiers on-post.

Buses in Columbia belonged to the South Carolina Electric and Gas Company, which controlled a statewide bus monopoly. Drivers followed South Carolina law regarding segregation of passengers. Whites seated themselves from front to rear while blacks did the same from rear to front. The color line depended upon the order of boarding. If African Americans

Getting Them "Off Our Neck" | 109

got on first and occupied all of the seats, then whites had to stand up. The reverse applied as well, but under no circumstances could the races sit together. The driver had legal authority to enforce this system. He could require whites to move forward and blacks to move to the rear in order to make more room. Furthermore, he had the power to arrest anybody who disobeyed.[3]

This system had galled African American servicemen stationed at Fort Jackson for years. It became a particular source of irritation after 1943, when the secretary of war ordered the desegregation of all on-post transportation. The new policy meant that drivers could not enforce the South Carolina law until after they left federal property. Buses literally stopped outside the post gates so that passengers could reseat themselves. For black soldiers, the rule brought into sharper focus the contradiction between the ideals they defended and the conditions under which they lived.

Many African American soldiers from Fort Jackson resisted during the next decade. In December 1944, for example, a driver asked one to move from the front seat to the rear of the bus. The latter responded by shaking his finger at the driver and making an obscene remark. Consequently, the man was arrested on charges of disorderly conduct and fined $10.[4]

In January 1945, a black soldier sat down next to a white male civilian. The driver told the serviceman to move. Even though he obeyed, his compliance apparently did not satisfy one of the other civilian white passengers. Words were exchanged, and a disturbance ensued at the rear of the bus. When the driver stopped to investigate, he said that he saw the soldier brandishing a knife. The driver then called the police, who arrested the soldier and turned him over to Fort Jackson authorities.[5]

In February 1946, another soldier refused to sit in the back of a bus even after the driver ordered him to move. The serviceman was refunded his fare and told to get off the vehicle. As he exited, he uttered a curse to the driver. This act of disrespect prompted several white soldiers to follow. The African American allegedly drew a knife, and a scuffle ensued. The whites beat him severely, but an investigation by the Fort Jackson provost marshal absolved them from any wrongdoing. An intelligence report stated that "his broken jaw and other injuries are attributed to a fall sustained as he attempted to escape apprehension."[6]

African American soldiers from Fort Jackson must have caused regular disruptions because sometimes the drivers tried to avoid confrontations. A lieutenant colonel working for the inspector general's office said

110 | BLACK, WHITE & OLIVE DRAB

after his trip to Fort Jackson in 1947 that "some of the soldiers questioned stated that quite frequently bus drivers would pass them up when they were trying to get back to the fort."[7]

Virtually no African Americans were stationed at Fort Jackson from 1947 until 1950. Large-scale segregation of soldiers on off-post buses resumed after the start of the Korean War. A special services officer explained the situation to Lee Nichols in 1952, saying: "We tell them the Army has no regulations but we're bound to obey the customs of the community."[8]

Bus disturbances involving Fort Jackson soldiers coincided with similar incidents involving Columbia civilians. Army domestic intelligence reports from 1944 provide a brief glimpse of the situation in Columbia and a comparison to other southern cities (see table 1).

One of these incidents involved a Columbia man named Joseph H. Benson Jr. In August 1944, he had gotten into an argument on a city bus with two white men and the driver. Benson was ordered off the vehicle at gunpoint. He took the matter to James Hinton, who acted in his capacity as head of the South Carolina Negro Citizens' Committee. Hinton wrote a letter to the South Carolina Electric and Gas Company.[9]

These efforts achieved nothing. In fact, they may have contributed to a white backlash. In 1945, the South Carolina House of Representatives considered whether or not to mandate the erection of partitions between black and white sections of all buses in the state.[10] The bill did not

TABLE 1 Racial incidents on southern buses, 1944

	Mar.	Apr.	May	Jun.	Jul.	Aug.	Sep.
South Carolina							
Charleston	2	0	5	3	5	8	1
Columbia	2	0	4	4	1	4	0
Spartanburg	7	2	1	7	1	0	0
Other states							
Birmingham, Ala.	7	7	9	6	10	7	5
Jackson, Miss.	0	0	1	0	0	1	0
Atlanta, Ga.	3	0	1	5	2	1	4
Augusta, Ga.	7	1	2	1	5	0	2
Greensboro, N.C.	0	1	0	3	2	2	1

Source: Domestic Intelligence Report, November 1944.

Getting Them "Off Our Neck" | 111

pass. Regardless, the continuing tensions fueled a growing movement against segregated transit. During late winter 1946, John McCray and J. W. Rhodes attempted to organize a bus boycott. They formed the Columbia Committee Against Jim Crow. McCray used his *Lighthouse & Informer* to announce that 2 March would be the first "Anti–Jim Crow Sunday." He encouraged blacks not to ride city buses on that day.[11]

The leaders announced their "complete satisfaction" with the boycott afterward, and they made plans to extend the protest to six other cities in South Carolina. They even dreamed of a national movement and announced that blacks would stage protests on the first Sunday of every month.[12] Meanwhile, white officials at the South Carolina Electric and Gas Company said that the attempted boycott had made no difference in the number of fares collected.[13] The Columbia Committee Against Jim Crow faded into obscurity as McCray and his associates became more deeply involved with the Isaac Woodard case and the fight over the all-white Democratic Party.

The year 1953 resembled 1946 in that considerable potential existed for a movement. Both years fell at the end of a protracted war, and both followed periods in which African Americans in the armed forces had made great strides toward achieving equal rights. The years differed, however, in that during 1953 civilian blacks seemed much more eager to change and to make the sacrifices necessary to effect that change. Racial tensions in South Carolina were at a peak.

The long battle over desegregation of the Clarendon County schools was approaching a crucial juncture. The U.S. Supreme Court would hear *Briggs v. Elliot* that December. Throughout the fall, news stories in the *State* and the *Columbia Record* detailed the state attorney general's preparation for defending segregation. African American leaders in South Carolina followed the impending proceedings with great anticipation. In October, the state conference of the NAACP held its thirteenth annual convention. Over eight hundred people from across South Carolina came to Charleston to attend the meeting. Reflecting their optimism and hope, the delegates passed an ambitious resolution to end Jim Crow within ten years.[14]

The NAACP convention came on the heels of another significant occurrence. A few weeks earlier, facilities at the Charleston Naval Yard had been desegregated. White civilian employees there had responded by boycotting the lunchroom. Many of them picketed outside of the cafeteria as the number of noon diners dropped from one thousand to four hundred.[15]

112 | BLACK, WHITE & OLIVE DRAB

Although events at the naval yard and the upcoming school desegregation lawsuit grabbed the most headlines in Columbia newspapers during late 1953, another civil rights incident attracted attention, too. This one came from outside the state, but it had important ramifications for the city's relations with Fort Jackson.

Earlier that year, an African American Air Force pilot from Craig Air Force Base, Alabama, was arrested for refusing to move to the rear of a civilian bus. The case took an unusual twist when the pilot's commander issued him a formal letter of reprimand for violating state segregation laws. This action generated protest across the United States. Air Force leaders relented under the pressure and ordered the reprimand removed from the pilot's file.[16]

The secretary of the Air Force issued a statement that officers from this service who violated civilian segregation ordinances would no longer receive reprimands. The decision coincided with an announcement by the assistant secretary of defense that the government would desegregate all schools located on federal property. Both stories appeared on the front page of the *State* in the 25 November 1953 edition. This article—along with the other actions and events of the fall—generated ample kindling to fuel a movement in South Carolina's capital city. Two days later on Thanksgiving, friction caused by fifty soldiers from Fort Jackson at the Taylor Street USO would create a spark.

Located in the Waverly District next to Allen University and Benedict College, the Taylor Street USO served as both a haven for African American soldiers and a reminder of their second-class status. It was one of the original five clubs to open during the Second World War, and it was one of two to reopen after the start of the Korean War. Whites went to a second, fancier club located at the corner of Laurel and Assembly Streets.

Although exclusion from the white facility no doubt caused some resentment among African American soldiers, the Taylor Street USO provided a place where they could feel comfortable during off-duty hours. Blacks could let their guard down there. They could take dancing lessons, listen to music, watch television, and read magazines. Saturday night dances and Sunday morning devotional services gave servicemen opportunities to meet local girls. "The USO in Col'a means a great deal to me and my buddies," wrote Pfc. James W. Luck in a 1955 essay. "This is our home away from home."[17]

The Taylor Street USO served additionally as a point of contact between the military and Columbia's African American community. Many members of the black elite belonged to the USO Senior Hosts' Commit-

tee, and at least three of the committee members also participated actively in the cause of civil rights. The chairman, Dr. Hemphill P. Pride, had battled to expose the abuses of Fort Jackson military police during World War II. Attorney Harold Boulware had represented Charleston teachers in the 1943 fight against unequal pay and was involved with *Briggs v. Elliot.* Lincoln Jenkins Jr. was also a lawyer involved with the Clarendon lawsuit. He would handle numerous antisegregation cases during the fifties and sixties. An Army veteran of World War II, Jenkins had been inducted at Fort Jackson. He knew firsthand how soldiers there felt.[18]

One other USO worker with civil rights ties merits attention, too. Schoolteacher Ethel Martin Bolden had worked with the USO since 1942. Her husband, Charles, had been inducted at Fort Jackson in 1943 and supported her efforts. She said: "My husband has been a great encouragement to me in my work at the USO. He understands and is helpful in every way." Bolden was additionally motivated by her two young sons, who had been born after the war. "The men are giving so much of themselves that it's the least I can do to give of my time—maybe one day a mother will do the same for my boys."[19]

One responsibility of these leaders entailed coordinating with the Columbia Interdenominational Ministerial Alliance to organize the annual USO "Pal Day." The program matched interested soldiers with families from local churches. On the second weekend of November, servicemen would meet with their sponsors for morning worship services followed by Sunday dinner. Pal Day also involved essay contests, spaghetti suppers, and other activities designed to foster good military-social relations.

Observance of this day in Columbia first began in 1952. Both black and white soldiers participated for years afterward through their respective USOs. Available records indicate, however, that African American soldiers took advantage of this opportunity in numbers that far exceeded their 25 percent proportion of the post population. For Pal Day in 1955, for example, the Taylor Street USO made arrangements for 250 servicemen (42 percent) while Laurel Street had only 350 (58 percent). These percentages suggest the limited alternatives for entertainment that African American servicemen at Fort Jackson had available as well as the rapport that they enjoyed with the local black community.[20]

On the evening of Thanksgiving, 27 November 1953, fifty soldiers left the Taylor Street USO to catch the bus back to their quarters at Fort Jackson. They were among the many servicemen who had not gone home for the holiday. Most of them probably had eaten a big meal at the post mess hall earlier during the day, as was Army custom. Although the feast would

114 | BLACK, WHITE & OLIVE DRAB

have satisfied the emptiness in their stomachs, it could not fill the loneliness of heart that many no doubt felt at being away from family and friends. Fortunately, the USO had once again helped to meet that need—just as it had two weeks earlier on Pal Day—by sponsoring a special dance.

The soldiers departed at approximately 11:30 p.m. Exactly to what unit each man belonged remains unknown. Their ages ranged from nineteen to thirty years. Some might have recently completed basic training and were enjoying the relatively greater freedom to go on "pass" that came during advanced individual training. Others might have belonged to the cadre of the Eighth Division. Still others might have recently returned from Europe or Korea, passing through Fort Jackson on their way to a new assignment elsewhere in the United States or to civilian life.[21]

The Columbia city bus had only a driver and four passengers aboard when it stopped in front of the USO, so all of the soldiers were able to crowd onto the vehicle. Space was limited, and many of the soldiers remained standing as the bus began to move again. Two of the soldiers, however, decided to sit on the bench located directly behind the driver. A twenty-two-year-old white waitress named Judy Mattox had already occupied this place. Affronted at this breach of racial etiquette, she told the pair to move. One of them went to the back immediately. The other one refused to budge. "I told him I didn't know where he was from, but here in Columbia the whites and Negroes don't mix," she later said.[22]

Mattox asked the driver, W. G. Brooks, for help. Brooks had driven the bus about a block east of the USO by this time. Most likely, the other soldiers on the bus had begun to encourage their rebellious comrade because Brooks chose not to exercise his legal authority as a law enforcement officer. He saw Columbia City police officer D. A. Neeley parked in his patrol car outside of Drake's Restaurant on the 2300 block of Taylor Street. The driver stopped, exited the bus, and approached the officer for assistance.

Meanwhile, the conflict onboard continued. Mattox testified that the soldiers took turns sitting next to her. She stood up. One of them "grabbed my wrist and told me if I was a lady I'd sit back down by him."[23]

When the bus driver returned with the patrolman, the original soldiers remained seated while Mattox stood next to him. The officer asked the man to get off of the bus so that they could talk. When he refused, Neeley grabbed him by the wrist and told him that he was under arrest. Other soldiers then intervened.

"We attempted to take the soldier off the bus," Neeley said, "but the

Getting Them "Off Our Neck" | 115

other soldiers pushed him in back and blocked the way. . . . All the time they were cursing us."[24]

The policeman left the bus, went back to his patrol car, and radioed for help. Officer J. D. Worthy responded to the call. When he arrived, the two of them went back to the vehicle.

This time, an African American Army officer became involved. First Lt. Austell O. Sherard, age twenty-four, had boarded the bus at the USO along with the others. A native of Anderson, South Carolina, he had received his commission as an infantry officer through the ROTC program at South Carolina State University. He had spent a year fighting in Korea, where he was wounded in action and earned the Purple Heart and Combat Infantryman Badge. After returning to his home state earlier in 1953, he worked in a basic training regiment at Fort Jackson.[25]

Lieutenant Sherard had been in Columbia visiting his girlfriend, who lived a block away from the USO on Laurel Street, so the other soldiers on the bus were probably strangers to him. Regardless, he knew that duty compelled him to act in their best interests. As a native of South Carolina, he no doubt had some familiarity with the ways of southern lawmen and knew the risks involved. He would have understood, however, that his position as a federally commissioned officer gave him a certain amount of protection. The recent article in the *State* about the Air Force pilot whose reprimand had been overturned may have further bolstered his confidence.

Sherard identified himself as an Army lieutenant. He asked Neeley and Worthy for their names, but they refused to tell him. He then wrote down the driver's name, the bus number, and the badge numbers of the policemen.

"We told him if he couldn't be of some service not to interfere," Neeley said. "Instead of cooperating he continued to agitate the crowd." The policeman later went so far as to say that Sherard "caused most of the trouble" by "agitating the others."[26]

The policemen decided that the two of them could not handle the situation alone. They told the driver to turn the bus around and take it directly to the police station. Neeley stayed onboard while Worthy took the woman with him and followed in a patrol car.

Authorities at the station arrested everybody on the bus. They did, however, permit the three white civilian passengers to leave after the white woman verified that the trio had done nothing. The remaining passengers were jailed for the night and brought before city recorder John I. Rice the next morning. As a high official in the state Democratic

116 | BLACK, WHITE & OLIVE DRAB

Party, Rice had earlier achieved notoriety as the defendant in the famous voting rights case filed in 1947 by Columbian George Elmore.[27]

Although Rice dropped charges against two soldiers who pleaded that they had no involvement, he assessed harsh penalties on the others. Forty-five of them were fined $25.50 for disorderly conduct. This difference in treatment suggests that the majority remained defiant. Indeed, another soldier was forced to pay the same amount plus $100 for contempt of court. The judge saved the stiffest fines for Lieutenant Sherard— $100 for disorderly conduct and $100 for interfering with a law enforcement officer.[28]

South Carolina NAACP president James Hinton learned about the incident the next morning, on 28 November. He was particularly outraged by Sherard's treatment. He announced later that day that his organization would help the officer appeal the $200 fine in state circuit court. He added that the NAACP would file another suit against the City of Columbia in federal court alleging that Sherard was denied due process of law. Lincoln Jenkins agreed to represent the young officer in both cases.[29]

News spread quickly beyond Columbia. Clarence Mitchell, the NAACP lawyer who had represented the reprimanded black pilot in Alabama, registered his protest on 10 December. In its annual report for 1953, the national organization of the NAACP gave the Fort Jackson arrests equal billing with the earlier Air Force incident. At least fifty local NAACP branches from across the country sent telegrams to President Eisenhower during December and January. Sixteen congressmen made official inquiries.[30]

Clearly, the potential existed for the kind of movement that would arise two years later in Montgomery after the arrest of Rosa Parks. Segregation of Columbia buses had been a long-standing grievance. It had mass appeal and provided a common cause for African American civilians and soldiers. Local civil rights leaders were in a strong position to build upon racial tensions that had simmered throughout the fall. They could count upon support from outside organizations.

Despite the presence of these factors, the case faded from the spotlight. Army domestic intelligence reports mentioned no further protests in the Columbia area during the winter of 1953–54. The *State* and *Columbia Record* published no follow-up stories. The only major local transportation story to appear during the following weeks concerned complaints by whites about the bus company. Over one hundred people attended a hearing on 14 December. Nobody brought up segregation, but

Getting Them "Off Our Neck" | 117

many whites voiced objections about having to walk through black neighborhoods to reach their stops.[31] Milton Kimpson, a resident of Columbia who had been drafted and was undergoing training at the fort, should have heard of the incident, but he had no knowledge of what had happened.

That a movement failed to coalesce is not surprising. Acts of rebellion against segregation laws rarely led to anything other than grief for those who committed them. Nevertheless, articulating the reasons why something did not happen in Columbia is important for understanding both the city's relationship with Fort Jackson and the military's role in the civil rights movement.

Primary responsibility for both the incident and its aftermath must lie with the soldiers themselves. However justified their protests, they surrendered the moral high ground by terrifying a young woman. Lieutenant Sherard weakened his position, too, by waiting to intervene until after the police arrived. Even if the soldiers' behavior did not raise the kind of interracial sexual taboos that the NAACP preferred to avoid, the servicemen were at the very least unchivalrous and rude. Indeed, most of them were charged with disorderly conduct, not violation of Jim Crow laws.

Potential for a mass movement also suffered from a lack of civilian black leaders who were committed to a course. John McCray, who in 1946 had pushed for the Anti–Jim Crow Sundays, attempted to organize black veterans, and come to the assistance of Isaac Woodard, had little to say seven years later. A recent stint on the South Carolina chain gang for libel had dispirited him. He would close the *Lighthouse & Informer* and leave town within six months.

The silencing of McCray left Columbia without a strong voice for anything like a boycott. By contrast, NAACP president James Hinton preferred working for change through formal petitions and lawsuits. He had remained conspicuously absent from McCray's 1946 boycott effort, and he would later purge Modjeska Simkins from the NAACP leadership in 1956 for suggesting similar militancy.[32]

Desegregation of Columbia buses eventually would come as a result of court action rather than boycotts or the protests of Fort Jackson soldiers. In 1955, a local black woman named Sarah Mae Flemming (later Brown) filed a civil lawsuit against the South Carolina Electric and Gas Company. She had refused in June 1954 to move to the back of a city bus "because there was no room in the back."[33] Although the driver did not have her arrested, he later elbowed her in the stomach as she got off the bus at her stop. Flemming said that she felt ill for days afterward as a re-

118 | BLACK, WHITE & OLIVE DRAB

sult. With the help of the NAACP, the twenty-one-year-old woman sued the bus company. She sought $25,000 in damages for the pain she suffered and for the violation of her civil rights. Attorneys Matthew Perry and Lincoln Jenkins used the then-recent *Brown* decision as the basis for their argument.

Federal judge George Bell Timmerman Sr. dismissed the complaint in 1955 just as he did most other civil rights cases that came into his court. He said that the *Brown* decision applied only to schools and the *Plessy v. Ferguson* still covered transportation. The Fourth Circuit Court of Appeals reversed Timmerman in December 1955, saying that *Brown* did apply. The state appealed to the Supreme Court in April 1956, but the justices criticized white South Carolinians for wasting the Court's time. This decision, combined with later decisions arising from Montgomery, marked the end of segregation on city buses.[34]

The Thanksgiving incident involving the Fort Jackson servicemen thus had little to do with the end of segregated busing in Columbia. Numerous conditions existed for a movement, but too many opposing factors prevented one from forming. These included questionable behavior by the soldier, the loss of key leaders who might have launched a direct-action protest, and reliance by the remaining leaders upon lawsuits. At best, Sarah Mae Flemming Brown may have taken inspiration from the example that these soldiers had set six months earlier. More likely, however, she was motivated by the *Brown* decision.

Meanwhile, the charges against Lieutenant Sherard were dropped quietly in June 1954. He went back to Fort Jackson, staying there until he left active duty in 1957. He never received another promotion despite six years of service and status as a decorated combat veteran. Sherard believed until his death in 1997 that the bus incident had put an end to his career advancement.[35]

The national publicity generated by the Fort Jackson arrests ultimately made little difference because the failure of a local movement to form left outsiders without an ongoing cause to support. Nevertheless, the telegrams sent to President Eisenhower and the Department of Defense — not to mention the congressional inquiries — caused genuine alarm within the Army. Their efforts to quell the uproar reveal much about the pressures that the high echelons of command placed upon military authorities at Fort Jackson and illuminate why the post had such a limited affect on desegregation in Columbia.

Officials at Fort Jackson — most likely the provost marshal, the public information officer, and post commander Maj. Gen. John A. Dabney —

Getting Them "Off Our Neck" | 119

learned about the arrests of the fifty soldiers early on the morning of 28 November. One or more of them tried to defuse the situation by asking the city recorder either to act more leniently or to release the soldiers into the custody of the military police. Judge Rice had to pick between maintaining favor with the Army or upholding white supremacy. He chose the latter. "It has always been my policy to cooperate with Ft. Jackson authorities," he said, "but I can't countenance such conduct as this."[36]

Having been thwarted initially, post leaders tried to minimize the damage. The information and public affairs officer issued the following statement on the morning of 28 November: "In accordance with current prescribed policy for the armed forces, segregation is not practiced at Fort Jackson, a federal military reservation. When military personnel go off the post they become subject to local laws the same as any other citizen. The Army expects its personnel, whether on the post or off, to be law abiding at all times."[37]

Representatives from Fort Jackson moved quickly to heal the rift in their traditionally close relationship with Columbia's white elite while quieting activists like Jenkins. They came to a new agreement with civilian authorities by the end of December, which said: "Fort Jackson military personnel taken into custody by Columbia police will be released to post military police under a new policy of close civilian-military police cooperation. No action except on traffic violations and major offenses will be taken by civil authorities. Instead, personnel involved will be tried by summary court martial appointed by the Commanding General, Fort Jackson."[38]

In other words, the City of Columbia agreed not to prosecute servicemen for violations of segregation law. Police would instead turn offenders over to military authorities. Any punishment that resulted would depend mainly upon the prejudices and whims of the court-martial's presiding officer, who had the power to restrict movement, withhold pay, reduce rank, and impose confinement in the post stockade. He could also suspend sentence or give no punishment at all.[39] Regardless of the outcome, the proceedings would take place out of the public eye. Local civil rights activists consequently lost any future chance to use soldiers as leverage.

Meanwhile, Major General Dabney ordered his inspector general, Lt. Col. Frank E. Smith, to conduct an investigation of the incident. Smith took approximately two weeks to complete his report, which was dated 16 December and unfortunately is not extant. Other sources indicate, however, that Dabney decided not to pursue any disciplinary action

120 | BLACK, WHITE & OLIVE DRAB

against Lieutenant Sherard or any of the other soldiers. He no doubt remembered the mistake that the commander at Craig Air Force Base had recently made with the black pilot.

Fort Jackson came under the direct control of the Third U.S. Army, located at Fort McPherson, Georgia. Army custom and regulation required that orders from the Department of Defense for the South Carolina post go through the Georgia headquarters and vice versa. The Third Army chief of staff, Maj. Gen. Louis W. Truman, received a copy of the Fort Jackson report on the same day that Lieutenant Colonel Smith completed it. The Third Army commander, Lt. Gen. A. R. Bolling, later saw the report and seems to have agreed with the findings and Major General Dabney's decision not to pursue the matter. General Bolling considered the case to be closed.[40]

The Columbia bus incident caused such a national uproar, however, that Pentagon officials remained worried. One of President Eisenhower's top aides instructed Secretary of Defense Charles Wilson to prepare a response to all of the NAACP telegrams and other inquiries that had flooded the White House. Wilson, in turn, gave the job to his assistant secretary of defense (manpower and personnel), John A. Hannah, who assigned the task to his assistant chief of staff for personnel (G1), Maj. Gen. John W. Young.[41]

Lt. Col. Steve Davis was the officer within the Personnel Branch who eventually drafted the responses. An African American himself, Davis had handled racial issues for the Department of Defense for several years. In fact, he had visited Fort Jackson on an inspection tour soon after it integrated in 1950 and had likely been the one who later advised Lee Nichols to go there. Lieutenant Colonel Davis worked for a Colonel Allen, who coordinated activities within the section. Davis had a deadline of 4 January to prepare a response to the first letters that had arrived in December, so he called to Fort Jackson to find out the facts.

The staff officer's jumping of the chain of command upset officers at Third Army. A handwritten note scribbled by an unidentified worker at the G1 branch said in January that "Gen Truman, C/S 3rd Army telephoned me to protest Col. Steve Davis calling an officer direct at Ft. Jackson—said Gen. Dabney had handled the affair."[42]

Officials at Fort McPherson themselves received another unusual inquiry from the Pentagon that did not follow the normal channels. Major Albert Parker, who worked for the civilian assistant to Assistant Secretary of Defense John A. Hannah, called the Third Army commanding general's office directly in January. Parker's boss, James C. Evans, occu-

Getting Them "Off Our Neck" | 121

pied essentially the same position that William Hastie and Marcus Ray had held years earlier. Like his predecessors, the civilian assistant provided advice on racial issues and worked closely with black groups and newspapers.

The Third Army commander did not protest Parker's violation of the chain of command in part because he did not know much about the major or what influence he might have with the secretary of defense. General Bolling instead allowed his inspector general, Col. Louis B. Rutte, to send a "bootleg" copy of the Fort Jackson report to Col. W. P. Grace, who headed the Complaints Branch of the inspector general's office in Washington. Colonel Rutte said in his cover letter to Colonel Grace: "I told you on the phone that I would informally send you a report. . . . General Bolling approved my recommendation we send this report to you for information and return. He further asked me to suggest to you that the report of investigation be shown to Major Albert Parker, Executive to the Civilian Assistant, Office of the Assistant Secretary of Defense. It was not clear to me why he should see it, except that it appears Major Parker is interested in segregation and/or discrimination matters."[43]

The report arrived at the Pentagon on 12 January. Colonel Grace forwarded it to Major Parker through Colonel Allen, whose staff immediately sent the file back to the inspector general's office with a handwritten note to Colonel Grace that said: "As you well know this paper was hand-carried back to us by Col Allen w/instructions to determine who Major Albert Parker was and what he did. Subsequently you mentioned you had the information which Allen presumably wants."[44]

Even with this detour, Major Parker received the report the same day that it came to the Pentagon. He returned it after a few hours. This haste says something about the urgency with which Pentagon officials viewed this matter. A handwritten memo-routing slip that Colonel Grace attached to the report also speaks volumes about the pressures that everyone there faced. It said: "This case was sent in informally by Col. Rutte IG Third Army because of the 'reverse discrimination' case that Sen. [Lister] Hill and The White House expressed interest in. . . . I think this is a potential press interest case. The Army appears over the barrel in this type situation."[45]

By the time the report arrived from the Third Army, Lieutenant Colonel Davis had already sent telegrams to the NAACP branches that had sent telegrams in early December. His phone call to Fort Jackson might have short cut the chain of command, but it provided him with enough information to give the protesters an adequate answer. The form

122 | BLACK, WHITE & OLIVE DRAB

letters stated that the Fort Jackson commander had decided not to take any further disciplinary action against the servicemen involved.[46]

Davis also coordinated with the Judge Advocate General Section at the Pentagon, which made the decision to forward the complaints to the Justice Department. Davis incorporated this information into the form letter, too. "This reply gets them off our neck but I don't know about [Attorney General Herbert] Brownell's," a staff member scribbled on a note attached to Defense Secretary Wilson's draft copy of the response.[47]

Responses to later complaints suggest that Davis eventually obtained the Fort Jackson report and updated the form letter. Two of these differed substantially from the others, however. They were addressed to Senator Hubert Humphrey and Representative Roy Wier. Of all the legislators who had written, these two were the only ones who had implied that they would push for the closing of Fort Jackson if Army authorities did not do more to protect African American servicemen. The responses said: "Fort Jackson is the only large basic training establishment in the southeastern United States and there is a need for such an installation in that area of the country. Should the military situation require deactivation of additional Army posts, Fort Jackson would be considered with the others."[48]

Just as the failure of a civilian movement to arise in Columbia is not surprising, neither is the desire of Army authorities to distance themselves from racial issues. Dealing with the press and the NAACP took time away from the armed forces' primary mission. The negative attention that came with incidents like the one on the bus had a greater potential to harm a general's career than to help it. Nevertheless, reactions to the 1953 arrests are noteworthy in that they demonstrate, from the post level to the Pentagon, the methods by which commanders and their staffs avoided the conflict.

7
★☆

School Desegregation on and around Fort Jackson
The Unintended Consequences of Federal Power

Even those who agree with the federal government's objectives in this gambit can only be horrified at the wasteful methodology.

—State, 4 March 1963

Reluctance at the Pentagon to use the military as an agent of social change did not stop other parts of the federal government from trying to do so. During the early sixties, the Department of Health, Education, and Welfare attempted to leverage school desegregation using funds earmarked for the children of parents stationed at Fort Jackson. The initiative did not accomplish its goal, and it actually made segregation profitable in the short run for local civilians. Post authorities meanwhile steered clear of the fray.

★☆

"Army brats" led the same transient lives as their parents. Rarely did they spend more than two or three years at one place. The Department of Defense provided two means of education for these children. Some installations had internal schools run by the federal government. Others had arrangements to send dependents to civilian facilities. Military pupils placed a strain on the latter because, on average, soldiers tended to pay fewer local taxes. The problem became acute as the Cold War gave rise to a massive standing army stationed at stateside bases. To compensate, Congress in 1951 enacted Public Laws 815 and 874. The first gave financial assistance for building off-post schools. The second authorized operational subsidies for "federal impact." By 1962, affected districts received $150 for each child who lived on-post and $75 for each whose family resided off-post.[1]

Fort Jackson did not have any of its own schools during the fifties and early sixties. The Korean War had brought the post back from extinction,

124 | Black, White & Olive Drab

but its status remained tenuous. Few people outside of South Carolina's congressional delegation wanted to appropriate funds at a place that might soon close. Even after the Army declared Fort Jackson to be a permanent training base in 1956, budget cutbacks hindered construction of schools or any brick structures until the mid-sixties.[2]

Children who lived on-post received their education through Richland County District 2, which lay on the outskirts of Columbia near the community of Dentsville. Service families who lived off-post sent their children either to this district or one of the county's two others. District 1 encompassed Columbia city schools. District 5 covered Richland County territory west of the Broad River and also included part of Lexington County. (Districts 3 and 4 had long since disappeared as a result of consolidation.) In 1963, approximately 3,000 military dependents went to District 1, 2,000 to District 2, and 1,200 to District 5. The city system had the best reputation of the three, so many parents tried to have their children sent there even if they did not actually live in District 1. The commanding general intervened with the school board in the case of at least one such request for a transfer.[3]

Fort Jackson commanders did not do anything, however, to help their African American subordinates whose offspring were forced to endure inferior facilities at the area's all-black schools. Although the Department of Defense had ended segregation at on-post schools several months before the *Brown* decision, the directive did not apply to civilian facilities.[4]

Anyone seeking to challenge the system faced formidable obstacles in South Carolina. During the early to mid-fifties, the governor and state legislatures approved a host of new measures designed to circumvent the U.S. Supreme Court. They repealed compulsory attendance laws so that schools could be closed if necessary. They also cut off funds to any district forced by a federal court to desegregate. Furthermore, they denied state money to any school *from* which a child was transferred by court order. Most significantly, the new laws placed authority for pupil transfers with local school boards.[5] Black parents wishing to send their child to a white school would have to make a formal request and then submit to whatever administrative procedures were required. They could not appeal to the courts until after they had exhausted this avenue. A black child seeking admission to a white elementary school could graduate from high school before jumping all of the hurdles set before him or her.

Parents additionally faced intimidation. The few who filed petitions lost their jobs or farm leases. If they owned businesses, they suffered boycotts. Threatening phone calls were commonplace. Groups of whites

School Desegregation on and around Fort Jackson | 125

formed across the state to coordinate pressure against blacks. They included the National Association for the Preservation of White People, the Grass Roots League, the States Rights League, and the Citizens' Council.[6] Although most white South Carolinians stated their disapproval of the Ku Klux Klan and violence, the group grew and assaults occurred with greater frequency. In January 1956, an unknown attacker fired a shotgun into the home of James Hinton. In December 1956, six masked men tied a Camden bandmaster to a tree and flogged him for making pro-integration remarks at a public meeting.[7]

State political leaders focused on what they saw as the root of the problem: the NAACP. Lieutenant Governor Ernest Hollings said in November 1955: "If there's one thing against our way of life in the South, it's the NAACP. And if the U.S. Supreme Court can declare certain organizations subversive, I believe South Carolina can declare the NAACP both subversive and illegal."[8] Soon thereafter, the legislature passed a resolution forbidding state employees from belonging to the NAACP. This law struck directly at the African American teachers who formed the core of the state conference.[9]

An antibarratry law enacted in February 1957 further hindered NAACP efforts by targeting for prosecution lawyers who filed suits on behalf of other people.[10] The state struck at two other centers of black power: Allen University and Benedict College. These schools had hosted NAACP meetings in the past, and in 1957 Allen had even admitted a white Hungarian refugee. Governor George Bell Timmerman Jr., the son of the federal judge, retaliated in 1958 by decertifying Allen's and Benedict's programs for teachers. Additionally, he pressured the deans to dismiss six supposedly subversive professors. Several Allen students responded by applying for admission to the School of Education at USC. The six faculty members were nevertheless fired, and the governor rescinded his decertification order.[11]

Intolerance for pro-integration supporters extended to white people as well. In 1955, the dean of the School of Education at USC lost his job after making a speech in favor of desegregation. In 1956, a USC student was fired as a page in the state senate for writing an article in the college newspaper that spoke out against the behavior of the government officials he had seen.[12]

White efforts to thwart desegregation succeeded brilliantly prior to 1960s. Besides Allen University, only three schools in the state had blacks and whites by the end of the fifties: an elementary school operated by the Department of Defense at Parris Island Marine Base, a Catholic School

126 | BLACK, WHITE & OLIVE DRAB

in Rock Hill, and the Lutheran Seminary in Columbia.[13] Even students in Clarendon County, source of the *Briggs* lawsuit, still attended separate schools. Through solid planning and ruthless execution, state officials had developed a system that stifled dissent and reduced implementation of the *Brown* decision to a snail's crawl.

Much of the change that occurred came as a result of external events. The 1957 Little Rock Crisis demonstrated that states lacked sufficient power to stop a determined federal government. In September of that year, President Eisenhower sent Army paratroopers to enforce a federal court order to desegregate a high school in the Arkansas capital. He also federalized the state's National Guard. Governor Orval Faubus could do nothing to stop the president short of civil war.[14]

The futile posturing of South Carolina politicians in the aftermath similarly reflected the impotence of states. Governor Timmerman resigned his commission as a Naval Reserve officer and called on draft board members to quit in protest. State senator James Hugh McFadden resigned his commission as an Army Reserve major. Legislators from Horry County withdrew funding for the local National Guard armory. Representatives from Union County authorized the purchase of submachine guns and ammunition to defend themselves against federal incursions. The legislature as a whole passed a resolution protesting Eisenhower's decision to use troops. They said that "such conduct more becomes the arrogance of a communistic dictator than the President of the world's first democracy."[15] These gestures came to naught.[16]

The 1962 riots at the University of Mississippi at Oxford provided what would become one of the final straws for many South Carolinians. There, Air Force veteran James Meredith tried to become the first African American to attend "Ole Miss." Governor Ross Barnett resisted the federal government with duplicity while he made fiery speeches to his constituents. The campus erupted into violence.[17]

The confrontations in Arkansas and Mississippi made a deep impression upon politicians in South Carolina. Lieutenant Governor Hollings had championed the backlash against the NAACP during the mid-fifties, but he began to change his mind when he became governor in 1959. "We won't have a Little Rock or an Oxford if integration comes to our state," he told a group of reporters in 1962.[18]

Desegregation also became a growing concern for state business leaders. South Carolina had a well-established program for recruiting industry. Throughout the fifties, the State Development Board and the chamber of commerce had lured manufacturers from northeastern states

School Desegregation on and around Fort Jackson | 127

with promises of tax incentives, nonunionized labor, and low wages. Meanwhile, city councils and local chambers such as the ones in Columbia actively sought recognition from the National Municipal League as "All-American Cities." Ugly incidents over school desegregation hindered these efforts.[19]

Charles E. Daniel owned one of South Carolina's largest construction firms and had close ties to the political elite. He had, in fact, served as an interim U.S. senator during the fifties. He made a dramatic public statement in August 1961, in which he said: "The desegregation issue cannot continue to be hidden behind the door. This situation cannot be satisfactorily settled at the lunch counter and bus station levels. We must handle this ourselves more realistically than heretofore or it will be forced upon us in the harshest way. Either we act on our own terms or we forfeit the right to act."[20]

Initially, politicians reacted with defiance. "Under my administration we will not have a policy of integrating any industry," Governor Hollings said in his initial response to Daniels's statement. The governor, however, could ill afford to offend—let alone impose sanctions upon—the powerful construction magnate. By 1962, Hollings had adopted a "firm policy of flexibility" on segregation that received a "new look" every day. This change of heart came in part because of events like those in Little Rock and Oxford and in part because of the influence of business leaders like Daniels.[21]

Even with external events and economic concerns taken into account, little would have changed in South Carolina without the perseverance of a few courageous blacks. They included people like state NAACP leader James Hinton and his successor, I. DeQuincey Newman. They also included local activists like Modjeska Simkins, who led the Richland County Citizens' Committee, and white liberals like James McBride Dabbs of the Southern Regional Council.[22] Most of all, they included everyday citizens who petitioned for their children to enter white schools despite intimidation and a wearisome administrative process.

Active-duty military families were not among these people. The Army's policy of transferring soldiers every few years provided insufficient time to follow through with challenges to the system and little incentive to become plaintiffs in lawsuits. Civilians who worked on the installations, however, had more opportunity to do so because they tended to stay in one place longer and because their federal paychecks gave them a certain amount of protection from local economic harassment. In August 1955, blacks seeking school desegregation in the district sur-

128 | BLACK, WHITE & OLIVE DRAB

rounding the Charleston Naval Yard submitted a petition with 250 signatures. Such examples were nevertheless rare.[23]

The single, childless adults who comprised the majority of the armed forces generally had more interest in attending college than the county school system. In August 1956, a black soldier from Cheraw applied for admission to Clemson University. He was stationed at Fort Sill, Oklahoma, and wanted to attend following his discharge. Another Cheraw native—this one a marine stationed in North Carolina at Camp Lejeune—applied that same month. Clemson administrators rejected both applications.

In October 1956, U.S. senator Herbert Lehman of New York drew national attention to the issue of segregated classes for off-duty servicemen stationed in South Carolina. He had received a complaint from an airman at Donaldson Air Force Base near Greenville, who alleged that blacks could not take extension courses offered by USC. Senator Lehman sent an official inquiry to the Department of Defense. Additionally, he issued a statement to the *New York Times* in which he decried the lack of higher educational opportunities for blacks not only at Donaldson but also at Fort Jackson. The publicity faded quickly after commanders at both installations responded that they had no jurisdiction in the matter. USC had no federal contract to teach soldiers or airmen, and the school held all classes on civilian property.[24]

The greatest credit for continuing the fight against school segregation during this period arguably could go to two African American Army veterans—Lincoln Jenkins and Matthew Perry. Both men had been inducted at Fort Jackson during World War II, and both decided to become lawyers after being discharged. The 1947 *Elmore v. Rice* case had helped inspire Perry to pursue a legal career. Soon thereafter, he became one of the first students at the segregated law school at South Carolina State. He found a job as an attorney in Spartanburg upon graduating and gaining admittance to the bar. Jenkins meanwhile earned a law degree from Howard University after leaving the Army. He practiced in Columbia.[25]

The two boyhood friends joined forces during the mid-fifties. Braving antibarratry laws and other harassment, they began representing the NAACP in a number of civil rights cases. During the late fifties and early sixties, they set the stage for desegregation by helping to bring about several key court rulings undermining the legal barriers erected by whites to maintain separate schools.[26]

They took a significant step in this direction in April 1960 when they filed a new lawsuit in Clarendon County. Forty-two students from fifteen

School Desegregation on and around Fort Jackson | 129

families had exhausted the administrative procedures with no success. Perry and Jenkins challenged both the bureaucratic requirements and the restrictions against class action cases. Two years later, they filed a similar action against Charleston County Schools after parents there followed all of the state rules and failed to get even one child transferred to a white school.[27]

Before either of these cases could ultimately be decided, a critical breakthrough came with the integration of Clemson University. In 1959, a black Charlestonian named Harvey Gantt expressed interest in attending the university, which had the best architecture school in the state. Clemson officials found various reasons to deny his request. Gantt received a South Carolina–funded scholarship to study architecture at Iowa State, but he continued to submit applications to Clemson. Perry and Jenkins agreed to represent Gantt. They filed a lawsuit in federal court.[28]

In January 1963, the Fourth Circuit Court of Appeals ordered Clemson to admit Gantt for the spring term. Other colleges and universities in South Carolina began to desegregate thereafter. The USC system opened its campuses to African Americans that fall. Among the first four to break the color barrier were a niece of Modjeska Simkins and Sgt. James H. Hollings, who was a marine stationed at Parris Island.[29]

The final obstacles to initial desegregation of elementary and secondary public schools fell in May 1963, when the Supreme Court declined to review the Clarendon lawsuit that Perry and Jenkins had filed in 1960. In July 1962, federal judge Charles C. Wyche had ruled that this case could not be tried as a class action. He then ordered that forty-one of the forty-two plaintiffs be stricken from the suit. The one remaining litigant had already graduated from a segregated school by this time, so the case seemed to have reached a dead end. The Fourth Circuit Court of Appeals, however, overturned Judge Wyche that December, and the Supreme Court's refusal to hear this case opened the door for class action suits across South Carolina.[30]

Three months later, federal judge J. Robert Martin ruled on the Charleston lawsuit that Perry and Jenkins had first filed in 1962. Martin (who in 1947 had been so appalled by the "not guilty" verdict for the whites who had brazenly lynched a black man that he walked out of the courtroom without thanking the jury) decided in favor of the plaintiffs. Moreover, he decreed that the case should be a class action. He warned the Charleston School Board not to create any new administrative obstacles and said that the plaintiffs could begin attending white schools in

130 | BLACK, WHITE & OLIVE DRAB

the fall of 1963. That September, eleven black children desegregated a South Carolina public school for the first time.[31]

The battle was far from over, however. Segregationists continued to fight efforts that would allow more than a token few African Americans to attend white schools. They might have delayed the struggle for many more years had federal aid to education not become a growing issue. Just as Columbia could withhold funds to school districts that did not toe the line, so could Washington deny money to South Carolina.

For many years, state leaders had expressed concerns about the strings that came with federal money. In 1945, the state legislature passed a resolution against an educational assistance measure pending in the U.S. Senate. "We may find federal interference following the money," one representative warned, "and see our schools directed by Negroes." Congress eventually passed the bill, but the state refused to participate. Such fears persisted into the next decade. In 1957, the legislature passed a concurrent resolution opposing federal aid to education.[32]

This behavior strikingly contradicted the willingness of these same officials to keep quiet while the Department of Defense spent billions on military installations in South Carolina. During the fifties and sixties, the state contained an Army post, a marine base, a navy yard, and three Air Force bases. It also had a plutonium-processing facility near the Savannah River. Moreover, South Carolina received bountiful federal aid for education despite the public protestations of state leaders. School systems near all of these places received assistance for building under Public Law 815 and federal impact subsidies under Public Law 874. After the Soviet Union launched its Sputnik I satellite, more money came to promote math and science education under the National Defense Act of 1958.

This seeming schizophrenia has a logical explanation: civil rights activists made an issue over federal aid to education whereas they did not do so for defense spending. In 1954, labor leader George Meany suggested withholding federal money as a method of implementing the *Brown* decision. In 1958, segregation opponents proposed an amendment to the impacted areas law that would have denied funds to schools refusing to integrate.[33] Few, if any, people on this side were willing to punish states by threatening to close bases. The perceived threat of the Soviet Union during this time left anybody who made such a linkage open to accusations of harboring Communist sympathies.

State officials, like civil rights activists, chose their battles carefully. Moreover, they could easily overlook the educational dollars that did flow into South Carolina from Washington because most of the coordi-

School Desegregation on and around Fort Jackson | 131

nation for those funds took place at the district level. School board minutes for Richland County, for example, indicate that District 2 superintendent E. L. Wright worked directly with the federal government to acquire assistance for several new schools. He was even investigated on one occasion for misappropriation.[34] Throughout, he received $75 to $150 for each child belonging to servicemen stationed at Fort Jackson.

The federal government did not attempt to use funding as an enforcement tool until the Kennedy administration. On 30 March 1962, Secretary of Health, Education, and Welfare Abraham Ribicoff announced that his department would no longer permit children who lived on federal installations to attend segregated schools in the civilian community. The policy would take effect no later than September 1963. If the schools concerned did not desegregate by that time, HEW would withdraw military dependents and build facilities for them on federal land. The local districts, meanwhile, would lose their impact subsidies under Public Law 874. Ribicoff's ruling covered only children in HEW's Category "A"—those who actually resided on an installation. It did not affect Category "B" children, who lived in civilian housing. In fiscal year 1961, South Carolina had received $3,356,252 in Category "A" funds. Statewide, 25,000 to 30,000 children would be affected.[35]

Politicians reacted angrily. Senator Thurmond called Ribicoff's announcement "a flagrant act of economic blackmail." Governor Hollings deemed it "an unconstitutional attempt to control the state public school systems." He added: "All of those who stated there would be no federal control when I opposed federal aid to education can at least get this part of the message clear." Meanwhile, the General Assembly considered legislation that would force military families to pay tuition in the event that the federal government withdrew funding.[36]

Ribicoff ignored these protests and threats as did his successor, Anthony J. Celebreeze, who took office in 1962. The new secretary authorized $2 million to survey armed forces installations where segregation persisted. HEW officials inspected Fort Jackson in February 1963.[37] Later that month, HEW announced that the post would become the site for a new, federally operated elementary school—one of eight nationwide and one of two in South Carolina.[38] High school students in Category "A" would continue to attend the segregated schools in District 2.

No exact breakdown exists of Category "A" students from Fort Jackson, but one news article from the time estimated three hundred. Figures from the 1960 Census suggest that they were disproportionately black. Most of the children from the post fell into Category "B." They in-

132 | BLACK, WHITE & OLIVE DRAB

cluded the 3,000 from District 1, the 1,700 from District 2, and the 1,200 from District 5. District 2, which had a total student population of 4,248 whites and 1,031 blacks, bore the brunt of this blow.[39]

Richland County school officials acted cautiously and kept quiet. They informed federal officials that they could not integrate. When HEW announced the building of new schools, Harvey Gantt had integrated Clemson University only a month earlier, and South Carolina's elementary and secondary schools remained completely segregated. No one knew for certain if the state would make good on its promise to withhold funds.

"I know nothing more than what's been in the papers," the Richland County superintendent told a journalist. District 2 superintendent E. L. Wright declined to speak to the press on the matter, and the school board minutes make no mention of the subject. One school board official, who wished to remain anonymous, questioned why HEW would consider the District 2 elementary schools unsuitable but not the secondary ones.[40]

Army officials displayed similarly restrained disapproval. The post commander at Fort Jackson, Maj. Gen. Charles D'Orsa, explained his position at a March 1963 press conference. "I'll go by the books," he said. "But they haven't sent me the book yet. They tell me what the rules are and I'll abide by them." He added that HEW would have to provide the money for any new schools because the post did not have sufficient internal funds.[41]

In April, the Lafaye-Tarrant Construction Company of Columbia won a contract to build an elementary school at Fort Jackson for $191,955. The firm agreed to complete the work within six months. On 31 August—days before public schools in Charleston were desegregated—the post commander held a ribbon-cutting ceremony for Fort Jackson Elementary School. The new facility employed nine teachers and served 245 pupils.[42]

Segregation proved profitable to the Richland County School system in the short run. Previously, the 245 students had brought in about $36,000 worth of federal funds, which had not covered the $40,000 that it cost to educate each child.[43] Under the new policy, the local economy enjoyed a boost from materials purchased and people hired to build the school. Nine additional civilian teachers obtained jobs. The *State* had earlier noted the lack of fiscal awareness exercised by HEW when the agency spent $2 million to make inspections of places it had already deemed unsuitable. "Even those who agree with the federal government's objectives in this gambit can only be horrified at the wasteful

School Desegregation on and around Fort Jackson | 133

methodology," the editorial read.[44] The same could be said for the entire endeavor.

The HEW program ultimately did little to change schools in the area around Fort Jackson, but the presence of the federal government did make a difference in at least two indirect, unintended ways. The first involved a former serviceman living in Columbia. In 1963, retired Army Sgt. Shelvie Wheeler began working through the Richland County Citizens' Committee to have his children admitted to white city schools.[45] The second involved fourteen airmen from Shaw Air Force Base who filed a federal lawsuit in 1963 on behalf of their thirty children to desegregate Sumter County Schools. Civilian officials retaliated by attempting to levy a fee upon the children of military personnel. On 29 July 1964, a federal judge ruled in favor of the Air Force dependents.[46]

This decision was the precipitating event in Richland County District 2. On 7 August 1964, Superintendent E. L. Wright announced that schools under his authority would be desegregated that fall. Although he did not mention the Shaw case explicitly, he alluded to it in the statement he made to the press: "Our board has followed certain school integration litigation with deep and responsible study because it felt that the result of that litigation would largely control in our situation due to the similarity of the factual and legal issues involved. Furthermore, this district is the school residence of a large number of defense and military families whose children must be educated. . . . The School District and Board of Trustees are genuinely concerned with the prospect of integration of schools but have been advised that . . . no useful purpose could be served in going to court."[47]

Desegregation of District 2 took place at the end of August 1964. The first two students, interestingly enough, had no connections to the military. "Army brats" were nevertheless credited with having a calming effect. Dentsville High principal C. E. Young referred to them when he said: "We really did not anticipate any difficultly here. Many of our students have attended integrated schools all their lives in other sections of the country."[48]

District 1 desegregated at the same time. Two of the first children there belonged to retired Sgt. Shelvie Wheeler. He said: "The way in which their admission was handled, and the smoothness that exists here, encourages me even more to want to fight for my country. I would also be willing to give my life, if necessary, for this great city, because it has shown me that I am a citizen."[49]

134 | BLACK, WHITE & OLIVE DRAB

The Civil Rights Act of 1964, passed in July of that year, provided added motivation to integrate. Giving force of law to the *Brown* decision, Title VI of this legislation denied federal funding to institutions that practiced racial discrimination. The Elementary and Secondary Education Act of 1965 raised the amount of money at stake to unprecedented levels.[50]

Regardless, the area near Fort Jackson had a long way to go before it was completely integrated. At the same time that the District 2 board voted to accept desegregation as mandated by the Civil Rights Act of 1964—which it did in 1965—it also adopted a plan to circumvent it. Students would have the privilege to attend the school of their choice, but their parents would have the responsibility of transporting them. Called "freedom of choice" by some people, this policy worked to the detriment of African American families, who were less likely to own automobiles.[51]

As a result, only eighteen districts in South Carolina had desegregated by the end of 1965. A scant one-tenth of 1 percent of African Americans in the state attended school with whites. In 1966, just 1,250 blacks from Richland County went to formerly white schools.[52] Lt. Col. Angelo Perri hardly noticed any change when he arrived at the post that year. "Columbia was still a segregated society," he said. "My children went to an all-white school. . . . Lower Richland was the all-white high school and then Hopkins was the black high school down there. Mill Creek Grade School was for whites, and another one was for blacks." (All were in District 1.)[53]

The situation changed a little bit by 1968. The number of blacks attending school with whites more than doubled to 3,100. District 5 selected an African American as the Athlete of the Year. In District 1, longtime USO volunteer Ethel Bolden became one of the first African Americans to integrate the faculty at Columbia's Dreher High School, where she worked as the librarian.[54]

Throughout the long struggle over school desegregation, the military played a ubiquitous, but not a leading role. Service in the armed forces helped inspire veterans like former navy sailor Harry Briggs to file suit in Clarendon County just as it did the soldier and marine who applied for admission to Clemson. Having a source of income that was safe from vengeful local whites emboldened the federal workers in Charleston who petitioned for better schools, the Donaldson airman who complained about the lack of college extension courses, and the Columbia retiree who wanted his children to have a brighter future. Military "brats"

School Desegregation on and around Fort Jackson | 135

who had attended integrated schools outside of the region contributed to the relative peacefulness of change when it did happen.

Institutionally, however, the armed forces had very little influence. Families of active-duty servicepeople usually did not stay in South Carolina long enough to go through the administrative procedures set forth by the state legislature or to serve as plaintiffs for the NAACP. The Department of Defense discouraged local commanders from getting involved or even speaking against Jim Crow. Furthermore, the key educational battles of the 1950s were fought over state, not federal law. As Matthew Perry noted, the South Carolina constitution and numerous state laws made racial segregation mandatory. Local officials had no choice but to obey. Military bases therefore had little influence.[55]

Not until the early sixties did the executive branch of the federal government—and armed forces installations—become directly involved. At first, Richland County officials allowed HEW to withdraw a small number of military children and create at Fort Jackson one of the state's first integrated elementary schools. This supposedly punitive action actually made segregation profitable in the short run. The superintendent and school board nevertheless realized that forgoing impact aid would eventually cost them dearly. The HEW action, though ineffective and even laughable, had provided a clear demonstration of Washington's resolve. Court decisions regarding a similar situation at Shaw Air Force Base made further resistance seem futile. In this way during 1964, Fort Jackson had the most direct influence it would ever have over school desegregation in South Carolina.

8
★☆

Fort Jackson and the Desegregation of Public Facilities

Military-Social Relations at the Local, State, and National Levels

Commanders were local heroes, and they had plenty of influence. . . . The trouble was most commanders were ignorant of the ferment among their own men on this subject [race]. In all my trips I hinted at sanctions and base closings. . . . I wanted the commanders to do the same.

—Judge Gerhard A. Gesell, 1972, chairman,
President's Committee on Equal Opportunity in the Armed Services

We knew that we would lose the battle. . . . Additionally, the Department of the Army was not yet ready to step out. I don't think they would have backed us. . . . Why would you want to make an enemy out of a powerful senator or congressman? You'd be stupid unless you wanted to become a martyr of some sort.

—Col. Angelo Perri, 1997, former Fort Jackson chief of staff

Commanders at Fort Jackson had the authority to place off-limits civilian establishments that cheated customers, spread disease, or otherwise harmed soldiers. Logic suggests that they would also have used this sanction to fight racial discrimination. Logic suggests further that fear of another base shutdown there would have caused civilians to be careful in their treatment of black servicemen who ventured away from post. Nevertheless, from the time of Fort Jackson's integration in 1950 until the end of the sixties, no commanding general ever wielded this power against Columbia businesses that catered to soldiers on a Jim Crow basis. Moreover, local civilians demonstrated no fear that he would.

The main reason for this state of affairs was that for much of the period in question, the Department of Defense forbade use of the off-limits sanction in matters concerning race. Pressure from higher headquarters, however, does not explain why Fort Jackson authorities declined to act even after the secretary of defense encouraged them to do so after 1963.

Fort Jackson and the Desegregation of Public Facilities | 137

The answers lie not in the uniformed chain of command, but within the connections that existed between post commanders and civilians at various levels of government. Five episodes from the fifties and early sixties highlight the relevant parameters of these installation-level military-social relations: Senator Thurmond's filibuster against the Civil Rights Act of 1957; Governor Timmerman's 1958 attempt to banish evangelist Billy Graham; the 1962 integration of Columbia lunch counters; area reactions to the 1963 Gesell Report; and the 1965 Citizens' Design for Progress. In every instance, whites saw no contradiction between their support for federal military spending within South Carolina and their states rights defense of segregation.

★☆

The commanding general at Fort Jackson technically answered to a higher headquarters in Georgia, but he dealt regularly with civilians who had tremendous power over his career. Every year or two, the installation played host to high-ranking civilians from the Department of Defense and the Department of the Army. The visitors were usually assistant secretaries or undersecretaries. Sometimes they came to the post as part of a larger regional tour. Other times they came to attend conferences about finance or to investigate some aspect of basic training. Still other times they came at the behest of people from the surrounding community.[1]

Civilians from the Departments of Defense and the Army received every courtesy while at Fort Jackson. An escort picked them up from the train station or airport. Besides accomplishing the stated purpose of the visit, the commanding general usually took the dignitaries on a tour of the basic training facilities and gave a reception or dinner at the officers' club. The entourage frequently played a round on the post golf course.

Although these representatives of the executive branch were important, they nevertheless had limited short-run influence. The commanding general could establish connections that might help his career later, but the assistant secretaries and undersecretaries did not have the power to do that much in their favor. Conversely, though, a negative report back to Washington could have grave consequences that would have reverberated back down the military chain of command. Everybody at Fort Jackson thus took these visits with requisite seriousness.

The Department of the Army maintained a permanent representative at Fort Jackson through use of civilian aides. The secretary appointed prominent local men who had an interest in military affairs. Together, they comprised the Army Advisory Board. The aides corresponded with

138 | BLACK, WHITE & OLIVE DRAB

the secretary as necessary and attended an annual meeting in Washington. Newspaper editors George Buchanan and Samuel Latimer served as aides at Fort Jackson for many years, as did Columbia banker J. Willis Cantey. Their power stemmed more from sources within South Carolina, however, than from any authority vested in them by the Department of the Army. Cantey, for example, was a leading figure in the Columbia Chamber of Commerce and was a relative by marriage to General William Westmoreland.

Members of the South Carolina congressional delegation wielded far more direct power over Fort Jackson and thus commanded greater attention. Although Army officials at the Pentagon developed the annual budget, the House Armed Services Committee approved each appropriation on an item-by-item, installation-by-installation basis before the bill went to a vote by the full House of Representatives. The goals of post commanders and congressmen often coincided. The former wanted new projects as a legacy of their tenure and justification for promotion. The latter wanted to bring federal money and jobs into their districts as justification for reelection. This symbiosis was crucial to the survival of Fort Jackson during the fifties because the post still did not have any permanent buildings. The lack of infrastructure made it highly vulnerable to closure during difficult economic times.

Representative John Riley labored mightily to secure a hospital for the post. So, too, did his widow, Corinne. Albert Watson won the seat in late 1962. His defection to the Republican Party the next year, however, diminished his ability to help Fort Jackson because the Democrats controlled Congress throughout his career.[2] William Jennings Bryan Dorn in the neighboring district played more of an active role in post affairs than did Watson. Dorn served for many years on the House Committee on Veterans' Affairs and eventually became its chair. He wanted to see a hospital built on-post that could serve retirees and disabled servicemen.[3]

The most influential member of the House with regard to Fort Jackson was L. Mendel Rivers. As a vice chairman of the House Armed Services Committee during the fifties, he held an excellent position to keep Fort Jackson open and obtain a hospital.[4] "It is a magnificent center," he said of the post during a committee hearing. "Everybody knows it. It not only trains boots, it is adjacent to the largest maneuver area you have in the east, along with Bragg. That is why I wondered why there is any even fleeting moment of reflection on the future of this installation."[5]

Given the influence of Rivers, Riley, and Dorn, the post commander at Fort Jackson accorded them every respect. They were invited to attend

Fort Jackson and the Desegregation of Public Facilities | 139

military parades and social functions. When Congress finally approved a hospital during the sixties, the commanding general asked Corinne Riley to turn the first shovel of earth for the new construction project.[6]

Fort Jackson commanders saved their greatest deference for South Carolina senators. These men stood at the apex of political power in the state. They also tended to have considerable seniority within the Senate because South Carolinians habitually reelected them until they died.[7] Most significantly for the military, senators had confirmation authority over promotions. The president appointed military officers just as he did cabinet secretaries and judges. Promotion lists therefore went to the Senate for final approval. If a senator held a grudge against any single officer, the legislator could easily prevent passage of the list until that person's name was stricken.

All of South Carolina's senators during the fifties and sixties were supportive of Fort Jackson and the military. Burnet Maybank was the post's chief senatorial advocate at the beginning of the fifties. He attempted to

In this 1966 photograph, an integrated group of soldiers moves into new barracks. Construction of the structures began in 1964, when Corinne Riley, the widow of Representative John Riley, turned the first shovelful of earth. Supporters of Fort Jackson campaigned for brick buildings like these because the expense would make the post less of a target for closure. (U.S. Army photograph, courtesy of the Fort Jackson Museum)

140 | BLACK, WHITE & OLIVE DRAB

use his personal friendship with President Truman to keep Fort Jackson open in 1949. Later, he worked toward acquiring a post hospital.

Senator Olin Johnston, who won his seat from Ellison D. "Cotton Ed" Smith in 1944, had an unusual personal interest in the installation. While serving as an enlisted soldier in the Army Corps of Engineers during the First World War, he had helped to lay out the first streets at Camp Jackson. He took pride in this fact. Johnston belonged to the Senate Civil Service Committee, so his office was the natural place for civilian employees who worked on-post to take complaints.[8]

After Burnet Maybank died suddenly in 1954, another senator with strong military ties took his place, J. Strom Thurmond, who became the first person to win Senate office as a write-in candidate. By this time, he was also a brigadier general in the Army Reserve. He switched over to the Republican Party to support Barry Goldwater for president in 1964. Unlike Albert Watson, he retained his statewide influence by virtue of his longer service, greater power, and possibly because South Carolinians were already accustomed to his maverick behavior. Thurmond began lobbying for a hospital at Fort Jackson as soon as he took office. He would eventually become chairman of the Senate Armed Services Committee during the nineties.

Senator Ernest Hollings, too, had military connections and an interest in Fort Jackson. After graduating from the Citadel, he had served thirty-three months during World War II as an infantry captain in Africa and Europe with the Thirty-sixth Division. He resigned the governorship to become a senator after Olin Johnston died in 1965.[9]

Three examples demonstrate how Fort Jackson commanders bowed to senatorial authority. In 1957, Maj. Gen. N. A. Costello attempted to reduce the number of civilian employees on-post. His secretary, Mrs. Ida Pride, had almost a decade of experience with such matters. She remembered that she rarely tried to give advice to her bosses, but on this occasion she volunteered the suggestion to the general that the workers be kept. He fired them anyhow. They complained to Senator Johnston, however, and won back their jobs.[10]

In 1964, Maj. Gen. Gines Perez attempted to place the post's barbershops, movie theater concessions, and vending machines under the auspices of the Army and Air Force Exchange Service (AAFES). Local contractors complained to Senator Johnston about the loss of business. Major General Perez tried to explain that the AAFES takeover was part of an Armywide process. The senator would not accept this answer. Perez

Fort Jackson and the Desegregation of Public Facilities | 141

backed down, and local contractors continued to provide these services for many years thereafter.[11]

In 1967, a group of retiree wives asked for help from Senator Thurmond. These women had belonged to the Fort Jackson NCO Wives Club, but they had been ousted after Major General Perez removed the slate of officers, annulled the club constitution, and designated the club for wives of active-duty personnel only. The dispute originated after the group held elections during the spring of 1967. A faction of retiree wives defeated an opposing bloc of active-duty wives by a vote of 43–40. Racial friction was possibly another factor because one of the retiree wives noted that the defeated candidate for president had walked out along with "several Negro ladies."

One of Thurmond's chief aides, Harry Dent, handled the case by calling Perez's assistant chief of staff for personnel, Col. Johnnie Duffie. His report of their conversation speaks volumes, both between the lines and at face value, about senatorial power. "I called Colonel Duffie Saturday night and informed him of the meeting," Dent said. "I told him of my impressions and that if the General would meet with the officers of the board of directors that he would be helping himself, even if he did not reverse himself. I told him that I had been asked to report this meeting to the Congressional delegation, which I felt a duty to do, although I did not wish to stir up any difficulties or try to second-guess the General."[12]

Perez received the message and quickly readjusted to the prevailing realities. He allowed the retiree wives to stay and proposed a six-month cooling-off period. In each of the three cases, the commanding generals probably had good reason for taking the measures that they took at first, but they understood the political situation and adjusted accordingly.

By contrast, Fort Jackson and the state government of South Carolina were relatively isolated from each other. Civilians at this level could do little to influence the military other than to work through their congressional delegation. Although the local commander always treated the governor and members of the General Assembly with respect, he did not go out of his way to court favor with them. By the same token, many South Carolina officials understood that the survival of Fort Jackson did not hinge upon their actions. This relative lack of connectedness allowed them to speak more openly about how they viewed armed forces integration.

Two men controlled the state legislature during the Second World War and for most of the following three decades. Edgar Brown served as

142 | BLACK, WHITE & OLIVE DRAB

president pro tempore of the South Carolina Senate from 1942 to 1972. Solomon Blatt served as Speaker of the House, with the exception of only a few years, from 1937 until 1973. Both of these powerful politicians came from the same county along the Savannah River, which led their opponents to call them the "Barnwell Ring." Other than attending occasional ceremonies as part of a larger group, neither man had much to do with Fort Jackson. Senator Brown's papers contain no files about the Army. Speaker Blatt actually served at Camp Jackson with the Eighty-first Infantry Division during World War I, but his papers have no files about the military either.[13]

The normal business of the General Assembly precluded almost any involvement with the post. "They had no reason to be," said former South Carolina senator Hyman Rubin, who had dealt closely with Fort Jackson officials as a city councilman before taking state office in 1967. "It was a national facility and a local installation."[14]

The governor often represented South Carolina at military parades, but the level of engagement rarely went deeper. Correspondence from the papers of Governor Timmerman made explicit the lack of connections. Whenever constituents wrote him for help with any situation at the post, they were told to contact the Department of Defense and given a standard response. "Although Fort Jackson is located in South Carolina," the letters read, "it is a military installation of the federal government and its officers and men are under the jurisdiction of the federal government."[15]

Relationships between governors and post commanders often rested upon other factors. Strom Thurmond had his Army connections. James Byrnes had a distinguished career at the federal level before becoming governor. By contrast, George Bell Timmerman Jr. had comparatively limited contact with the Army or the federal government. He had served in the navy during World War II and maintained a commission in the Reserve of that service. He had never held political office at the federal level. Consequently, Timmerman seemed to be the most detached from Fort Jackson of the South Carolina governors from this era.

Officials from Fort Jackson interacted most closely on a day-to-day basis with civilian leaders at the local level. The post itself was a small city, so cooperation with Columbia was essential for coordinating such things as crime control, public transportation schedules, electric power, road building, property development, and other municipal services. The Army also contracted with area businesses for food and supplies. Commanding generals and their staffs rarely stayed in their positions for

Fort Jackson and the Desegregation of Public Facilities | 143

more than two years. This limited span of time placed them at a relative disadvantage to local officials, who often held office for years or decades. Success for them, and thus their military careers, depended heavily upon how quickly they could establish and maintain good community relations. Likewise, Fort Jackson was a major part of the city's economy. Decisions made by the post commander could make civilian businessmen wealthy or drive them to bankruptcy. Policies regarding troop housing, for example, could affect tax revenues and the prices of real estate. Local civilians therefore had a vested interest in maintaining rapport with the military.

The government of Columbia consisted of a mayor and four council members, all elected at large. A city manager was hired in 1950, but the mayor remained the central figure. The two mayors who served during the peak years of the city's civil rights movement were J. Clarence Dreher (1954–58) and Lester L. Bates (1958–70). Another prominent Columbia politician was Hyman Rubin, who served on the council and as mayor pro tempore from 1952 to 1966 before his election to the South Carolina Senate.

As Rubin's election as a senator suggested, city leaders did have connections within the state Democratic Party. They communicated regularly with legislators and members of the South Carolina State Development Board. They also kept in touch with the congressional delegation in Washington. Both Mayors Dreher and Bates wrote occasional letters to the president of the United States, often when something notable was going to take place at Fort Jackson.

The Greater Columbia Chamber of Commerce played a role in post affairs equal to if not more prominent role than that of the city. Members of the chamber persuaded the Department of War to build Camp Jackson in 1917 and later to designate it as a fort in 1940. The organization continued to lead efforts to keep the post open during the decades after World War II. It operated primarily through its Armed Services Committee. This group consisted of businessmen who had financial interests in the Army as well as a substantial number of military retirees, many of whom moved to Columbia because of the year-round warm climate, friendliness of the people, and proximity to post facilities. Not all of the retirees had necessarily served at Fort Jackson, but their knowledge of the armed services helped the chamber in dealing with the post. Moreover, the experiences that many of the retired generals and colonels had with logistics and large-scale organization made them ideal candidates to lead community-development projects.

144 | BLACK, WHITE & OLIVE DRAB

The Richland County government did not have many ties to Fort Jackson other than through the District 2 school superintendent and the board. A former aide-de-camp to the post commander during the sixties remembered that this lack of contact remained the case even after the post's chief engineer, a lieutenant colonel named John Brewer, retired in 1962 and went to work as a county administrator.[16] Neither did the commander at Fort Jackson deal much during the fifties and sixties with leaders across the Congaree River in Lexington County or in the towns of Cayce and West Columbia. Not until subsequent decades would this connection develop.

The close relationship between Fort Jackson and Columbia was cemented further in March 1963 with the announcement of the Columbia–Fort Jackson Community Relations Council. The organization met every other month and had five subgroups: police and safety; legal and education services; religion and welfare services; recreation and public relations; and housing, commercial services, and health. Council leaders planned to add a sixth field, training, at a later date. William DeLoache, a city administrator and retired Army lieutenant colonel, served as the coordinator.[17]

Despite the upbeat rhetoric that accompanied the creation of the council, it lay at the periphery in terms of influence. Col. Angelo Perri, who dealt with the committee as a senior staff officer at Fort Jackson and who later served on several such committees after his retirement from the Army, summed up the role of this and other committees. "The relationship between Columbia and the downtown community is the relationship established by the commanding general with the key business and industry leaders," he said. "The councils are the kind where they send their deputies."[18]

The events that followed the announcement of the committee bore out the truth of Perri's observation. Neither the post commander nor the mayor attended the first meeting. Major General D'Orsa sent his deputy commander. Mayor Bates sent his city manager, Graydon Olive. In a 1995 conversation, former coordinator William DeLoache could not even recall having served in this capacity.[19]

The Fort Jackson Officers Club was actually more significant than the committee for maintaining good civilian-military relations. The post commander held a reception there every month or two. Besides honoring visitors from the Department of the Army or Congress, he hosted them to welcome new senior officers or city leaders. The commanding general's secretary, Mrs. Ida Pride, kept the guest list and continually up-

Fort Jackson and the Desegregation of Public Facilities | 145

dated it. A version of this list survives in the papers of Assistant Secretary of the Army Chester Davis, who attended a finance conference at Fort Jackson in 1955. The invitees for this particular reception included the Third Army commander, the commanding general's staff, South Carolina Adjutant General James Dozier, civilian aide George Buchanan, civilian aide Samuel Latimer, mayor Clarence Dreher, city manager Thomas Maxwell, and chamber of commerce president Arthur W. Williams Jr.[20]

Mrs. Pride remembered that the receptions provided one of the most important settings for making contacts. Indeed, the military custom of the receiving line literally forced people to introduce themselves. After making small talk, they could then plan for future appointments at the golf course or in their offices. Columbia native Charles Wickenberg, who was involved with the receptions both as Governor Timmerman's secretary and as a political correspondent for the *State* newspaper, noted that the affairs were probably more helpful for the military people than for the civilians because of the high personnel turnover rate at Fort Jackson.[21]

A variety of ceremonies also allowed for post officials to meet with civilian leaders at all levels. The South Carolina National Guard normally held a parade at the conclusion of summer training. The dignitaries who sat with the commanding general in the reviewing stand ranged from city councilmen to governors to senators. Other ceremonies celebrated special events such as Representative Corinne Riley's groundbreaking for the new hospital in 1963 or Mayor Lester Bates's presentation from the City to the post of thirty-nine dogwood trees.[22]

The Fort Jackson Officers Club was also an important venue for less formal meetings. Many of the influential civilians in Columbia had served in the military, and many of them retained commissions in the Reserves. This status allowed them to join the club. Membership was coveted not only because of the excellent golf course and dining facilities but because Fort Jackson was the only place in the area prior to 1974 that served liquor by the drink. Columbian John Harden, a World War II enlisted soldier who rose to the rank of full colonel in the Army Reserve, became a member during the fifties. Speaking as a person who regularly attended the town's more exclusive balls and parties, Harden said that Fort Jackson was one of the most popular nightspots in the city.[23]

People who did not belong to the club sometimes tried desperately to obtain an invitation. "The Fort Jackson Officers Club every Wednesday, Friday, and Saturday night had a band," said Colonel Perri. "Most of the state legislators had memberships to our officers club and a lot of the

146 | BLACK, WHITE & OLIVE DRAB

lawyers downtown would do anything . . . just to get somebody to bring them out to dinner."[24]

Civilians in Columbia took their turn at playing host as well. Every spring, the chamber of commerce held a reception for senior officers from Fort Jackson. Twice a year, on Armed Forces Day in May and on Veterans Day in November, the mayor invited the commanding general to join him on the reviewing stand in town. The post commander often attended luncheons and banquets sponsored by the chamber or various civic organizations such as the Lions and Rotarians.[25] "The relationship with the leadership of Fort Jackson and Columbia was superb, remembered Hyman Rubin. "I can recall having commanders from Fort Jackson at my home for dinner. And whatever they did out there—they'd have their events and affairs—as far as possible, the local officials and leadership would go out there and share it with them, and what we had here, the parades and celebrations, they'd come in, too. . . . I suppose from an institutional standpoint, we just couldn't have had a warmer, friendlier relationship."[26]

This cordiality reached a peak in 1968 when the city actually annexed the post. No American municipality had ever taken a federal reservation into its boundaries before. Mayor Bates initiated the step because it would allow for annexation of several expensive housing developments that had been built along the post's periphery. Additionally, the boost in population made the city eligible for increased federal aid and block grants. L. Mendel Rivers had become chairman of the House Armed Services Committee by this time, and he made certain the Congress approved the measure.[27]

To commemorate this union and to celebrate the Fort Jackson's fiftieth anniversary, Columbia leaders raised $82,000 so that the city could give the post a statue of Andrew Jackson. Local banker, chamber of commerce member, and civilian aide to the secretary of the Army J. Willis Cantey led the effort. Artist Felix De Weldon, who also designed the Marine Corps War Memorial in Washington, was commissioned to sculpt and cast the bronze monument. The statue was presented in 1970 and erected at what was then the main gate.[28]

Sociologist Carl David Sutton said in his 1973 sociology dissertation that one reason why armed forces installations had a limited ability to affect the civil rights movement was that civilians in the surrounding community "captured" the commanding general and his staff. Certainly this aspect of Sutton's thesis rang true at Fort Jackson and in Columbia. Although the local white power structure gave due respect to the post

Fort Jackson and the Desegregation of Public Facilities | 147

commander, they clearly held the upper hand through their longer tenures in office and their connections to the South Carolina congressional delegation.[29]

"Capture" by the city government and chamber of commerce had the effect of excluding local African Americans. Institutionally, civil rights groups such as the NAACP held no influence over the Fort Jackson command. Racial matters were never a topic for discussion at meetings of the Columbia–Fort Jackson Community Relations Council or at the chamber of commerce's Armed Forces Committee.[30] Socially, members of the civilian black middle class had few counterparts on-post with which to interact.

Whereas white South Carolinians could sway the Army through the chamber of commerce, the city government, and their congressional delegation, the African American community had no corresponding access. Even though blacks in South Carolina had begun to vote in larger numbers, they still did not have sufficient voice in Congress to pressure the military. Years of racial confrontations at both the national and local level had sown distrust between the NAACP and white armed forces leaders.

In addition, the state civil rights movement stayed in chaos throughout the fifties and sixties. The 1950 libel charge against John McCray, anti-NAACP laws, and the various sanctions taken against South Carolina black colleges succeeded in splitting the African American leadership. McCray and Modjeska Simkins exchanged bitter words. During the next two years, James Hinton maneuvered Simkins out of the NAACP in a dispute over tactics.[31]

Furthermore, African Americans in Columbia had no social counterparts who could invite them to receptions or dinner at the Fort Jackson Officers Club. Although a large number of black NCOs and company-grade officers were assigned to the post along with a few majors, the post did not have any permanently assigned officers of that race above the rank of lieutenant colonel until 1971. The effect of this social vacuum cannot be overstated given the class-consciousness exhibited by South Carolinians of all races.[32]

The lack of influence in Congress by South Carolina blacks allowed legislators from the state to live within a seemingly illogical, topsy-turvy world. Southern congressmen had the freedom to rail against national civil rights laws as unconstitutional intrusions upon the rights of states. Simultaneously, they could lobby for increased federal spending that far exceeded the taxes collected. They were almost never forced to wrestle

148 | BLACK, WHITE & OLIVE DRAB

with this contradiction. The actions of Senator J. Strom Thurmond during August 1957 make this point clear.

The future of Fort Jackson again came into question during the late fifties. An economic recession had placed increased pressure upon the Department of Defense to make cutbacks. A reduction in force took place within the officer corps and among civilian workers. By 1957, Pentagon officials had begun to consider closing installations. Even though it had permanent status, Fort Jackson remained a prime candidate because the post did not have any brick buildings and other major infrastructure.

South Carolinians learned that Fort Jackson was on the chopping block in June 1957. They immediately jumped into action. Columbia mayor J. Clarence Dreher sent a telegram to President Eisenhower while George Buchanan assembled a group of prominent citizens to make a trip to Washington. Among them were state legislators A. Fletcher Spignor and Floyd D. Spence, city councilman Hyman Rubin, newspaper editor Samuel Latimer, District 2 school superintendent E. L. Wright, lawyers, realtors, and members of the chamber of commerce.[33]

The delegation arrived in Washington on 27 August 1957. They visited with Senators Thurmond and Johnston as well as Representatives Riley and Dorn. The meetings consisted of office calls and a breakfast. They were not entirely successful, however. "We were supposed to appear before a committee dealing with these matters," remembered Hyman Rubin. "Curiously enough, we didn't get before a committee. We got before one member of the committee. That was what we sort of call in Yiddish *chutzpah*, that's nerve."[34]

At the same time that the South Carolinians were pleading their case, the Civil Rights Act of 1957 was pending before Congress. The Senate had reached an impasse over this bill because one of its provisions allowed for persons accused of obstructing voting rights to be tried before a judge without the defendant having the option of a jury trial. Although this stipulation arguably violated the Sixth Amendment, proponents had fought to keep it because in cases involving black victims, all-white juries had often voted to acquit whites despite clear evidence of guilt.

The provision gave southern legislators an excuse to derail the entire bill. Many wanted to do exactly that, but Senate majority leader Lyndon Johnson persuaded or coerced them to remain quiet. J. Strom Thurmond would not acquiesce, however. Within a day after the delegation from Columbia had departed his office, he began a filibuster. He spoke for over twenty-four hours, urinating into a glass container to avoid giving up the floor. Although he did not stop the bill from becoming law, he set a record

Fort Jackson and the Desegregation of Public Facilities | 149

for the longest filibuster by a single person. Moreover, he forced an amendment to the bill that permitted trials by jury.

Given that Fort Jackson's fate was pending during this same time, the possibility existed that Johnson or another congressman might have tried to have the post closed in retaliation for Thurmond's intransigence on the civil rights bill. Given that many South Carolinians already attributed the attempted closing of the installation in 1949 to Thurmond's run for president against Truman, the connection and its political implications might have worried the senator.

None of the available evidence suggests, however, that Thurmond or any of the congressmen from South Carolina were concerned that opposition to the civil rights bill might jeopardize Fort Jackson. The senator's papers contain nothing to that effect, and Thurmond himself said in a letter written forty years later that the delegation from Columbia had no influence on his decision to mount the filibuster. In fact, he did not even remember the visitors.

Thurmond implied that his close ties to President Eisenhower and Vice President Nixon would have prevented any such closing. "There would have been no concern that my speech might have an adverse effect on the future of Fort Jackson," he wrote. "The thought that the post in Columbia might suffer never entered into my mind when I decided to speak out in favor of the sanctity of the jury system."[35]

Correspondence written in 1957 by Senator Olin Johnston also made apparent that the two issues were not related. He sent a form letter to each member of the delegation from Columbia. "It was certainly good to have the opportunity of meeting you and the other members of the South Carolina delegation at the breakfast yesterday in the Speaker's Dining Room in the Capitol regarding the Fort Jackson situation," he said. "You may rest assured that I am doing everything possible to protect South Carolina and the South not only in such matters as this but also with regard to the so-called civil rights bill which I vigorously oppose and which I am doing my utmost to defeat during this session of Congress."[36]

Constituents in South Carolina did not see a connection either. Two recipients of the above letter—Hyman Rubin and Floyd Spence—said in response to questions posed forty years later that they did not remember being concerned that the filibuster would affect the decision by the Department of Defense.[37] Another South Carolinian, C. M. Tucker of Pageland, wrote to Thurmond in July 1957 to thank the senator for support of a local watermelon festival. Tucker said: "The Fort Jackson band was the outstanding band in the parade, and we certainly appreciate your going

150 | BLACK, WHITE & OLIVE DRAB

to bat for us to get them to come. . . . Good luck on the fight against the so-called civil rights bill."[38]

Rather than worry that opposition to civil rights legislation would close Fort Jackson, one person worried that the continued existence of the post would undermine the state's system of segregation. W. Legare McIntosh did not wield any special influence, but his views were reflective of those of many constituents. He wrote Senator Johnston in March 1957: "Several weeks ago I noticed the howl that you put up when it was stated that 12% of the personnel at Fort Jackson would be cut. Instead of cutting it 12%, they had better cut it 100% and get rid of the niggers and loafers."[39]

McIntosh expressed similar sentiments in a letter he wrote to Senator Thurmond in 1959: "I notice that you insist on spending $5,000,000 on a hospital at Fort Jackson. The best thing that could happen in this state and its people would be to close that place up entirely. For a number of years I kept my commission in the Air Force Reserve. About 2½ years ago I went out to Fort Jackson to take my annual physical. The things I saw made me sick to my stomach. Black negroes in every bed. The receiving room filled with negroes and their families. To top it all off I saw a negro patient being pushed around in a rolling chair by a white Captain nurse. This was too much for me and I resigned my commission."[40] Given this kind of feedback, South Carolina congressmen had no reason to question the contradiction that existed between championing states rights while lobbying for disproportionate amounts of federal spending.

For a brief period during the mid- to late fifties, the integrated armed forces provided a convenient target for state-level politicians in South Carolina. This tendency was most pronounced in Governor Timmerman. Besides having the fewest connections to the Army of any recent chief executive from South Carolina, he held office during a time in which a growing number of southern governors began to use racial demagoguery as a tactic. Moreover, he sought to gain stature among southern Democrats as a possible presidential candidate.[41]

Timmerman made his first public attack upon military racial practices in December 1955 after he received a letter from the National Security Committee. The message had requested that governors in all states assist with encouraging voluntary enlistments because the number of new recruits had dropped off in the wake of the passage of that year's Reserve Forces Act. The South Carolina governor replied to the committee with a well-publicized letter that referred obliquely to Fort Jackson. "So

Fort Jackson and the Desegregation of Public Facilities | 151

long as our basic training installations are used as sociological camps for compulsory race mixing," he said, "it is reasonable to expect a continued lack of voluntary enlistments, and a continued lessening of morale and esprit de corps in our armed forces."[42]

The South Carolina General Assembly followed suit by passing a resolution on 24 February 1956. Agreeing with the governor, legislators from both the state senate and House of Representatives blamed the low level of recruitment on integration. They concluded by calling for the president "to restore segregation of the races in the Armed Forces of this county [sic]."[43]

Two months later, the president of South Carolina's state-supported military academy, the Citadel, also spoke out. Retired Army Gen. Mark Clark, who had commanded Allied forces during the Italian campaign of

This photograph of Brigadier General McConnell (*left*) and Gen. Mark Clark (*right*) was taken during the fall of 1950. Clark commanded the Army Field Forces, an organization one echelon above the Third Army and two above Fort Jackson. At the time of this picture, Clark called Fort Jackson, which he presumably knew had just been integrated, a "Mecca" for training. He would make headlines in 1956 for disparaging black troops and calling integration a mistake. (Quotation from the *Columbia Record*, 17 October 1950.) (U.S. Army photograph, courtesy of the Fort Jackson Museum)

152 | BLACK, WHITE & OLIVE DRAB

World War II, disparaged both black troops and Army policy in a speech before the Southern Regional Conference of State Governors. He said that in Italy "the worst division I had was a Negro division." The general added that "I did not feel that we should integrate then, and I don't think so now."[44]

Clark's motivations for making this statement are unknown. Possibly he was positioning himself for a run at state office because he hedged his remarks carefully. He seemed mindful that he had served as commander of Army Field Forces when Fort Jackson was desegregated in 1950 and had visited the post in November of that year. In 1952, the post commander had said of Clark, "He saw them all mixed up, and he was quite in favor of it."[45]

The Citadel president justified his role during the early fifties by saying integration "was expedient from a military standpoint." He further buttressed his vulnerability on this issue by drawing a line between racial mixing in the ranks and in the civilian population. "There were no social problems involved" when he integrated troops in 1950. "There we had no schools, no buses[,] and no families to consider."[46]

Pentagon officials made no public response to Timmerman or the South Carolina General Assembly, but they took Clark's challenge seriously. They defended the decision to integrate, but at the same time sought to smooth southern fears of any larger social motives. Speaking for them was Gen. Anthony McAuliffe, the hero of Bastogne during World War II and Army assistant chief of staff for personnel in 1950. "I don't agree with him at all," McAuliffe said of Clark to the *New York Times*. "We didn't do it to improve the social situation. It was merely a matter of getting the best out of the military personnel that was available to us."[47] Despite condemnation by the governor, the legislature, and Clark, the Department of Defense tried to stay above the fray in South Carolina. This attempt to keep military and social considerations separate is evidenced not only by McAuliffe's statement but by the announcement in April 1956 that Fort Jackson would be designated a permanent installation.

The governor and his colleagues learned from experience that they could make public attacks upon the military with impunity while continuing to reap the economic benefits of defense spending. Timmerman's antimilitary rhetoric reached a climax in October 1958, after a racially mixed contingent of troops from Fort Jackson arrived at the South Carolina Statehouse to set up stands for a rally by Billy Graham. Even though the evangelist had addressed a joint session of the General As-

Fort Jackson and the Desegregation of Public Facilities | 153

sembly in 1950, the governor based his opposition to the meeting primarily on the grounds that the state should not sponsor church activities. He attempted to use the issue of blacks in the armed forces to strengthen his case further, and he implied once again that the Army had ulterior social motives.

"In apparent defiance of this well-known principle of law," Timmerman said in reference to the separation of church and state, "an integrated Army detachment has erected Army property in front of the approach to the South steps of the State House in preparation for the Graham rally." He added that "there is, in fact, no reason to select the State House unless the real purpose is to capitalize, for propaganda purposes, on the appearance of a widely-known advocate of de-segregation [sic] preaching from the South Carolina State House to his followers."[48]

The governor's comments received attention from President Eisenhower and the national press, all of whom honed in upon the racist aspects of the remarks. Realizing that the integration issue was backfiring at a national level, Timmerman and his supporters responded with a vigorous constitutional defense of the separation of church and state. At least among South Carolinians, the governor succeeded in confining the debate to these boundaries. Almost all of the constituents who wrote to Timmerman mentioned religion rather than race. Favorable letters outnumbered negative ones by a ratio of approximately four to one.[49]

Billy Graham meanwhile decided to relocate his rally. He used his influence as a friend of President Eisenhower to secure use of the parade field at Fort Jackson. The commanding general issued a public invitation, and former Governor Byrnes lent his support by appearing on the stand with Graham. Local newspapers published maps of where to drive and park on-post. In contrast to earlier outbursts by the governor, state legislators remained conspicuously silent.

The most effective repudiation of Governor Timmerman on both racial and religious grounds, however, came from the thousands of South Carolinians who crowded the post. Black and white, worshipping together, they demonstrated their acceptance of Fort Jackson as an oasis of integration. The governor's term expired soon thereafter. Timmerman's presidential ambitions fell flat, and he retreated to the judiciary to spend the rest of his career as a state circuit judge.

South Carolinians clearly believed that the Department of Defense would remain neutral on the issue of desegregated civilian facilities for black service members. Congressmen displayed no fear that the Pentagon would relocate southern installations on this account. State politi-

154 | BLACK, WHITE & OLIVE DRAB

cians did not hesitate to criticize military racial practices. Conversely, officials at the local level did not use their success at integration as a selling point with the military. Black and white leaders in Columbia desegregated Main Street lunch counters peacefully in 1962. They took justifiable pride in this accomplishment and touted it in their campaign to win All-American City status in 1963. They did not seem to feel, however, that integration improved their standing with the military. The 1962 effort by Columbia citizens to locate a corps headquarters at Fort Jackson provides an example.

The sit-in movement that started in 1960 alarmed many people in the Columbia area. African American students from Allen University and Benedict College had conducted protests during the spring of that year and also in 1961. Several minor incidents of violence and one near-riot had already taken place. City leaders were concerned about the possibility of more serious incidents as the spring of 1962 began to warm.[50]

Mayor Lester Bates consulted with approximately sixty to seventy leading citizens during the early part of 1962. From them, he selected a group of eighteen people. They included whites such as Hyman Rubin as well as African Americans such as John McCray and James Hinton. The races met in separate groups, but they shared a common goal of peacefully integrating lunch counters. The biracial committee had another characteristic common in South Carolina—secrecy. Mayor Bates made no public mention of the group. After the committee members quietly persuaded local businessmen to desegregate lunch counters, editors at the *State* and *Columbia Record* agreed to keep the news out of print for several days.[51] On 21 August 1962, James Hinton became the first African American in Columbia to receive service at a Main Street lunch counter. Even though Columbia journalist Charles Wickenberg reported the event the next day in the *Charlotte Observer,* city newspapers did not release the information until seventy-two hours later.[52]

At the same time the news appeared about the desegregation of Columbia lunch counters, another delegation from the city went to Washington, D.C. This group sought to persuade the Department of Defense to move the Twelfth Corps headquarters from Atlanta to Fort Jackson. This organization controlled Army Reserve units in North Carolina, South Carolina, Georgia, and Tennessee.[53]

Mayor Bates himself led the group. Other members included representatives from the chamber of commerce, the General Assembly, and the South Carolina Military Affairs Committee. Once they arrived in Washington, they were joined by Senators Johnston and Thurmond as

Fort Jackson and the Desegregation of Public Facilities | 155

well as Representatives Rivers, Dorn, and (Corinne) Riley. This impressive show of unity probably helped to sway Pentagon officials, for the Department of Defense soon relocated the headquarters to Fort Jackson.[54] Significantly, nobody on the delegation tried to use the peaceful desegregation of Columbia lunch counters as a selling point. The lack of dialogue regarding this subject says much about the priorities of not only white South Carolinians but also of Army officials.

The silence surrounding the successful desegregation of lunch counters is intriguing because the treatment of black servicemen in civilian communities surrounding federal installations had become an important issue in Washington by 1962. Only a few months before the delegation from Columbia visited, President Kennedy had appointed his Committee on Equality of Opportunity in the Armed Forces. He named Judge Gerhard A. Gesell as the chairman and gave the committee the task to examine, among other things, off-base conditions.

The Gesell Committee conducted hearings and toured installations across the United States. It investigated at least one case involving Fort Jackson. Three African American civilians who worked at the post warehouse testified before the committee that they had been denied promotions on account of their race. The men later complained that they had suffered retaliation for speaking out.[55]

The work of the Gesell Committee did not become a concern for most white Columbians until 26 July 1963, when Secretary of Defense McNamara gave local commanders the power to place off-limits any civilian establishment that discriminated against black servicemen. He exerted pressure upon them to use this tool by implying that their next promotion might hinge upon their making measurable progress in this area. McNamara based the new policy upon the initial report of the Gesell Committee.[56]

The secretary's announcement prompted fury in South Carolina. The *Columbia Record* published six editorials against McNamara and the Gesell Committee during late July and August.[57] The articles stated that the secretary of defense intended to turn local commanders into Russian "commissars" and noted that few of the committee members had served in the military or knew much about the South. "All are extreme exponents of revolutionary civil rights actions," one editorial read. "They are willing to destroy the morale, mission, and effectiveness of the armed forces to gain their sociological ends by federal vindictiveness." The editorial also lamented with unintended irony that the Columbia–Fort Jackson Liaison Committee, which had never even discussed desegrega-

156 | BLACK, WHITE & OLIVE DRAB

tion, would be undermined. (George Buchanan, incidentally, had left the newspaper several years earlier to become dean of the USC School of Journalism.)

Several South Carolina congressmen expressed their disapproval, too. "This is the beginning of police state and commissar government in the United States," said Mendel Rivers.[58] Strom Thurmond called the new policy "economic blackmail in its rawest possible form." He said that it would cause economic hardship for civilians while hurting military families. "What we are witnessing today is the imposition in America of a second Era of Reconstruction."[59]

At least two South Carolina towns near Columbia courted sanctions openly during the next month when the Army held its annual Swift Strike exercise. These maneuvers involved mock battles in the Carolina countryside between Forts Jackson and Bragg. Even though the military brought money into the local economy, the town of Whitmire placed its facilities off-limits to soldiers.[60] Police in Sumter harassed black servicemen, and officials at the National Guard armory there refused to allow African Americans to use the snack bar even though a four-star Army general was using a briefing room in the same building.[61]

The commander at Fort Jackson treaded cautiously. Soon after McNamara made his announcement, Maj. Gen. Charles D'Orsa issued a brief, noncommittal statement to the press. "I'll do my duty as God guides me to do it," he said. The post commander tried to soothe white feelings by making a speech before the Columbia Lions Club titled "What the Army and Columbia Mean to Each Other."[62]

The speech brought praise from the *Columbia Record*, which devoted an editorial to him. "Fort Jackson is a racially integrated 'town,'" the article said. "Columbia observes many customs of social segregation that are traditional in the South offering many opportunities to the people of both races in their respective spheres. . . . Quite properly, he would not commit at this time on the effect the new policy might have on two good neighbors, Columbia and Fort Jackson."[63]

Major General D'Orsa's caution proved to be a wise career move because the chairman of the Senate Armed Services Committee soon made a blatant threat against local commanders who might have been inclined toward using their new power. Mississippi senator John Stennis referred to the Senate confirmation of promotion lists when he warned, "Those who might be ranked high by the President's Commission when it comes to 'measuring progress' might not be ranked quite so high by those who finally act on the proposed promotion."[64]

Fort Jackson and the Desegregation of Public Facilities | 157

Secretary of Defense McNamara backed down in the face of this up-roar. He attempted to minimize the political damage by noting that no-body had yet to apply the off-limits sanction and that local commanders could not impose it without first gaining approval from the civilian sec-retary of the service involved. He emphasized the limited nature of his proposal by adding that "the commander will be concerned only with the welfare of his men and their dependents; unequal treatment of oth-ers by the community—whatever the commander's personal feelings about such treatment—is not his concern."[65]

Consequently, no commanding general at Fort Jackson or anywhere else applied the off-limits sanction for racial discrimination. Two instal-lation commanders elsewhere apparently tried, but the service secre-taries disapproved the requests.[66] The assassination of President Kennedy blunted the impact of the final Gesell Committee report, which was re-leased two days before the shooting. The issue of off-limits sanctions died with the president.

Although Secretary of Defense McNamara lost this battle, he did win minor victories in four other areas. First, he persuaded the USO to de-segregate nationally.[67] Second, he forbade officers of the armed forces from speaking in uniform before civilian groups that advocated segrega-tion.[68] Third, he restructured his staff to include an assistant secretary of defense for civil rights and then appointed Albert Fitt to the position. Fourth, McNamara initiated a series of "Equal Opportunity Climate Sur-veys," which commanders at all installations containing over five hun-dred people were required to conduct.[69]

At Fort Jackson, national desegregation of the USO resulted in the closing of the Taylor Street facility. Although black soldiers gained access to the Laurel Street USO, they lost one of their refuges within Columbia's African American community. USO Pal Day had meanwhile been can-celed a year earlier because of the Cuban Missile Crisis.[70] The prospect of integrated churchgoing and Sunday dinners ensured that the event would not be held again.

The policy against speaking before segregated audiences had no effect in South Carolina. The Fort Jackson Public Information Office suppos-edly began screening invitations for speakers, but not once did the staff reject a request.[71]

The appointment of Fitt created an opportunity for at least one black Columbia family. Charles F. Bolden Jr., the son of USO board member Ethel Bolden and World War II veteran Charles Bolden, was graduated from high school in 1964. He had tried several times to secure an ap-

158 | BLACK, WHITE & OLIVE DRAB

pointment to the U.S. Naval Academy. Even though he was a star athlete with grades that had already won him admission to Harvard, Duke, and the University of North Carolina, Senator Hollings and Representative Watson had told him that he was unqualified to be a midshipman. Senator Thurmond had also rejected Bolden's request to go to Annapolis and instead offered to send him to the Merchant Marine Academy. Assistant Secretary of Defense Fitt intervened personally to give the young man a direct appointment to the Naval Academy. "I have forgotten just how we turned up Bolden," Fitt remembered in a 1968 interview, "but somehow, as part of our case-finding effort, I learned about him." The Columbian fulfilled his promise by graduating in 1968 and becoming a pilot in the Marine Corps. Fitt recalled that while at Annapolis, Bolden "had been president of his junior class. He had a B average. And it was just a happy ending."[72]

Equal Opportunity Climate Surveys at Fort Jackson raised Fitt's concern about the lack of interaction between the commanding general and black civilians in the Columbia area. In March 1964, he directed that a follow-up survey be conducted and that post officials provide additional information about the "effort and results by command to change racial composition of military-civilian advisory committee."[73]

Regardless of efforts the Fort Jackson commander might have made in the wake of Fitt's request and regardless of what the Gesell Committee said, white Columbians at this time felt little pressure from the military regarding off-post treatment of African American soldiers. This fact is evident in the report of the Citizens' Design for Progress (CDP). The chamber of commerce initiated the CDP in April 1964. Retired Army Brig. Gen. O. P. Newman was appointed to lead it. Thirty-six committees investigated ninety-six different aspects of life in the city and then made reports, which were consolidated into a final document released in February 1965.[74]

Two of the groups dealt specifically with Fort Jackson: the Liaison Committee and the Military Installations Committee. The latter omitted the topic of race entirely in its report. The former, however, noted that black soldiers using local recreational facilities was a "problem" that was "not to be ignored."[75] Liaison Committee members were also aware of the HEW secretary's 1962 threat to build schools on-post if local ones did not desegregate. They expected that the Army would soon construct more educational facilities at Fort Jackson, but this development did not appear to bother them. In fact, they took the position in their report that any sanctions arising from the Gesell Committee report would hurt fam-

Fort Jackson and the Desegregation of Public Facilities | 159

ilies at the post more than they would hurt civilians: "It is anticipated that continued practice of segregation by the area council may, in the future, deprive Fort Jackson children of participation in Scouting activities."[76]

The Citizens' Design for Progress did have a few black representatives, but none of them served on the installations or liaison committees. Their absence spoke volumes about the state of relations between the African American community and Fort Jackson.

Desegregation of public facilities in Columbia came about through civilian, not military effort. The process began with the biracial committee of 1962 that worked to eliminate Jim Crow lunch counters. Mayor Bates resurrected the organization the next year and made it more public. He selected fifty prominent citizens—twenty-five black and twenty-five white. They included many longtime civil rights leaders such as James Hinton, John McCray, Lincoln Jenkins, and Ethel Bolden. Bates called them the Greater Columbia Relations Council. Some of the city's more radical blacks criticized the group. "They're just a buffer state," said Modjeska Simkins. "They jump when the mayor says 'frog.'"[77]

Nevertheless, the council did succeed in persuading most area businessmen to comply with the Civil Rights Act of 1964. "Colored" and "White" signs were removed peacefully and without fanfare from most water fountains, waiting rooms, restaurants, and other places. The council also worked to find jobs for qualified African Americans. By 1968, its members claimed to have helped over 1,200 blacks.

Given Fort Jackson's record of near-closures, a historian could be forgiven for assuming that fear of losing the installation might have contributed to this success. The evidence, however, does not bear out the hypothesis. Institutional constraints imposed by civilians from the local to the national level blunted the effect of the post even when the Pentagon encouraged post commanders to use the off-limits sanction.

9
★☆

Staying Out of Trouble
Fort Jackson Soldiers and Columbia Sit-ins

The very least any soldier can contribute to community relations is to stay out of trouble.

—YOU AND YOUR COMMUNITY, Department of the Army
Pamphlet 355-12, April 1958

That the Army discouraged its members from becoming involved in civilian demonstrations against Jim Crow should come as a surprise to no one. Nevertheless, assessing the extent to which servicemen participated in the desegregation struggle is important when considering the sixties. This decade was the era of mass-based protest, driven to a large extent by draft-age young people who tended to question authority. How they reconciled their personal beliefs with the requirements of uniformed service says much about the way the integrated military was perceived in relation to the civil rights movement. Equally revealing is the way armed forces authorities worked to thwart potential activists in the ranks.

Few, if any soldiers stationed at Fort Jackson joined Columbia's sit-ins of the early 1960s. Those who had previous experience with the movement elsewhere declined to take part until after their military service ended. Nevertheless, the commanding general at Fort Jackson felt compelled to take steps beyond what the Pentagon required of him to ensure that soldiers stayed out of local protests. The focus of efforts against segregation by black civilians in Columbia and South Carolina meanwhile shifted from lunch counters to the ballot box. Here, a number of former soldiers played key roles.

★☆

The first major protest of the sixties in South Carolina took place in January 1960 at the Greenville Airport. The dispute, which had a number of connections to the armed forces, had simmered throughout the previous

Staying Out of Trouble | 161

year. In August 1959, a civilian Air Force worker visiting from Michigan had filed a lawsuit after municipal airport authorities denied him access to the all-white waiting room. Judge George Bell Timmerman Sr. had dismissed the case in his typical fashion. Two months later, baseball star Jackie Robinson (an Army veteran of World War II) encountered the same situation when he passed through Greenville. The local NAACP rallied its members and staged the demonstration.[1]

Although the Greenville incident did not have the national impact of the Greensboro sit-ins that occurred a month later, it did show that South Carolina blacks were ready for change and willing to fight. Indeed, the February protests in North Carolina set in motion numerous spontaneous uprisings across the Palmetto State. Some of the most effective ones took place in Rock Hill.[2] The largest occurred at South Carolina State in Orangeburg, where one thousand students marched on 14 March 1960. The police arrested three hundred of them and used fire hoses and tear gas to disperse the rest. The climax for Orangeburg, however, would not come for another eight years.[3]

Sit-ins began in Columbia on 2 March 1960, when approximately fifty students from Allen University and Benedict College occupied lunch counters at Woolworth's and Kress's department stores on Main Street. The demonstrations lasted about ten minutes because the managers at both places shut down their facilities almost immediately. The students left peacefully. The next day, five hundred young people met for a rally at Allen and Benedict. Two hundred of them then marched into the downtown business district. All of the stores there closed when the students arrived.[4]

Events took an ominous turn on 4 March after someone burned a cross near the campuses. A crowd of about fifty students congregated in the aftermath, and they took out their anger about the cross on whites dining at an adjacent drive-in restaurant. Several car windows were broken in the fracas. Soon thereafter, Columbia mayor Lester Bates announced that the police would arrest any person who attempted a sit-in. The student leadership at Allen and Benedict agreed to cease their protests for the moment.[5]

The truce did not stop everybody. Arnold M. Smith became the first student arrested on 5 March. City recorder John I. Rice fined him for loitering. An unusual sleet and freezing rain storm brought all activity to a standstill for the next few days, but the unrest persisted. Two more students—Simeon Bouie and Talmadge Neal—were later arrested for demonstrating at a local lunch counter. Five others were apprehended at

162 | BLACK, WHITE & OLIVE DRAB

the Greyhound bus terminal. Despite these efforts, the movement in the state capital ground to a halt.[6]

The initial failure of the Columbia sit-ins resulted largely because whites there wielded overwhelming power at both the city and state levels. The student movement also suffered because the African American community in Columbia remained largely conservative, divided by class distinctions, and fragmented over tactics. Neither Allen University nor Benedict College had recovered fully from the damage inflicted during the late fifties when Governor George Bell Timmerman Jr. had tried to withdraw from the two schools the privilege of certifying teachers. The American Association of Colleges and Universities had censured both institutions for bowing to white pressure and firing several faculty members deemed subversive. The two colleges would experience accreditation problems throughout the sixties. More often than not, students directed their protests at the faculty and administration rather than any white racists in town.[7]

Columbia's leading civil rights activists stayed divided, too. I. DeQuincey Newman was the state president of the NAACP in 1960. He initially supported the students' tactics, but his organization labored under harassment by the state as well as the conservatism of its membership. Newman would quickly lose his taste for civil disobedience a year later when he led a "wade-in" at Myrtle Beach State Park. He barely escaped from there with his life after a high-speed automobile chase. Thereafter he seemed to prefer the legal approach that NAACP lawyers Matthew Perry and Lincoln Jenkins were then taking against segregated schools.[8]

Such older leaders as James Hinton and John McCray remained factors as well. They had ushered in a new, radical approach to change during World War II and the following decade. Hinton and McCray had stood on the cutting edge in 1941, but they had become more conservative in their old age. Hinton did not voice any public opinions about the sit-ins, but he worked diligently behind the scenes with other black and white leaders to achieve a peaceful solution. In 1962, he himself became the first African American to be served at a Columbia lunch counter.[9]

McCray publicly criticized the young people for their activism. He still lived in Columbia, and he witnessed some of the protests firsthand. He thought that the students had acted irresponsibly. In his opinion, they courted disaster by confronting whites in a blatant, threatening manner. "For close to two hours," he said, "mostly unguided young people wandered and roamed about Main Street, a breath away from an ugly explosion."[10]

Staying Out of Trouble | 163

The Richland County Citizens' Committee (RCCC) became the students' most vocal, supportive ally. In conjunction with the South Carolina Council on Human Relations, the group helped provide legal assistance for those people arrested. The RCCC also issued public rejoinders to McCray. One letter to the editor by a member of the committee reminded McCray that black Carolinians—him included—had acted with equal boldness during the MP brutality incidents of World War II.[11]

This difference of opinion was not new. It had carried over into the sixties from the earlier shake-up of the NAACP and the *Lighthouse & Informer* that had put Modjeska Simkins at odds with Hinton and McCray. Simkins served as the secretary of public relations for the RCCC throughout the sixties. Although she belonged to the older generation, Simkins became Columbia's most outspoken proponent of direct-action protest.

Despite dissension among local blacks, the sit-in movement in Columbia achieved its ultimate purpose because city leaders desperately wanted to avoid conflict. They considered such behavior to be unseemly and beneath the dignity of upper-class white South Carolinians. Racism also hurt business. Outbursts of student protest eventually prompted the mayor to assemble his biracial committee that accomplished desegregation of lunch counters in 1962.

John McCray provided some insights into the situation through his *Pittsburgh Courier* column. He said white people "have done more to help Negroes in this connection in two years than Negroes have done for themselves." He agreed with Mayor Bates, who had said recently at Allen University that "Negroes in Columbia are more busy fighting each other for the title of leader than their common enemy for the title of citizen." He implied that black adults were the force behind the student protests, and he recommended they stop pushing young people to act. The boycotts would not be successful, he said, "because Negroes in Columbia aren't organized."[12]

One month later, McCray wrote another column in which he focused on the military ramifications that students faced for participating in the sit-in movement. He wrote that Simeon Bouie, one of the first students arrested in Columbia, had called him on the telephone. Bouie had been inducted into the armed forces during his final month of college. He had gone to Fort Jackson and had passed his mental and physical examinations. Later he received notification that he had been rejected for service because he was considered to be subversive.

Bouie checked his records and learned that his draft board had disqualified him because of his sit-in activities and arrest. McCray called the

164 | BLACK, WHITE & OLIVE DRAB

Fort Jackson Public Information Office, and an officer assured him that participation in a sit-in would not prevent anyone from joining the Army. Nevertheless, the Selective Service Board stood "politely adamant, restrained, and noncommittal" in its decision.[13]

The sit-in movement alarmed authorities at the Pentagon, especially after groups of black airmen actually joined in several protests during the spring of 1960. The judge advocates of each service quickly formulated a plan, which the secretary of defense approved. The new policy declared civil rights protest to be "inappropriate" for members of the armed forces. Additionally, local commanders received the power to place civilian lunch counters off-limits and to restrict servicemen to their garrisons as necessary.[14]

The Freedom Rides of 1961 also disturbed officials in Washington. During the spring of that year, students tried to desegregate interstate bus facilities across the South. Their attempt resulted in violence in Alabama, mass imprisonments in Mississippi, and embarrassment for the Kennedy administration. Consequently that year, the secretary of the Army gave explicit guidance regarding travel to lower-echelon commanders. Racially mixed groups of soldiers would continue to ride civilian buses traveling interstate routes, but they would move under supervision and only after receiving briefings about local and state segregation laws. Commanders would make every attempt to avoid "known trouble areas" and would feed soldiers box lunches if integrated lunch counters were unavailable. In the event that servicemen were arrested, Army leaders would try to have them released to military authorities.[15]

The post commander at Fort Jackson somehow felt compelled to restate these established Army policies. On 15 June 1961, Maj. Gen. H. D. Ives ordered soldiers there "not to loiter in the vicinity of or participate in" civil rights demonstrations while in uniform. He warned that those who violated the directive would be "subject to the laws of the area in which he may be participating."[16]

Major General Ives's announcement attracted attention as far away as New York City. During July, an article about Fort Jackson appeared in the *New York Post* and was broadcast over radio station WLIB. Apparently the stories were unfavorable to the Army because the Fort Jackson Public Information Office responded with a reiteration of the order and the assurance that segregation was not practiced on-post and that "men and women have been given equality of treatment and opportunity in the U.S. Army in a manner unparalleled in history."[17]

Why the commanding general chose to issue the directive remains a

Staying Out of Trouble | 165

mystery. No new guidance had come from the Pentagon, and the newspaper articles from the time state that "there is no record of Ft. Jackson soldiers having been involved" with any demonstration in Columbia. Local editors did appear worried about outside agitators from the North who might have been assigned to the post, and this concern might have prompted Major General Ives to act. "Most of the inductees are from Southern states," said both the *State* and the *Record*, "but a number come from Pennsylvania, Michigan, and other Northern states."[18]

Through tightened supervision and administrative restrictions, officials at the Pentagon and at Fort Jackson attempted to squelch activist impulses within the ranks. Although military authorities did not expressly forbid former protesters from enlisting, they did little or nothing to stop local draft boards from screening out individuals who had joined civil rights demonstrations in the past. By its nature, the Army was a conservative institution and filled with people who—whether by disposition, training, or economic necessity—were not inclined to question authority. Combined with these elements, the new prohibitions had their intended result.

Ironically, a South Carolinian who had been a civil rights activist reported to Fort Jackson for basic training only a few months later. He was James Felder, and his story provides an excellent example of how military service could temporarily still the voice of protest.[19] Born during the early forties, Felder grew up in Sumter, South Carolina, an area both rich in civil rights history and military tradition. The town had one of the state's earliest and most active NAACP chapters. It also adjoined Shaw Air Force Base, which had integrated its ranks two years before Fort Jackson did.

As a child, Felder and other young African Americans in the civilian community had a high regard for the Air Force. The commanding general there allowed local children of all races to swim at the base pool and participate in Scout programs. Felder belonged to the Explorer post at Shaw and rode an Air Force plane on at least one occasion.

Despite a relatively happy upbringing, Felder felt the sting of racism. His parents belonged to the black middle class and had ties to the NAACP leadership in town. Through this connection, the young man learned more than the average teenager about the racial struggles of the fifties. He also remembered vividly going north to appear on the *Today* show with his school. He resented having to stay in segregated hotel rooms during the trip.

Felder attended Clark College in Atlanta, Georgia. He had high am-

166 | BLACK, WHITE & OLIVE DRAB

bitions, first wanting to become a doctor and then deciding later to attend law school. Handsome, intelligent, and articulate, he was elected president of his student body just as the sit-in movement began. He went to the 1960 Shaw University conference that gave birth to the Student Nonviolent Coordinating Committee (SNCC), and he later worked with student leaders at other Atlanta colleges to coordinate protest efforts. Along with other notables such as Julian Bond and Lonnie King, he helped to draft and then signed the famous "Appeal for Human Rights" that appeared in the city newspapers.[20]

He remained in Atlanta after graduation from college in 1961. He married and took a job at the post office, but he still faced the draft and two years of active service. Rather than take that course, he decided instead to volunteer for the Air Force and become an officer. He traveled to Maxwell Air Force Base in Alabama, where he was accepted for duty.

Before the Air Force could process him, however, the Army sent him a draft notice. Apparently the Selective Service board in Sumter County did not know that he had been arrested during an Atlanta demonstration. Felder's parents appealed to Congressman John Riley to let him join the Air Force, but to no avail. On 19 January 1962, Felder reported as ordered to Fort Jackson. The Army normally assigned South Carolinians to posts farther from their homes, but Felder's Atlanta residence made him an exception.

Private Felder had a positive experience in basic training, both professionally and socially. He had no complaints about his living conditions or the instruction he received. He also got along well with the other members of his platoon. The racial situation within this group was far less tense than in the civilian world of this time. Felder remembered that his comrades segregated themselves more along lines of common hometowns than color. The platoon sergeant was an African American as were many of the officers. In Felder's eyes, everybody appeared to receive equal treatment and respect.

Race became a factor primarily when soldiers went off-post to Columbia. According to Felder, everybody received a briefing beforehand telling them about local segregation practices and warning them to avoid trouble. The sit-in movement in town had waned by the winter of 1961–62, but concerns persisted. In fact, Mayor Bates's biracial committee was formulating its plan to desegregate Columbia lunch counters during the same spring that Felder was assigned to Fort Jackson.

Felder usually visited his parents in Sumter when he had free time, but he did go on occasion to the segregated USO on Taylor Street. Al-

Staying Out of Trouble | 167

though the facility was located next to the campuses of Allen and Benedict, he did not attempt to contact students, nor did he try to organize his fellow soldiers. As he said in an interview over thirty years later, the idea never occurred to him. The former student activist conformed so well to Army discipline that his superiors selected him to attend Fort Jackson's leadership school and receive an accelerated promotion to sergeant.

While at the leadership school, Felder was chosen to become one of the first black members of the Old Guard, the Army's elite ceremonial unit stationed in Washington, D.C. He departed Fort Jackson in June 1962 for Fort Myer, Virginia, where he underwent additional training and a background check for a higher security clearance. Once again, his past activism did not pose a problem. Felder eventually became part of a casket-bearing team that conducted burials in Arlington National Cemetery. The pinnacle of his military career came in 1963, when he served as the sergeant in charge of the team carrying President Kennedy's body to its final resting place. Soon thereafter he left active duty to enroll in law school at Howard University.

The armed forces became more embroiled in civil rights issues as the decade progressed. Amid the public controversy over the Gesell Committee's 1963 recommendations regarding off-limits sanctions, Secretary of Defense McNamara quietly lifted the order that had prohibited service members from participating in civil rights demonstrations. Some limitations still applied, however. Nobody could wear uniforms or conduct protests during duty hours. Furthermore, any activities that could possibly lead to violence remained forbidden.[21] McNamara's announcement thus had little impact on Fort Jackson, where the preponderance of soldiers had long been required to wear uniforms whenever they left post and where the commanding general had broad discretion to determine what activities might lead to violence.

The post commander also received power to limit the access of civilian activists to the installation. In a 1964 memorandum, Assistant Secretary of Defense for Civil Rights Albert Fitt clarified how the regulations applied to the current movement. He said that representatives from organizations such as the SNCC and the NAACP could not speak to military formations or groups of soldiers while on-post. Local commanders could decide whether or not to let people go door to door in family housing areas, but Fitt discouraged any on-post chapters, solicitation of funds, or membership drives. He suggested that service members who wanted to support such groups could exercise their legal right to do so by contributing to national organizations rather than local ones.[22] Given

168 | BLACK, WHITE & OLIVE DRAB

the gulf that already separated Columbia's civil rights activists and Fort Jackson officials, Fitt's guidance had no more effect than did McNamara's directive of the previous year.

The Civil Rights Act of 1964 had similarly mixed results for the military in South Carolina. The landmark legislation wrought the greatest change upon the state's National Guard, which had been one of the country's last to allow African Americans. Adjutant General Frank Pinckney, who had replaced James Dozier in 1958, had won election for this office on a segregationist platform.[23] He had succeeded in keeping the force all-white, but the 1964 law left him with little choice but to admit blacks. According to Albert Fitt, "The Adjutant General of the State [South Carolina] called the Chief, National Guard Bureau to inform him within a day or two after enactment of the Civil Rights Act of 1964 he had called in the senior troop leaders to inform them that Negroes were no longer barred from National Guard membership."[24] Six African Americans joined by December 1964. Their numbers tripled by the end of the next year, but they remained a token presence in a statewide force of almost ten thousand whites.[25]

The Army Reserve in South Carolina made greater progress than did the National Guard, but it also lagged behind most of the nation. Efforts to desegregate began in earnest during 1962, after Army Chief of Staff Gen. George Decker visited Fort Jackson. He proclaimed publicly that there would be "no great falling off of morale" if blacks joined previously white Reserve units. "I think there will be no ill effects generated by integration," he said.[26] General Decker had served as post commander of Fort Jackson during the late forties and was highly regarded in Columbia, so his word carried considerable weight. In 1963, South Carolina blacks in the Army Reserve numbered 42 officers and 813 enlisted out of a total force of 1,737 and 6,118 respectively.[27]

By contrast in the Regular Army, a disproportionately large number of African Americans participated in Project 100,000. This program was the military's contribution to Lyndon Johnson's War on Poverty program and had some civil rights ramifications. Under it, the armed forces allowed the annual enlistment of 100,000 men classified as Category IV on the entrance examination. The military normally preferred those in Category III or higher. Project 100,000 operated under the assumption that many of those in Category IV suffered from the effects of poverty or inadequate education. These men had the potential—proponents said—to become good soldiers if given extra training. The program began in 1965 with 40,000 people. A total of 215,000 entered the Army via

In this 1965 photograph, soldiers undergoing advanced individual training to become radio communications specialists learn how to climb and work safely at Fort Jackson's "pole orchard." (U.S. Army photograph, courtesy of the Fort Jackson Museum)

170 | BLACK, WHITE & OLIVE DRAB

this avenue by the time the experiment ended in 1969. Thirty-eight percent of the total was black. An undetermined but large number of these men came to Fort Jackson.[28]

The Army's training and indoctrination system underwent a massive, pivotal overhaul during this same period. Two years before Project 100,000 started, Undersecretary of the Army Stephen Ailes issued a seminal report on the status of Army basic training. It had been sparked by public outrage over a 1957 incident in which several marines were drowned at Parris Island. The Ailes Report drew upon a wealth of practical experience and sociological research that stretched back to the Second World War. It established a standard, Armywide curriculum for the initial eight weeks of training. Instructors would no longer "break down" recruits and build them into a common mold. Instead, they would try to enhance already existing qualities within each individual. The report also called for cadre members themselves to undergo two weeks of special training so that they could learn the specifics of the new philosophy.[29]

Most memorably, the Ailes Report gave rise to the Army drill ser-

In this 1966 photograph, a black sergeant oversees soldiers at a rifle range. (U.S. Army photograph, courtesy of the Fort Jackson Museum)

Staying Out of Trouble | 171

geant. Qualified NCOs at the platoon level would thenceforth receive elite treatment. New privileges and perks included extra uniform allowances, a distinctive badge, and the right to wear special headgear— the "Smoky Bear" campaign hat from World War I.[30] A select group of sergeants from Fort Jackson went to the Marine Drill Instructor School at Parris Island during early 1964. Upon graduation, they returned to Fort Jackson, where they helped to establish the Army's first drill sergeant academy. Elsewhere on-post, sociologists studied basic trainees undergoing the new program of instruction.[31]

Although the Ailes Report did not address civil rights specifically, the resulting reforms highlighted the scientific, managerial, and standardized solutions that Army leaders increasingly applied to human relations. As outright restrictions loosened on participation by soldiers in racial demonstrations, military officials would come to rely upon these new methods of indoctrination in their attempts to instill discipline.

While training methods in the Army evolved, the nature of black protest changed within the civilian sector. Mass demonstrations against segregated public facilities climaxed nationally with the 1963 marches in Birmingham, Alabama. The emphasis of the movement shifted toward voting rights. With the help of the Kennedy administration, the major civil rights groups pooled their resources through the Southern Regional Council's (SRC) Voter Education Project (VEP). This organization coordinated registration across the South. The best-publicized of these efforts was the "Freedom Vote" in Mississippi, which was followed by an attempt to unseat the state's delegation to the 1964 Democratic National Convention.

Activists in South Carolina waged a similar, but less well-known battle. The state offered perhaps the best chance in the Deep South to mobilize the black vote. African Americans there had already won the right to vote in the primaries after the *Elmore v. Rice* victory of 1948. "Here's our ticket to freedom, right here," an old black man in Columbia told reporter John Egerton in 1965. "We're gonna take that piece of paper and be free. Best way to demonstrate is on 'lection day with this little 'ol piece of paper. We don't have to raise hell."[32]

The white Democratic establishment remained powerful, but weakened. White voters increasingly opted for Republican presidential candidates. A Republican had made a strong bid for the Senate in 1962. Senator Thurmond defected to the Grand Old Party in 1963. Soon afterward, the congressman who represented the district surrounding Fort Jackson also defected to the Republicans. Albert Watson, who had replaced John

172 | BLACK, WHITE & OLIVE DRAB

Riley's widow in 1963, would later become a controversial candidate for governor.

The SRC and the Southern Christian Leadership Conference (SCLC) seized upon the opportunity presented in South Carolina. In 1965, the two groups organized the Summer Community Organization and Public Education (SCOPE) Project under the auspices of the VEP. The primary function of SCOPE was to utilize the large number of students who became available during the summers. These volunteers would go door to door encouraging blacks to vote. SCOPE included representatives from older civil rights groups like the NAACP and the Congress of Racial Equality (CORE) as well as a relatively new group, the Southern Student Organizing Committee, or SSOC, which was a white counterpart to the increasingly black separatist SNCC.[33]

SCOPE brought together longtime state activists such as Modjeska Simkins, Matthew Perry, and Billie Flemming. The latter was a World War II Army combat veteran who had been involved as an adult with the original Clarendon County school desegregation case. He later had become a mortician in Columbia. Many newcomers, too, established a presence in South Carolina. William Treanor, for example, was an outsider who became a full-time SCOPE worker within the state. After serving as an Army infantryman, he had gone to college, where he became interested in civil rights.

Treanor headed the registration effort in Newberry County, one of the most dangerous parts of the South Carolina Upstate. Located in this county was the town of Whitmire, which had banned soldiers in 1963 after the Gesell Committee proposed using off-limits sanctions to ensure fair treatment of troops. Here, too, was the county seat of Newberry, where in 1950 Olin Johnston had called Strom Thurmond a liar for saying that he did not oppose armed forces desegregation vehemently enough in 1948 and where the latter had challenged the former to a fistfight. Prevailing attitudes appeared to have changed little in this county. SCOPE workers there faced police harassment and an ever-present threat of violence. Indeed, a young activist was almost lynched in April 1965.[34]

Passage of the Voting Rights Act in August 1965 gave additional impetus to the movement. Among other provisions, the new law banned literacy tests and authorized the federal government to intervene directly in counties having low levels of registration and participation. The number of registered blacks in South Carolina jumped from 138,544 in 1964 to 190,017 in 1967. The percentage went from 37.3 of eligible African Americans to 50.8.[35]

Staying Out of Trouble | 173

The South Carolina VEP gained a full-time executive director that year.[36] Organizers found a South Carolinian who had recently graduated from Howard University with a law degree. He was James Felder, the former Atlanta student activist and presidential casket bearer. Now that he no longer had any constraints placed upon him by the military, he pursued civil rights with vigor. The leadership skills that he had learned at the Fort Jackson NCO Academy served him well, as did the celebrity he gained from the Kennedy funeral. He would become a prominent figure in the state.

James Felder's example shows that administrative restrictions imposed upon soldiers during the early sixties—combined with American ideas about the military as an institution in general—helped to squelch social activism in the ranks at the height of the sit-in movement. His case also suggests that even radically minded people did not have problems with this situation. Felder took for granted that he would give up some of his rights when he joined the military. He considered that to be part of his duty. "I characterize myself as being a pragmatic realist," he said in a 1971 interview. "I am very proud of the two years I spent in the service of the United States Army."[37]

That Felder had done well in the Army and was supportive of the military did not come as a surprise to at least one of his colleagues from the Atlanta student movement. Jean Toal, a native of Columbia, had attended Agnes Scott College at the same time Felder was at Clark. She belonged to the SNCC and had participated in the Mississippi "Freedom Summer" of 1964 before returning to Columbia for law school in 1965 and working in voter registration. She later married a navy veteran and became chief justice of the South Carolina Supreme Court.

"Being in the Army was not necessarily incompatible with very strongly held civil rights views," she said. In the early sixties, it wasn't a negative thing at all." Toal felt the disjuncture that later arose between the protest community and the armed forces came largely as a result of the Vietnam War. "A lot of us who were involved in civil rights activity were a little 'pre the curve' of antiwar feeling," she said. "The Army was a liberating thing for a lot of southerners. It gave them a broader view. It gave them opportunities, particularly with black kids."[38]

Surprisingly, the conflict in Vietnam would also help to undermine the military's effort to end housing discrimination against black servicemen.

10
★☆

Counting Bodies in Columbia
Fort Jackson and Equal Housing

McNamara's fight for open housing demonstrates, as nothing had before, his determination to use, if necessary, the department's economic powers in the civilian community to secure equal treatment and opportunity for servicemen.

—Morris MacGregor, INTEGRATION OF THE ARMED FORCES

An analysis of the narrative and statistical housing reports filed by Fort Jackson in South Carolina, has revealed that the base's statistics do not illustrate what we believe to be the true housing situation for Negro servicemen in the number of open assurances received by the base housing office.

—1969 letter to the Department of Defense

When the Department of Defense actively tried to do something about racism in communities surrounding military installations, the initiatives did not work. The 1967 effort to use the off-limits sanction to stop discrimination by landlords and realtors is a good example. The commanding general at Fort Jackson misled his superiors and avoided any situation where he might have to use the off-limits sanction. The failure resulted in part from the dynamics of military-social relations at the local level. It also reflects the climate of distrust and dishonesty that arose within the military during the 1960s as a result of the management style of Secretary McNamara and the pressures of the Vietnam War.
★☆

The vast majority of soldiers who brought spouses and children with them to Fort Jackson during the early to mid-sixties lived in the civilian community. The post had 3,682 officer and enlisted families in 1964 but only 413 sets of quarters.[1] Most of the government houses were part of the Jackson Homes development that the New Deal–era Works Progress Administration had built on the western edge of post in early 1941. The

Counting Bodies in Columbia | 175

remainder consisted of apartments created by partitioning the old wooden buildings of an abandoned hospital from the Second World War. Although the Census Bureau did not classify any of the structures as deteriorating or dilapidated, the quarters offered few comforts or modern conveniences such as air-conditioning. Only 31 out of 382 surveyed in 1960 met minimum Army square-footage requirements for military residences, but they did have plumbing and electricity. Furthermore, families who lived in them did not have to pay rent or utility bills.[2]

Service members who resided off-post in Columbia received a "Basic Allowance for Quarters," or BAQ. A staff sergeant in 1964, for example, earned $110 in addition to his normal $200 to $300 monthly salary.[3] This supplement helped to offset the cost of rent or mortgage payments. Drawing BAQ required special authorization, so every installation had a family housing office where soldiers and their spouses could go to complete the necessary paperwork. Administrators there tried first to fill any available on-post vacancies before granting permission to live off-post. They also offered assistance in locating civilian landlords or realtors. Army Community Services (ACS) provided similar aid. This agency helped newcomers to get children enrolled in school and to obtain telephone hookups, newspaper subscriptions, and electrical service. Like the family housing office, ACS had information about where to find a place to live.[4]

Although the typical BAQ far exceeded the $41 median rent for Richland County, leasing a suitable house or apartment in the civilian community presented a considerable challenge.[5] Many buildings posed fire hazards, needed repair, or did not meet basic standards of construction. The housing committee for the 1965 Citizens' Design for Progress (CDP) of the Greater Columbia Chamber of Commerce classified one-fifth of all dwellings for lease in the Columbia area as dilapidated or deteriorating.[6] Competition with employees of the state government and students from the University of South Carolina kept demand high and drove up prices for quality properties even further.

The shortage meant that many families from Fort Jackson either inhabited substandard homes or paid rents that exceeded their BAQ. According to a 1964 report by the Fort Jackson Housing Office, 79 officers and 364 enlisted families lived in places that the Army considered to have inadequate floor space. They totaled 443 and comprised 13.5 percent of the families who lived off-post. Telephone directories from the 1960s indicate that many of them clustered in trailer parks that dotted the outskirts of the federal reservation along Percival and Two Notch Roads.

An even larger number of people spent amounts of money that

176 | BLACK, WHITE & OLIVE DRAB

exceeded their authorized BAQ. In 1964, 294 families paid at least $10 more rent, 521 paid at least $25 more, and 431 paid at least $50 more. In addition, 511 families incurred other costs that they would not have had to pay if they lived on-post. Purchasing a house was rarely an option despite the availability of federal loans, especially for enlisted personnel. Tours of duty at Fort Jackson averaged two years, which meant that most soldiers had insufficient time to recoup a real estate investment. Military authorities estimated that 1,800 of the 3,272 families who lived off-post in 1964 would have moved onto Fort Jackson if given the choice.[7]

This situation did not go unnoticed by local civilians. In 1960, Congressman John Riley tried to arrange for the Federal Housing Authority to purchase and convert into government quarters a civilian apartment complex located adjacent to the post. The owners had defaulted on their mortgage. The congressman thought the move would improve Fort Jackson's chances of staying open while helping to alleviate the housing shortage. He could not obtain funding for the purchase, however.[8]

Members of the CDP housing committee recognized the problem, too. "Large numbers of officers and noncommissioned officers with moderate rental allowances are stationed at Fort Jackson," they wrote in their 1965 report. "The present situation requires most of them to purchase houses and sell them after two or three years at a financial sacrifice." The committee made a dire prediction if nothing changed. "The failure of Columbia to provide these rental units . . . will undoubtedly result in a large number of housing units being constructed at Fort Jackson, thus withdrawing a considerable source of income from Columbia."[9]

In fact, planning for more on-post quarters had already begun by the time the CDP made its report. The House Armed Services Committee set aside money in the 1964 budget for 250 new housing units at the post, and it authorized another 180 in 1965. Members of the CDP housing committee expressed nonchalance at this news: "This quantity of family housing will generally replace the existing family housing occupied by both officers and noncommissioned officers and, therefore, is not really an addition."[10]

Columbia landlords and realtors were nevertheless concerned about the potential economic effects. Although local civilians lamented the shortage of available housing in reports to the chamber of commerce, they proclaimed an abundance of the same in letters to their congressmen.[11]

Col. Angelo Perri arrived at Fort Jackson during the fall of 1966. A lieutenant colonel at the time, he was serving as interim public information officer when the issue of this new construction came to fore. "We . . .

Counting Bodies in Columbia | 177

made a conscious decision, it was an unwritten agreement, with the real estate interests downtown," he remembered. "If they would not object to us building all of this enlisted housing . . . then we would build no officer housing. . . . Otherwise, the real estate interests in town were ready to go to the mat with us about all of this housing that we were building."[12]

Construction began during the spring of 1967. Fort Jackson had a total of 645 units by 1970. Though an improvement, the number still did not come even close to meeting demand.[13]

Finding housing created a special hardship for African Americans. Lieutenant Colonel Perri took command of a basic training battalion in early 1967. He recalled that "black NCOs that came here just faced a terrible time finding anything decent."[14] Segregation limited many African American military families to living in some of Columbia's worst slums. In 1965, the Columbia Planning Department and Planning Commission conducted a study of neighborhoods. The predominantly black ones had significantly higher rates of crime, fire, and disease.[15] Many African Americans joined the military to escape this kind of environment. Moreover, they earned far higher than the median income for local blacks and could afford better homes. Perhaps for these reasons, or for the schools, a disproportionate number of African American families lived on-post. Blacks comprised 11 percent of the population at Fort Jackson in 1960, but they made up 18 percent of the families who lived in on-post housing.[16]

Race played a part in the 1966 deal made between Fort Jackson officials and local realtors. Colonel Perri remembered: "The feeling was we were not going to force integration downtown, period. So the downtown real estate community said, well, if you all want to build housing out there for the black NCOs, you know, essentially fine. And we said we won't build any officer housing other than those few around the club here for the senior commanders."[17]

The story of Capt. Ernest Porter gives added poignancy to these statistics and gives lie to the notion that all officers wanted to purchase houses. An African American ophthalmologist from Ohio, Dr. Porter worked at the Fort Jackson Hospital. He and his wife moved to Columbia in 1966. A year later, he made a statement under oath in which he described the difficulties they had in finding housing. He said: "I was, to say the least, very despondent because we were going to have to purchase a home to have a place to live. It seemed to be outlandish for just a two-year tour." Living off-post increased his transportation costs and subjected him and his wife to other kinds of racism. She, for example, had been thrown out of an all-white laundromat near their home. "I felt that

178 | BLACK, WHITE & OLIVE DRAB

my first venture into the Southland was rather a negative one," Dr. Porter said.[18]

Local civil rights activist Modjeska Simkins related a similar account on a July 1967 radio program. She described an African American lieutenant who could not find housing in Columbia. He already had orders to go to Vietnam, and he wanted to find a place for his wife to live. The lieutenant had tried for three weeks without success, and he had informed his commanding officer, who said that he could do nothing to help. Simkins concluded her story about the plight of this young serviceman with a prescient observation: "The matter of housing for Negro servicemen has become acute to the point where the federal government is being forced to threaten to put off-limits all rental properties that refuse to house Negro personnel."[19]

John F. Kennedy had promised during his 1960 presidential campaign that he would end housing discrimination "with the stroke of a pen." He tried to fulfill that pledge on 20 November 1962 by issuing Executive Order 11063.[20] This directive required federal agencies to take action against anybody who discriminated on the basis of race in the sale

This 1967 photograph shows housing at Fort Jackson for noncommissioned officers. A disproportionate number of black sergeants and their families lived in dwellings like these because they could not rent or buy places in Columbia. (U.S. Army photograph, courtesy of the Fort Jackson Museum)

Counting Bodies in Columbia | 179

or leasing of federal housing. It also applied to any homes purchased with loans from or insured by the federal government.

Robert McNamara implemented the president's order within the Department of Defense by issuing a letter to the service secretaries on March 8, 1963. He directed that all contracts for private housing rented by the military for use by servicemen contain a nondiscrimination clause. This policy did not apply, however, to service members who rented or bought housing privately. McNamara seems to have recognized this inherent shortcoming because he added a requirement for all installations to maintain lists only of nonsegregated housing available in surrounding civilian communities.[21]

A few months later in June 1963, the Gesell Committee also noted the problem of housing for black military families. Its initial report urged leaders at all levels to "make every effort to eliminate discriminatory practices as they affect members of the Armed Forces and their dependents within the neighboring civilian communities."[22]

Secretary of Defense McNamara apparently heeded these words. In November 1963, Pentagon information packets about housing discrimination were distributed to all installations. Local commanders received orders to work on improving the situation by promoting open housing, emphasizing the lists at family housing offices, and using biracial community committees.[23] The assassination of President Kennedy that same month put these efforts on hold. The new president, Lyndon Johnson, focused on persuading Congress to pass the Civil Rights Act of 1964, which he signed in July of that year. The new law made sweeping changes in the areas of education, employment, and public facilities. In housing, however, it did little more than validate President Kennedy's 1962 executive order.

For the next year or two, Secretary McNamara contented himself with consolidating the tiny gains he had made. In February 1965, the Department of Defense entered into a formal arrangement with the Federal Housing Authority (FHA). The FHA agreed to provide local commanders with lists of all housing in their area covered by the president's executive order and to arrange for the lease of foreclosed properties to military personnel.[24]

Interest in housing began to rise as President Johnson submitted open housing legislation to Congress in 1966 and 1967. Although both bills failed, they generated nationwide debate. Secretary of Defense McNamara meanwhile worked on his own plan. He appointed one of his assistant secretaries to devise a way to foster integration of civilian hous-

180 | BLACK, WHITE & OLIVE DRAB

ing for service members living in the vicinity of Washington, D.C. He hoped that the area could then serve as a model for other installations. Members of the Maryland legislature lent their support on 16 February 1967 by passing a resolution calling for an end to discrimination against airmen stationed just outside of the nation's capital at Andrews Air Force Base. McNamara responded by expanding his efforts across the entire United States. In April 1967, he ordered all posts and bases having five hundred or more people to conduct a survey of housing conditions in their surrounding civilian communities. More decisive action would follow later.[25]

The directive took a couple of weeks to filter down the chain of command. Officials at Fort Jackson did not receive guidance until the second week of May, when memoranda from the Third Army headquarters at Fort McPherson, Georgia, arrived with instructions on how to proceed.[26] The commanding general and his staff immediately swung into action. The post commander, Maj. Gen. Gines Perez, assigned the mission of conducting the Department of Defense survey to Colonel Johnnie D. Duffie, who served as the G1, assistant chief of staff for personnel. Colonel Duffie in turn delegated tasks to his subordinates. A first lieutenant named Terry A. Carr, who worked in the personnel services section, performed most of the legwork.[27]

Although Lieutenant Carr did not consult specifically with any African American organizations or individuals, he did a thorough job of querying the various agencies on-post that might have had reason to deal with housing discrimination. He confirmed, for example, that the Fort Jackson inspector general's office had no case files regarding this matter.

He also learned that the family housing officer did not appear to have taken the shortage of quarters for African Americans very seriously. The most that this person—a civilian named Fred Stuck—did was to hang upon a bulletin board a list of nondiscriminatory landlords and realtors. Despite the severe housing shortage and the large number of black families at Fort Jackson, Stuck did not aggressively seek to find places for them to live. He waited instead for a landlord or realtor to call. Only then did he update the list.

Judging from the lieutenant's report, Stuck appeared somewhat defensive about his previous inaction and uncomfortable about the scrutiny under which McNamara's forthcoming survey had placed him.[28] He said that he had received no recent guidance from the installation commander and was continuing to follow a memorandum Major General Perez had issued two years earlier forbidding discriminatory landlords

Counting Bodies in Columbia | 181

or realtors from advertising on-post. Stuck could not, however, find a copy of the letter. While not evidence of wrongdoing, this kind of bureaucratic "tap dancing" suggests that black service members had found little assistance at the Family Housing Office during the mid-sixties.

Nor would they have received much help from Army Community Services. As Lieutenant Carr noted, "Military personnel who request ACS assistance in selecting off-post housing are provided a copy of the most current newspaper and instructed to use the want ads therein."[29] This policy perpetuated rather than alleviated segregation because the classified advertisements in the *Columbia Record* and the *State* normally did not say anything about race except for an occasional few that specified "For Colored."

Lieutenant Carr also talked to the military recorder of the Civil/Military Liaison Committee and the post's representative to the Greater Columbia Chamber of Commerce Armed Forces Committee. According to these people, neither group had ever discussed the issue of housing discrimination. The lieutenant consulted them because the person in charge of the Civilian Liaison Office, a Mr. Ingram, considered them to be the primary points of contact regarding this issue. Ingram apparently had never asked leaders of the black community for their opinions.

Indeed, the civilian liaison officer displayed bureaucratic defensiveness similar to that shown by Mr. Stuck at the Family Housing Office. Ingram made a point of saying that the Columbia community was, as Carr paraphrased his words, "generally non-discriminatory." The comment revealed both an ignorance of the black housing situation and some very elastic logic regarding race. "This opinion is predicated on the fact," as Carr continued in his summary of Ingram's position, "that all requests from the local community for guest speakers have been checked to ensure that the requesting activity is non-discriminatory—and a request has never been denied because of discrimination."[30]

Carr did not have to take Ingram at his word because he had additional orders to conduct an informal survey of civilian landlords and realtors. This sample would help Fort Jackson authorities to prepare an initial report as well as get mechanisms in place to complete the larger Department of Defense survey scheduled to begin on 22 May.

Informal telephonic inquiries started on 12 May and lasted for two or three days. The people called included landlords, real estate brokers, and public housing supervisors. The properties sampled encompassed a relatively broad range of locations and prices. Indeed, the lieutenant did a thorough job. He omitted from his survey only the all-black housing

units. The responses varied. Two of the places contacted—the Federal Housing Authority and the public housing agency—fell under President Kennedy's 1962 executive order. (Even so, only two of the public housing projects were integrated.) Five private landlords said that they had already desegregated their properties. Five others had all-white tenants but said they might rent to blacks under certain conditions. One said that he would take African Americans from Fort Jackson but not "local trash." Two people, including the only realtor contacted, refused to comment. Only two apartment owners would state forthrightly that they would not lease to blacks.[31]

Lieutenant Carr concluded in his 16 May report that "renters, leasers, and sellers in the Columbia area are predominantly non-discriminatory," but he added a few caveats. "More than a few," he said, "have never been forced to make a decision because they have never received a minority group application for tenancy. Hence, they say they are non-discriminatory but reserve the right to reject any tenant, white, or negro, who does not appear to be of a high moral character, etc." He similarly hinted at, rather than described, a more complex racial picture in his earlier comments regarding the civilians who supervised the Family Housing Office and Civilian Liaison Office.[32]

The data gathered by Lieutenant Carr formed the basis of the post commander's report to his higher headquarters at Third Army. All of the nuances within the initial document disappeared, however, as the information went up the chain of command and into Major General Perez's 17 May report. The final product contained unprovable assertions, misleading statements, implausibilities, and falsehoods.

"Equal treatment of all military personnel seeking off-post housing has long been a matter of concern to me," Major General Perez wrote. Perhaps the issue did interest him personally, but nothing in the record of the time indicated that he did anything about it officially until after Secretary McNamara issued his directive.

He mentioned, as Lieutenant Carr did, that many civilian landlords and realtors claimed that they did not discriminate even though they catered exclusively to whites. Using reasoning that rivaled that of Messrs. Stuck and Ingram for bureaucratic contortedness, Perez explained that blacks had not applied to live at these places because "there is generally sufficient housing of the type that is obviously integrated, ranging from moderately priced one family homes to lower cost multiple unit subdivisions." This statement directly contradicted all contemporary evidence about the availability of housing for blacks near Fort Jackson.

Counting Bodies in Columbia | 183

"We have rigidly adhered to a policy of advertising available housing only if the owner or agent will positively state that they practice nondiscrimination toward all applicants," Perez continued. Indeed, he fulfilled the Army regulation to the letter. Posting a list on a bulletin board and updating it only at the initiative of civilian landlords, however, hardly fulfilled the spirit of the requirement. Moreover, the family housing officer's inability to produce the policy letter indicates that the issue was of limited priority.

Major General Perez's report included not only misleading statements but ones that had, at best, only a minimal basis in fact. "I have, at every opportunity made the leaders of the local civilian community aware that I sought equal treatment for every Soldier of my command, particularly in their efforts to attain suitable housing for themselves and their families," he said. "The local community leaders are continually made aware of the Department of Defense policy towards equal treatment of all races through daily contact with key personnel of the post and through various joint military and civilian councils. This will continue." The minutes and records of the groups checked by Lieutenant Carr prove the exact opposite. In addition, Perez made no mention of having solicited the opinions of leaders in the black community.

Regardless, the commanding general boasted that his handling of the matter was worthy of emulation. He said that "these actions have, I feel, been very useful in this installation's gaining and maintaining excellent relations with the City of Columbia, and has minimized related problem areas. I would recommend this approach for consideration by other installations."[33]

Why would Major General Perez display such a disregard for the information provided him? Why would he compromise his integrity? The general was a fine officer by other measures. He had commanded infantry battalions during World War II and Korea and had won the nation's second-highest award for heroism under fire, the Distinguished Service Cross. He had a master's degree, possessed a photographic memory, and was multilingual.[34] Fear of negative reactions from local civilians is the best explanation for the post commander's behavior. Perez voiced this concern on several occasions, and he took clear steps to minimize friction.

The possibility of interference from powerful legislators like Senator J. Strom Thurmond and Representative L. Mendel Rivers caused perhaps the most worry. Perez noted in his 17 May report that "the potential exists for this census to generate special or congressional inquiries,"

184 | BLACK, WHITE & OLIVE DRAB

writing that "it may be worthwhile for Headquarters, Department of the Army to apprise Congress of this census."[35] Colonel Duffie, the G1, reiterated this point a week later when acting as the commander's representative at a 24 May meeting held at the Third Army headquarters. "DOD and DA should keep Congress apprised of such programs being implemented," he had said.[36]

If congressmen did become involved, Major General Perez wanted to make certain that local civilians understood that the order to conduct the housing survey originated at the Pentagon and not with him. After all, he had only a few months earlier made a deal with real estate developers over new construction at Fort Jackson. He requested that the Department of Defense ensure that "information officers at all echelons are kept current in this matter."[37]

Colonel Duffie added that "DOD and DA should reissue their policies on this housing matter on a periodic basis and through news media."[38] Although the local civilian papers never took much interest in the story, the *Fort Jackson Leader* began to run features about the nationwide activities of the Department of Defense in regard to housing discrimination. The articles said nothing, however, about the local situation.[39]

Major General Perez and his staff sought as well to soothe local civilians using more direct methods. On 19 May, the deputy commanding general spoke before the Civil/Military Liaison Committee. He told the assembled group that representatives from Fort Jackson would be calling Columbia realtors and landlords and described to them the information needed, adding: "The forthcoming survey can be made less painless for all if we can enlist your help. . . . General Perez discussed this already with Mayor Bates. . . . Johnnie Duffie has been and will be down in the Mayor's office to get some advice, guidance and assistance which will help us. We really appreciate his support, and we sincerely solicit yours."[40]

Post officials also tried to avoid any ugly confrontations over race that might arise once the formal surveys began. A "party line" was developed for Army survey takers to read aloud over the telephone. These instructions told the caller to "gently and tactfully advise the owner or operator of the DOD policy and concern on welfare and morale of its members and particularly of the matter of lack of discrimination in their search for off-post housing."

If anybody refused to answer questions or stated outright that they would not allow blacks, the survey taker was supposed to tell the person that his or her response "*may* cause a follow-up visit by Colonel Duffie or higher." The instructions emphasized that "this is *not* a threat, of course."

Counting Bodies in Columbia | 185

They further warned callers: "CAUTION: Be courteous at all times. If hostility is evidenced, gracefully withdraw. NO debates."[41]

While Fort Jackson authorities went to great lengths to avoid upsetting local civilians, they faced an equally prickly situation in their dealings with the Pentagon. The command climate of the sixties encouraged neither candor nor mistakes. Secretary McNamara, for example, had instituted his "Zero Defects" program only a year earlier in an attempt to apply civilian production-line management techniques to military leadership.

Major General Perez ushered in the Zero Defects program at Fort Jackson with a ceremony held in April 1966. The effects filtered down the chain of command. "There was terrible pressure then—this was '67, '68, '69, '70, all that time," Colonel Perri said, to pay attention to statistical measurements like absentee rates and disciplinary rates. The close focus on numbers "created a lot of duplicity. . . . Even at the lieutenant colonel level, a lot of these people were career-punching."[42]

Similarly, Major General Perez sought to avoid the negative attention that an accurate assessment of the racial situation at Fort Jackson would surely have brought. As the commanding general's initial report of May 1967 made clear, the attitude that led to inflated body counts in Vietnam had a parallel within the United States. The response of post officials to McNamara's next phase of his fight against housing discrimination further confirms this viewpoint.

The secretary of defense took his boldest action yet to secure equal housing for service members during the summer of 1967. On 17 June, he used the off-limits sanction against discriminatory landlords surrounding four armed forces installations in Maryland. A month later, he ordered that housing referral offices across the United States (like the one supervised by Fred Stuck at Fort Jackson) keep lists of nonsegregated places to live. He additionally required that all married personnel obtain clearance from one of these offices before signing a lease or mortgage. Unless they selected from the approved list, they would not be able to draw the BAQ. The policy thus imposed the off-limits sanction upon discriminatory landlords automatically.[43]

McNamara supervised the program tightly. Starting in July 1967, installations began submitting monthly reports up their chains of command to the Pentagon. Reflecting the obsession with statistics that characterized McNamara's tenure, the format required detailed percentages and raw figures. The Department of the Army housing coordinator at the Pentagon consolidated the data from fifty-three Army installations into

186 | BLACK, WHITE & OLIVE DRAB

a quarterly report for the chief of staff. Table 2 summarizes the extant information submitted from Fort Jackson.[44]

At first glance, the reports paint a rosy picture of the situation at Fort Jackson. Most civilian landlords agreed to permit mixed occupancy. Two who had refused to allow blacks in July 1967 capitulated by November. The four who considered changing did so. The one who initially refused to talk eventually broke his silence. The number of written assurances climbed steadily.

Nevertheless, the figures do not bear close analysis. A journalist for the *Fort Jackson Leader,* for instance, used the May 1968 data for one of the few articles written about the local situation. The writer said that the family housing officer told him that 106 landlords out of 117 had stated they were open to all races. The story implied that the remaining eleven still practiced segregation.[45] The information that went to the Pentagon indicated, however, that only two places would not allow blacks and that the remaining nine had given "other" assurances.

This discrepancy could very well have arisen from a journalistic error or the idiosyncrasies of the Department of Defense reporting format, but other numbers also suggest that Fort Jackson authorities manipulated the figures to their advantage. For example, the percentages coming from the post consistently reflected that over 90 percent of landlords had agreed to comply with the new policy. These figures put Fort Jackson within the majority of Army installations across the United States and thus did not draw unfavorable notice. Only as recalcitrant landlords

TABLE 2 Results of Fort Jackson off-post housing surveys

Date	Total facilities/ units	Did not allow blacks	Would consider change	Would not talk	Signed assurances	Other assurances
31 Jul. 67	88/11,037	2	2	1	n/a	n/a
31 Oct. 67	96/11,353	—	4	1	2	89
30 Nov. 67	96/11,353	—	4	1	2	89
31 May 68	117/15,006	—	2	—	106	9
30 Jun. 68	129/15,404	—	2	—	118	9
31 Aug. 68	145/15,759	2	—	—	143	—
30 Sep. 68	155/16,129	4	—	—	151	—

Source: DCSPER-DAHC, Fact Sheet, Subject: Equal Opportunity in Off-Post Housing, 20 December 1967 and 28 October 1968, MacGregor Papers, Center of Military History.

Counting Bodies in Columbia | 187

agreed to comply did anybody at the post discover new places that discriminated and that might skew the statistics.

Indeed, the director of the Office of Federal Programs questioned the validity of these reports in a 1969 letter to the deputy assistant secretary of defense for manpower, writing: "An analysis of the narrative and statistical housing reports filed by Fort Jackson in South Carolina, has revealed that the base's statistics do not illustrate what we believe to be the true housing situation for Negro servicemen in the number of open assurances received by the base housing office. These statistics infer *that there has been little integration of housing facilities since our staff visit, at which time we found that the only facilities housing Negroes were trailer courts and slum-type dwellings. Our report also recommended that a dialogue be established between the base command, their Negro personnel, and the local Negro community, but the narrative reports from these bases make no mention of any minority group contact.*[46]

Major General Perez had good reason, however, for interpreting the data loosely: submitting marginal results to the Pentagon would have brought unwelcome consequences. As a 1967 fact sheet from the Department of the Army housing coordinator said, posts having problems received "some form or another of special and intensive attention, such as high-level dinner meetings, special reporting requirements, special visits, or the imposition of sanctions by the Secretary of Defense or Secretary of the Army."[47]

Exposing racism thus made local commanders look incapable of handling the situation on their own. Major General Perez already had enough trouble on his hands without having to worry about defending his record over this issue. The court-martial of an Army doctor at Fort Jackson during the spring of 1967 had attracted negative international press coverage.[48] Ladies from the NCO Wives Club had complained to Senator Thurmond about their charter.[49] To top things off, the general had health problems that required several weeks of hospitalization at Walter Reed Army Medical Center in Washington. He certainly would have wanted to avoid any further scrutiny from the Department of Defense.

In addition, Fort Jackson authorities would not have wanted the increased administrative burdens mentioned in the Pentagon fact sheet. They had many other personnel issues with which to contend. These included McNamara's Project 100,000 and the surge in the number of basic trainees brought about by escalation in Vietnam.[50] Colonel Duffie had earlier made explicit his worries about time and resource constraints in his 24 May briefing at Fort McPherson, writing that "the job of coming

188 | BLACK, WHITE & OLIVE DRAB

up with a complete listing of facilities to survey is time consuming." He added that, "if as indicated, there is to be special and possibly additional offices and staffing in this program, it should be expedited."[51]

McNamara's directive on housing discrimination thus put installation commanders in a bind. On one hand, the lack of publicity and involvement by the legislative branch placed them at the forefront of educating citizens and implementing policy. They—not the secretary of defense—risked the ire of local congressmen and their constituents. On the other hand, they received negative attention for reporting an unfavorable situation to the Pentagon. Here, too, they took great risks with their careers. Like battlefield commanders in Vietnam who inflated body counts, post authorities in the United States had more to lose than they had to gain by telling the truth.

As a result, the situation for African Americans at Fort Jackson grew worse by the time of the 1970 Census. While the percentage of assigned blacks grew from 11 to 17, the percentage living in on-post facilities increased from 18 to 29.[52] Secretary McNamara's attempt to use the off-limits sanction to end housing discrimination clearly failed in Columbia.

11
★☆

Fighting at Home and in Vietnam
Howard Levy, the UFO Coffeehouse, and the Fort Jackson Eight

Is civil rights organizing a usual pastime for ANY *army officer* ANYWHERE?
—letter to the editor, COLUMBIA RECORD, 4 July 1967

Close ties between Fort Jackson and Columbia's white elite helped prevent soldiers from protesting not only against racial discrimination but also the war in Vietnam. The two issues became increasingly intertwined as the 1960s progressed. Military and civilian authorities coordinated efforts to undermine activists such as Capt. Howard Levy, the civilian owners of the UFO Coffeehouse, and the Fort Jackson Eight. This kind of cooperation further alienated local civil rights leaders and helped to overshadow the accomplishments of African Americans who chose to serve in the armed forces and fight in the war.

★☆

The year 1965 marked the introduction of U.S. ground combat troops into South Vietnam. American soldiers assigned there previously had technically been considered advisors rather than combatants even though many of them had already perished in the fighting. The effects of the escalation rippled back to Fort Jackson. An advanced infantry training brigade, the Third, was activated in order to prepare young men to go to Southeast Asia. Toward that end, several returning veterans created among the South Carolina pines a mock Vietnamese village that they nicknamed "Bau Bang."

The intensifying war temporarily thwarted full implementation of the Ailes reforms to basic training at Fort Jackson because overseas transfers and a swell of draftees caused a perpetual shortage of drill sergeants. To compensate, the post commander instituted a drill corporal program. Basic trainees who demonstrated superior ability were held at Fort Jackson, given additional instruction, and used as cadre.[1]

190 | BLACK, WHITE & OLIVE DRAB

The Vietnam War helped to transform some of the success of integration into ironies. Whereas activists during World War II had decried the exclusion of African Americans from frontline duty, many of them now complained that blacks in Vietnam died disproportionately.

This situation arose for several reasons. First, blacks did not have as many opportunities to join the Reserves or National Guard. Second, African Americans as a group scored lower on qualification tests and were more likely to end up in the infantry rather than in a technical, rear-echelon branch of service. Third, blacks often volunteered for duty as paratroopers because of the prestige and extra "jump pay." The Army's airborne and airmobile infantry brigades bore the brunt of the early battles in Vietnam. Some sociologists later claimed that African Americans did not suffer any more than whites, but this assertion holds true only when the war is examined as a whole. African Americans comprised approximately 10 percent of the Army, but they accounted for 25 percent of the deaths in 1965, 16 percent in 1966, and 13 percent in 1967.[2]

The war also called into question the wisdom and justice of Project 100,000. Although many young men found opportunities in the military that they otherwise would not have had, few of them could quality for the more technical Army jobs that would have given them marketable civilian skills. The vast majority found themselves in the infantry with orders for Vietnam. Although color-blind racial policies allowed these inequities to arise within the Army, some civil rights activists ascribed the failure not to a flawed, perhaps unrealistic, policy but to evil motives on the part of Pentagon officials.[3]

In the eyes of a growing number of African Americans, the military became more of an enforcer of a white-dominated capitalist system than an avenue of opportunity. The use of all- or mostly white National Guard and Regular Army troops to quell urban riots in Harlem, Watts, and Detroit reinforced this view. Although the older, more conservative generation of blacks such as NAACP director Roy Wilkins continued to support the military and its war effort, most of the younger ones began to see similarities between the plight of African Americans at home and the treatment of the Vietnamese people. These activists included Stokely Carmichael, who had purged whites from the leadership of the SNCC and raised the cry "Black Power" in 1966. They also included Martin Luther King Jr., who in the years before his assassination began to question the viability of his dream within a market economy.[4]

Amid these events, a white officer named Capt. Howard Levy arrived at Fort Jackson during the third week of July 1965. A twenty-eight-year-

old doctor from Brooklyn, New York, he had recently completed his residency in dermatology before being drafted. He would spend his two-year term of service as the post's primary specialist on skin diseases.[5]

The young physician seemed ill at ease with the constraints of many traditional institutions, yet he appeared reluctant at first to break away from them completely. Though he professed the Jewish faith, he rejected the orthodox practices of his parents. Though married, he had separated from his wife. Being in the Army, Levy followed in the footsteps of his father, a World War II veteran. Nevertheless, the son clearly felt uncomfortable in the military. He wore his hair longer than Army custom, if not regulation, dictated. He paid little attention to the appearance of his uniform. He refused to join the Fort Jackson Officers Club, where membership was virtually obligatory for officers assigned to the post.

Levy also had a growing interest in social activism, one that would eventually force him to take sides against the established order. He had become attuned to the plight of poor minorities while working as a medical resident in the slums of New York City. He began subscribing to publications such as the *New Left Review, Studies on the Left*, the *Militant*, and the *Nation*. He attended meetings of the Militant Labor Forum and on one occasion listened to Malcolm X give a speech before the group.

Levy waited less than a week after his arrival at Fort Jackson before becoming involved with civil rights causes. While eating breakfast in a diner on Saturday, 17 July, he read in that morning's *State* about the attempted lynching that April of a person who had tried to register black voters in Newberry County.[6] He decided to make the hour-long drive there in order to see for himself what had happened. While there, he met William Treanor, a U.S. Army veteran who headed the SCOPE effort in that part of the state. Levy quickly volunteered to become part of the project.

By an odd twist of fate, Newberry County also happened to be home of Special Agent James West, who belonged to the U.S. Army Counter-Intelligence Corps (CIC). West had served as a soldier during World War II and afterward had gone to work for the Department of Defense as a civilian investigator. He held membership in the same American Legion post and attended the same church as the local chief of police. West could possibly have learned from him about the automobile with New York state license tags and Fort Jackson registration sticker that had seen been in town on Saturday. Although West later testified under oath that local police had told him nothing about Levy's weekend visit, a note dated the following Monday appeared in the doctor's official personnel file. Instructions on it said to "determine whetver [sic] loyalty investiga-

192 | BLACK, WHITE & OLIVE DRAB

tion should be made 19 July, 1965." West would become the lead investigator for this case.[7]

Practicing dermatology normally did not require a high-level security clearance, but somebody scrutinized Levy's records thoroughly. Within a month after his trip to Newberry County, a discrepancy was discovered on his Armed Services Security Questionnaire. Levy apparently had failed to mention his involvement with the Militant Labor Forum on the form, although he had done so when questioned six months earlier. After being confronted, Levy wrote a statement explaining that the omission was simply an act of forgetfulness.

Levy meanwhile gave Army operatives ample grist for their mill by attracting unusual attention. For example, he socialized with African American officers in nonmilitary settings. Two of them were Capts. Ernest Porter and David Travis. Porter worked as an Army doctor in the same clinic as Levy. Travis served as an infantry officer and had attended Levy's undergraduate alma mater in New York. Both men and their wives went out dining and dancing with Levy. Travis's children called Levy "Uncle Howard."

Levy's sometimes churlish behavior did not improve his image in the eyes of Army authorities. The military police stopped him for a traffic violation on one occasion. As a consequence, he had to explain himself to a lieutenant colonel. That officer's report is revealing. "When told to come to attention and salute," the colonel said, "subject smirked, came to attention on one leg and half-heartedly put his hand near his head with his fingers in a crumpled position, then threw his hand in the direction of the wall. His left hand remained in his pocket." The officer added that "throughout the conversation CPT LEVY was insubordinate by facial expression, body movement, and vocal inflection. Subject needed a hair cut and his branch insignia and U.S. insignia were in reverse manner. CPT LEVY was wearing only one rank insignia on his blouse."[8]

Levy did follow Army regulations by shedding his uniform whenever he participated in civil rights activities. He spent much of his off-duty time working for SCOPE. William Treanor later testified: "He came up practically every night and on weekends."[9] Matthew Perry said: "I personally encountered Dr. Levy from time to time in conferences with the various officials of the Voter Education Project, and during those times . . . he would attend and participate in deliberations and in helping to direct the programming of the organization."[10]

The doctor went door to door registering voters. He met Billie Flemming in Columbia and traveled to Orangeburg to meet SCOPE director

Fighting at Home and in Vietnam | 193

Charles Thomas. Richland County Citizens' Committee secretary Beatrice McKnight remembered that he attended their meetings at Zion Baptist Church. Levy organized a talent show in order to raise money for civil rights causes and coordinated with Modjeska Simkins to advertise the show on her radio broadcast. He even contributed $700 of his own money to purchase a printer. Levy proved his personal bravery by standing up to a mob of thirty to forty men while registering voters in Whitmire.

Although Levy encountered potentially violent situations during the course of his civil rights activities, he felt optimistic. He had a high opinion of the progress being made in Columbia. Ernest Porter said in 1967: "Dr. Levy tried to explain to me that there were lots of opportunities here in Columbia, and that Columbia was coming along very rapidly. And I must say at this point, I have to concur with his opinion."[11]

Levy felt less positive about the Vietnam War. He began trying to learn more about the conflict as well as its racial implications. William Treanor gave him the address of Sgt. 1st Class Geoffrey Hancock, an old Army buddy of Treanor's who had stayed on active duty and who had gone to Vietnam. Hancock was a white man who had a black wife. Levy wrote him a letter asking him about his interracial marriage and how he felt about the war. Such a personal letter from an officer to an enlisted man was highly unusual regardless of the content. Moreover, Levy made some strong comments against the war as well.

Levy also began discussing the war with African American soldiers at his clinic. Some of the men worked there; others had come for treatment. The doctor tried to persuade them individually of the war's unjustness and the cruel irony that it posed for blacks. Preaching politics to subordinates was shocking enough, but Levy was quite vocal about his views. "In the heat of argument, he's very aggressive, very volatile, and very strong in trying to put his point across," David Travis said of him.[12] Levy told one patient that if he were black, he would not go to Vietnam if ordered to do so.

As a dermatologist with a two-year commitment to the Army, Levy faced virtually no chance of assignment overseas. He found another way, however, to take a stand against the war. The Army Special Forces, or Green Berets, regularly sent medics to the Fort Jackson Hospital to receive training on the various rashes, parasites, and other skin disorders they might encounter in a tropical, Southeast Asian environment. Twelve-man Special Forces A-teams often worked far away from regular support. They conducted commando operations and organized guerrilla battalions from local populations of Vietnamese Montagnards and Laotians.

194 | BLACK, WHITE & OLIVE DRAB

Green Beret aid men frequently functioned as doctors, treating both soldiers and natives. Levy made a point to let an assistant provide dermatology instruction whenever classes were held. He believed that the Special Forces used medical knowledge for political and military advantage rather than humanitarian concern. He did not hesitate to express his opinion to those men he encountered at the hospital.

Levy's refusal to train Green Beret medics gave Agent West an opportunity to test the doctor's loyalty to the Army. The dermatologist had remained the subject of investigation, and his personal file had been flagged since May 1966. West visited Levy's supervisor on 2, 7, and 10 October 1966. The commander, Col. Henry Fancy, had recently taken charge of the hospital. West apparently informed Fancy about Levy's eccentricities and the way he handled the aid men.

On 11 October, Colonel Fancy called Levy into his office and gave him a direct order to train the Special Forces medics. A class had been scheduled for 25 November. Levy politely refused. Fancy gave a statement to West the next day. On 14 October, the hospital commander put his order to Levy in writing. The doctor again refused to comply.

Clear-cut disobedience could not be established legally until after the date of the class had passed, so Agent West and Colonel Fancy waited. Levy stood firm in his refusal. On 14 December, Fancy initiated legal action. He intended to recommend that the commanding general administer nonjudicial punishment under Article 15 of the Uniform Code of Military Justice (UCMJ). Levy would have received a fine or reprimand at most for his behavior.

Although Levy was a draftee who would have left the service soon, somebody higher up the chain of command apparently wanted to make a harsher example of the young doctor by requiring him to undergo a court-martial instead. That somebody was most likely the court-martial convening authority, Maj. Gen. Gines Perez.

"It was a real drag-out to get the hospital commander to finally prefer charges," said Angelo Perri, who at that time was a lieutenant colonel in the Public Information Office.[13] He saw General Perez regularly at staff meetings and would have known about any push for a court-martial. The general's personal secretary remembered that the mere mention of Levy's name made the post commander extremely angry, and his aide-de-camp said that General Perez considered Levy enough of a threat to good order that he had the doctor's mail screened.[14]

Agent West returned to Colonel Fancy's office. West showed the hospital commander Levy's G2 dossier. At this point, Colonel Fancy decided

Fighting at Home and in Vietnam | 195

to withdraw his recommendation for an Article 15. On 28 December 1966, he recommended that Levy receive a court-martial. The doctor was charged with disobeying a direct order by refusing to train the Green Berets, promoting disloyalty and disaffection by his statements at the clinic, and conduct unbecoming an officer and gentleman. After Sergeant First Class Hancock learned about the court-martial through the news, he turned over Levy's letter to the authorities. They then added another charge of promoting disloyalty and disaffection.

The court-martial began at Fort Jackson on 10 May 1967. Attorney Charles Morgan of the Atlanta, Georgia, branch of the American Civil Liberties Union (ACLU) served as Levy's defense lawyer. A five-man panel of officers—including one African American and one Japanese American—sat in judgment. The trial received international attention primarily because Levy's lawyers invoked the Nuremburg defense, which held that a soldier had an obligation to disobey orders that promoted genocide. No American serviceman had tried this defense before.

The proceedings are equally fascinating in retrospect because they reveal the variety of attitudes that African Americans at Fort Jackson held about the military and the civil rights movement. Further, they made even more apparent the disjuncture between Columbia black activists and post soldiers and authorities.

Sgt. Clifton Henry Davis was one of the Green Beret medics whom Levy refused to train. His testimony for the prosecution demonstrates a detachment similar to that with which James Felder seemed to view the military. Prior to enlisting in the Army, Davis had belonged to SNCC in his hometown of Danville, Virginia. He had participated in protests there during June and July 1963. The police had arrested him, but the U.S. Supreme Court eventually overturned his conviction. At Fort Jackson, Levy had asked Davis how he could reconcile belonging both to SNCC and the Special Forces at the same time. Davis explained to the prosecutor: "I told him [Levy] that presently I was inactive in SNICK [transcriber's rendering], and that I joined special forces because of the medical training they offered."[15]

Like James Felder during the early sixties, Davis's sense of patriotism transcended his opposition to Jim Crow. The medic continued: "During the course of the conversation Dr. Levy said he didn't think the Negro soldier should go to Vietnam because they didn't have anything to fight for, because they were being discriminated against here in the states." Davis replied to Levy "that this could be partly true, but for most of us this is the only country that we have, this is our home country, and it may

196 | BLACK, WHITE & OLIVE DRAB

not be the best place in the world, but at least it is home, and we should defend it like everybody else."[16]

The economic opportunity offered by the military overrode concerns that some African Americans had about Vietnam. A young soldier from Georgia made this point explicit in his testimony against Levy. A private first class, he had come to Fort Jackson for basic training and had gone to the clinic to seek treatment. The doctor gave him a full dose of antiwar rhetoric. The private first class liked the Army, however, and did not resist the idea of going to war. He said that "I had a couple of brothers in and they were making it O.K. One was in the Air Force and the other in the Navy. Well I was taking care of my mother, so I decided if I came in the service, maybe I could do a little better, you know."[17]

Two other black soldiers who testified against Levy at the court-martial indicated that they objected less to the war in Vietnam than they did to the violent turn that the civil rights movement had taken during the mid-sixties. Spc. Warren Charles Gerig Jr. was a Green Beret medic who met Levy in the spring of 1966. He disagreed with the doctor over the legitimacy of sit-in tactics. Gerig thought that such behavior "would lead on to further outbreaks of lawlessness and so forth, such as the case of riots."[18] Special Forces medic Richard Wayne Gillem had similar views. He had no qualms about blacks going to Vietnam, but he did object to the "Black Power" movement that was gaining popularity among many younger African American. He said: "In some of the movement, the Stokely Carmichael I'm particularly referring to. This I can't agree with. I don't agree with the violence that he advocates in getting their desires fulfilled."[19]

Sgt. John Robert Ware indicated that some blacks tried to achieve "manhood" through military service. Ware had attended basic training at Fort Jackson and had met Levy before going to Vietnam. He said: "I explained to him that I thought that great progress was being made in the civil rights struggle." He also told Levy that the racial situation in the South had no bearing on his decision to go to Southeast Asia. "I thought it was in my duty in the tradition of a man to go."[20]

That African American officers walked a tightrope during the sixties is apparent in the words of Levy's friend Capt. David J. Travis. The prosecution called Travis back to Fort Jackson all the way from Vietnam in order for him to appear at the court-martial. Travis had not always agreed with Levy, especially about the war, but he respected him. The infantry officer told a reporter that "to fuse civil rights and Vietnam is erroneous . . . but people have a right to air their opinions."[21]

Fighting at Home and in Vietnam | 197

The prosecution and the *Record* seemed to hold Travis up as a refutation of Levy's claim that the Army was persecuting him for civil rights activism. Both missed or chose to ignore Travis's subtlety. In his testimony, Travis hinted that he himself might have worked with the VEP. He said that "Howard was very involved in voter registration at that time. He asked me about it and indicated his interest, and I knew various people that were involved in it, and I sort of referred him to them and vice versa."[22]

Even if Travis had connections to the VEP, he belonged to a tiny minority. Levy was virtually the only serviceman from Fort Jackson to take a prominent role in the local civil rights movement. "You didn't have many soldiers from Fort Jackson who would get involved in racial justice initiatives," said Jean Toal.[23] She remembered only one or two people from the post ever helping, and they were all officers. Matthew Perry knew only of Levy.[24]

The testimony of Billie Flemming confirms this fact. As a World War II Army veteran who had seen combat in the South Pacific, he was an ideal person to attract soldiers to work in voter registration. When asked directly at the court-martial if he had indeed tried to recruit black officers, he said "yes." He added, however, that "we could not get participation."[25]

The Levy trial focused initially on the doctor's civil rights activities and the opinions of black soldiers, officers, and local civilians. Later, it shifted to the Army's main contention that Levy had disobeyed orders. He was ultimately convicted of disobedience as well as promoting disloyalty and disaffection by his letter to Geoffrey Hancock. He was sentenced to three years in prison, given a dishonorable discharge, and stripped of all pay and allowances.

The court-martial reinforces several important conclusions about the effect of civil rights activities in Columbia upon Fort Jackson and vice versa. First, military authorities at the post did not approve of their soldiers taking an active role in local protests. Levy's work in voter registration attracted the attention of Army counterintelligence operatives. Rather than allowing the draftee to finish his two-year term of service and leave, they honed in upon his antiwar pronouncements. The doctor was either too arrogant or too ignorant to avoid the trap set for him, and he paid a steep penalty. As Jean Toal said: "He made the trouble for himself in the sense that had he simply stayed out there and registered people to vote and been a liberal voice in the community, I don't think he would have been court martialed."[26]

198 | BLACK, WHITE & OLIVE DRAB

Second, virtually no servicemen from Fort Jackson participated in Columbia demonstrations or registration activities. They did not do so in part because of the restrictions imposed upon them by the command, but they often had motives that superseded any imperative for social activism. Some, particularly the older ones, made a mental distinction between their rights as citizens and their obligations as soldiers. Others valued economic security or validation of their manhood above other concerns. The disillusionment that many of these young men expressed about the urban riots or "Black Power" exposed a growing division among African Americans about the course of the movement that often seemed to split along military-nonmilitary lines. Conversely, the soldiers' almost unanimous support for the Vietnam War highlights their increasing alienation from the black civilian leadership.

Finally, the Levy court-martial exposed once again the chasm that existed between African Americans in Columbia and the command at Fort Jackson. The frustration that James Hinton felt toward local military authorities during World War II had a sixties parallel in the person of Modjeska Simkins.

This woman became the dominant voice of black protest in Columbia during the sixties. Although she was already disinclined to admire white authorities at Fort Jackson, she became vastly more outspoken against Army inequities as a result of the Levy case. Her antimilitary pronouncements over her radio program heightened as soon as Major General Perez approved the court-martial on 3 March 1967. For example, she spoke out against Project 100,000 on 26 April. She said the program was designed "to get more Negroes into the service as cannonfodder."[27]

Gen. William Westmoreland visited Columbia that same month. He came to see his ailing mother, who lived in the city, but he also took time to speak before the South Carolina General Assembly. He made an effort in his speech to make positive comments about the contributions of African Americans to the war effort in Vietnam.[28]

Rather than laud the general for saying something favorable about black soldiers, Simkins lashed out at him on her 10 May program. She said that "the black soldier needs no syrupy praise from General Westmoreland or anyone else to show that he fights as well as white soldiers. The black soldier fights like a soldier, not like some other soldier."[29]

Simkins was angry at the Army for what it had done to Howard Levy, and she believed that the court-martial was part of an attempt to suppress local civil rights activity. She said in her broadcast of 15 November: "The citizens committee expressed grave concern over the persecution

Fighting at Home and in Vietnam | 199

and plight of Captain Howard Levy, detained at Fort Jackson since June. Members reiterated their conviction that Levy's persecution and trial were due in large measure to the interest and cooperation he offered in the local political action and civil rights program."[30]

The RCCC leader's anger spurred her to greater involvement with the post. In addition to assisting soldiers with housing and segregation issues, she began discussing job discrimination among civilian employees at Fort Jackson.[31] She questioned why Columbia leaders would annex Fort Jackson and not the poor black neighborhoods that lay to the southeast.[32]

In 1968, she tried to derail a job appointment for Major General Perez. The Fort Jackson post commander had decided to retire from the Army, and white city leaders nominated him to become the executive director of the Lexington–Richland County antipoverty program.[33] Simkins wrote a letter opposing this move. She said that the retired general was unqualified, had ample income from his pension, and was denying employment to other people. She added that "persistent reports on hiring and promotion policies at Fort Jackson, particularly with relation to civilian personnel, give the definite impression that . . . racial discrimination prevails at high degrees."[34] Perez got the job over Simkins's objections, but he resigned little more than a year later. According to one source who knew the general well, he thought that the black women who worked in his office complained too much.[35]

With tragic prescience, Simkins drew attention to the lack of progress toward integration of the South Carolina National Guard. She said during her show on 16 August 1967: "After much pumping and priming, we have learned that there are less than a dozen black folks in the S.C. National Guard numbering 11,000 men, and perhaps one little Ink Spot on the Highway Patrol. Well, they can say these units are not segregated."[36]

Given a truly integrated National Guard, South Carolina might have avoided the tragedy that took place six months later. On 8 February 1968, white authorities opened fire on a gathering of black students from South Carolina State University in Orangeburg. The young people had been protesting the refusal of a local bowling alley owner to comply with the Civil Rights Act of 1964. As tensions mounted, the National Guard and State Highway Patrol were summoned to the area. The virtually all-white composition of both forces did little to help matters. Shooting began after a few black protesters threw rocks at highway patrolmen. Three students were shot to death, and twenty-eight were wounded by gunfire in what came to be known at the Orangeburg Massacre.[37]

200 | BLACK, WHITE & OLIVE DRAB

The National Guard did little to promote racial harmony in Columbia either. Fires and window breakings occurred there in April 1968 after the assassination of Martin Luther King Jr. Mayor Bates quickly announced a curfew, and National Guard troops began patrolling the streets.[38] These actions quelled any more violence, but they did nothing to change the sentiments among blacks that Simkins had voiced earlier in September 1967. She had said then that: "All evidence points to the fact that 'riot control' definitely means CONTROL TO HOLD BLACKS IN CHECK no matter what their protests may be. . . . The national guard [sic] is composed, police dogs are quietly licking themselves, entertaining their fleas, because there are no blacks to pounce upon and tear up."[39]

Simkins saved her most caustic barbs for the Army's handling of the Vietnam War and its use of black soldiers. She said on her 5 April 1972 radio program that "American blacks are forced into military slavery along with hundreds of thousands of unwilling white youth, and made to kill people thousands of miles away who never did them one bit of harm. Black military slaves—for military service is a vicious type of slavery."[40]

The woman who had given presentations for the Army's Negro Health Week in 1943 and who had organized veterans after World War II had changed her opinion of the military drastically by the end of the 1960s. Bitterness over the Levy case did much to bring about this change as did her growing disillusionment over the Vietnam War. Indeed, her views reflect the antiwar stance that many national-level civil rights leaders had taken by this time. By so doing, she and these other activists distanced themselves from the genuine gains that African Americans had made in the armed forces.

The response of Fort Jackson officials to the antiwar movement did nothing to bridge this widening gap. Indeed, one of the ways that Army officers at the post curbed dissent within the ranks was to tighten their relationship with the same white civilians who had enforced segregation in Columbia. Their behavior suggests what might have happened had soldiers there decided to organize against racism.

An antiwar movement in Columbia began to take shape during the spring of 1967. Fierce battles in the Central Highlands of Vietnam were producing mounting casualties while the steady escalation of U.S. forces led to increased draft calls. These factors—as well as the parade of horrors on the evening television news—brought the war home to most Americans.

In South Carolina, the Levy court-martial provided a local angle

Fighting at Home and in Vietnam | 201

through which many people, particularly the younger ones of draft age, began to question the war. The visit of William Westmoreland in April 1967, however, was the catalyst that led to the first organized protests in Columbia. Students of the University of South Carolina started to unite after school officials announced their intention to confer an honorary degree upon the general.[41]

Soldiers at Fort Jackson meanwhile began to ask questions, too. Antiwar sentiments ran especially strong among the servicemen who worked at the post hospital. Medical units normally did not undergo as much indoctrination as did the infantry training organizations there. They had weaker cohesion and were under less supervision. They also had fewer Vietnam combat veterans, who tended to support the war if only because they had come to have a personal stake in it. Medics and aid men concentrated on honing their technical skills rather than on the art of killing. Moreover, hospital staffers comprised Fort Jackson's largest contingent of permanently assigned junior enlisted personnel. They seemed to be more concerned about the war than issues of race.

Several medics tried to organize soldiers to discuss it soon after the Tet Offensive of 1968 shattered the illusion that the U.S. involvement would end quickly and painlessly. "Some of them wanted to go AWOL, but I told them that was not the way," said one serviceman. "I encouraged them to express their doubts about the war in a legal way and suggested that we meet and meditate in the chapel." Post officials initially approved the meeting but canceled it when they learned about the intended topic of discussion. The soldiers defied this decision by passing out leaflets in downtown Columbia announcing a "pray-in." Five of them arrived at the chapel at the appointed hour.[42] Military police escorted them back to their barracks as newspaper photographers snapped pictures.

According to Paul Cowan of the *New Republic*, soldiers attempted a second meeting at the chapel a week later. The military arrested them, and the command made preparations for a court-martial. After Howard Levy's lawyer, Charles Morgan, threatened to defend the two, however, the charges were dropped.[43] Antiwar activity among servicemen continued through an underground newspaper and a new group called "GIs United Against the War in Vietnam."[44] Occasionally, a draft protester at Fort Jackson would make the news.[45]

USC students and soldiers from Fort Jackson had a venue to mingle and interact in Columbia at the UFO Coffeehouse. Opened in January 1968 by antiwar activists from outside of South Carolina, the establish-

202 | BLACK, WHITE & OLIVE DRAB

ment was one of several nationwide in cities located next to Army basic training posts. The coffeehouse sat on Main Street next to the Elite Epicurean Restaurant and across from the city hall. Patrons at the UFO could drink nonalcoholic beverages and listen to folk music. They could also read antiwar literature, discuss Vietnam with like-minded people, listen to guest speakers, or coordinate demonstrations.[46]

The UFO was not a profit-making enterprise. It relied upon summer fund-raisers to stay in business. Its purpose was to foment dissent. To that end, its owners had a Spanish-speaking employee who tried to make Puerto Rican soldiers feel more at home. The coffeehouse attracted one hundred people per night on average, but attendance rose higher during special events such as the visit from author Norman Mailer in August 1968 and the free dinner that Thanksgiving. Here was a place where soldiers could meet easily with people such as Brett Bursey, an SSOC member who had enrolled at USC in 1967 and who became a prominent part of the local effort against the war.

Columbia's conservative elite was aghast at the appearance of the UFO. "The so-called coffeehouse is a sore spot in our craw," said Thomas Fitzpatrick, the executive manager of the chamber of commerce.[47] He shared this sentiment with Army leaders at Fort Jackson. The spirit of cooperation that they had long upheld carried over into the suppression of the coffeehouse and the undermining of antiwar dissenters.

Just as had happened during the integration of Fort Jackson in 1950, local leaders tried to control the flow of information. For example, military policemen detained reporters at the post gate when soldiers attempted the second chapel protest in 1968.[48] News of this censorship did not make the *Record* or the *State*. Ultimately, however, this strategy did not work very well because journalists from outside of South Carolina had kept a close eye on the post since the Levy trial. Many of the articles in the *Record* and the *State* about the local antiwar movement were not breaking news. Rather, they tended to be responses or follow-ups to stories that had already appeared in the *New York Times*.

Blatant harassment worked much more effectively than silence in combating the UFO. Columbia police strictly enforced city noise ordinances. They arrested people outside of the coffeehouse for loitering. They ordered posters of scantily clad women to be taken down. "We check them every night to see if we can get something on them," chief of police L. J. Campbell told a *New York Times* reporter. "I think they're terrible. They have such a slouchy, beatnik crowd. I've never been used to anything like that."[49] Campbell apparently had forgotten about the rough

Fighting at Home and in Vietnam | 203

crowd that frequented the Blue Palace when he first became police chief during the early days of World War II.

Just as Campbell permitted Fort Jackson military police to patrol the streets of Columbia then, he allowed Major General Perez to post MPs outside of the UFO. In fact, Campbell wanted the Army to declare the coffeehouse off-limits. The post commander never took this step because Department of Defense policy would not permit them to do so.[50] Nevertheless, several incidents occurred in which MPs stationed outside the UFO took names, asked questions, and generally intimidated soldiers who wanted to enter.

Fort Jackson authorities also relied upon the Columbia police to keep pressure on the UFO. Col. Angelo Perri returned to Fort Jackson after a year in Vietnam. He would eventually become acting chief of staff at the post before leaving again in 1972. He remembered that "we just called the police department, the chief, and he closed the coffeehouses. And the way they did it . . . the fire department went in, and said, 'Ah! Fire hazard here, fire hazard there, you know, gotta be closed. Whether it was true or not, you know, you could go to court and sue them to reopen it."[51]

Eventually, in early 1970, the city shut down the UFO and charged the owners with maintaining a public nuisance. The trial revealed extensive cooperation between civilian and military law enforcement agencies. Operatives from the State Law Enforcement Division (SLED) had infiltrated the coffeehouse, as had at least one undercover MP from Fort Jackson.[52] The owners were convicted, sentenced to six years in prison, and fined $10,000. In return for not appealing the verdict, they agreed to leave South Carolina immediately and never return.

Officials at Fort Jackson behaved with equal ruthlessness against antiwar protesters on-post. The GIs United Against the War had become very well organized. A cadre of them apparently were failing advanced individual training on purpose and recycling through to the next class. This tactic allowed them to spread dissent to a larger number of trainees.[53]

Articles in the *Fort Jackson Leader* countered this threat with warning about leftists and other radicals. "Don't be a sucker—play it smart," advised one.[54] Basic trainees received briefings to avoid the UFO Coffeehouse and places like it. The Laurel Street USO established its own coffeehouse in the basement, complete with folk music.[55] Nevertheless, the situation called for sterner measures.

Major General Perez retired during the summer of 1968, but as he did so, he fired the commander of the company that contained the recycling antiwar organizers. He replaced him with his aide-de-camp, Capt. Eli

204 | BLACK, WHITE & OLIVE DRAB

Wishart, a South Carolinian who had graduated from the Citadel and who had already served a tour of duty in Vietnam. Wishart was assigned a new first sergeant, an African American who took enjoyment from declaring to trainees, "Black Power is standing before you."[56] Together, the two worked to undermine the protesters. They arranged for one soldier to infiltrate the leadership and gather information. After obtaining sufficient evidence to file charges, they waited for an appropriate time to act. That moment came on 20 March 1969, when the GIs United held a meeting in the barracks with over two hundred servicemen in attendance.

Soon thereafter, nine soldiers were arrested for various offenses that included breach of peace, disrespect toward an officer, failure to obey an order, and agitation against the Vietnam War. The number of prisoners shrank to eight after the informant was released. The remaining group attained a brief, national notoriety as the "Fort Jackson Eight." Military police held them in the stockade for over a month. Army officials held a pretrial hearing to determine whether or not to hold a court-martial. Fearing a repeat of the negative publicity that had surrounded the Levy case, and facing defense accusations that the informant had provoked the other eight, they decided instead to discharge the soldiers as undesirables.[57]

The antiwar movement in Columbia peaked and collapsed during the first part of 1970. In January, Howard Levy returned after serving three years in prison to address students at USC. This visit occurred soon after the city shut down the UFO and prosecuted the owners. Students held a "Freak the Army" festival at the state fairgrounds in March. That same month, Brett Bursey and a fellow activist broke into the local Selective Service Office and splashed red paint on the draft records. Bursey's accomplice turned out to be an undercover state policeman, whose testimony put him in prison for two years.

The largest antiwar demonstration in Columbia took place in the wake of the Kent State Massacre in May, where Ohio National Guardsmen shot and killed four protesters. USC students reacted to the tragedy by taking over their union building, which was named Russell House. A tense standoff with police and the National Guard followed, but the confrontation ended quickly and without bloodshed. Antiwar celebrity Jane Fonda's visit during the next week seemed anticlimactic. Columbia settled back to its conservative pace and politics.[58]

Throughout the episode, Fort Jackson authorities demonstrated their

ability to annihilate organized dissent within the ranks and in the surrounding community. Their efforts gave a good indication of what might have happened had any African American soldiers tried to form a movement within the ranks against segregation. The willingness of Army leaders to collaborate with the same civilians who had upheld Jim Crow further tarnished the image of the post in the eyes of civil rights leaders.

12
★☆

The Forgotten Decade of the Civil Rights Movement

The Seventies

An essentially blue-collar organization that has overcome its own grim racial history to achieve a remarkable degree of racial integration and fairness perhaps has something to say to the rest of us.

—William Raspberry, WASHINGTON POST, 20 November 1996

Fort Jackson did not have much of an impact on the racial practices of its civilian neighbors until the start of the seventies, when African Americans in South Carolina began voting in sufficient numbers to influence the state's congressional delegation. This development coincided with the aftermath of the Orangeburg Massacre, a federal court decision regarding schools, and a bitter gubernatorial election. It also coincided with institutional and generational changes within the armed forces. As South Carolinians reconciled themselves to the inevitability of desegregation, the post served as a model of racial harmony. Its failure to have done so when the military stood in advance of civilian society was conveniently forgotten.

★☆

Fort Jackson did not experience the racial violence that rocked several nearby installations during the late sixties.[1] Besides antiwar protests, disruptions at the post tended to involve marijuana and AWOLs. An occasional soldier might have raised a "Black Power" salute or grown a bushy Afro hairstyle, but no black-white confrontations of note were reported up the chain of command. Relative calm prevailed in part because authorities at Fort Jackson had tighter control over their soldiers in a basic training environment than did leaders of combat units. Additionally, they did not have to contend with as many returning Vietnam veterans trying to readjust to life back in the United States.

By contrast, the Camp Lejeune Marine Base in North Carolina

The Forgotten Decade of the Civil Rights Movement | 207

seethed with turmoil. At least 160 incidents took place there during the first part of 1969. They culminated that spring when a mob of black leathernecks beat to death one of their white comrades.[2] A few months later at Fort Bragg, two hundred black and white troops rioted. Twenty-five of the soldiers required hospitalization.[3] In the aftermath, Congress tasked a subcommittee to investigate while the Department of Defense dispatched researchers to conduct interviews across the country.[4]

Several Armywide changes resulted. African American soldiers were allowed to wear their hair longer. Commanders tried to avoid unfair prosecution of black soldiers under UCMJ. The Army chief of staff directed that "instruction on race relations be incorporated into the Army educational system."[5]

Meanwhile, a generation of black officers who had virtually no experience with Jim Crow units was starting to move into the upper ranks and affect policy. African Americans increasingly began to command battalions, brigades, and divisions. Black generals wearing multiple stars became more commonplace. In no part of American society did as many nonwhites supervise whites as in the Army.

The reforms made commanders at Fort Jackson much more attuned to issues of race. For example, a white captain assigned to the post's Third Brigade described to an *Army Digest* reporter in 1970 how he dealt with soldiers in his company. "To make certain that a man is heard," he said, "I have a standing policy that he does not have to go through the chain-of-command to see me. In this regular weekly session, eight men on average come to talk to me. Most have problems other than racial—usually financial, family, or both. In my time in the service, I have heard of isolated incidents of racial discrimination but have never witnessed any."[6]

The military's climate of equal opportunity bolstered confidence among African American servicemen that working hard within the system would bring results. It made them less likely to nurse grievances or claim status as victims. As one black NCO at Fort Jackson said in 1970: "The black soldier should be encouraged to undertake programs to help himself. . . . He should be given more challenging leadership positions. I feel that many of the statements of prejudice in the Army are unwarranted—too many people blame their own shortcomings on racial prejudice."[7]

Although no black versus white violence occurred at the post during this period, the reaction of officials there to a 1971 incident involving Hispanics demonstrates how they might have behaved in such an event. In August of that year, ten Puerto Rican basic trainees attacked an Italian

208 | BLACK, WHITE & OLIVE DRAB

American soldier after he called one of them a "dumb foreigner" or something similar. The brigade commander reacted quickly to the fight. He made certain that the participants received punishment from field grade officers under Article 15 of the UCMJ. The colonel also hosted special events for Puerto Ricans and ensured that the mess hall regularly served ethnic foods.[8]

In keeping with the rest of the Army, Fort Jackson began to have its share of higher-ranking black officers. One of the most notable was Porcher Taylor. He had left Fort Jackson in 1953 still holding the rank of lieutenant. He then completed a tour of combat duty in Korea. Later, he commanded a company in Hawaii and taught ROTC at Virginia State University, where he earned a master's degree. He also attended the infantry officer advanced course and airborne school at Fort Benning, Georgia.[9]

In 1962, he became one of the first African Americans to attend the prestigious Command and General Staff College at Fort Leavenworth, Kansas. After working at the Pentagon and spending a year of combat in Vietnam, he returned to Fort Jackson in 1968 holding the rank of lieutenant colonel. On 15 July, he took command of a training battalion. He was not the first black at the post, incidentally, to reach this milestone. Two or three other African Americans had preceded him a year or two earlier.

Taylor came back to Fort Jackson because of the new post commander, Maj. Gen. James F. Hollingsworth, who had taken the younger officer under his wing at a previous assignment. "He was my mentor," Taylor said. The general soon moved him to a higher-level position. In 1969, Taylor became the deputy chief of staff for personnel and community affairs (G1).

Later that year, General Hollingsworth helped Taylor enroll in the doctoral program at the University of South Carolina in Columbia to study counselor education and personnel work. He would become one of the first African Americans to earn a Ph.D. there. Taylor achieved another distinction while attending graduate school. In October 1971, he pinned on the eagles of a full colonel. This promotion made him the highest-ranking black officer to have been assigned to Fort Jackson up to that date.

Ironically, the rise of Taylor's career corresponded with the decline of his old nemesis and company commander from his earlier tour of duty at the post. Captain R. Smith lost his officer's commission during the budget cutbacks of the late fifties not because of the rough way he treated blacks, but because he did not have a college degree. He accepted his de-

The Forgotten Decade of the Civil Rights Movement | 209

motion and stayed in the Army as a first sergeant. He occasionally had to work for African Americans he had once commanded. The discomfort he felt contributed to his decision to leave the service and go to work for a car dealership in Columbia. Even so, he could not avoid bearing witness to the extent to which the Army had changed by the seventies. Smith said, not without some bitterness, that he "went to work at Pulliam Ford, and Porcher Taylor came in to get his car repaired, full colonel, oh yes, that's one of the stepping stones that got me to the retirement building over there."[10]

While reforms took place within the military, bloodshed in the area surrounding Fort Jackson began to change attitudes among many white civilians. South Carolinians had taken pride in having avoided racial confrontations like the ones that had occurred in Arkansas, Mississippi, and Alabama. They had congratulated themselves for the peaceful integration of Clemson University and of lunch counters in Columbia.

Fallout from the Orangeburg Massacre of February 1968 undermined this genteel image. In May 1969, nine highway patrolmen were tried on federal charges of using excessive force when they shot to death three black students from South Carolina State and wounded many others. A jury of ten whites and two blacks found the troopers not guilty. State prosecutors subsequently focused their efforts on making civil rights activist Cleveland Sellers a scapegoat. Sellers had been wounded with shotgun pellets during the incident. He was charged with incitement to riot, participating in a riot, and conspiracy to incite others to riot. As the case dragged into the seventies, publication of a book about the shootings by Jack Nelson and Jack Bass drew national attention to the case.[11]

Other incidents erupted amid the Orangeburg controversy that further eroded the state's reputation for peacefulness. An altercation took place in June 1969 when African American hospital workers went on strike in Charleston. In January 1970, Governor Robert McNair sent National Guard troops to the campus of all-black Voorhees College in the town of Denmark. In May of that year, he ordered state soldiers to quell the antiwar protests at the University of South Carolina in Columbia.[12]

Meanwhile, the situation regarding desegregation of public schools came to a critical juncture. When lawsuits put a stop to freedom-of-choice plans in 1968, a federal judge allowed South Carolina districts to eliminate their dual systems gradually. The Fourth Circuit Court of Appeals overturned this decision in early 1970 and ordered the immediate desegregation of schools in Darlington and Greenville Counties. As a result, thousands of students were transferred literally overnight during

210 | BLACK, WHITE & OLIVE DRAB

the middle of the academic year.[13] The rest of South Carolina, including the districts surrounding Fort Jackson, followed suit that September.

Appalled by the decision, many whites opted for private institutions. The transformation had costs for blacks, too. Segregated schools, though unequal, had served as centers of community. Those were lost. Many African American principals were demoted to assistant status. Disproportionate numbers of black children were transferred and faced lengthy bus rides.[14]

More racial tension came as a result. Fights broke out in many of the recently integrated schools. Bomb threats frequently interrupted classes. The most serious incident took place in Darlington County in March 1970, when a mob flipped over a school bus near the town of Lamar.[15]

The flare-up of violence at the turn of the decade shattered the notion that the Palmetto State was somehow different from the rest of the country and that it would avoid the kinds of mass demonstrations and urban riots that had occurred elsewhere. South Carolinians understood that these kinds of confrontations threatened to undermine the state's hard-won economic progress. Whites—especially businesspeople in cities like Columbia—become more willing to make concessions.

The elections of 1970 made apparent that a paradigm shift had taken place. The Republicans nominated Albert Watson, who served as congressman of the district containing Fort Jackson. Like Strom Thurmond, he had switched parties during the early sixties. Watson campaigned for whites to defy the recent court orders regarding freedom of choice. In fact, he made one such speech in the town of Lamar just a few days before the bus-flipping incident. A majority of South Carolinians rejected his call for continued massive resistance. Tired of the struggle and fearful of more violence, they elected Democrat John C. West with 51.7 percent of the ballots cast.[16]

The increase in African American voters over the previous three decades made a definite difference. The number of registered blacks had climbed from 3,000 in 1940 to 58,000 by 1960 to over 200,000 by 1970. They comprised 24.6 percent of the total registered population and 22.9 percent of the 482,145 who participated in 1970.[17] They provided far more than the margin of victory for the new governor, who won by fewer than 30,000 votes. In places like Columbia Ward 9, where only 24 of 1,904 registrants were white, the results were 1,006 to 19 in favor of West.[18]

Black voters affected other races that year, too. They helped elect three African Americans to the South Carolina House of Representatives. These men were the first to gain office in the legislature since the

The Forgotten Decade of the Civil Rights Movement | 211

Reconstruction period after the Civil War. One of them was Army veteran and Voter Education Project director James Felder.

White politicians who had previously engaged in racist demagoguery began to alter their stances. "An appeal to race is no longer a vote-getter," advisor Dolly Hamby wrote to Strom Thurmond two days after the election. The senator's aide Harry Dent said: "We've got to get him on the high ground of fairness on the race question. We've got to get him in a position where he can't be attacked like Watson by liberals as being a racist." As a result, Thurmond hired an African American Army veteran named Thomas Moss to work on his staff as project director of black voter registration.[19]

The new assessment of the situation by politicians had a profound effect on military-social relations at the post level. Previously, commanders at Fort Jackson had hesitated to act against local discrimination because they knew that elite whites in Columbia had connections to members of the congressional delegation who in turn controlled budgets and promotions. Once African Americans began to vote in sufficient numbers, those same representatives and senators became more willing to support, if not push military authorities on civil rights issues.

Involvement by politicians finally brought about an improvement to conditions for civilian black workers at the post. As mentioned previously, women at the laundry had complained of mistreatment during World War II. African American warehouse employees had testified to the 1963 Gesell Committee about the prejudice they faced. The Richland County Citizens' Committee had tried to help in 1967. The lack of results led civil rights activist Modjeska Simkins to describe the post as "a hotbed of color discrimination, which has caused hundreds of workers through the years to yearn for relief."[20]

Although he never met Simkins, Porcher Taylor worked to solve the same problem. One of his responsibilities as G1 was enforcement of federal equal opportunity laws in the hiring of civilians. He did the job personally instead of assigning it to a subordinate. "I made myself EEO Officer because it was not being carried out," he said. Taylor began trying to do something during early 1969.

"The laundry workers, they had all kinds of legitimate complaints at the time," he remembered. "I said I'm going to stop this damn foolishness. I'm going to get things straight and get those laundry workers to where they get equal pay and . . . trained jobs . . . rather than . . . doing all the scrub work and so forth."

The then–lieutenant colonel had insufficient power to prevail. "That

could be my only failure at Fort Jackson," he said. "I could not get the civilian part of the house to comply with all of those EEO regulations. . . . They were too well entrenched. Military, hey no problem with that, but [with] the civilians I failed. I totally failed."[21]

Taylor had left his position as G1 to work on his doctorate by time of the 1970 elections, but Simkins persevered. Moreover, she had a firm grasp of the new reality. As she said in her radio program of 10 March 1971, Senator Thurmond "is a politician and nothing more or less. His stock trade is votes. If black votes will keep him in Washington, that is what he wants."[22]

Simkins launched a letter-writing campaign to the senator two months later. Under the auspices of the RCCC, she organized forty-five black civilians who worked at Fort Jackson. They came from the laundry, the post exchange, the hospital, and the Adjutant General's office. All were women. Each one of them wrote a letter detailing her complaints. Most of the problems involved overtime compensation, rest breaks, and whether or not workers could have chairs.

The reaction to this case differed markedly from previous ones. Senator Thurmond's office immediately contacted post authorities, who then worked to correct many of the concerns that the women had voiced. At the senator's behest, Fort Jackson administrators went to great effort to find home addresses for each of the people who had sent a letter. Every woman received a written response from Thurmond containing assurances that corrective actions had been taken.[23]

Senator Thurmond's office had a reputation for outstanding constituent service. After 1970, post commanders at Fort Jackson understood that their careers depended upon helping local blacks as well as whites from the chamber of commerce.

The year 1970 also marked a new initiative in the capital of South Carolina to foster better race relations, the Greater Columbia Human Relations Council (GCHRC). This group evolved out of the biracial committee created by Mayor Bates in the wake of the sit-in movement. The governments of Richland County and the City of Columbia funded the new organization while the chamber of commerce provided "in-kind" services such as office space.

These backers supplied sufficient resources to hire a full-time director. They chose Milton Kimpson. As described earlier, Kimpson had grown up in the area and had completed basic training at Fort Jackson in 1953. He had pursued a career in public education after leaving the Army. He had not participated in civil rights activity until the late sixties,

The Forgotten Decade of the Civil Rights Movement | 213

after the city began relocating black neighborhoods to make room for development.

Aware that many African Americans had been skeptical about the mayor's earlier committee, Kimpson worked to establish his credibility with the black community. He consulted with Modjeska Simkins and attended meetings of the RCCC. He said that he gained the confidence of almost everybody after about six months.

The GCHRC served as a clearing house for racial concerns. Organizations such as the Urban League could contact Kimpson over matters such as slum clearance. Individuals could also lodge complaints by phone or in person at his chamber of commerce office. Kimpson dealt with some issues privately, but he also strove to create a public forum for discussion. Every week, he hosted a radio show called *Focus* and a television program called *Infomat*.

Soldiers from Fort Jackson soon learned about the GCHRC and began to channel racial complaints through the organization. Kimpson said he handled several instances of discrimination involving military people during his tenure as executive director. On one occasion, a near-riot occurred at a Lexington County bar after an African American from the Army danced with a white woman. Another time, a black soldier complained that the owner of the Elite Epicurean Restaurant refused him service. Kimpson said that in each case, post officials cooperated with him and the local businesspeople to resolve the conflicts.[24]

The GCHRC and Fort Jackson were also unified in their opposition to racial discrimination by local landlords and realtors. Much had changed since 1967, when Robert McNamara had tried unsuccessfully to force open housing upon an unwilling community and an equally unwilling post commander. The turnaround began in April 1968 when Congress passed the Fair Housing Act. Although some of the support for the law came as a result of the King assassination, its passage hinted strongly that civilian society was catching up with the military.

The replacement of McNamara by Clark Clifford also contributed to the new outlook. Clifford became the secretary of defense in early 1968. An old school liberal who had advised President Truman to issue his 1948 executive order against segregation in the armed forces, the new secretary left no doubt that he wanted to end the problem with housing. On 20 June 1968, he directed that all installation commanders provide legal aid to any service member encountering discriminatory landlords or real estate agents.[25] Four months later, he approved publication of Army Regulation 600-4, *The Fair Housing Enforcement Program*.

214 | BLACK, WHITE & OLIVE DRAB

When the Nixon administration took power in 1969, the new secretary of defense, Melvin Laird, indicated that Clifford's policies would continue. In fact, he loosened restrictions on the ability of local commanders to use the off-limits sanction in cases of racial discrimination against servicemen in civilian communities.[26]

Civilian landlords and realtors apparently took this possibility to heart. Kimpson said: "If you were a soldier, a renter wouldn't dare refuse renting you a house because that was the Army's practice. Of course now, the Army didn't do a whole lot to try to break patterns. . . . [If a] black soldier comes in, more than likely he's going to try to find a new community where most of the people are black. . . . But when that black soldier says 'I want to go out there' that place would not discriminate against him."[27]

Statistics from the federal census suggest that the housing situation for African Americans stationed at Fort Jackson improved during the seventies. In 1960, blacks had comprised 11 percent of the military population and 18 percent of the ones who lived on-post. In 1970, the situation appeared to have worsened as the percentages rose to 17 and 29 respectively. By 1980, however, they comprised 39 percent in both categories.[28]

The extent to which Fort Jackson affected housing or any other aspect of race relations in Columbia during the early seventies can never be known precisely. Too many forces were at play to make an exact determination. Furthermore, the post's presence was not a necessary condition for change. Numerous cities and towns in South Carolina and across the United States underwent desegregation peacefully without the benefit of a military installation nearby. Fort Jackson nonetheless contributed to the civil rights movement in the civilian community by the example it set and by the lifelong influence it had on individuals who served there.

During the fifties and sixties, the presence of the post bore daily witness to the reality that blacks and whites could work together. It undermined the dire predictions by some die-hards that desegregation would lead to anarchy or worse. After 1970, the greater likelihood of sanctions for mistreatment of soldiers gave incentive for white civilians to rethink their positions on race. The post further encouraged this process by providing a model to follow. Milton Kimpson remembered a Fort Jackson commander emphasizing these aspects in a speech made before the chamber of commerce during the early seventies.

According to Kimpson, the general said: "We are not going to be a part of segregation, and our people who are transferred to Fort Jackson will not be discriminated against whether it's school, whether it's hous-

The Forgotten Decade of the Civil Rights Movement | 215

ing, whether it's whatever accommodations. . . . We've been integrated in the Army since Truman. . . . We haven't had any problems. In fact, we are better off because of it, and we support full integration, and none of my people will be subjected to discrimination."[29]

Kimpson's vivid recollection of the speech underscores the extent to which he and others in Columbia credit the post with helping to bring about desegregation. South Carolinians pride themselves on the relative peace they enjoyed during the fifties and sixties as compared to the rest of the Deep South. Emphasizing Orangeburg as an aberration, historians of the state's civil rights movement emphasize the "calm and exemplary" behavior of citizens and the way change came about with "dignity" as well as "grace and style." They interpret leaders as working with "firm flexibility" toward the "good order" and "harmony of the whole community." The successful integration of Fort Jackson in 1950 fits neatly into this mold, as does its influence in Columbia during the 1970s.[30]

The danger with this interpretation in regard to the post is that it overlooks the missed possibilities of the intervening two decades. Fort Jackson had a negligible effect on civilian race relations during the period it stood at the forefront of integration. When soldiers ran afoul of Jim Crow bus laws in 1953, the chain of command from the post to the Pentagon worked to minimize the incident. Fort Jackson officials kept a low profile during the early sixties when HEW threatened to take money from segregated public schools and when the Gesell Committee encouraged use of the off-limits sanction against civilians who discriminated against servicemen. When the secretary of defense actively encouraged penalization of racist landlords and realtors in 1967, the post commander gave half-hearted support and submitted misleading reports. The only time a commanding general took a strong public stance regarding civil rights was to discourage soldiers from participating in sit-ins and demonstrations.

The failure of Fort Jackson to have had a greater impact on desegregation in Columbia is not necessarily a negative thing. Allowing the armed forces to dictate law and custom in local communities does not befit a democratic republic. Civilian control over the military has been a cornerstone of American freedom for hundreds of years. Ironically, the power that segregationist politicians had over local commanders speaks well for the system. That change occurred as soon as African Americans began voting in significant numbers speaks even more favorably.

Although integration did not spread beyond post boundaries during the fifties and sixties, the success of military integration in the midst of

segregated South Carolina offers some positive lessons about leadership, secrecy, and timing.

Leadership made a clear difference at Fort Jackson. Integration there in 1950 contrasted with that which took place on the battlefields of Korea in that the shared desire for survival in combat was not the primary motivation. Post authorities in South Carolina took charge of a fluid situation, worked discreetly with local whites to ease possible friction, and firmly enforced a new policy. Civil rights activists like James Hinton and John McCray exercised good faith by holding their tongues and pens.

Secrecy was a kind of leadership in that it required those in power to decide in the best interests of others without necessarily consulting them. It worked particularly well in the tightly knit hierarchy of South Carolina politics. Indeed, state leaders would later rely upon it to achieve several important civil rights reforms. These included the desegregation of Columbia lunch counters in 1962 and that of Clemson a year later. The silence surrounding the integration of Fort Jackson suggests an alternative to such confrontational methods of bringing about social change as mass marches, civil disobedience, and political mobilization. Open conflict tends to bring about faster change, but it also can result in long-term factionalism and feuds. Movements lose momentum.

Of course, secrecy had drawbacks. It did not permit a celebration of success in the case of Fort Jackson. The self-censorship by Columbia newspapers meant that few people ever learned about the post's path-breaking part in integration. Working behind closed doors also led to corruption. Both post and city elites abused their authority in 1968 when the provost marshal teamed up with the city police in order to conduct undercover surveillance at the UFO Coffeehouse.

Timing was as important as the other two factors. Several disparate courses of events came together in 1950 to bring about change at the South Carolina post. They included the decision a year earlier to close Fort Jackson, the end of race-based draft calls, the start of the Korean War, the timing of the state's primary election, and the retirement of Lt. Gen. Alvan Gillem. A similar convergence occurred during the early 1970s with the reform of Army racial policies, publication of *The Orangeburg Massacre,* the Fourth Circuit Court decision to require immediate desegregation of schools, and the registration of a critical mass of black voters. Sometimes contingency overshadows any larger cause or intent.

Nevertheless, the most important moral to come from the story of Fort Jackson is that individuals can and did make a difference. This level is where the post ultimately had its greatest effect on the civil rights

The Forgotten Decade of the Civil Rights Movement | 217

movement. Millions of young men donned uniforms as a result of the Cold War draft. Time spent in the integrated services caused whites and blacks alike to question their prejudices about race. It was especially valuable to African Americans, however, because few places in the United States at the time offered as much as did the armed forces. The military provided career opportunities and educational benefits. It helped to instill intangible qualities like self-discipline, confidence, courage, and an enlarged perspective of the world. Numerous blacks who passed through Fort Jackson's gates went on to become leaders in the struggle against Jim Crow and major contributors to their community.

Being in the Army sharpened the racial awareness of such people as desegregation lawyer Matthew Perry, who painted barracks at the post in 1941 and who was inducted there in 1943. Perry took advantage of the GI Bill to earn a law degree during the years following World War II. After orchestrating the desegregation of Clemson University in 1963, he continued to file lawsuits against public school systems. In 1975, Senator Thurmond nominated him to become a judge on the U.S. Military Court of Appeals. Senator Hollings recommended him for a federal district judgeship four years later.[31]

Perry's partner and fellow Fort Jackson inductee Lincoln Jenkins also had a distinguished career. He became one of the first African Americans to sit on the Richland County School Board. In 1974, he was appointed as a municipal judge for the City of Columbia. Ironically, he occupied the same position as John I. Rice, whom Jenkins had opposed in the 1953 bus case. To what extent Jenkins attributed his success to the armed forces is unknown because he died suddenly in 1986. His involvement with the USO and willingness to represent Austell Sherard, however, suggest that his time in the military did make some impression upon him.[32]

Greater Columbia Human Relations Council director Milton Kimpson remembered his days at Fort Jackson warmly because basic training gave him the confidence that he could compete with white people. After leaving the GCHRC, he went on to a successful career in the state government. Governor Richard Riley selected him as an executive assistant for health and human services. Later, Kimpson served as the associate commissioner of the state higher education committee.[33]

Fort Jackson trainee James Felder built upon his military experience, too. After a term in the state legislature, he became the first African American in South Carolina to serve as assistant solicitor. His career took a nosedive in 1975, however, when he was disbarred for misappropriating a client's money. He was convicted of breach of trust in 1978 and

218 | BLACK, WHITE & OLIVE DRAB

spent time in jail. Later, he became executive director of the state NAACP. He resigned in 1995 after pleading guilty to cashing a counterfeit check for $96,000 and being sentenced to another term of imprisonment.[34]

The personal impact of armed forces service among black Columbians sometimes crossed generational lines. Charles Bolden was inducted at Fort Jackson in 1943, and he worked for a while as the coordinator for a veterans' program after World War II. His wife, Ethel, volunteered for decades at the USO. Their experiences with the military did not dissuade their son Charles Jr. from applying to the Naval Academy in 1964. After his graduation in 1968, the younger Bolden fought in Vietnam as a Marine Corps pilot. He was later selected to train as an astronaut and commanded the space shuttle mission that launched the Hubble Telescope. He rose to the rank of two-star general before retiring from the marines.[35]

Besides these prominent individuals, countless other African Americans in Columbia used the armed forces as a way to escape poverty, acquire useful skills, and build productive lives. They included not only active-duty personnel but civilians who worked on-post. Blacks found jobs at the Fort Jackson laundries, exchanges, warehouses, and social clubs.

Family members of servicemen were influenced as well. Porcher Taylor's wife, Ann, for example, contributed to the relatively smooth desegregation of local schools during the late sixties. She worked with the local Upward Bound program and served as human relations coordinator for Richland County District 1. She also was active in the Fort Jackson Officer Wives Club and worked as a volunteer in the post thrift shop.[36]

The eldest son, Porcher Taylor III, attended Spring Valley High School, which had been built during the late sixties in Richland County District 2 to replace all-white Dentsville High and all-black Hanberry High. The younger Taylor compiled an impressive record at the integrated school that included election as president of both his senior class and National Honor Society chapter. He subsequently gained admittance to the United States Military Academy at West Point.

The effect of the post radiated beyond the Columbia area. Austell Sherard, who had been arrested in the 1953 bus incident, became a college teacher after leaving the Army. He taught industrial education at South Carolina State and Tuskegee Institute. He eventually oversaw thirteen two-year colleges as the dean of the Indiana Vocational Technical System. He passed away in 1997.

Porcher Taylor also had a distinguished career away from Fort Jack-

The Forgotten Decade of the Civil Rights Movement | 219

son after retiring from the Army in 1976 as a colonel. He rose to the position of vice president of Virginia State University. Among other important activities, he served as chairman of the Petersburg School Board and as an aide-de-camp to two state governors.[37]

★☆

In *Breakthrough on the Color Front*, Lee Nichols loosely organizes his book around the metaphor of a military campaign. He uses the early pages to describe the terrain on which black servicemen operated and how pressure for change began to build during World War II. He sees the "breakthrough" taking place during the mid- to late 1940s, culminating with desegregation of the Army during the Korean War. He gives the title "Mop-up Campaign" to the second-to-last chapter, in which he describes the situation in 1953. Jim Crow within in the military has not been eliminated completely by this time, but it appears to have been confined to isolated pockets. Writing from the perspective of 1954, he says in the final chapter that "there was no way to bottle up racial integration within military precincts" and that "integration was spilling over uncontrollably" as a result of "direct military contacts with outside communities."[38]

In retrospect, and in the context of larger American society, the "breakthrough" Nichols witnessed in 1953 turned out for the next two decades to have been more of a salient. White civilian elites successfully managed to contain the bulge in places like Columbia. They could not cut it off or destroy it, however, nor could they stop the countless African Americans whose personal achievements chipped away at segregation like so many partisan raids. By 1970, most of the United States had caught up to the armed forces. Now the opponents of segregation found themselves to be the ones surrounded. Rather than fight to the death, however, they surrendered. The presence in the South of posts like Fort Jackson provided a salve for wounded feelings on both sides.

Notes

Abbreviations

CMH   Center of Military History
DIR   Domestic Intelligence Report
NARA National Archives and Record Administration
USC   University of South Carolina

Introduction

1. Quoted in Nichols, "The Military's Secret War against Racism," *Freeman* 40, no. 7 (July 1990). The article is a condensed version of Nichols's unpublished memoirs. The magazine is available online at http://www.fee.org/publications/the-freeman; Nichols interview.

2. Nichols, *Breakthrough*, 98–99; MacGregor, *Integration*, 427, 435. MacGregor interviewed Nichols and obtained his notes, which are located at the National Archives in Record Group 319. Dalfiume, *Desegregation*, 203; Lanning, *African-American Soldier*, 230; Mershon and Schlossman, *Foxholes and Color Lines*, 230; Stillman, *Negro Integration*, 49–50; Wright, *Soldiers of Freedom*, 208.

3. Nichols interview. In the introduction to the 1993 edition of *Breakthrough*, Nichols writes that James Evans from the Department of Defense provided the copy to the justices (xix). Evans later identified one of the two as Chief Justice Fred Vinson, who died and was replaced by Earl Warren. Evans died before naming the other one.

4. In *Integration*, MacGregor writes, "The fact and example of integration in the armed forces was an important cause of change in the communities near military bases" (621). He does not present much supporting evidence, which is understandable given that his task was to focus on the services as a whole. Nalty addresses the military's involvement with the civil rights movement in chapters 17 and 18 of *Strength for the Fight*. He contradicts MacGregor by citing examples from installations where commanders, community leaders, and congressmen worked together to thwart attempts to involve the services with efforts to desegregate civilian facilities. The scope of Nalty's book does not allow for analysis of any one place across time, however. Historians writing since MacGregor and Nalty have added little new about the effect of integrated bases or posts on their surrounding areas.

5. The "new military history" became popular over thirty years ago. Although this approach steers away from campaigns and battles, it tends not to focus on peacetime

222 | Notes to Pages 2–10

activities or domestic civil-military relations. Paret makes this point clear in his article "The History of War."

6. For examples, see McGuire, *Taps for a Jim Crow Army;* Terry, *Bloods;* Bussey, *Firefight at Yechon;* B. Moore, *To Serve My Country;* and Colley, *Blood for Dignity.*

7. For examples, see Lee, *Employment of Negro Troops;* MacGregor, *Integration;* Dalfiume, *Desegregation;* Mershon and Schlossman, *Foxholes and Color Lines;* and Nalty, *Strength for the Fight.*

8. For examples, see Chafe, *Civilities and Civil Rights;* Payne, *I've Got the Light of Freedom;* and Norrell, *Reaping the Whirlwind.* Norrell does touch upon the importance of the Tuskegee Army Air Field and local veterans' hospital in that area's civil rights movement (27–30, 47–52, 62, 70, 105).

9. A good start in this direction is Dudziak, *Cold War Civil Rights.*

10. A quarterly, interdisciplinary journal about civil-military relations called *Armed Forces & Society* has been published since 1962. Military sociologists are the main contributors. This field arose out of such studies as Stouffer, *The American Soldier;* Janowitz, *The Professional Soldier;* and Moskos, *The American Enlisted Man.* One of the most notable recent sociology books on the effects of military integration is Moskos and Butler, *All That We Can Be.* Anthropologist Catherine Lutz is the only recent scholar to focus on military-social relations at the local level. In *Homefront,* she devotes sixteen pages (115–30) to the effect that Fort Bragg had upon race relations in Fayetteville, North Carolina, during the fifties and sixties.

1. Organizational Racism at Fort Jackson during the Second World War

1. Franklin and Moss, *From Slavery to Freedom,* 332; Megginson, *Black Soldiers in World War I,* 8–14, 27–29. The Medal of Honor recommendation for Stowers was submitted during the war but not approved until 1991. *New York Times,* 6 April 1991.

2. Lee, *Employment of Negro Troops,* 3–20.

3. Fort Jackson, Fiftieth Anniversary History, 1917–1967, 50–84; Weigley, *History of the United States Army,* 393–482. Unless otherwise noted, general information about the post and the Army comes from these two sources.

4. *Army Times,* 14 December 1940.

5. The Spartanburg, South Carolina, induction station provides an example of what could occur in this region when the races were processed at the same time. A white inductee complained to Senator Ellison D. Smith in 1941 about having to sit next to black soldiers. He said that it was not "the South Caroline way" and that such integration could lead to violence. Edward Watson to Senator E. D. Smith, 28 March 1941, NARA, RG 407, Records of the Adjutant General, Decimal File 291.2.

6. Information about the details of basic training at Fort Jackson comes from the following sources: *Second to None! The Story of the 305th Infantry in World War II;* Lopez, *From Jackson to Japan: The History of Company C, 307th Infantry, 77th Division, in World War II; The Story of the Century, Yearbook of the 100th Infantry Division;* Ernest Schichler, written personal reminiscence, Seventy-seventh Infantry Division File, Fort Jackson Museum; Thompson interview.

7. For in-depth information about the AGF and ASF, see Palmer, Wiley, and Keast, *United States Army in World War II: The Army Ground Forces;* Millett, *United States Army in World War II: The Army Service Forces;* and U.S. Army, *Logistics in World War II.*

8. Lander, *From Clemson College to India.*

9. Wyatt, "United States Policy toward German Prisoners of War"; J. Moore, "Nazi

Troopers in South Carolina." See also Fort Jackson General Order Number 26, 3 April 1942, which activated the Enemy Prisoner of War Detachment, and Fort Jackson General Order Number 7, 24 June 1946, which closed it.

10. *State*, 21 October 1942; *Army Times*, 1 February 1941, 15 August 1942.

11. *Army Times*, 11 January 1941, 22 February 1941, 27 September 1941, 15 August 1942.

12. The number of five thousand black soldiers is a very rough estimate based on personnel statistics and lists of units found in Domestic Intelligence Reports from 1942 to 1943. If anything, the estimate is high. The peak number of whites at Fort Jackson during the war was over sixty thousand.

13. Testimony of 1st Sgt. Bennie Perry, 19 May 1941, Report of Investigation of Alleged Unwarranted Assaults on and Mistreatment of Colored Civilians in Columbia, South Carolina by Military Police Made by Colonel Andrew Krieger, Inspector General's Department, Assistant Inspector General, First Army, at Columbia, South Carolina on May 16–24 inclusive, NARA, Record Group 407, Dec. file 291.21. Copy also in RG 159, Records of the Inspector General (declassified), Fort Jackson file. Subsequent references appear as "Krieger Investigation."

14. *Army Times*, 1 February 1941; see also Fort Jackson General Orders for this period, NARA, RG 338, Records of the Third United States Army, box 505.

15. Lee, *Employment of Negro Troops*, 348–70.

16. Statement of Col. R. E. Beebe, 5 February 1942, Investigation of Alleged Mistreatment of Negroes by Military Police at Columbia, South Carolina, Made by Colonel Charles Richtel, February 1942, NARA, RG 159, Fort Jackson file. Subsequent references appear as "Richtel Investigation."

17. DIR, Fourth Service Command, 21 June 1942 (declassified), NARA, RG 319, box 57.

18. Earley, *One Woman's Army*, 62. A letter to the editor in the *State*, March 1960, also mentions the denial of arms to black MPs.

19. Lee, *Employment of Negro Troops*, 130–31; Fort Jackson General Order No. 21, 20 March 1942, activated the 723rd Medical Sanitation Company; Fort Jackson General Order No. 31, 5 May 1942, activated the 710th; Fort Jackson General Order No. 36, 6 September 1943, mentions both companies as well as a third, the 792nd.

20. B. Moore, *To Serve My Country*, 69.

21. Alleged Mistreatment of Colored Employees in Laundry #2, Fort Jackson, S.C., 24 August 1944, NARA, RG 107, entry 91, box 208.

22. *Army Times*, 20 November 1943.

23. Center of Military History, Organizational History Branch, History Card for the 367th Infantry Battalion; DIR, November 1942, December 1942, January 1943; *Columbia Record*, 20 October 1942, 10 November 1942, 21 November 1942; Lee, *Employment of Negro Troops*, 366. In the latter, Lee erroneously states that the 367th was stationed at Fort Jackson during what he calls the "Columbia friction" between black civilians and Fort Jackson MPs (350). As will be discussed in the next chapter, these tensions had largely subsided by the time the 367th arrived.

24. Stanton, *Order of Battle*, 590; Furr, *Democracy's Negroes*, 71–72.

25. P. L. Prattis to Truman Gibson, 27 March 1943, NARA, RG 107, Records of the Office of the Secretary of War, entry 91, William Hastie files, box 208; DIR, 30 October 1943, 20 November 1943; *Army Times*, 20 November 1943.

26. Quoted in Edgar et al., *A Columbia Reader*, 139.

224 | Notes to Pages 13–19

27. Quoted in Shortal, *Forged by Fire*, 29.

28. Map Collection, Fort Jackson Museum; Map Library, University of South Carolina.

29. *Army Times*, 22 February 1941.

30. Ibid., 23 August 1941, 11 October 1941.

31. Fort Jackson Public Relations Office Press Release, 25 October 1941, NARA, RG 107, entry 91, box 208; *Army Times*, 25 October 1941; *Army Times*, 6 December 1941. By comparison, one of the white service clubs had a 7,000-volume library, and the white USO cost $200,000. Given the numbers of whites to blacks, the ratio of books and money spent was equitable.

32. *Army Times*, 30 August 1941; *Columbia Record*, 10 November 1942.

33. *State*, 17–18 January 1944; *Palmetto Leader*, 15 January 1944.

34. DIR, 29 January 1944, summarizes what the *Lighthouse & Informer* printed.

35. *Army Times*, 28 June 1941, 2 August 1941, 21 November 1942, 10 April 1943, 23 April 1943.

36. Ibid., 28 July 1941, 10 April 1943, 12 February 1944; *Palmetto Leader*, 7 August 1943.

37. Fort Jackson General Order Number 23, 25 April 1941; *Army Times*, 19 July 1941.

38. *Army Times*, 30 January 1943, 14 August 1943, 23 August 1943; *Columbia Record*, 11 January 1944.

39. *Army Times*, 29 August 1942.

40. For an example, see the case of M.Sgt. Linwood Beverly later in this chapter.

41. For details about the violence of 1943, see Lee, *Employment of Negro Troops*, 366–79.

42. *Army Times*, 11 September 1943. Originally, blacks at Fort Jackson were allowed to swim only at the YMCA and Legion Lakes. For signs, see "Survey of Negro Conditions at Fort Jackson and Columbia, S.C.," 14 February 1947, NARA, RG 159, Records of the Inspector General, box 241.

43. For information about the Camp Van Dorn incidents, see Lee, *Employment of Negro Troops*, 368–70.

44. *Army Times*, 22 March 1941.

45. *Ibid.*, 1 November 1941.

46. *Palmetto Leader*, 11 December 1943.

47. DIR, 26 June 1943.

48. *Pittsburgh Courier*, 14 June 1941; DIR, March-April 1943.

49. Documents pertaining to the alleged burning of the *Pittsburgh Courier* at Fort Jackson, NARA, RG 107, entry 91, box 208; memo to commanding generals from the adjutant general, 29 November 1943, Subject: Restriction of Commercial Publications, NARA, RG 319, MacGregor Papers, box 1.

50. *Pittsburgh Courier*, 14 June 1941.

51. Lee, *Employment of Negro Troops*, 262–63, contains a substantial excerpt of this report.

52. Cpl. George G. McDemmond to Lt. Col. Campbell C. Johnson, 16 May 1943; Lt. Col. Johnson to Truman Gibson, 26 May 1943, NARA RG 107, entry 91, box 208.

53. B. Moore, *To Serve My Country*, 70.

54. Unsigned letter dated 1 April 1944 from Fort Jackson. Papers of Modjeska Simkins, Murphy file.

55. DIR, 30 October 1943.

56. Ibid., 2 November 1943, 20 January 1945.

Notes to Pages 19–25 | 225

57. Ibid., 20 November 1943.

58. Ibid., 14 July 1945, 28 July 1945.

59. Anonymous letter from soldier in the 1700th Engineer Battalion to *Pittsburgh Courier*, 31 August 1944, NARA, RG 107, entry 91, box 208.

60. Anonymous letter from soldier in the 1700th Engineer Battalion to *Pittsburgh Courier*, 1 September 1944, NARA, RG 107, entry 91, box 208.

61. The intelligence officer became interested in the prison population after the 250 whites attacked the 45 blacks with rocks and attempted to burn down their quarters. Apparently a black prisoner had struck a white one. Guards ended the fight by shooting two of the three white leaders and moving the blacks temporarily out of the stockade. DIR, 27 October 1945.

62. *Army Times*, 25 July 1942.

63. Perry testimony, Krieger Investigation.

64. Case of M.Sgt. Linwood Beverly, NARA, RG 407, Dec. file 291.2.

65. E. B. Hamer to Ellison D. Smith, 15 December 1943, NARA, RG 407, Dec. file 291.2. The author also wrote to Senator Burnet R. Maybank, but the original was not filed. See Burnet Maybank to Secretary of War Stimson, 20 December 1943, NARA, RG 407, Dec. file 291.2.

66. Perry testimony, Krieger Investigation.

67. *Pittsburgh Courier*, 14 June 1941.

68. *Army Times*, 12 July 1943.

69. Ibid., 29 May 1943, 5 June 1943.

70. Ibid., 29 November 1941.

71. DIR, 15 January 1944.

72. *Army Times*, 12 February 1944. The *Army Times*, 16 October 1943, announced that 1st Lt. Llewellyn Thornhill would be the first black chaplain and that he would be assigned to the 274th Quartermaster Battalion. Later articles in the *Palmetto Leader* mention Thornhill's activities at the local USO. George W. Williams claimed to have been the first permanent chaplain, and an *Army Times* article erroneously supports this assertion, but he arrived several months after Thornhill did. For more biographical information on Williams, see the *Palmetto Leader*, 3 November 1956, and the alphabetical entry in Fleming and Burckel, *Who's Who in Colored America*.

73. DIR, 12 June 1943.

74. In *Employment of Negro Troops* (349, 350), Ulysses Lee misidentifies the unit involved as the Forty-eighth Quartermaster Regiment because he relied upon incomplete information. Fort Jackson General Order Number 7, 23 January 1941, says that the Forty-eighth Quartermaster Regiment furnished cadre for Company G, 28 QM, effective 25 January.

75. Report of Investigation, Civilian Conservation Corps, 23 April 1941, and "Report of Proceedings of Board of Officers at Fort Jackson, S.C.," 28 April 1941, NARA, RG 407 (declassified), Dec. file 291.2. Duplicate copy in RG 159, 333.1; *Columbia Record*, 21 April 1941; *State*, 21 April 1941; *Pittsburgh Courier*, 3 May 1941, 14 June 1941; *Militant*, 3 May 1941, reprinted in James et al., *Fighting Racism in World War II*, 93–94. The *Militant* article mentions use of a machine gun. Robert Scott McConnell, who wrote a master's thesis about the Eighth and Thirtieth Divisions at Camp Jackson, says that a veteran of the Thirtieth Division described how he and his fellow Guardsmen mounted a machine gun on a fire truck for use against the black soldiers. McConnell telephone conversation.

76. See previous note for the dates of these publications.

77. Lee, *Employment of Negro Troops*, 349–57.

226 | Notes to Pages 25–37

78. Lt. Col. Frank L. Whittaker to Commanding General, I Army Corps, 5 June 1941, NARA, RG 407, Dec. file 291.2.

79. Sixteen of the eighteen National Guard division commanders were relieved during early 1942. This decision generated much debate as to whether Marshall had "purged" the National Guard to further the interests of the Regular Army or whether the relieved officers were simply unfit for command by education, experience, or ability. For additional information, see Russell, *Purge of the Thirtieth Infantry Division,* and McConnell, "Refuting the National Guard 'Purge Theory.'"

80. Carmichael and Hamilton, *Black Power,* 3–6.

81. *Pittsburgh Courier,* 14 June 1941.

2. Alienating Black Civilians

1. Unless otherwise noted, information about Columbia comes from J. Moore, *Columbia and Richland County,* 389–400. Information about Fort Jackson comes from the *Army Times,* Fort Jackson supplement, December 1940–June 1944.

2. Buchanan file, The *State* Newspaper Reference Library, Columbia, South Carolina. According to Buchanan's grandson Bruce LeGrand, the editor did not leave behind any significant correspondence or personal documents that might have supplemented his writings as a newsman. LeGrand telephone conversation.

3. J. Moore, *Columbia and Richland County,* 397.

4. *State,* 27 March 1941.

5. Allen University is actually a small college sponsored by the African Methodist Episcopal Church. It is located across the street from Benedict College, which is a Baptist institution.

6. Fleming and Burckel, *Who's Who in Colored America,* 1950); obituary, *Palmetto Leader,* 20 March 1943.

7. *Palmetto Leader,* 28 June 1941; *Pittsburgh Courier,* 17 October 1942.

8. Lofton, "A Social and Economic History of Columbia, South Carolina," 227.

9. Krieger Investigation, 12.

10. J. Moore, *Columbia and Richland County,* 416; Report to Post Commander through the Office of the Provost Marshal, 27 December 1941, NARA, RG 159, Fort Jackson file; Krieger Investigation, 21.

11. Krieger Investigation, 233.

12. Ibid., Exhibit E.

13. Statement of Seymour Carroll, Krieger Investigation, 104–8.

14. Statement of Cpl. Kie Haithcock, Richtel Investigation.

15. Statement of Patrolman Isaac F. Garner, Krieger Investigation, 218–28.

16. Statement of Henry Dore, Krieger Investigation, 73–76.

17. Statement of Nezzie Young, Krieger Investigation, 77–82.

18. Statement of Hardy Hopkins, Krieger Investigation, 83–86.

19. Statement of Dr. Robert W. Mance, Krieger Investigation, 69–72.

20. Krieger Investigation, Exhibit F.

21. *State,* 13 January 1941.

22. Statement of Mildred Jackson, Krieger Investigation, 40–44.

23. Statement of Raymond White, Krieger Investigation, 36–39.

24. Statement of Willis Johnson, Krieger Investigation, 21–28; statement of Corporal William Musselwhite, Krieger Investigation, 208–14.

25. Statement of Dr. Robert Mance, Krieger Investigation, 69–72.

26. Statement of Mildred Jackson, Krieger Investigation, 40–44.

Notes to Pages 37–44 | 227

27. Statement of George Williams, Krieger Investigation, 49–52.

28. Vertical file, James M. Hinton, South Caroliniana Library, University of South Carolina; Fleming and Burckel, *Who's Who in Colored America*, 1950.

29. *State,* 27 March 1941.

30. Statement of James M. Hinton, Krieger Investigation, 245–54; statement of Lt. Col. Lewis Page, Krieger Investigation, 229–41.

31. Statement of Robert Pearson, Krieger Investigation, 192–95; statement of Private John Bassett, Krieger Investigation, 162–70.

32. Modjeska Simkins erroneously told historian Jacquelyn Hall that the committee was first organized in May 1944. Simkins collapsed the creation of the Colored Citizens' Committee with that of the Richland County Citizens' Committee, which was a later offshoot. Modjeska Simkins, interview by Jacquelyn Hall, 28–31 July 1976, Southern Oral History Program Collection, Southern Historical Collection of the University of North Carolina, 87. Transcription available in the Simkins Papers. See also *State,* 27 March 1941.

33. Statement of Pfc. John Calhoun, Krieger Investigation, 141–46.

34. Statement of James P. Reeder, Krieger Investigation, 1–6; *State,* 27 March 1941.

35. James Hinton to Gen. George Marshall, 25 March 1941; Hinton to Secretary of War Henry L. Stimson, 27 March 1941; John P. Davis, secretary of National Negro Congress, to Secretary of War Stimson, telegram, 2 April 1941, NARA, RG 407, Dec. file 291.21; Claude A. Barnett, Associated Negro Press, to Judge William Hastie, 31 March 1941; Hinton to Walter White, 22 April 1941; White to Hastie, 23 April 1941, NARA, RG 107, entry 91, box 208.

36. Report of Investigation, 18 April 1941, NARA, RG 407, Dec. file 291.21.

37. The tactical units at Fort Jackson answered to the First Corps Headquarters. The service units at the post belonged to the Fourth Service Corps Area. Why the investigation went through the former instead of the latter is unknown.

38. Krieger Investigation, 14.

39. Ibid., 5.

40. Ibid., 46.

41. Ibid., 41.

42. Report of Investigation—Fort Jackson and Columbia, South Carolina, to Major General H. D. Russell, 30 October 1941, NARA, RG 407, Dec. file 291.21.

43. Statement of Seymour Carroll, Krieger Investigation, 104–8.

44. Ibid.

45. Special Investigation: Character, Reputation, and Conduct of Sidney Joseph Friedman, 5 June 1941, and Report of Investigation of Complaint on Sergeant Carl L. Stone and Pvt. Lewis, 18 June 1941, NARA, RG 159, Fort Jackson file.

46. Krieger Investigation, 18–19.

47. James Hinton to Capt. Carey Robinson, 28 July 1941, NARA, RG 159, Fort Jackson file.

48. Memorandum to provost marshal, dated 31 July 1941, Subject: Corporal M. A. Musselwhite, NARA, RG 159, Fort Jackson file.

49. James Hinton to Lt. Col. Frank L. Whittaker, 23 August 1941, NARA, RG 159, Fort Jackson file.

50. James Hinton to Lt. Col. Frank L. Whittaker, 23 September 1941, NARA, RG 159, Fort Jackson file.

51. James Hinton to William Hastie, 23 September 1941, NARA, RG 107, entry 91, box 208.

228 | Notes to Pages 45–52

52. Lee, *Employment of Negro Troops,* 349–57.

53. James Hinton to commanding officer, Fort Jackson, 27 September 1941, NARA, RG 159, Fort Jackson file.

54. *University of South Caroliniana Society: Fifty-fourth Annual Meeting, 1990,* 12–17; Vertical file, John H. McCray, South Caroliniana Library, University of South Carolina.

55. DIR, 7 April 1945, NARA, RG 319, box 62. McCray sold all of the file copies of the *Lighthouse & Informer* to a scrap-paper dealer when he closed the newspaper in 1954. Only a few issues and fragments remain extant.

56. *Palmetto Leader,* 3 May 1941. Richards, "Osceola E. McKaine" See also Egerton, *Speak Now Against the Day,* 227–28.

57. Osceola McKaine to Franklin D. Roosevelt, 24 September 1941, NARA, RG 407, Dec. file 291.2.

58. "Friction with MPs Again in Columbia," certified transcription of *Lighthouse & Informer* article, NARA, RG 159, Fort Jackson file.

59. Capt. William D. Nixon to William H. Hastie, 23 December 1941, and joint affidavit of Pfc. John A. Miller and Dorothy A. Miller, 26 December 1941, NARA, RG 159, Fort Jackson file.

60. Proceedings of a Board of Officers . . . in the case of Privates Kie Haithcock and Peter F. McCarthy, 27 December 1941, NARA, RG 159, Fort Jackson file.

61. Colonel Royden Beebe to James Hinton, 29 January 1942, NARA, RG 159, Fort Jackson file.

62. James Hinton to commanding officer, Fort Jackson, 30 January 1942, NARA, RG 159, Fort Jackson file.

63. Statement of Mayor Fred D. Marshall, Richtel Investigation, 14–17.

64. Statement of Columbia chief of police L. J. Campbell, Richtel Investigation, 17–21.

65. Richard Broome to commanding officer, Fort Jackson, 14 February 1942, exhibit in Richtel Investigation.

66. Richtel Investigation, 3.

67. Ibid.

68. Lee, *Employment of Negro Troops,* 131.

69. *Columbia Record,* 11 November 1942; James Hinton to Truman Gibson, 15 February 1943, NARA, RG 107, entry 91, box 255.

70. See previous chapter for details about these three incidents.

71. Record of Investigation, 31 December 1942, NARA, RG 107, entry 91, box 255.

72. Investigation of Matters Pertaining to Advertising Billboards in Vicinity of Fort Jackson, S.C., 8 September 1942, NARA, RG 159, Fort Jackson file.

73. DIR, 20 November 1943.

74. *Palmetto Leader,* 23 October 1943; Mayor Fred D. Marshall to John McCray, 20 March 1943, McCray Papers, Journalism Files, box 1; Racial Tensions in War Production Centers, 1 December 1943, Truman Library, Oscar D. Chapman Papers, box 38.

75. Alleged Mistreatment of Colored Employees in Laundry #2, Fort Jackson, South Carolina, 24 August 1944, NARA, RG 107, entry 91, box 208, Fort Jackson Post Laundry file.

76. Charles Payne, "Men Led, but Women Organized," in Hine, *Black Women in United States History: Trailblazers and Torchbearers.*

77. Hine, *Black Women in America,* 1032–34: *Palmetto Leader,* 10 April 1943; Simkins, interview by Jacquelyn Hall, Simkins Papers.

Notes to Pages 52–59 | 229

78. Statement of Captain John McVoy, Richtel Investigation, 36; *Columbia Record*, 16 August 1944.

3. Tangled Connections and Lost Opportunities

1. Newby, *Black Carolinians*, 281.

2. DIR, 16 December 1944, 5 January 1945.

3. As early as March 1943, James Hinton began writing letters concerning Fort Jackson soldiers on Negro Citizens' Committee stationery and dropped the word "Colored." Hinton to Lt. Frank J. Kelly, 21 March 1943, NARA, RG 107, entry 91, box 208. I. A. Newby says in *Black Carolinians*, 281, that the committee was formed in 1942 as an ad hoc group.

4. Newby, *Black Carolinians*, 281.

5. DIR, 18 August 1945.

6. Ibid., 25 August 1944, 24 March 1945, 31 March 1945, 14 April 1945, 9 June 1945, 18 August 1945, 15 September 1945, 22 September 1945, 13 October 1945.

7. James Hinton to Mayor Fred Owens, 3 November 1945, McCray Papers, box 3, correspondence with James Hinton file.

8. Report made from Savannah, Georgia, dated 9–10–46, Osceola McKaine FBI file. The informant told the provost marshal that McKaine was receiving a salary from Communist sympathizers. McKaine was indeed receiving a salary from the Southern Conference for Human Welfare (SCHW). McCray knew this because the SCHW had offered him a similar salary in 1945. Furthermore, he did not like the SCHW and thought that its leaders were Communist sympathizers. McKaine biographer Miles S. Richards obtained the information under the Freedom of Information Act and provided copies to the author. For additional information, see Richards, "Osceola E. McKaine and the Struggle for Black Civil Rights, 1917–1946."

9. 1947 Survey of Negro Conditions at Fort Jackson and Columbia, S.C., 14 February 1947, NARA, RG 159, IG General Correspondence, 1939–1947, box 241, Fort Jackson file. The original *Lighthouse & Informer* article is not extant, but this Army report contains an excerpt of the McCray column. Subsequent references appear as "1947 Survey."

10. DIR, 22 December 1945, 21 April 1945, 4 March 1949, 18 March 1949.

11. Simkins Papers, UNAVA file; DIR, 24 October 1947.

12. Perry interview; *Official Roster of South Carolina Servicemen and Servicewomen*, 3:3238.

13. DIR, 17 November 1945, 15 December 1945, 15 February 1946, 15 March 1946; Memorandum 1–2–46, General File, Fort Jackson, Truman Papers.

14. Chapter 6 contains details of several additional incidents involving black soldiers on city buses.

15. DIR, 29 December 1945, 12 January 1946.

16. Ibid., 29 March 1946, 9 April 1946.

17. Ibid., 28 April 1945, 5 May 1945, 19 May 1945.

18. Ibid., 15 December 1945.

19. *Pittsburgh Courier*, 24 August 1945.

20. McCray mentions this incident in "The Isaac Woodard Story," McCray Papers.

21. Portions of this account appear in Andrew H. Myers, "The Blinding of Isaac Woodard," *Proceedings of the South Carolina Historical Association* (2004): 63–73.

22. Alton Blackwell testimony, 1947, *Papers of the NAACP*, reel 30, frame 240.

230 | Notes to Pages 59–66

23. Ibid., frame 246. Blackwell's 1947 testimony varied slightly from statements attributed to him in 1946. He apparently threatened to leave Woodard behind. His use of "boy" to address Woodard stayed consistent.

24. Isaac Woodard testimony, 1947, *Papers of the NAACP*, reel 30, frame 125. Also quoted in *Lighthouse & Informer* clipping, 6 February 1946, McCray Papers.

25. Isaac Woodard testimony, 1947, *Papers of the NAACP*, reel 30, frame 127.

26. *New York Times*, 18 August 1946.

27. Egerton, *Speak Now Against the Day*, 366–70.

28. *Le Monde*, 31 July 1946; Captain D. Mochalin, "In the Armed Forces of the Bourgeois Nations: The Status of the Negro in the United States Army," declassified, translated U.S. intercept of Soviet Army document, 1949, Combined Arms Research Library, Fort Leavenworth, Kansas.

29. Gardner, *Harry Truman and Civil Rights*, 16–17.

30. Ibid., 17–18.

31. Franklin H. Williams to Thurgood Marshall, memorandum, *Papers of the NAACP*, reel 29, frame 1006.

32. Yarborough, *A Passion for Justice*, 52.

33. Reel 30, *Papers of the NAACP*, contains a complete transcript of the 1947 civil suit.

34. *Columbia Record*, 6 November 1946, 22 November 1946.

35. Yarbrough, *A Passion for Justice*, 42–43.

36. Waring to J. Heyward Gibbes, 12 June 1945, Waring Papers, quoted in Yarbrough, *A Passion for Justice*, 46.

37. *Elmore v. Rice*, quoted in Yarbrough, *A Passion for Justice*, 64.

38. Harry Truman to Ernest W. Roberts, 18 August 1948, quoted in Ferrell, *Off the Record*, 146–47.

39. For biographical information, see Cohadas, *Strom Thurmond*, and Bass and Thompson, *Ol' Strom*.

40. Quoted in MacGregor, *Integration*, 312. Fahy was selected because he was a southerner who held liberal views on race. See MacGregor, 314, 349–50, and 354, for additional information about him.

41. Quoted in Quint, *Profile in Black and White*, 6.

42. *Columbia Record*, 27 July 1948, 29 July 1948.

43. MacGregor, *Integration*, 223–24. MacGregor cites War Department Memo 615–500–4, 21 November 1946, subject: Flow of Enlisted Personnel from Induction Centers to Central Examining Stations.

44. The location and composition of the Fifth Training Regiment can only be surmised. The 1947 Survey notes that Fort Jackson authorities had planned to build a recreation area near the Boyden Arbor Pond, which apparently was near the Fifth Regimental area. This stipulation would place the regiment either in the North Post area or in the barracks south of the pond where the Seventy-seventh Infantry stayed during World War II.

45. MacGregor, *Integration*, 223–24. The custom of having an African American serve as an assistant secretary for racial matters began during World War I with the appointment of Emmett Scott. The position went unfilled for two decades until 1941, when Judge William Hastie received the job. He was followed by Truman Gibson, then Marcus Ray. The latter commanded an artillery battalion during World War II as a lieutenant colonel with the Ninety-second Infantry Division. Nalty, *Strength for the Fight*, 111, 140, 148, 225–26.

46. *Pittsburgh Courier*, 25 January 1947.

Notes to Pages 66–73 | 231

47. W. I. Gibson, editor of Afro-American Newspapers, to Secretary of War Robert Patterson, 1 February 1947; air mail from Fort Jackson to the inspector general, Washington, D.C., 18 February 1947. Both letters are attached to the 1947 Survey.

48. 1947 Survey.

49. Statement of 1st Lt. Ronald Mordecai, 17 January 1947, NARA, RG 107, entry 91, box 208.

50. 1947 Survey.

51. Outgoing Clear Message, 18 February 1947, NARA, RG 107, entry 91, box 208; AGF message to commanding general, Second Army, 30 October 1947, NARA, RG 319, MacGregor Papers, box 4; for impact of Greenville lynching, see Walter White to Robert Patterson, 18 February 1947, NARA, RG 107, entry 91, box 208.

52. Ronald Mordecai to Marcus Ray, 19 March 1947, NARA, RG 107, entry 91, box 208; General Orders 11, 23, and 35, dated respectively 26 February, 1 April, and 16 May 1947, give some indication of the swell of out-processing African American soldiers from Fort Jackson. Located in NARA, RG 338, box 505.

53. James Hinton to Marcus Ray, 16 April 1947, and Marcus Ray to James Hinton, 18 April 1947, NARA, RG 107, entry 91, box 208, Fort Jackson file.

54. Hogan interview.

55. Questionnaire: The President's Committee on Equality of Treatment of Opportunity in the Armed Services: Fort Jackson, South Carolina, NARA, RG 319, MacGregor Papers, box 6.

56. Most of the former Station Complement was redesignated 1458th Army Services Unit by Fort Jackson General Order 17, 13 September 1946. Fort Jackson General Order 26, 10 October 1946, changed the 1458th Army Services Unit to the 3431st. All orders in NARA, RG 338, box 505.

57. The TDA and civilian status are enclosures to the Fahy Committee questionnaire on Fort Jackson.

58. Fahy Committee questionnaire; Fort Jackson Athletic and Recreation Memorandum Number 3, 11 February 1950, NARA, RG 338, box 507.

59. *Columbia Record,* 23 August 1949.

60. Ibid., 23 August 1949, 25 August 1949.

61. The second visit occasioned the writing of a document that has become widespread to various libraries, museums, and archives. It is titled "To the Honorable Louis A. Johnson, Secretary of Defense: The Honorable Gordon Gray, Secretary of the Army: In support of its Petition that Fort Jackson be preserved as a training and tactical base for the use of the Army," September 1949. Mayor Owens commissioned attorney David W. Robinson to write it on 30 August 1949 and gave him a deadline of 12 September. George Buchanan suggested the outline. Copy available in NARA, RG 319, Dec. file 333.1, box 653.

62. Esther Bonnet to President Truman, 7 October 1949, Truman Papers, Official File 300B, box 982; E. C. Townsend to Senator Olin Johnston, 21 September 1949, Johnston Papers, box 15; John Riley to Strom Thurmond, 29 June 1955, Thurmond Papers, Subject Correspondence, MS100, box 17.

63. Memorandum for Record, 29 August 1949, Subject: Inactivation of Fort Jackson, South Carolina, NARA, RG 319, entry 26, Dec. file 323.3, box 653.

64. See, for example, Truman Library, Official File 8B, box 91. For a contrast, see Truman's correspondence with Olin Johnston, General File, box 1239, and correspondence with Second District congressman John Riley, General File, box 2034.

65. J. Strom Thurmond to author, 21 April 1997.

232 | Notes to Pages 74–80

4. The Open Secret of 1950

1. Fort Jackson, "Fiftieth Anniversary History," 82, 84, 105; *Columbia Record*, 17 July 1950. General McConnell was a native of Cicero, Indiana, and had served in the Army since 1921. For additional biographical details, see Eighth Infantry Yearbook, 1951, at the Fort Jackson Museum.

2. U.S. Army, "Fiftieth Anniversary History," 105; *Columbia Record*, 17 July 1950, 1 August 1950, 23 August 1950.

3. The *Columbia Record*, 21 August 1950, estimated 15,000 soldiers. A 1952 memorandum for record by Army Vice Chief of Staff Gen. J. E. Hull indicated that the Eighth Infantry Division had a training capacity of 13,000 to 14,000 soldiers. See NARA, RG 319, entry 26, Dec. file 333.1, box 1167.

4. The Sixty-first Regiment would later convert to a training unit as administrative support became more established. Information about the organization and personnel of the Eighth Division comes from Report of Command Inspection of Fort Jackson, South Carolina, 30 November 1950, NARA, RG 319, entry 26, Dec. file 333.1, box 1167.

5. The Navy began desegregating ships at the end of World War II. The Air Force complied with President Truman's order within a year, if not sooner. Neither service had as many African Americans as the Army. Integration of the Marine Corps tracked roughly with that of the Army. For a comprehensive narrative about desegregation of the armed forces on a national scale, see Nalty, *Strength for the Fight*, 218–69.

6. MacGregor, *Integration*, 153–57.

7. Nalty, *Strength for the Fight*, 227.

8. Nichols, *Breakthrough*, 97–98; Incoming Clear Message to the Adjutant General dated 29 January 1949, NARA, RG 319, MacGregor Papers, box 7.

9. MacGregor, *Integration*, 364.

10. *Congressional Record* excerpt "Extension of Remarks of Hon. Jacob K. Javits, 21 April 1950," in NARA, RG 330, Dec. file 291.2.

11. Nalty, *Strength for the Fight*, 253.

12. SR 600–629–1, *Utilization of Negro Manpower*, Pentagon Library; quoted in MacGregor, *Integration*, 371.

13. MacGregor, *Integration*, 373–74.

14. Ibid., 430. These figures refer to first-time enlistments, not reenlistments.

15. The states were North Carolina, South Carolina, Tennessee, Alabama, Georgia, Florida, Mississippi, Pennsylvania, Maryland, Virginia, and Indiana. Included also was the District of Columbia. *Columbia Record*, 11 September 1950.

16. Nichols, *Breakthrough*, 98.

17. Ibid.

18. Ibid., 99.

19. Nichols gave his notes to Morris MacGregor. They are located in NARA, RG 319, MacGregor Papers, box 11. See *Columbia Record*, 5 September 1950, for article about Hodge.

20. *Columbia Record*, 21 August 1950, 23 August 1950; *State*, 26 August 1950; McConnell already had a means of silencing subordinates. A general order dated 27 June 1950 said: "No material or information pertaining to the activities of the Post or incidents occurring thereon, will be submitted to any newspaper, wire service, house organ, newsreel service, magazine (including trade or religious publications) or radio station for publication or broadcast, unless approved by the Post Commander," NARA, RG 338, box 506.

21. *Columbia Record*, 21 July 1950.

Notes to Pages 80–83 | 233

22. *State,* 20 August 1950.

23. The use of "cantonment" and "non-segregated" implies familiarity with Fort Jackson and the situation. A. G. Kennedy to Secretary of Defense Louis Johnson, 21 August 1950, NARA, RG 330, Dec. file 291.2.

24. *State,* 27 August 1950.

25. The documentary evidence does not say specifically to which regiments each race belonged, but the above interpretation fits the available facts for several reasons. First, the Army during this period normally segregated the races at the regimental level. Second, the *Columbia Record* said on 11 September that the Thirteenth had twelve companies and that the Twenty-eighth had six. The article added that Fort Jackson had a total of eighteen companies, twelve white and six black, without identifying regiments. Third, a 1 September article in the *Record* describes the first three companies of the Thirteenth Regiment without specifying race. The *Record* almost always made mention of color if the soldiers involved were African Americans. Fourth, even though the Twenty-eighth Regiment took its nickname during World War I from a European coat of arms, "Black Lions" would have been a fitting nickname for a segregated unit even though the term "black" to describe an African American was not as fashionable as it would later become.

26. *Columbia Record,* 16 September 1950, 2 October 1950; Report of Command Inspection, 30 November 1950.

27. This inspection was part of the larger Report of Command Inspection, 30 November 1950.

28. Information on the committee system comes from various interviews with six men who served as cadre during the early 1950s: Dale Abbott, Whit Anderson, Albert Hamilton, R. Smith, Walter Thompson, and Porcher Taylor.

29. Army yearbooks make questionable sources because public information officers used them as propaganda tools. They nevertheless make useful gauges of racial demographics. Several of these books are available at the Fort Jackson Museum.

30. The yearbook does not depict any African American officers in the rank of captain or higher. The lack of captains, or of any of the lieutenants in command positions, suggests that racism continued at Fort Jackson. The absence of black majors, lieutenant colonels, and generals reflects that only forty-six African Americans in the entire Army held these ranks at the start of the Korean War. Forty-six more received promotions in December 1950.

31. Outgoing Clear Message to Honorable James E. Folsom, Governor of Alabama, and Outgoing Clear Message to Honorable Fielding L. Wright, Governor of Mississippi, Subject: Ordering National Guard Units into Active Service, 16 December 1950, NARA, RG 168, entry 344, box 1330.

32. *Columbia Record,* 23 January 1951.

33. "A Year in Columbia with the Dixie Division," *State Magazine* (Sunday insert), 30 November 1951.

34. *Pittsburgh Courier,* 21 April 1951.

35. *Investigation of the Preparedness Program, Tenth Report of the Preparedness Committee of the Committee on Armed Services, United States Senate: Fort Jackson, S.C., 1951.*

36. *State Magazine,* 30 November 1951.

37. Nichols, *Breakthrough,* 122.

38. A. C. McAuliffe, ACofS, G1, to General Hull, memorandum, 25 January 1952, and "Arrival of G-1 Representative at Fort Jackson, S.C.," 27 July 1951, NARA, RG 319, entry 26, Dec. file 333.1, box 1167.

234 | Notes to Pages 84–88

39. Col. Samuel E. Mays, chief of legislative liaison, to Senator Spessard L. Holland, 29 June 1951, NARA, RG 407, Dec. file 291.2.

40. Quoted in MacGregor, *Integration*, 322.

41. "Policy Regarding Negro Separation," 7 December 1950, NARA, RG 319, MacGregor Papers, box 7.

42. Representative Jacob K. Javits to Secretary of Defense General George C. Marshall, 2 October 1950, NARA, RG 319, MacGregor Papers, box 7.

43. The performance of the Twenty-fourth Regiment was a source of controversy as early as September 1950, when articles in the black press featured a young combat engineer named Charles Bussey, who claimed that the Army was conducting a smear campaign aimed at African American troops. The issue arose again during the 1980s, and Bussey again led the way with his book *Firefight at Yechon*. The renewed interest prompted the Army Center of Military History (CMH) to take a second look at its official history of the Korean War, written by Ray Appleman. After seven years of interviewing veterans and assessing the evidence, the CMH committee concluded that the Twenty-fourth Regiment as a whole deserved its reputation for unreliability. The committee attributed the unit's problems to racism. See "Black Soldier, White Army: The 24th Infantry in Korea Executive Summary," at http://www.army.mil/cmh-pg/books/korea/24th.htm.

44. Nichols, *Breakthrough*, 120.

45. Cross Reference Sheet dated 1 March 1950, Truman Library, Official File 93, box 544.

46. *Pittsburgh Courier*, 30 September 1950, 9 December 1950, 31 March 1951.

47. *Columbia Record*, 26 June 1950. Thurmond made a similar statement that May at a rally in McCormick. For text, see Thurmond Papers, Clemson University, MSS 100, 11A, 00493.

48. Thurmond said in a 21 April 1997 letter to the author: "Regrettably, I do not have any recollection of when or how I learned of the integration of Fort Jackson."

49. Sims was a World War II hero who at the age of twenty-eight unseated incumbent John Riley in the 1946 election. According to the *Columbia Record*, 28 July 1950, he lost his bid for reelection because of his support for organized labor, the Fair Employment Practices Commission, and other liberal policies of the Truman administration. The article notes that Sims did not support the president's stance on civil rights. See the *State*, 11 July 2004, for Sims's obituary. Regrettably, the author had not known that Sims lived such a long life and did not attempt an interview.

50. Corrine B. Riley to Olin Johnston, 9 October 1962, Johnston Papers, box 94.

51. James Byrnes to Dwight D. Eisenhower, 27 August 1953, Eisenhower Library, Anne Whitman file, Name Series, James Byrnes Correspondence.

52. Dorn to Kennedy, 12 April 1951, Dorn Papers, box 37, file 38, Civil Rights.

53. Rivers to Vinson, 2 April 1952, NARA, RG 335, Dec. file 291.2. The deputy chief of staff for the Army for personnel, Gen. Anthony McAuliffe of Bastogne fame, did investigate the matter and concluded that the woman had overreacted.

54. For example, see Acting Secretary of the Army Karl R. Bendetson to Maybank, 1 August 1952, NARA, RG 319, entry 26, Dec. file 333.1, box 1167.

55. *Columbia Record*, 22 August 1950.

56. Brown Papers, Clemson University. See *Columbia Record*, 28 November 1950 and the *State* 29 November 1950 for the first public announcement of this project.

57. *Columbia Record*, 15 July 1950.

58. *Investigation of the Preparedness Program, Tenth Report of the Preparedness Com-*

Notes to Pages 88–94 | 235

mittee of the Committee of the Armed Services, United States Senate: Fort Jackson, S.C., 1951; Columbia Record, 20 April 1951, 21 July 1951.

59. Bates to Truman, 1 December 1951, Truman Library, Official file 200–4-D, box 763.

60. The football teams were all-white, which reflects the general predominance of whites in the sport at the time. Commanders from both sides packed their teams with draftees who had been star college or professional athletes. According to John S. Poppell, who ran on the track team at Fort Jackson from 1952 until 1954, African Americans did participate on sports teams. Poppell, personal conversation, January 1998.

61. Nichols, *Breakthrough,* 147.

62. DIR, 20 July 1951, 14 December 1951.

63. *Columbia Record,* 6 November 1950; *State,* 6 November 1950.

64. Order for advertisement from Third Army titled "Four Good Reasons to Join the Army Organized Reserve," McCray Papers, Journalism file, January-August 1951, box 1.

65. DIR, 13 January 1950; *Pittsburgh Courier,* 25 August 1951; DIR, 16 January 1953.

66. *Pittsburgh Courier,* 21 January 1951.

67. DIR, 17 June 1949, 25 November 1949, 23 December 1949, 5 May 1950, and 6 October 1950; *State,* 19 August 1950.

68. *Pittsburgh Courier,* 21 January 1951.

69. Nichols notes, NARA, RG 319, MacGregor Papers, box 11.

70. *Investigation of the Preparedness Program.*

71. Maj. Gen. James Reber, legislative liaison, to Senator Maybank, 22 July 1952, NARA, RG 407, Dec. file 291.2.

5. Turning Out Soldiers

1. Copies of reports located in NARA, RG 319, entry 26, Dec. file 333.1, box 1167; RG 319, entry 26, Dec. file 323.3, box 1468; RG 319, entry 26, Dec. file 323.3, box 1659. See also *Investigation of the Preparedness Program.*

2. "Report of Command Inspection of Fort Jackson, South Carolina," 30 November 1950, NARA, RG 319, entry 26, Dec. file 333.1, box 1167.

3. *Investigation of the Preparedness Program,* 2.

4. "Report of the Inspection of the 8th Infantry Division, Fort Jackson," 21 May 1951, NARA, RG 319, entry 26, Dec. file 333.1, box 1167.

5. "Report of Semiannual Inspection of the 8th Infantry Division," 2–4 March 1954, NARA, RG 319, entry 26, Dec. file 323.3, box 1659; Lee Nichols indicates in his notes that venereal disease was a problem during previous years as well. For records of earlier problems with segregated Section 2 of the 3431st Army Service Unit, see "Annual Report of Medical Activities," 27 February 1950, NARA, RG 338, box 509.

6. Memorandum Number 175, Taxicab Regulations, 26 December 1950, NARA, RG 338, box 506, outlines the off-limits areas for African American soldiers. Sexual morality classes mentioned in "Report of Staff Visit to Fort Jackson," 16 January 1952, NARA, RG 319, entry 26, Dec. file 333.1, box 1167. Prophylactic kits mentioned in "Report of Semiannual Inspection of the 8th Infantry Division (Training) and Annual Command Inspection of Fort Jackson (Post)," 1 October 1952, NARA, RG 319, entry 26, Dec. file 323.3, box 1167.

7. Headquarters, 3431st Army Service Unit Reception Center, Statistical Report for Year 1952, NARA, RG 319, entry 26, Dec. file 323.3, box 1468.

8. Herbert Powell, assistant deputy chief of staff, G1, to Major General John Dab-

236 | Notes to Pages 94–103

ney, commanding general of Fort Jackson, memorandum, 18 November 1953, NARA, RG 319, entry 26, Dec. file 323.3, box 1468.

9. Unidentified civilian woman from Maryland to Anna Rosenburg, assistant secretary of defense for manpower, 25 March 1952, NARA, RG 335, OSA 291.2.

10. "Problems Confronting the Post Commander, Fort Jackson, South Carolina," and "J. E. Hull, Vice Chief-of-Staff, to Harry Collins," 21 January 1952, both in NARA, RG 319, entry 26, Dec. file 333.1, box 1167. A native of Chicago, Collins had served in the Army since 1917. For additional biographical details, see Eighth Infantry Yearbook, 1951, at the Fort Jackson Museum.

11. If the post commander did not read the *Courier*, he nevertheless knew about the reporter through weekly intelligence summaries and had time to prepare for his arrival. DIR, April 1951. George was fired a year later from his job as managing editor for allowing articles to be printed in the *Courier* that "closely resembled news and editorials appearing in the Communist Michigan edition of *The Worker*." DIR, April 1952.

12. *Pittsburgh Courier*, 21 April 1951.

13. Ibid.

14. *Detroit Free Press*, 15 May 1953. Copy in MacGregor Papers, NARA, RG 319, box 7.

15. *Pittsburgh Courier*, 9 June 1951. "In short, in liberal Wisconsin, a worse racial policy is maintained at Camp McCoy than I saw in any of the camps I visited below the Mason-Dixon line."

16. Ibid., 5 May 1951, 23 June 1951, 21 July 1951.

17. *Pittsburgh Courier*, 21 April 1951. George's story about the Thirty-first is repeated in David Mandelbaum's *Soldier Groups and Negro Soldiers*, 117–99.

18. Bogart, *Finding Out*, 98.

19. Bogart, *Project Clear*, xxxiii. The introduction to this volume contains an excellent account of the background of Project Clear. The text is a reprint of the first two reports, which were originally published in 1969 under the title *Social Research and the Desegregation of the United States Army*. Original copies of the reports are located in the NARA, RG 319, and at the Combined Arms Research Library, Fort Leavenworth, Kansas. The text of the reprints matches that of the original. For additional information about Bogart's role in Project Clear, see Leo Bogart, *Finding Out*, 97–107.

20. Bogart, *Finding Out*, 99.

21. Bogart, *Project Clear*, xliv.

22. Ibid., 349.

23. Ibid., 186–87.

24. Ibid., 265.

25. Bogart, *Finding Out*, 98.

26. Quoted in Nichols, "The Military's Secret War."

27. Cross Reference Sheet, Central files, Alphabetical file, Fort Jackson, Eisenhower Library. A Private Appelt wrote to Mrs. Eisenhower asking to be transferred back to Fort Jackson from his current duty station of Fort Sam Houston, Texas. He threatened to kill himself or "get into trouble" if he were not returned to Jackson.

28. Smith interview.

29. Taylor interview.

30. Meadowlark Lemon was a native of Lexington, South Carolina. He served in the Army from 1952 until 1954. Matney, *Who's Who Among Black Americans*, 1975–76, 1:385.

6. Getting Them "Off Our Neck"

1. Memorandum for Maj. Gen. James F. Collins, Subject: Information on Fort Jackson, South Carolina, 30 October 1953, NARA, RG 319, entry 26, Dec. file 323.3, Fort Jackson file, box 1468.

2. Kimpson interview.

3. *Columbia Record*, 16 August 1944.

4. DIR, 20 January 1945.

5. Ibid.

6. Ibid., 26 February 1946, 1 March 1946.

7. 1947 Survey.

8. Nichols, *Breakthrough*, 131.

9. DIR, 18 August 1944.

10. Ibid., 24 March 1944.

11. Ibid., 8 March 1946.

12. Ibid., 22 March 1946.

13. Ibid., 8 March 1946.

14. *State*, 26 October 1953.

15. Ibid., 20 October 1953.

16. MacGregor, *Integration*, 480–81.

17. *Palmetto Leader*, 26 November 1955.

18. Ibid., 5 November 1955.

19. *State*, 23 April 1968.

20. *Palmetto Leader*, 5 November 1955, 26 November 1955.

21. Unfortunately, detailed official records of this incident are lost. The Columbia City Police Department routinely destroyed incident reports after ten years. Names and ages of the soldiers are available, however, at the Municipal Court. These records also detail the punishments meted out to each of them. Criminal Docket, July 1, 1953, to December 31, 1953, Recorders Court, City of Columbia, S.C., 326–27.

22. *Pittsburgh Courier*, 5 December 1953.

23. Ibid. *Columbia Record*, 28 November 1953, is the only account that mentions the soldiers taking turns.

24. *Charlotte Observer*, 28 November 1953.

25. Paralee Means Sherard telephone conversation. Mrs. Sherard is the widow of Austell, who died in March 1997. Sherard served with the 160th Infantry Regiment of the Fortieth Infantry Division. He was wounded in action by a missile on 27 October 1952 while fighting in North Korea. He was hospitalized for his injuries, but later returned to duty. See http://www.kellnet.com/veterans/use4offs.htm and http://www.2id .org/40-160-s.htm.

26. *Charlotte Observer*, 28 November 1953.

27. See chapter 3 for details about this case.

28. Criminal Docket, July 1, 1953, to December 31, 1953, Recorders Court, City of Columbia, S.C., 326–27.

29. Matthew Perry was practicing law in Spartanburg at this time and had no involvement with the case. He has no memory of it and does not remember Jenkins ever saying anything about it. Perry interview.

30. "Mass Jailing and Fining of Negro Soldiers in SC," NARA, G1 Staff Files, RG 319, Dec. file 291.2; NARA, RG 335, Dec. file 291.2; Eisenhower Library, Central File, Official File 124-A, box 910; Complaints re Incident, Columbia, S.C.—Military Personnel in Custody of Civil Authorities, NARA, RG 407, Dec. file 291.2.

238 | Notes to Pages 117–124

31. *Columbia Record*, 15 December 1953.

32. Interview with Modjeska Simkins by Jacquelyn Hall.

33. *Columbia Record*, 25 April 1956.

34. Ibid., 24–28 April 1956; *New York Times*, 15 July 1955. Another desegregation incident took place in October 1954 involving a woman named Sadie Brevard. "You try to run us over," she said. "You want us to work for you, but you can't get along with us." A judge suspended her sentence, saying that "I think the spirit of cooperation would accomplish a great deal in such matters." Apparently Brevard cleaned the house of an influential white family.

35. Sherard telephone conversation; Criminal Docket, July 1, 1953 to December 31, 1953, Recorders Court, City of Columbia, S.C., 326–27.

36. *Charlotte Observer*, 28 November 1953.

37. Ibid., *Columbia Record, State,* 28 November 1953.

38. *Fort Jackson Leader,* 31 December 1953. This issue is bound at the front of the 1954 volume of collected newspapers in the Fort Jackson Museum. The year 1954 was the first in which somebody on-post began to keep and bind the papers systematically. No other papers for 1953 besides the 31 December edition are extant.

39. The Army did not preserve records of proceedings at this level, so how many black soldiers were prosecuted under the new agreement remains unknown.

40. "Rpt of Inv by Lt Col Smith re segregation incident in Columbia, S.C.," NARA, RG 159, box 1935, 631/40/57/4. This file contains routing slips and other papers about the report. Unfortunately, the inspector general's office at the Pentagon returned the actual report to Third Army after using it. A search of the Third Army records available at the NARA revealed no trace of it.

41. Cross Reference Sheet, "Fort Jackson," Eisenhower Library, Central File, Alphabetical File; "Mass Jailing and Fining of Negro Soldiers in SC," NARA, RG 314, G1 Staff files, Dec. file 291.2.

42. Ibid.

43. "Letter from Colonel Louis B. Rutte to Colonel W. P. Grace," 2 January 1954, in "Rpt of Inv by Lt Col Smith."

44. Handwritten note attached to "Rpt of Inv by Lt Col Smith."

45. Memo routing slip attached to "Rpt of Inv by Lt Col Smith."

46. Memorandum signed by Col. Charles W. Hill, 4 January 1954, in "Mass Jailing and Fining of Negro Soldiers."

47. MacGregor notes, NARA, RG 319, box 8. See also MacGregor, *Integration*, 480. MacGregor found this information in the papers of the secretary of defense, RG 330.

48. Complaints re Incident, Columbia, S.C.—Military Personnel in Custody of Civil Authorities, NARA, RG 407, Dec. file 291.2.

7. School Desegregation on and around Fort Jackson

1. MacGregor, *Integration*, 487–88; *Southern School News*, September 1961, April 1962.

2. During the Second World War, the post did have one small elementary school located in the Jackson Homes area, but that was turned over to civilian authorities in 1951. This school was operated on a segregated basis. "List of States and Whether or Not Segregation Is Practiced in Schools for Dependents," 16 October 1951, NARA, office of the secretary of the Army, RG 335, 291.2. *Columbia Record*, 17 May 1950, 2 September 1950.

3. *State*, 6 February 1963. Richland County Board of Education, Minutes, 1946–63,

Notes to Pages 124–129 | 239

South Carolina State Archives; Memorandum Number 33, Information on Schools for Dependent Children Residing on the Fort Jackson Reservation, 29 August 1950, NARA, RG 338, box 506, Fort Jackson file; "List of States and Whether or Not Segregation Is Practiced in Schools for Dependents," 16 October 1951, NARA, RG 335, Dec. file 291.2.

4. Memorandum from secretary of defense, 12 January 1954, Subject: Schools on Military Installations for Dependents of Military and Civilian Personnel, NARA, RG 319, MacGregor Papers, box 8; *Southern School News*, March 1960; MacGregor, *Integration*, 489.

5. *Southern School News*, September 1954, February 1956; Quint, *Profile in Black and White*, 15–17, 104; Edgar, *South Carolina: A History*, 523.

6. Quint, *Profile in Black and White*, 38–54.

7. *Southern School News*, February 1956, January 1957, February 1957, March 1957; Quint, *Profile in Black and White*, 36–37.

8. *Southern School News*, November 1955.

9. Ibid., April 1956; Quint, *Profile in Black and White*, 116.

10. *Southern School News*, March 1957; Quint, *Profile in Black and White*, 116.

11. *Southern School News*, February 1958; Quint, *Profile in Black and White*, 116–24.

12. *Southern School News*, December 1955, April 1956; Quint, *Profile in Black and White*, 175–78.

13. Quint, *Profile in Black and White*, 117; Edgar, *South Carolina: A History*, 529; *Southern School News*, March 1960.

14. *Southern School News*, October 1957, November 1957.

15. Copy of resolution located at Eisenhower Library, Central File, General File 123, box 903, S.C. Senate Resolutions file.

16. *Southern School News*, October 1957, November 1957; *Columbia Record*, 28 September 1957.

17. *Southern School News*, November 1962; Franklin and Moss, *From Slavery to Freedom*, 501.

18. *Southern School News*, November 1962.

19. Egerton, "Weep No More, Columbia."

20. *Southern School News*, August 1961.

21. Ibid., January 1962.

22. Edgar, *South Carolina: A History*, 527, 540, 498; Quint, *Profile in Black and White*, 74.

23. *Southern School News*, September 1955. How many of the 250 signers were on active duty or had jobs at the Navy yard is unknown, but the *Southern School News* made note of the federal government presence in the district. This petition was submitted before the requirement for individual petitions went into effect.

24. *Southern School News*, November 1956; memorandum for the secretary of the Army, Subject: Racial Discrimination—Allegations by Senator Lehman That Negro Servicemen Are Denied Access to Educational Courses, 18 October 1956, NARA, OSA, RG 335, 291.2; *New York Times*, 11 October 1956. The available documents indicate that Lehman never received any correspondence from Fort Jackson, only from Donaldson.

25. Perry interview. See also Burke and Gergel, *Matthew J. Perry*.

26. Perry interview; Jenkins obituary, *State*, 16 May 1986.

27. *Southern School News*, May 1960.

28. Ibid., August 1962. See also Orville Vernon Burton, "Dining with Harvey Gantt," in Burke and Gergel, *Matthew J. Perry*, 188.

29. *Southern School News*, October 1963. Most accounts of desegregation at USC

240 | Notes to Pages 129–138

mention the three blacks who desegregated the Columbia campus (Henri Monteith, Robert Anderson, and James Solomon), but Sgt. James H. Hollings also rode the spearhead of integration by attending classes at USC-Beaufort.

30. Ibid., July 1962, October 1962, January 1963, June 1963.

31. Ibid., September 1963.

32. DIR, 7 April 1945, 15 February 1946; *Southern School News*, May 1957.

33. *Southern School News*, April 1955, April 1962.

34. Richland County Board of Education, Minutes, 1946–63, South Carolina State Archives.

35. *Southern School News*, April 1962.

36. Ibid., June 1961, March 1963, April 1964.

37. *State*, 27 February 1963.

38. Ibid., 22 February 1963; *Southern School News*, March 1963.

39. *State*, 6 February 1963.

40. Ibid., 23 February 1963, 6 March 1963; Richland County School Board Minutes; *Southern School News*, March 1963.

41. *State*, 27 February 1963; *Southern School News*, March 1963.

42. *State*, 3 April 1963, 20 April 1963, 31 August 1963, 3 September 1963, 6 September 1963.

43. *Southern School News*, September 1963, estimated that the average cost for educating a child in South Carolina totaled $163 per year.

44. *State*, 4 March 1963. In *Southern School News*, May 1963, Congressman John H. Dent of Pennsylvania also questioned the $4 million cost of building the schools and suggested moving the bases instead.

45. *Southern School News*, September 1964.

46. Ibid., August 1964.

47. *State*, 8 August 1964.

48. *Southern School News*, September 1964.

49. Ibid.

50. Franklin and Moss, *From Slavery to Freedom*, 516, 626–27.

51. *State*, 2 February 1965.

52. J. Moore, *Columbia and Richland County*, 427.

53. Perri interview.

54. USO "Veterans' Render Constant Service," *State*, circa April 1968. Copy provided to the author by the journalist who wrote the article, Jane Brewer.

55. Perry interview.

8. Fort Jackson and the Desegregation of Public Facilities

1. Trip report of 1955 visit to Fort Jackson by Assistant Secretary of the Army (Financial Management) Chester R. Davis, Davis Papers, Eisenhower Library, box 3; trip report of 1955 visit to Fort Jackson by Undersecretary of the Army Charles C. Finucane, Finucane Papers, Eisenhower Library, box 15; trip report of 1957 visit to Fort Jackson by Undersecretary of the Army Charles C. Finucane, Finucane Papers, box 11.

2. After Watson left Congress in 1970 to run for governor, a Republican named Floyd Davidson Spence won the seat. He served for more than three decades and eventually became chairman of the House National Security Committee, a position that gave him tremendous leverage in matters concerning Fort Jackson. He died in office during 2001.

Notes to Pages 138–147 | 241

3. The Veterans Administration Hospital in Columbia is named for Dorn, and his papers at the University of South Carolina contain several files about Fort Jackson.

4. Mrs. Ida Pride, who served as the personal secretary to every commanding general at Fort Jackson from 1948 until 1979, agreed during her interview that Rivers was the most influential congressman.

5. *Hearings before the Committee on Armed Services, House of Representatives, Eighty-seventh Congress, Second Session, Military Construction Authorization Fiscal Year 1963,* 4110. For additional information about Rivers, see Huntley, "Mighty Rivers of Charleston."

6. *Columbia Record,* 17 July 1964.

7. Strom Thurmond stayed in office until the beginning of 2003 and died less than six months later; his long term in office, however, was unusual only because of his longevity. In a 19 October 1917 editorial, the *Columbia Record* discussed the fitness of Senator Benjamin R. "Pitchfork Ben" Tillman to complete another term. The article noted that Senator John C. Calhoun had died in office, too.

8. Huss, *Senator for the South,* 34–35.

9. Lois T. Shealy, 1981 *South Carolina Legislative Manual,* 265.

10. Johnston Papers, box 52; Pride interview.

11. Johnston Papers, box 94; Pride interview; Thurmond Papers, box 16.

12. Thurmond Papers, box 24.

13. Brown Papers, Clemson University; Blatt Papers, Clemson University. For biographies of each man, see Calhoun, *Speaker Blatt,* and Workman, *The Bishop from Barnwell.* The latter book has a good overview of the Barnwell Ring on pages 99–129. See also J. Moore, "The Barnwell Ring."

14. Rubin interview.

15. Papers of Governor George Bell Timmerman Jr., South Carolina State Archives, box 52, Servicemen file.

16. Wishart interview. The author had the opportunity to meet Lieutenant Colonel Brewer during a 1997 interview with his wife, Mrs. Jane Brewer, who wrote a newspaper column about military families for the *State* called "The Service Set."

17. *State,* 3 April 1963; *Columbia Record,* 12 May 1963; Fort Jackson Public Information Office, Press Release Number 199, 29 March 1963, copy located at Fort Jackson Museum.

18. Perri interview. Perri served on the chamber of commerce Armed Services Committee after his retirement from the Army.

19. DeLoache conversation.

20. Trip report of 1955 visit to Fort Jackson by Assistant Secretary of the Army (Financial Management) Chester R. Davis, Davis Papers, Eisenhower Library, box 3.

21. Wickenberg to author, 2 May 1995.

22. *Columbia Record,* 5 July 1968.

23. Harden conversations.

24. Perri interview.

25. *State,* 5 April 1963; Jane Brewer interview.

26. Rubin interview.

27. *Columbia Record,* 4 September 1968.

28. *State,* 12 November 1970.

29. Sutton, "The Military Mission against Off-Base Discrimination," 118–29.

30. The records of both committees are no longer extant. They were available, however, to 1st Lt. Terry Carr in 1967. He went through these records in an attempt to

242 | Notes to Pages 147–155

determine whether either committee had discussed housing discrimination. He concluded that the issue had "never" been a topic. Memorandum from First Lieutenant Carr to Major McCracken, Subject: Equal Opportunity for Military Personnel in Rental or Off-Post Housing, 12 May 1967, Fort Jackson Housing Staff Study, Fort Jackson Museum.

31. McCray Papers, box 1, Journalism File, 1953; Modjeska Simkins interview by Jacquelyn Hall.

32. Fort Jackson was not unusual in its shortage of high-ranking African Americans. In 1969, blacks made up only 3.2 percent of the Army officer corps, whereas they comprised 10.3 percent of the total force. African American colonels numbered only nine in 1965. By 1968, their strength had risen to forty-two. Brooks and Miller, *The Gathering Storm*, 5–6.

33. Mayor Dreher to President Eisenhower, 21 August 1957, Eisenhower, General file, box 260; Johnston Papers, box 52, contain the most comprehensive and detailed information about the proposed closing of Fort Jackson.

34. Rubin interview.

35. Thurmond to author, 21 April 1997.

36. Johnston Papers, box 52.

37. Rubin interview; telephone conversation with Craig Metz, chief of staff for Representative Floyd D. Spence, 30 May 1997. Metz called in response to a letter to the congressman from the author.

38. C. M. Tucker to Thurmond, 12 July 1957, Thurmond Papers, box 4, Fort Jackson file.

39. McIntosh to Johnston, 18 March 1957, Johnston Papers, box 52.

40. McIntosh to Thurmond, 9 April 1959, Thurmond Papers, Subject Correspondence File, 1959, box 13. The word "Negro" is not capitalized in the original.

41. For information on Timmerman's presidential ambitions, see Henry, "Governor George Bell Timmerman and the 1956 Southern Solidarity."

42. *Columbia Record*, 1 December 1955. See also *Southern School News*, January 1956.

43. Copy of resolution located at Eisenhower Library, Central File, General File 123, box 903, S.C. Senate Resolutions file.

44. *Columbia Record*, 28 April 1956.

45. Quoted in Nichols, *Breakthrough*, 99.

46. *Columbia Record*, 28 April 1956.

47. *New York Times*, 6 May 1956.

48. Timmerman Papers, box 52. See also various articles in *Columbia Record*, October 1958.

49. Timmerman's secretary, journalist Charles Wickenberg, wrote an article for the *Charlotte Observer* that appeared on 25 October 1958. Wickenberg reiterated this position during an interview with the author on 27 March 1995. Correspondence from constituents regarding the Graham rally located in Timmerman Papers, box 52.

50. These events will be discussed in greater detail in the next chapter.

51. This account of lunch-counter desegregation comes from four major sources: the Rubin interview; J. Moore, *Columbia and Richland County*, 423–24; Egerton, "Weep No More, Columbia," 27–35; Lofton, "Calm and Exemplary," 70–82.

52. *Charlotte Observer*, 22 August 1962; *Columbia Record* and *State*, 24 August 1962.

53. *Columbia Record*, 24 August 1962; Johnston Papers, box 80.

54. Within a few years, the Twelfth Corps would be renamed the 120th Army Re-

Notes to Pages 155–159 | 243

serve Command (ARCOM). Three decades later, this headquarters would again be reorganized and redesignated the Eighty-first Regional Support Group.

55. Report of Proceedings by Investigating Officer, 9 October 1962, NARA, RG 407, file 291.21.

56. *Columbia Record*, 27 July 1963; MacGregor, *Integration*, 544; Department of Defense Directive, Subject: Equal Opportunity in the Armed Forces, 26 July 1963, MacGregor Papers (for unfinished sequel to *Integration*), U.S. Army Center for Military History. Subsequent references will appear as "MacGregor Papers, CMH."

57. *Columbia Record*, 27, 29, 30 July and 3, 5, and 6 August 1963.

58. Ibid., 8 August 1963.

59. Ibid., 27 July 1963.

60. Ibid., 8 August 1963. According to Whitmire officials, black and white soldiers were fighting each other at a local pool hall. Police there also arrested an African American soldier for disorderly conduct.

61. Various statements and documents concerning discrimination at Sumter Air Force Base, NARA, RG 335, Dec. file 291.2, 1962.

62. *Columbia Record*, 31 July 1963, 1 August 1963.

63. Ibid., 1 August 1963. Although the *State* was noticeably less strident than its sister journal, the *Columbia Record* appeared to speak for the leadership of Columbia. On 2 August, a five-man delegation from the chamber of commerce departed for Washington to lobby against the bill that would become the Civil Rights Act of 1964. *Columbia Record*, 2 August 1963.

64. Quoted in Sutton, "The Military Mission against Off-Base Racial Discrimination," 128. Originally in *Congressional Record*, CIX, 13784.

65. Memorandum for the General Counsel, Subject: Use of the Off-Limits Power, 4 September 1963, NARA, RG 319, MacGregor Papers, box 10.

66. I was unable to locate copies of the Equal Opportunity Surveys, which apparently are still under the control of the Department of Defense. Carl David Sutton obtained the documents for his 1973 dissertation, and the figure of two is based on his research. Sutton, "The Military Mission against Off-Base Racial Discrimination," 132–33.

67. MacGregor, *Integration*, 539–40.

68. The *Columbia Record*, 26 October 1964, cites a Department of the Army message dated 14 July 1964 as the source of this directive. See also *State*, 17 July 1964.

69. Memorandum for Under-Secretaries of the Services, Subject: Off-base Equal Opportunity Inventory, 24 September 1963, NARA, RG 335, OSA, 291.2.

70. Thurmond Papers, Subject Correspondence Series 1960, box 18, Fort Jackson file, discusses the end of Pal Day.

71. Memorandum from First Lieutenant Carr to Major McCracken, Subject: Equal Opportunity for Military Personnel in Rental or Off-Post Housing, 12 May 1967, Fort Jackson Housing Staff Study, Fort Jackson Museum.

72. Albert Fitt, interview by Dorothy Pierce, October–November 1968, MacGregor Papers, CMH. Original copy in Lyndon B. Johnson Papers.

73. Memorandum to Mr. Davenport from Albert Fitt, Subject: Off-base Equal Opportunity Follow-Up Reports, 4 March 1964, NARA, RG 335, OSA, 291.2.

74. "Citizens' Design for Progress," Greater Columbia Chamber of Commerce, 1965. Copies located at the Greater Columbia Chamber of Commerce and at the Richland County Public Library. See also *Columbia Record*, 2 February 1965.

75. "Citizens' Design for Progress," 151.

76. Ibid. Liaison Committee chairman John Gibson declined to be interviewed

244 | Notes to Pages 159–168

during a telephone conversation in May 1995. A retired Army colonel, he had served as the senior advisor to the South Carolina National Guard from 1957 until his retirement in 1962. See *Columbia Record,* 24 August 1962.

77. Egerton, "Weep No More, Columbia."

9. Staying Out of Trouble

1. *Southern School News,* August 1959, January 1960, February 1960.

2. For a detailed analysis of the sit-in movement in South Carolina, see Sproat, "Firm Flexibility." For additional information about the Rock Hill protests, see *Southern School News,* March 1960.

3. *Columbia Record,* 15 March 1960.

4. Ibid., 2–3 March 1960.

5. Ibid., 5 March 1960; *Southern School News,* April 1960.

6. *Columbia Record,* 6 March 1960.

7. For an example of a student boycott against Allen University, see *Columbia Record,* 5 March 1967.

8. *State,* 25 March 1984; *Columbia Record,* 7 July 1961.

9. *State,* 1 February 1994; *Charleston News,* 24 August 1962.

10. *Columbia Record,* 14 March 1960.

11. Ibid., 7 March 1960.

12. *Pittsburgh Courier,* 24 March 1962.

13. Ibid., 28 April 1962.

14. MacGregor, *Integration,* 514.

15. "Instructions for Army Commanders," July 1961, NARA, RG 335, OSA, file 291.2.

16. *Columbia Record,* 20 July 1961; *State,* 21 July 1961; *Southern School News,* August 1961.

17. *Columbia Record,* 20 July 1961; *State,* 21 July 1961.

18. *Columbia Record,* 20 July 1961; *State,* 21 July 1961.

19. Unless otherwise noted, information on James Felder comes from an interview conducted by the author on 26 April 1995 and from his book, *I Buried John F. Kennedy.*

20. The "Appeal for Human Rights" contains a reference to the role played by African Americans in the armed services. Felder said in his 1995 interview with the author that the idea came from Lonnie King, who was a Navy veteran.

21. MacGregor, *Integration,* 516.

22. "Participation by Military Personnel in Civil Rights Activities," 12 June 1964, NARA, RG 335, OSA, file 291.2.

23. *Southern School News,* July 1958. As a major during World War II, Pinckney was the ordnance officer for the Thirtieth Division at Fort Jackson during the time when the Georgia National Guardsmen from his organization fired shots into the "colored area" of the post. Pinckney appears in a photograph in the yearbook of Lt. Col. Oran Hydrick, which was donated to the Fort Jackson Museum.

24. Memorandum for Deputy Assistant Secretary of Defense (Civil Rights) from Chief of National Guard Bureau, Subject: Desegregation in the National Guard, 22 July 1964, MacGregor Papers, NARA, RG 319, box 9.

25. National Guard Bureau Statistics, 1965, MacGregor Papers, CMH; *Columbia Record,* 29 December 1964.

26. *Columbia Record,* 27 April 1962.

27. "U.S. Army Reserve Strength by Race for Specified Geographic Areas as of 31 March 1963," NARA, RG 319, MacGregor Papers, box 2.

Notes to Pages 170–176 | 245

28. Morris MacGregor, "Project 100,000: Training the Marginal Soldier," typescript, MacGregor Papers, CMH. Also see Albert Fitt, interview by Dorothy Pierce, October–November 1968, original transcript in Lyndon B. Johnson Library, copy in MacGregor Papers, CMH. For general information, see Nalty, *Strength for the Fight*, 299, or *Southern Educational Report*, March 1967. The Army also had an interesting program for veterans called Project Transition, in which solders at the end of their enlistments received job training and counseling. See Louis J. Prost, "Project Transition: A Unique Social Reform Program for the Army," U.S. Army War College, Carlisle Barracks, Pennsylvania. Copy located at the Combined Arms Research Library, Fort Leavenworth, Kansas.

29. Ailes Report, 26 December 1963, NARA, RG 335, file 353, entry 5. See also *Army Information Digest*, November 1964, 32–39.

30. For more information on drill sergeants, see *Infantry*, March–April 1965, and *Journal of the Armed Forces*, September 1964.

31. "Fiftieth Anniversary History," 155–58. For an example of one sociological study conducted at Fort Jackson during this time, see Albert Elkin, *The Development of a List of Minimal Training Goals for Basic Combat Training*, HumRRO Technical Report, December 1967, Fort Benning Infantry School Technical Library.

32. Egerton, "Weep No More, Columbia."

33. For additional information about SSOC, see Michel, "We'll Take Our Stand."

34. *State*, 17 July 1965. Information about Treanor is contained the records of the court-martial of Captain Howard Levy.

35. U.S. Commission on Civil Rights, *Political Participation*, 252–53.

36. *Columbia Record*, 20 July 1967.

37. *State*, 3 January 1971.

38. Toal interview.

10. Counting Bodies in Columbia

1. Family housing on a military installation is divided into officer and enlisted neighborhoods. Regulations specify the allocated amount of square footage per person based upon rank, and units are built accordingly.

2. *Hearings before the Committee on Armed Forces, House of Representatives, Eighty-eighth Congress, Second Session, Military Construction Authorization, Fiscal Year 1965*, 8689–701. This document contains a report conducted in 1964 by the Fort Jackson Housing Office. See also the United States Census tract for 1960 and the Fort Jackson Annual Report for Fiscal Year 1961 located at the Fort Jackson Museum.

3. Pay depended upon not only rank but also the number of years served. Those people who lived on-post did not receive BAQ, but they did not have to pay rent or utilities. *Army Register*, 1964.

4. Memorandum from First Lieutenant Carr to Major McCracken, Subject: Equal Opportunity for Military Personnel in Rental or Off-Post Housing, 12 May 1967, Fort Jackson Housing Staff Study, Fort Jackson Museum. This memorandum explains both the role of the Family Housing Office and Army Community Services.

5. Census tract, 1960.

6. "Citizens' Design for Progress," 105.

7. *Hearings before the Committee on Armed Forces, 1965*, 8689–8701.

8. Thurmond Papers, Subject Correspondence Series 1960, Fort Jackson file.

9. "Citizens' Design for Progress," 98, 102.

10. Ibid., 152.

246 | Notes to Pages 176–184

11. Thurmond Papers, Subject Correspondence Series 1960, Fort Jackson file.

12. Perri interview.

13. Census tract, 1970.

14. Perri interview.

15. *Columbia Record*, 17 June 1965.

16. Census tract, 1960.

17. Perri interview.

18. Testimony of Capt. Ernest Porter, 26 May 1967, Howard Levy court-martial transcript, 2068–87.

19. Simkins Papers, Radio Broadcast files, 12 July 1967.

20. MacGregor, *Integration*, 506.

21. Ibid., 516–17.

22. Quoted in ibid., 542.

23. Ibid., 600–601.

24. Ibid., 601.

25. Ibid., 603–4; Nalty, *Strength for the Fight*, 299.

26. Memorandum to Commanding General, Third United States Army, 17 May 1967, Subject: Equal Opportunity for Military Personnel in Rental Off-Post Housing, Fort Jackson Housing Staff Study.

27. Major General Perez is deceased. Colonel Duffie settled in the Columbia area after his retirement from the Army. He declined to answer questions about his role in the housing survey, cited illness in his family as a reason, and abruptly hung up the phone. Duffie telephone conversation. The author has not located Lieutenant Carr. A Major McCracken (first name unknown) was also involved.

28. After a brief telephone conversation with the author, Fred Stuck agreed to an interview at his home on 12 February 1997. The house was empty at the appointed hour for the meeting, and he did not return subsequent calls. The assessment of Mr. Stuck as "defensive" was made before I knew how to contact him. Stuck's later evasiveness appears to have confirmed this conclusion.

29. Memorandum from First Lieutenant Carr to Major McCracken, Subject: Equal Opportunity for Military Personnel in Rental or Off-Post Housing, 12 May 1967, Fort Jackson Housing Staff Study.

30. Ibid.

31. Memorandum for Record, 16 May 1967, Subject: Equal Opportunity for Military Personnel in Rental of Off-Post Housing, Fort Jackson Housing Staff Study.

32. Ibid.

33. Memorandum to Commanding General, Third United States Army, 17 May 1967, Subject: Equal Opportunity for Military Personnel in Rental of Off-Post Housing, Fort Jackson Housing Staff Study.

34. Pride interview; Wishart interview. Perez Fitness Center at Fort Jackson has a large portrait of the general and several display cases containing his personal artifacts.

35. Memorandum to Commanding General, Third United States Army, 17 May 1967, Subject: Equal Opportunity for Military Personnel in Rental of Off-Post Housing, Fort Jackson Housing Staff Study.

36. Memorandum for the Commanding General, 24 May 1967, Subject: Resume of Oral Presentation Given at 1000 hours Meeting, subject: Rental of Off-Post Housing, Fort Jackson Housing Staff Study. Colonel Duffie also misrepresented the facts in this briefing when he said, "We have received no outright negative responses to our

question of "Are you open to all races?" Lieutenant Carr's 16 May memorandum clearly states otherwise.

37. Memorandum to Commanding General, Third United States Army, 17 May 1967, Subject: Equal Opportunity for Military Personnel in Rental of Off-Post Housing, Fort Jackson Housing Staff Study.

38. Memorandum for the Commanding General, 24 May 1967, Subject: Resume of Oral Presentation Given at 1000 hours Meeting, subject: Rental of Off-Post Housing, Fort Jackson Housing Staff Study.

39. For example, see *Fort Jackson Leader*, 7 July 1967, Fort Jackson Museum.

40. Text of speech, 19 May 1967, Fort Jackson Housing Staff Study.

41. Sheet titled "Party Line," Fort Jackson Housing Staff Study; emphasis in original document.

42. Perri interview.

43. MacGregor, *Integration*, 604–5.

44. DCSPER-DAHC, Fact Sheet, Subject: Equal Opportunity in Off-Post Housing, 20 December 1967 and 28 October 1968, MacGregor Papers, Center of Military History.

45. *Fort Jackson Leader*, 12 July 1968.

46. *In the United States District Court for the Middle District Court for the Middle District of Pennsylvania. Howard B. Levy, Petitioner, v. Jacob J. Parker, as Warden of the United States Penitentiary, Lewisburg, Pennsylvania, and Stanley R. Resor, as Secretary of the Army*, 137. This source is heavily biased against Fort Jackson authorities. The lawyers who quoted this source appeared to have been looking for information to discredit their opponents. Regardless, it is likely accurate for two reasons. First, if untrue, the claim could easily have been disproved. Second, the claim is extremely tangential to the matter discussed in the appeal. If a lawyer were going to make up something, one would think he would create something more germane. The emphasis was in the original.

47. DCSPER-DAHC, Fact Sheet, Subject: Equal Opportunity in Off-Post Housing, 20 December 1967, MacGregor Papers, CMH.

48. See next chapter for details about this court-martial.

49. Dent to Thurmond, 22 May 1967, Thurmond Papers, Subject Correspondence File 1967, box 24. See chapter 8 for additional information about the NCO wives controversy.

50. See chapter 10 for information about Project 100,000.

51. Memorandum for the Commanding General, Subject: Resume of Oral Presentation Given at 1000 hours Meeting, 24 May 1967, subject: Rental of Off-Post Housing, Fort Jackson Housing Staff Study.

52. Census tract, 1970.

11. Fighting at Home and in Vietnam

1. "Fiftieth Anniversary History," 167.

2. Year-by-year statistics can be found in John Perazzo, "Black Patriotism vs. Liberal Lies," *FrontpageMagazine.com*, 20 March 2002 (http://www.frontpagemag.com). For an example of how overall figures can be used to reach the opposite conclusion, see Moskos and Butler, *All That We Can Be*, 8. See also Nalty, *Strength for the Fight*, 298–99.

3. Nalty, *Strength for the Fight*, 299; MacGregor, "Project 100,000: Training the Marginal Soldier," typescript, MacGregor Papers, CMH.

4. Nalty, *Strength for the Fight*, 294–96. For additional information about the origins of the term "Black Power," see "Growl of the Panther."

248 | Notes to Pages 191–199

5. Unless otherwise noted, information on Howard Levy comes from one of two sources. The first is the thousands of pages of transcripts from his court-martial. The Office of the Clerk of Court, United States Army Judiciary, maintains control of those documents, which are located at the National Records Center, Suitland, Maryland. Subsequent references to this source will be cited as "Levy transcript." The second is Levy's appeal: *In the United States District Court for the Middle District Court for the Middle District of Pennsylvania. Howard B. Levy, Petitioner, v. Jacob J. Parker, as Warden of the United States Penitentiary, Lewisburg, Pennsylvania, and Stanley R. Resor, as Secretary of the Army.* Copies located with the transcript at Suitland and also at the South Caroliniana Library, University of South Carolina. Subsequent references will be cited as "Levy appeal."

6. *The State* indeed carries a story about the April incident in its 17 July 1965 edition.

7. Levy appeal, 114.

8. Quoted in *New York Times*, 1 January 1967.

9. Levy transcript, 1057.

10. Ibid., 858.

11. Ibid., 2087.

12. Ibid., 2348.

13. Perri interview.

14. Pride interview; Wishart interview.

15. Levy transcript, 673–76.

16. Ibid., 750.

17. Ibid.

18. Ibid., 701–2.

19. Levy transcript, 723. For additional information about the Black Power movement, see Carmichael and Hamilton, *Black Power.* See also "Growl of the Panther."

20. Levy transcript, 693.

21. *Columbia Record,* 22 July 1967.

22. Levy transcript, 2346.

23. Toal interview. She did say that the name Ernest Porter rang a bell, but that she did not have any clear memories of Levy's physician friend.

24. During the trial, the defense lawyer tried to ask Perry exactly how many officers from Fort Jackson worked in the voter-registration project. The prosecution successfully objected to the question, so Perry could not answer then. In 1997, Perry said that he knew of no other officers than Levy. Levy transcript, 858; Perry interview.

25. Levy transcript, 906.

26. Toal interview.

27. Simkins Papers, Radio Broadcast files, 26 April 1967.

28. *Columbia Record,* 26 April 1967.

29. Simkins Papers, Radio Broadcast files, 10 May 1967.

30. Ibid., 15 November 1967.

31. Ibid., 31 May 1967.

32. Ibid., 15 November 1967.

33. *Fort Jackson Leader,* 5 July 1968.

34. Simkins Papers, RCCC Folder, 9 January 1969.

35. Pride interview.

36. Simkins Papers, Radio Broadcast file, 16 August 1967.

Notes to Pages 199–206 | 249

37. Nelson and Bass, *The Orangeburg Massacre*, 76–98; Edgar, *South Carolina, A History*, 542.

38. *Columbia Record*, 8 April 1968. Fort Jackson's role during these civil disturbances was limited to securing the perimeter of the installation against sabotage. Capt. Eli Wishart, for example, remembered placing guards around one of the water towers during this time. The use of Regular Army troops to control riots required higher authorization and usually involved line units, not basic training organizations like those stationed at Fort Jackson. Wishart interview.

39. Simkins Papers, Radio Broadcast file, September 1967. The transcript does not capitalize "National Guard."

40. Ibid., 5 April 1972.

41. Giles, "The Anti-War Movement in Columbia."

42. *Columbia Record* and *State*, 14 February 1968.

43. Paul Cowan, *New Republic*, 8 March 1968, 23.

44. One issue of the underground Fort Jackson newspaper is on file at the South Caroliniana Library, University of South Carolina.

45. *Columbia Record*, 9 March 1967.

46. Unless otherwise noted, information about the UFO comes from the following sources: *New York Times*, 12 August 1968; *Columbia Record*, 13 August 1968; *Columbia Record/State* (combined Sunday edition), 22 December 1968; McAninch, "The UFO"; J. Moore, *Columbia and Richland County*, 408; Giles, "The Antiwar Movement in Columbia."

47. *New York Times*, 12 August 1968.

48. Paul Cowan, *New Republic*, 8 March 1968, 23.

49. *New York Times*, 12 August 1968.

50. DOD Directive, 12 September 1969, MacGregor Papers, CMH.

51. Perri interview.

52. *State*, 24 April 1970, describes the activities of the Fort Jackson MP.

53. Wishart interview.

54. *Fort Jackson Leader*, 1 November 1968.

55. *New York Times*, 12 August 1968.

56. Wishart interview.

57. *Columbia Record*, 2 April–21 May 1969 (articles almost daily). For copy of pamphlet regarding the GIs United, see Heath, *Mutiny Does Not Happen Lightly*, 406–11; Foner, *Blacks and the Military*, 212–13. The soldiers were a mixture of whites, blacks, and Puerto Ricans.

58. Novelist Pat Conroy bases the climax of his book *Beach Music* on the Bursey paint-splashing incident and the Russell House demonstrations.

12. The Forgotten Decade of the Civil Rights Movement

1. The *Washington Post*, 24 September 1969, lists Fort Jackson as one of the posts that experienced racial violence during that year. Jack Foner uses this source in his history of blacks in the military. No other source could be found to confirm this allegation. The Randall Subcommittee that investigated racial violence in the military did not request anything about Fort Jackson when it asked the Army for information about a long list of other posts. See Memorandum from Chief, Investigations Division, to Assistant Secretary of the Army (Manpower and Reserve Affairs), 31 October 1969, MacGregor Papers, CMH.

250 | Notes to Pages 207–215

2. Nalty, *Strength for the Fight*, 306–8.

3. Brooks and Miller, *The Gathering Storm*, 20–21; Lutz, *Homefront*, 139–140.

4. For examples, see "Racial Discrimination: An Analysis of Serviceman Opinions," April 1970. This survey was authorized in 1969 by the assistant secretary of defense for manpower and reserve affairs. Copy located at the CARL, Fort Leavenworth. See also, Memorandum for Assistant Secretary of the Army (Manpower and Reserve Affairs), Subject: Race Relations in the Army—Visits to Fort Bragg and Fort Riley, 8 September 1969, MacGregor Papers, CMH.

5. Deputy Chief of Staff for Personnel document dated 1970, MacGregor Papers, CMH.

6. *Army Digest*, April 1970, 11.

7. Ibid.

8. Army message dated August 1971 and "Case Studies of Racial Incidents," 26 October 1971, both in MacGregor Papers, CMH. Story also appeared in the *Columbia Record*, August 1971.

9. Taylor interview. See also *State*, 21 November 1971 for an article about Taylor and his family.

10. Smith interview.

11. Nelson and Bass, *The Orangeburg Massacre*, 138–46; Sellers was eventually convicted of one charge, sentenced to a year in prison, and fined $250. Edgar, *South Carolina, A History*, 672 n. 73.

12. Nelson and Bass, *The Orangeburg Massacre*, 234. See the previous chapter for details about the aftermath of the King assassination in Columbia and the antiwar protests at USC.

13. Edgar, *South Carolina, A History*, 543.

14. Ibid., 544–45.

15. Ibid., 544.

16. State of South Carolina Web site about Governor John C. West, http://www.sciway.net/hist/governors/west.html.

17. Garrow, *Protest at Selma*, 7, 11, 19, 189, 200.

18. Bass and DeVries, *Transformation*, 262–63.

19. Ibid., 272; Bass and Thompson, *Ol' Strom*, 253–56; Moss obituary, *State*, 24 April 2004. The Hamby memo was discovered in 2004 and reported in the *State* on 3 October 2004.

20. Thurmond Papers, Subject Correspondence files, 1971, box 19.

21. Taylor interview.

22. Simkins Papers, Radio Broadcast file, 10 March 1971.

23. Thurmond Papers, Subject Correspondence files, 1971, box 19.

24. Kimpson interview.

25. MacGregor, *Integration*, 605.

26. Sutton, "The Military Mission against Off-Base Discrimination," 102.

27. Kimpson interview.

28. Census tracts, 1970 and 1980.

29. Kimpson interview.

30. Lofton, "Calm and Exemplary"; George McMillan, "Integration with Dignity"; Stall, "With Grace and Style"; Sproat, "Firm Flexibility"; Edgar, *South Carolina*, xx, 541. Stephen O'Neill criticized this consensus approach to the state's history in a thoughtful paper titled "Facing Facts: The 'Voluntary' Desegregation of Greenville, South Carolina," which he presented at the Citadel Conference on Civil Rights, Charleston, S.C.,

Notes to Pages 217–219 | 251

March 2003. Although Orville Vernon Burton notes that "with grace and dignity is better than without it," he also expresses reservations about the overemphasis on consensus in "Dining with Harvey Gantt," in Burke and Gergel, *Matthew J. Perry*, 183–220.

31. *State*, 14 October 1979.

32. Ibid., 16 May 1986.

33. Kimpson interview.

34. *State*, 24 May 1996.

35. Ibid., 6 December 1995. For information about Bolden's father, see the *State*, 19 October 1979; *Official Roster of South Carolina Servicemen and Servicewomen*, vol. 1 (Columbia, undated), 360; and 1999 Program Dedication, Biographical Vertical File, Local History Room, Richland County Public Library. For information about Bolden's mother, see the *State*, 22 October 2002. For information about Bolden's retirement from the Marine Corps, see the *State*, 10 August 2002.

36. Ann Taylor was present for part of the 2001 interview with her husband. Some of her activities are also detailed in the *State*, 21 November 1971.

37. Taylor interview. Taylor published an autobiography in 2004 titled *Damn the Alligators*.

38. Nichols, *Breakthrough*, 199.

Sources Consulted

The sections below describe the various libraries and archives that provided the thousands of documents consulted in writing this book. They also detail the people interviewed and provide alphabetical lists of relevant secondary materials and paper collections.

National Archives and Record Administration (NARA)

The National Archives has custody of the largest collection of official records pertaining to Fort Jackson. The bulk of it is divided into the following record groups:

Record Group 107, Department of War
Record Group 138, National Guard Bureau
Record Group 159, Inspector General
Record Group 319, General Staff
Record Group 330, Department of Defense
Record Group 335, Secretary of the Army
Record Group 338, Third Army
Record Group 407, Adjutant General

Within each record group, documents are organized according to the War Department classification system. Three decimal files were particularly relevant:

Decimal file 291.2, Racial Matters
Decimal file 333.1, Installations
Decimal file 323.3, Inspections

Three concentrations within the record group merit special consideration. Record Group 107 has the papers of William Hastie, who in 1941 became the secretary of war's special advisor for civil rights. Record Group 319 contains domestic intelligence reports collected by the G2 Intelligence section of the Fourth Service Command. These provide weekly situation updates on racial incidents, labor unrest, and subversive activities in the South. Record Group 319 also has material that Morris MacGregor used to write *Integration of the Armed Forces*. MacGregor's papers include the notes—both handwritten and typewritten—that Lee Nichols used to write *Breakthrough on the Color Front*.

254 | Sources Consulted

Records Held by the United States Army

The U.S. Army Center of Military History (CMH) has another collection of Mac-Gregor papers at its main facility in Washington, D.C. MacGregor gathered these notes in order to write a sequel to *Integration*. (He retired before completing it.) The CMH facility also has an excellent library containing annual historical reports submitted by the U.S. Army Continental Army Command (CONARC) and the Training and Doctrine Command (TRADOC). This saved me a trip to the archives at the TRADOC headquarters in Fort Monroe, Virginia.

Several other Army facilities warrant mention. The Combined Arms Research Library at Fort Leavenworth, Kansas, has such items as an original Project Clear manuscript and declassified field manuals regarding the treatment of African American soldiers. The Infantry School Technical Library at Fort Benning, Georgia, has one of the best collections of reports prepared by the Human Resources Research Organization (HumRRO). The Pentagon Library has a set of regulations that is well cross-referenced and enables a researcher to trace the evolution of a particular subject across time.

The Army keeps records of court-martial proceedings at the National Records Center in Suitland, Maryland. Researchers must make special coordination through the Office of the Staff Judge Advocate in Charlottesville, Virginia, to gain access to such records as the Howard Levy transcripts because they fall under army control, not that of the National Archives.

The Army War College at Carlisle Barracks, Pennsylvania, has a massive number of documents, including the papers of Special Assistant for Civil Rights James C. Evans. Within these papers are transcripts from the Fahy and Gesell Committees. Unfortunately, much of the material at Carlisle was not catalogued and in boxes at the time this book was researched. I did not have an opportunity to use this facility.

Fort Jackson Museum

The Fort Jackson Museum belongs to a nationwide network of museums run by the Department of the Army. From this facility came one of this book's most important documents, the study created by the commanding general's staff in reaction to Secretary of Defense McNamara's 1967 policy regarding segregated housing. Somebody apparently recognized the historical significance of the document and kept it, which was fortunate because army regulations do not require the preservation of most installation-level records. In addition, the museum has a bound collection of the post newspaper, the *Fort Jackson Leader*. It also has a bound edition of the *Army Times* from World War II, which contains a local supplement published at Fort Jackson. Scattered copies of other installation newspapers are available, too, as are the old clipping files from the Public Information Office. Besides the newspapers, the museum has an eclectic collection of photographs, yearbooks, maps, press releases, and files for divisions that were stationed at the post.

Sources Consulted | 255

During the late 1990s, the museum acquired a large number of maps and blueprints from the post engineering section.

Presidential Papers

Presidential papers were useful primarily for learning about political activity regarding South Carolina. I visited the libraries of Harry Truman, Dwight Eisenhower, and Lyndon Johnson. None contained much information about individual soldiers because the presidents' staffs tended to forward military-related correspondence to the Department of Defense. A look through the subject correspondence files and subject cross-reference files turned up some important nuggets of information. The Eisenhower Library, for example, had a few documents about the 1953 Columbia bus incident that were not preserved in the Office of the Army Inspector General records at the National Archives. The Johnson Library has the papers of Albert Fitt, who served as the assistant secretary of defense for civil rights. The Truman Library has papers related to the Fahy Committee.

More fruitful were name searches through the individual correspondence files of such South Carolina politicians as James Byrnes, Burnet Maybank, John Riley, L. Mendel Rivers, and Strom Thurmond. These letters reveal the efforts of state leaders to keep Fort Jackson open during the forties, fifties, and sixties.

The papers of Franklin D. Roosevelt, John F. Kennedy, and Richard Nixon would probably be worth a look as well. The Kennedy Library has the papers of Gerhard Gesell, who chaired the 1963 Committee on Equality of Opportunity in the Armed Forces. I did not have the opportunity to visit these facilities.

Legislative Papers

Searching for the papers of South Carolina politicians is a relatively painless task. There are few people to track, and they leave an easy-to-follow trail. Clemson University has the largest concentration, which includes the papers of Strom Thurmond, James Byrnes, Edgar Brown, and Solomon Blatt. The Modern Political Collections at the University of South Carolina has the papers of two other important figures, Olin Johnston and William Jennings Bryan Dorn.

The papers of Thurmond, Johnson, and Dorn have the most files about Fort Jackson. The Thurmond papers are especially well organized. Papers were not available at this writing for the following legislators: Ernest Hollings, Floyd D. Spence, John Riley, and L. Mendel Rivers. The best sources of information about Rivers are the records of the House Armed Services Committee, which researchers should be able to find in any government document repository.

University of South Carolina

Located in Columbia, the University of South Carolina has the most comprehensive collection regarding the state's civil rights movement. The South Caroliniana Library there has the papers of African American leaders John McCray and Mod-

256 | Sources Consulted

jeska Simkins. It also has the papers of Samuel Latimer, editor of the *State* newspaper. Unfortunately, no institution has the papers of George Buchanan or James Hinton. A Freedom of Information Act inquiry to the Federal Bureau of Investigation revealed no files on Hinton. Buchanan's grandson said the *Columbia Record* editor was notorious for his messy desk and left no organized papers.

USC has an extensive collection of material about Fort Jackson, but most of it dates back to the World War I era, when the installation was known as Camp Jackson. These documents include the diary of the engineer who built the original cantonment and a superb collection of postcards. USC's more recent information about Fort Jackson pertains mostly to the antiwar movement. The South Caroliniana Library has a copy of an underground GI newspaper as well as Howard Levy's federal court appeal. It also has an excellent unpublished term paper about the antiwar movement in Columbia written by Doris B. Giles. The Map Library within USC's Thomas Cooper Library has aerial photographs of the region.

The South Caroliniana Library has an extensive collection of microfilmed newspapers from across the state. These include fragments of the *Lighthouse & Informer* and a relatively complete set of the *Palmetto Leader*. The staff there has recently obtained microfilm copies of some issues of the *Lighthouse & Informer* that historian Wim Roeffs discovered in Belgium at the University of Ghent. Apparently Osceola McKaine subscribed to the paper after he left the United States. Excerpts and clippings from the *Lighthouse & Informer* can occasionally be found in the domestic intelligence reports stored at the National Archives.

Richland County Public Library, City Hall, and the Municipal Court
Although the South Caroliniana Library has microfilmed sets of the *Columbia Record* and the *State*, a researcher will do better looking for these at the Richland County Public Library (RCPL). This facility allows open access to the microfilm collection and charges less for copies. The RCPL has a superb local history room, which contains unpublished documents like the chamber of commerce's Citizens' Design for Progress. The room also has telephone directories, legislative handbooks, and other reference materials of local and state interest.

Additional local facilities of note are the Columbia City Hall and the Municipal Court. The former has minutes of the city council locked in the vault. The latter has a room full of docket books.

State of South Carolina
The state, not the county, maintains control of the Richland County School Board records. A researcher can find these at the State Department of Archives and History in Columbia. This facility has public papers of all South Carolina governors, too. The ones for George Bell Timmerman Jr. have extensive correspondence about the 1958 Billy Graham rally, but in general, the gubernatorial papers did not have much information about Fort Jackson or racial issues.

The State Library has at least two important documents pertaining to Fort

Sources Consulted | 257

Jackson. The first is a Camp Jackson yearbook dating to World War I. The second is a study of the economic effect of Fort Jackson upon Columbia in 1979. Conducted by the USC School of Business and the Greater Columbia Chamber of Commerce, this analysis was part of an effort to prevent the army once again from closing Fort Jackson.

Oral Sources

Documents, not interviews, form the basis for this book. Personal interviews generally provided corroborating evidence and leads to other sources rather than standing on their own. Barracks rumors are the scourge of military life, and I have found that those rumors often grow worse with age. Interviews were conducted not in order to collect oral histories or preserve memories but to gather information. Several people did not want their interviews taped. Considerable information came as a result of serendipitous meetings. Except where noted, I conducted the interviews listed below. Important conversations and failed interview attempts are also included. The interviews and conversations took place in Columbia, South Carolina, unless otherwise noted.

Abbot, Dale. Drill sergeant at Fort Jackson during the fifties. Interview. Tape recording. February 1995.

Anderson, Whit. Maintenance officer at Fort Jackson during the fifties. Interview. Tape recording. June 1995.

Baker, Vivian. Schoolteacher for Richland County District 1 whose husband was stationed at Fort Jackson during the sixties. Telephone interview. March 2001. (She lived in Columbia, S.C., at the time of the interview.)

Brewer, Jane. Wrote column about military families for the *State*. Interview. Tape recording. 14 April 1997.

Brewer, John. Post engineer for Fort Jackson during early sixties; civilian worker for Richland County after retirement. Conversation as part of the tape-recorded interview with his wife, Jane. 14 April 1997.

Burgess, Joe. Basic trainee at Fort Jackson during early fifties. Various conversations. Spartanburg, S.C. Fall 2003.

Cassedy, Jim. Basic trainee at Fort Jackson in 1968; archivist at the NARA facility in Suitland, Md. Conversation. November 1995.

Cross, Joe. Basic trainee at Fort Jackson during late sixties. Interview. Tape recording. 8 June 1995.

DeLoache, William. Personal conversation with author. May 1995.

Duffie, Johnnie. Deputy chief of staff for personnel (G1) at Fort Jackson during late sixties; key participant in implementing Defense Secretary McNamara's 1967 housing initiative. Telephone conversation and failed request for interview. October 1996.

Felder, James. Basic trainee at Fort Jackson; JFK pallbearer; state legislator. Interview. No tape recording. 26 April 1995.

258 | Sources Consulted

Gibson, John. Chairman of Military Liaison Committee for Citizens' Design for Progress; retired army colonel. Telephone conversation and failed request for interview. May 1995.

Gibson, Julie. Civilian worker at Fort Jackson during early seventies; librarian at Pentagon. Arlington, Va. Conversation. April 1995.

Hamilton, Al. First sergeant at Fort Jackson during fifties. Interview. Tape recording. June 1995.

Hammond, James. Basic trainee at Fort Jackson during late sixties; president of Columbia Veterans of Foreign Wars. Conversation. October 1996.

Hampton, George. Lieutenant at Fort Jackson during early 1950s; member of 3431st Area Service Unit, which was the last unit at the post to be desegregated. Telephone interview. March 2001. (He lived in Dale City, Va., at the time of interview.)

Harden, John M., III. Colonel in the Army Reserve; member of the Fort Jackson Officers Club since late fifties. Various conversations between 1996 and 1998.

Harms, Roy. Fort Jackson public information officer during the Howard Levy court-martial. Interview. 29 May 1995.

Hogan, Helen. Columbia woman who met husband at USO. Interview. Tape recording. February 1995.

Hogan, Roy. Served at Fort Jackson during forties, fifties, and sixties. Interview. Tape recording. February 1995.

Johnson, Spencer. Basic trainee at Fort Jackson during mid-fifties; enlisted aide to Major General Costello. Spartanburg, S.C. Various conversations. Spring 2001.

Johnson, Thomas. Basic trainee at Fort Jackson during late fifties. Archivist at South Caroliniana Library. Conversation. Fall 1995.

Joyner, Charles. Basic trainee at Fort Jackson during late fifties; civil rights worker in Columbia during sixties; historian. Telephone conversation and failed request for interview. Spring 2004. (He lived in Myrtle Beach, S.C., at the time of the conversation.)

Kimpson, Milton. Basic trainee at Fort Jackson during early fifties; executive director of Greater Columbia Human Relations Council. Interview. Tape recording. 4 and 12 December 1996. Telephone interview. 15 December 2005.

Legrand, Bruce. Grandson of George Buchanan. Telephone conversation. 19 March 1996.

MacDonald, Laughlin. Basic trainee at Fort Jackson during early sixties; lawyer for Howard Levy; regional director of American Civil Liberties Union. Charleston, S.C. Conversation. March 2003.

MacGregor, Morris J., Jr. Author of *Integration of the Armed Forces*. Interview. Arlington, Va. 19 June 1995.

McConnell, Robert Scott. Author of master's thesis about the Eighth and Thirtieth Divisions during World War II; librarian at the Fort Jackson Soldier Support Institute. Telephone conversation. February 1998.

Sources Consulted | 259

McKnight, Beatrice. Secretary of the Richland County Citizens' Committee during the sixties. Conversation. April 1997.

Metz, Craig. Chief of staff for Congressman Floyd D. Spence. Telephone conversation. 30 May 1997.

Nichols, Lee. Newspaper reporter who visited Fort Jackson in 1952; author of *Breakthrough on the Color Front*. Interview. Rockville, Md. 21 June 1995.

Parks, William. Basic trainee at Fort Jackson during mid-sixties. Criminal justice professor at the University of South Carolina Upstate. Spartanburg, S.C. Various conversations. 2004.

Perri, Angelo. Basic trainee at Fort Jackson during the late forties; senior officer at Fort Jackson during the late sixties and early seventies. Interview. Tape recording. 30 January 1997.

Perry, Matthew. Civilian worker and World War II inductee at Fort Jackson; federal district judge. Interview. Tape recording. 12 February 1997.

Phillips, James. Served at Camp Jackson with the Sixth Division in 1939; Pearl Harbor attack survivor. Conversation. November 1996.

Pickus, Sigmund. Basic trainee at Fort Jackson during early fifties. Spartanburg, S.C. Various conversations. 1999–2004.

Poppell, John S. Basic trainee and track team member during early fifties. Conversation. January 1998.

Pride, Ida. Fort Jackson post commander's personal secretary from 1948 to 1979. Interview. 29 April 1995.

Rubin, Hyman. Mayor pro tempore of Columbia; city councilman; state senator. Interview. Tape recording. 27 January 1997.

Sherard, Paralee Means. Widow of Austell Sherard; army wife in Columbia from 1954 to 1958. Telephone interview. 10 December 1997. (She lived in Indiana at the time of the interview.)

Simkins, Modjeska. Interview by Jacquelyn Hall. 28–31 July 1976. Southern Oral History Program Collection, Southern Historical Collection of the University of North Carolina, 87. Transcription available in the Simkins Papers, USC Columbia.

Smith, R. (pseudonym). Company commander at Fort Jackson during early fifties. Interview. Tape recording. June 1995.

Steedly, Homer. Served on cadre at Fort Jackson during late sixties. Various conversations. 1999–2002.

Steedly, Tibby Dozier. Granddaughter of South Carolina adjutant general James Dozier. Various conversations. 1995–98.

Stuck, Fred. Civilian housing coordinator at Fort Jackson in 1967. Telephone conversation and failed interview request. February 1997.

Taylor, Porcher. Lieutenant at Fort Jackson during early fifties; first African American full colonel stationed at Fort Jackson. Interview. Petersburg, Va. March 2001. Telephone interview. 28 November 2005.

260 | Sources Consulted

Thompson, Walter P. Served at Fort Jackson during forties, fifties, and sixties; three-time Combat Infantryman Badge–awardee. Interview. Tape recording. February 1995.

Toal, Jean. SNCC worker; friend of Howard Levy; state Supreme Court justice. Interview. Tape recording. 16 December 1996. (An associate justice at the time of the interview, Toal later became chief justice.)

Walker, Harold. National Guardsman at Orangeburg and Columbia during 1968. Conversation in Charlotte, N.C. Fall 1995.

Waltrip, Les. Cadre member at Fort Jackson during early fifties; civilian worker at Fort Jackson until nineties. Various conversations. 1996–97.

Wapinski, Sean. Engineer who supervised construction of Trainfire Ranges at Fort Jackson during late fifties. Conversation. November 1996.

Wickenberg, Charles. Secretary to Governor George Bell Timmerman Jr.; reporter for *Charlotte Observer* who broke story about lunch-counter desegregation in Columbia. Interview. 27 March 1995.

Wishart, Eli. Aide-de-camp to post commander during late sixties. Interview. 1 June 1995.

Newspapers, Periodicals, and Film
The *Columbia Record* provides the most comprehensive day-to-day information about Fort Jackson during the period in question. No longer published, it was an afternoon paper that tended to focus more on local news than did its morning counterpart, the *State*. The *Charlotte Observer* carried reports about Columbia, too, and is sometimes useful in cases where editors in South Carolina suppressed stories. The *Pittsburgh Courier* has the best coverage of Fort Jackson and the military from a black perspective.

Articles about desegregation of South Carolina schools can be found in the *Southern School News*. Published in Nashville from September 1954 until June 1969 by the Southern Education Reporting Service, this periodical concentrated exclusively on the *Brown* decision and its implementation across the South. The editors strove for objectivity and tried to take stories only from what they considered to be "responsible" sources. Each issue of the paper provides a state-by-state breakdown of the latest news regarding desegregation as well as excerpts from relevant speeches, court decisions, and legislation.

National news magazines contain almost no mention of Fort Jackson or Columbia. The main exception is an article written by John Egerton that appeared in the 3 May 1965 edition of *Newsweek*. Titled "Weep No More, Columbia," it describes how the area had changed since Sherman's army marched through a hundred years earlier. The *New York Times* also published a number of stories about the Columbia area in the mid- to late sixties. The focus of these articles is more on Howard Levy and the antiwar movement than on race, however. The *New York Times* covered the Isaac Woodard case of 1946, too.

A crew from CBS News did initial filming in 1967 for a documentary about

race relations at Fort Jackson. The story was not broadcast, however, so the footage is not available to the general public.

Books and Other Secondary Sources

Bartley, Numan. *The New South, 1945–1980: The Story of the South's Modernization.* Baton Rouge, 1995.

Bass, Jack, and Marilyn W. Thompson. *Ol' Strom: An Unauthorized Biography of Strom Thurmond.* Atlanta, 1988.

Bass, Jack, and Walter DeVries. *The Transformation of Southern Politics: Social Change and Political Consequence since 1946.* New York, 1976.

Bogart, Leo. *Finding Out: Personal Adventures in Social Research—Discovering What People Think, Say, and Do.* Chicago, 2003.

———, ed. *Project Clear: Social Research and the Desegregation of the United States Army.* New Brunswick, N.J., 1992.

———, ed. *Social Research and the Desegregation of the U.S. Army.* Chicago, 1969.

Brooks, Harry W., and James Miller. "The Gathering Storm: An Analysis of Racial Instability within the Army." Carlisle Barracks, 1970.

Bruce, Catherine Flemming. *Rivers of Deliverance: A Visitor's Path through African-American History in Columbia and Richland County.* Columbia, 1994.

Burke, W. Lewis, and Belinda F. Gergel, eds. *Matthew J. Perry: The Man, His Times, and His Legacy.* Columbia, 2004.

Bussey, Charles M. *Firefight at Yechon.* Washington, 1991.

Calhoun, John K. *Speaker Blatt: His Challenges Were Greater.* Columbia, 1965.

Carmichael, Stokely, and Charles V. Hamilton. *Black Power: The Politics of Liberation in America.* New York, 1967.

Chafe, William. *Civilities and Civil Rights: Greensboro, North Carolina, and the Black Struggle for Freedom.* New York, 1980.

Chesnutt, David R., and Clyde N. Wilson, eds. *The Meaning of South Carolina History: Essays in Honor of George C. Rogers Jr.* Columbia, 1991.

Cohadas, Nadine. *Strom Thurmond and the Politics of Southern Change.* New York, 1993.

Colley, David P. *Blood for Dignity: The Story of the First Integrated Combat Unit in the U.S. Army.* New York, 2002.

Conroy, Pat. *Beach Music.* New York, 1995.

Dalfiume, Richard M. *Desegregation of the U.S. Armed Forces: Fighting on Two Fronts, 1939–1953.* Columbia, Mo., 1969.

Davidson, Chandler, and Bernard Grofman, eds. *Quiet Revolution in the South: The Impact of the Voting Rights Act, 1965–1990.* Princeton, 1994.

Dudziak, Mary L. *Cold War Civil Rights: Race and the Image of American Democracy.* Princeton, 2000.

Earley, Charity Adams. *One Woman's Army: A Black Officer Remembers the WAC.* College Station, 1989.

Edgar, Walter B. *South Carolina: A History.* Columbia, 1998.

262 | Sources Consulted

————. *South Carolina in the Modern Age.* Columbia, 1992.

Edgar, Walter B., et al. *A Columbia Reader, 1786–1986.* Columbia, n.d.

Egerton, John. *Speak Now Against the Day: The Generation before the Civil Rights Movement in the South.* Chapel Hill, 1994.

————. "Weep No More, Columbia." *Newsweek,* 3 May 1965, 27–35.

Felder, James. *I Buried John F. Kennedy.* Columbia, 1994.

Ferrell, Robert H., ed., *Off the Record: The Private Papers of Harry S. Truman.* New York, 1980.

Fleming, G. James, and Christian E. Burckel, eds. *Who's Who in Colored America.* Yonkers-on-Hudson, 1950.

Fletcher, Marvin E. *America's First Black General, Benjamin O. Davis, Sr., 1880–1970.* Lawrence, 1989.

Flynn, George O. *The Draft, 1940–1973.* Lawrence, 1993.

Foner, Jack D. *Blacks and the Military in American History: A New Perspective.* New York, 1974.

Franklin, John Hope, and Alfred A. Moss Jr. *From Slavery to Freedom: A History of African Americans.* New York, 1994.

Furr, Arthur. *Democracy's Negroes: A Book of Facts Concerning the Activities of Negroes in World War II.* Boston, 1947.

Gardner, Michael R. *Harry Truman and Civil Rights: Moral Courage and Political Risks.* Carbondale and Edwardsville, 2002.

Garrow, David J. *Protest at Selma: Martin Luther King, Jr., and the Voting Rights Act of 1965.* New Haven and London, 1978.

Giles, Doris B. "The Antiwar Movement in Columbia, South Carolina, 1965–1972." Term paper for History 858, USC, Spring 1987, South Caroliniana Library, University of South Carolina.

Graves, John Temple. *The Fighting South.* New York, 1943.

"Growl of the Panther." *Newsweek,* 30 May 1966, 33–36.

Heath, G. Louis., ed. *Mutiny Does Not Happen Lightly.* Metuchen, N.J., 1976.

Henry, Hallie B. "Governor George Bell Timmerman and the 1956 Southern Solidarity." Master's thesis, University of South Carolina, 1972.

Hine, Darlene Clark. *Black Women in America: An Historical Encyclopedia.* New York, 1993.

————, ed. *Black Women in United States History: Trailblazers and Torchbearers, 1941–1965.* New York, 1990.

Huntley, Will F. "Mighty Rivers of Charleston." Ph.D. diss., Department of History, University of South Carolina, 1993.

Huss, John E. *Senator for the South: A Biography of Olin D. Johnston.* Garden City, N.Y., 1961.

James, C.L.R., George Brietma, Edgar Keemer et al. *Fighting Racism in World War II.* New York, 1980.

Janowitz, Morris. *The Professional Soldier.* Glencoe, Ill., 1960.

Sources Consulted | 263

Lander, Ernest M., Jr. *From Clemson College to India in World War II by a GI Who Never Saw the Enemy.* Spartanburg, 1992.

Lanning, Michael Lee. *The African-American Soldier: From Crispus Attucks to Colin Powell.* Secaucus, N.J., 1997.

Lee, Ulysses. *The United States Army in World War II, Special Studies: The Employment of Negro Troops.* Washington, 1966.

Lofton, Paul S., Jr. "Calm and Exemplary: Desegregation in Columbia, South Carolina." In *Southern Businessmen and Desegregation,* edited by Elizabeth Jacaway and David Colburn, 70–82. Baton Rouge, 1982.

———. "A Social and Economic History of Columbia, South Carolina, during the Great Depression, 1929–1940." Ph.D. diss., University of Texas at Austin, 1977.

Lopez, Henry D. *From Jackson to Japan: The History of Company C, 307th Infantry, 77th Division, in World War II.*

Lutz, Catherine. *Homefront: A Military City and the American 20th Century.* Boston, 2001.

MacGregor, Morris J., Jr. *Integration of the Armed Forces, 1940–1965.* Washington, 1981.

Mandelbaum, David G. *Soldier Groups and Negro Soldiers.* Los Angeles, 1952.

McAninch, William Shepard. "The UFO." *South Carolina Law Review* 46 (1995): 363–79.

Matney, William C., ed. *Who's Who Among Black Americans, 1975–76,* Vol. 1. Northbrook, Ill., 1976.

McConnell, Robert Scott. "The 1940–41 United States Army Mobilization: A Comparison of the 8th and 30th Divisions—Refuting the National Guard 'Purge Theory.'" Master's thesis, History Department, University of South Carolina, 1993.

McGuire, Phillip, ed. *Taps for a Jim Crow Army: Letters from Black Soldiers in World War II.* Santa Barbara, 1983; Lexington, 1993.

McMillan, George. "Integration with Dignity: The Inside Story of How South Carolina Kept the Peace. *Saturday Evening Post,* 16 March 1963, 16–18.

Megginson, W. J. *Black Soldiers in World War I: Anderson, Pickens, and Oconee Counties, South Carolina.* Seneca: Oconee County Historical Society, 1994.

Mershon, Sherie, and Steven Schlossman. *Foxholes and Color Lines: Desegregating the U.S. Armed Forces.* Baltimore and London, 1998.

Michel, Gregg. "'We'll Take Our Stand': The Southern Student Organizing Committee and the Radicalization of White Southern Students, 1964–1969." Ph.D. diss., Department of History, University of Virginia, 1999.

Millet, John D. *United States Army in World War II: The Army Service Forces, The Organization and Role of the Army Service Forces.* Washington, 1954.

Moore, Brenda L. *To Serve My Country, To Serve My Race: The Story of the Only African-American WACs Stationed Overseas during World War II.* New York, 1996.

Moore, John Hammond. "The Barnwell Ring." *Sandlapper* (Spring 2004): 26–28.

264 | Sources Consulted

———. *Columbia and Richland County: A South Carolina Community, 1740–1990.* Columbia, 1993.

———. "Nazi Troopers in South Carolina." *South Carolina Historical Magazine* 81 (October 1980): 306–15.

Moskos, Charles C. *The American Enlisted Man: The Rank and File in Today's Military.* New York, 1970.

Moskos, Charles C., and John Sibley Butler. *All That We Can Be: Black Leadership and Racial Integration the Army Way.* New York, 1996.

Myers, Andrew H. "Black, White, and Olive Drab: Military-Social Relations during the Civil Rights Movement at Fort Jackson and in Columbia, South Carolina." Ph.D. diss., Department of History, University of Virginia, 1998. (This work contains additional material not found in this volume.)

Nalty, Bernard C. *Strength for the Fight: A History of Black Americans in the Military.* New York, 1986.

Nalty, Bernard C., and Morris J. MacGregor Jr., eds. *Blacks in the Military: Essential Documents.* Wilmington, Del., 1981.

Nelson, Jack, and Jack Bass. *The Orangeburg Massacre.* New York, 1970.

Newby, I. A. *Black Carolinians: A History of Blacks in South Carolina from 1895 to 1968.* Columbia, 1973.

Nichols, Lee. *Breakthrough on the Color Front.* New York, 1954. Colorado Springs, 1993.

———. "The Military's Secret War against Racism." *Freeman* 40, no. 7 (July 1990). Available online at http://www.fee.org/publications/the-freeman; Nichols interview.

Norrell, Robert J. *Reaping the Whirlwind: The Civil Rights Movement in Tuskegee.* New York, 1985. Chapel Hill, 1998.

Official Roster of South Carolina Servicemen and Servicewomen. Columbia, n.d.

O'Neill, Stephen. "Facing Facts: The 'Voluntary' Desegregation of Greenville, South Carolina." Paper presented at the Citadel Conference on Civil Rights, Charleston, S.C., March 2003. Available at http://www.citadel.edu/civilrights/papers/oneill.pdf.

Palmer, Robert R., Bell I. Wiley, and William R. Keast. *United States Army in World War II: The Army Ground Forces, The Procurement and Training of Ground Combat Troops.* Washington, 1948.

Papers of the NAACP. Microfilm edition. Frederick, Md., 1988.

Paret, Peter. "The History of War." *Daedalus* 100 (Spring 1971): 376–96.

Payne, Charles. *I've Got the Light of Freedom: The Organizing Tradition and the Mississippi Freedom Struggle.* Berkeley, 1995.

Putney, Martha S. *When the Nation Was in Need: Blacks in the Women's Army Corps during World War II.* Metuchen, N.J., 1992.

Quint, Howard H. *Profile in Black and White: A Frank Portrait of South Carolina.* Washington, 1958. (This work is virtually a word-for-word transcription of the master's thesis that I. A. Newby wrote at USC.)

Richards, Miles S. "Osceola E. McKaine and the Struggle for Black Civil Rights, 1917–1946." Ph.D. diss., Department of History, University of South Carolina, 1994.

Russell, Henry D. *The Purge of the Thirtieth Infantry Division*. Macon, n.d., ca. late forties.

Scanlan, Tom. *Army Times Guide to Army Posts*. Harrisburg, 1963.

Shealy, Lois T., ed. *1981 South Carolina Legislative Manual*. Columbia.

Shortal, John F. *Forged by Fire*. Columbia, 1987.

South Carolina War Stories. Columbia, 1995.

Sproat, John G. "'Firm Flexibility:' Perspectives on Desegregation in South Carolina." In *New Perspectives on Race and Slavery in America: Essays in Honor of Kenneth M. Stampp*, edited by Robert H. Abzug and Stephen E. Maizlish, 164–84. Lexington, 1986.

Stall, Betty. "With Grace and Style: The Desegregation of the Greenville County Schools in 1970." *Proceedings and Papers of the Greenville County Historical Society* 9 (1990–91): 80–92.

Stanton, Shelby L. *Order of Battle, U.S. Army, World War II*. Novato, Calif., 1984.

Stillman, Richard J. *Integration of the Negro in the U.S. Armed Forces*. New York, 1968.

"The Story of the Century." Yearbook of the 100th Infantry Division. Fort Jackson Museum

Stouffer, Samuel A., Arthur A. Lumsdaine, Marion Harper Lumsdaine, Robin M. Williams Jr., M. Brewster Smith, Irving L. Janis, Shirley A. Star, and Leonard S. Cottrell Jr. *The American Soldier*. Princeton, 1949.

Sutton, Carl David. "The Military Mission against Off-Base Racial Discrimination: A Study in Administrative Behavior." Ph.D. diss., Department of Political Science, Indiana University, 1973.

Taylor, Porcher. *Damn the Alligators—Full Speed Ahead*. Bloomington, 2004.

Terry, Wallace. *Bloods: An Oral History of the Vietnam War by Black Veterans*. New York, 1985.

Treadwell, Mattie. *The Women's Army Corps*. Washington, 1954.

U.S. Army, U.S. Army Training Center, Fort Jackson. War Department General Staff. *Logistics in World War II: Final Report of the Army Service Forces*. Washington, 1947.

———. "Fiftieth Anniversary History, Fort Jackson, South Carolina, 1917–1967." Fort Jackson, 1967.

U.S. Commission on Civil Rights. *Political Participation*. Washington, May 1968.

Weigley, Russell F. *History of the United States Army*. Bloomington, 1984.

West, Charles O., Philip C. Wood, Neil F. Wender, and Harold R. Butler, eds. *Second to None! The Story of the 305th Infantry in Worls War II*. Washington, 1949.

Whiting, Charles. *Death of a Division*. New York, 1981.

Workman, William D. *The Bishop from Barnwell: The Political Life and Times of Edgar Brown*. Columbia, 1963.

266 | Sources Consulted

Wright, Kai. *Soldiers of Freedom: An Illustrated History of African Americans in the Armed Forces.* New York, 2002.

Wyatt, Judy L. "United States Policy toward German Prisoners of War and Its Application in South Carolina." Term paper, University of South Carolina, 27 April 1984. Copy in Fort Jackson Museum.

Yarbrough, Tinsley. *A Passion for Justice: J. Waties Waring and Civil Rights.* New York, 1987.

Who's Who Among Black Americans, 1975–76. Vol. 1. Northbrook, Ill., 1976.

Paper Collections

Blatt, Solomon. Special Collections, Clemson University Library.

Brown, Edgar. Special Collections, Clemson University Library.

Byrnes, James F. Special Collections, Clemson University Library.

Davis, Chester. Eisenhower Presidential Library, Abilene, Kans.

Dorn, William J. B. South Caroliniana Library, USC Columbia.

Evans, James C. Army War College Library, Carlisle Barracks, Pa.

Fahy Committee. Transcripts located in the Evans Papers at the Army War College Library, Carlisle Barracks, Pa.

Finucane, Charles. Eisenhower Presidential Library, Abilene, Kans.

Fitt, Albert. Johnson Presidential Library, Austin, Tex.

Gesell, Gerhart. Kennedy Presidential Library, Boston, Mass.

Gesell Committee. Transcripts located in the Evans Papers at the Army War College, Carlisle Barracks, Pa.

Hastie, William. NARA, RG 107.

Johnston, Olin. South Caroliniana Library, USC Columbia.

Latimer, Samuel. South Caroliniana Library, USC Columbia.

Levy, Howard. Transcript of court-martial located at National Records Center, Suitland, Md. Contact the Office of the Staff Judge Advocate, Charlottesville, Va., for access.

MacGregor, Morris J. NARA, RG 319. Second collection at U.S. Army Center for Military History, Washington, D.C.

McCray, John. South Caroliniana Library, USC Columbia. Available on microfilm.

NAACP Papers. Library of Congress. Available on microfilm.

Nichols, Lee. Located in the MacGregor Papers, NARA, RG 319.

Simkins, Modjeska. South Caroliniana Library, USC Columbia.

Thurmond, J. Strom. Special Collections, Clemson University Library.

Timmerman, George Bell, Jr. South Carolina Department of Archives and History, Columbia.

Index

Italicized page numbers refer to illustrations

Adams, Charity, 51

Adams, E. A., 4, 38–39, 51

advanced individual training (AIT): antiwar movement and, 203; Fort Jackson, 108, *169*; race-based assignments for, 94, 106; training division concept of, 75; Vietnam escalation and, 189

advancement and promotion: black enlistment and, 17–18; black officer, 14, 207–8, 218–19, 233n30; civilian employee, 199; equality of opportunity for, 76; leadership academies for, 75, *106*, 167; military appropriations and, 138; officer efficiency reports (OER), 102; politics and officer, 139, 156; racial incidents and, 118; "Zero Defects" program and, 185

African Americans in military history: civil rights movement and, 198; as historical research topic, 2–4; Korean War, 84–85, 89; Reconstruction era, 6; Regular Army segregated units, 10; Vietnam War and, 190; women and, 10–11, 51; WWI and, 6; WWII and, 26. *See also* military units, black, combat

Agnes Scott College, 173

Aiken, SC, 60

Ailes, Stephen, 170

Ailes Report of 1963, 170, 189

Air Force. *See* U.S. Air Force

Alabama: Birmingham march (1963), 171; Craig Air Force Base, 112; Freedom

Rides of 1961, 164; Maxwell Air Force Base, 166; John McCray and, 45; National Guard, 82, 96, 101–2; racism, 34

alcohol: black soldiers and, 52; Columbia "Congo Square" and, 33; Fort Jackson Officers Club and, 145; police searches for, 35

Allen University: church affiliation, 226n5; Columbia and, 31; desegregation retaliation toward, 125; Kappa Alpha Psi at, 32; sit-in movement and, 154, 161–62; social activities with, 13, 56–57, 67–68, 95; sports competition with, 15

American Association of Colleges and Universities, 162

American Broadcasting Company, 60

American Civil Liberties Union (ACLU), 195

American Dilemma, An (Myrdal), 63

American Legion, 58, 89

Anderson, Robert, 240n29

Anderson, SC, 115

anti-Semitism, 37, 41, 43

antiwar movement: Army response to, 200; Brett Bursey and, 202, 204; "Fort Jackson Eight," 204; "GIs United Against the War in Vietnam," 201, 203–4; Howard Levy and, 191–97, 247n46; off-limits sanctions and, 202; Modjeska M. Simkins and, 198–200; soldiers and, 201–2; UFO Coffeehouse, 201–3. *See also* student protests

268 | Index

"Appeal for Human Rights," 166, 244n20
Arkansas, 126
Arlington National Cemetery, 167
Armed Forces: as economic opportunity, 195–96, 198, 218; equality of opportunity, 76, 155–59; Executive Order 9981 and, 1, 54, 65, 74–77; integration, 221n4; racial discrimination and, 135; racism in command structure of, 26; school desegregation and, 134–35; training inspections, 92–93; Truman integration of, 1, 64, 232n5. *See also* racial policy, Armed Forces
Armed Services Security Questionnaire, 192
Army Advisory Board, 137–38
Army Air Forces (AAF): black units in, 12; as major U.S. command, 9; Myrtle Beach Army Airfield, 58, 99; 702nd Maintenance Company, 19; Tuskegee Airmen, 14, 17, 222n8. *See also* Columbia Air Base; U.S. Air Force
Army and Air Force Exchange Service (AAFES). *See* post exchange (PX)
Army Community Services (ACS), 175, 181
Army Digest, 207
Army General Classification Test (AGCT), 18, 75, 93–94, 168. *See also* Project 100,000
Army Ground Forces (AGF): basic training for, 66; black units in, 12; Mark Clark and, 152; First Corps, 227n37; as major U.S. command, 9. *See also* military units; National Guard
Army Nursing Corps, 10–11, 57
Army Reserve. *See* U.S. Army Reserve
Army Service Forces (ASF). *See* Fourth Service Command; Fourth Service Corps; military units, black, other
Army Times, 15–16
Arthur, Henry, 37
assignment: court-martial rates, 92–93; limitations on black officer, 14, 22, 66; race-based, 93; segregation and limitations on, 67; and TDA, 70
Associated Negro Press, 40
Atlanta, GA, 154–55, 165–66
Avon School for the Blind, 62

awards and decorations: Combat Infantryman Badge, 115; Distinguished Service Cross, 89; Good Conduct Medal, 23; Medal of Honor, 6, 222n1; Purple Heart, 115
AWOLs, 59, 201, 206

Bamberg, SC, 17
Barnett, Ross, 126
basic training: Ailes Report on, 170–71, 189; antiwar movement and, 203; assembly-line concept for, 9, 13; at Fort Bragg, 18; integration of, 81–82, 94; segregation in, 7–9; training division concept of, 75; Vietnam escalation and, 187. *See also* training; training units
Bassett, John, 35, 39
Bates, Lester L., 88, 143–45, 154–55, 163, 200, 212
Batesburg, SC, 59–61
Beaufort, SC, 240n29
Beebe, Royden, 23, 25, 28, 45, 47–48, 50
Benedict College: church affiliation, 226n5; Columbia and, 31; desegregation retaliation toward, 125; Kappa Alpha Psi at, 32; Milton Kimpson and, 107; sit-in movement and, 154, 161–62; social activities with, 13, 56–57, 67–68, 95
Benson, Joseph H., Jr., 110
Beverly, Linwood, 21, 23
Birmingham, AL, 64
"Black Power" movement, 190, 196, 198, 204, 206
black separatism, 190–91
Blackwell, A. C., 59
Blatt, Solomon, 142
"Blinding of Isaac Woodward, The" (Guthrie), 60
Bogart, Leo, 96–99, 101
Bolden, Charles F., Jr., 157–58, 218
Bolden, Charles F., Sr., 113, 218
Bolden, Ethel Martin, 4, 113, 134, 218
Bolling, A. R., 120–21
Bond, Julian, 166
Bouie, Simeon, 161–64
Boulware, Harold, 113
boycotts: Anti–Jim Crow Sundays, 117; Charleston cafeteria, 111; Columbia bus, 111; leadership issues and, 163

Boykin, Lonnie, 20
"boys," black men as, 5, 59, 230n23
Bradley, Omar N., 65
Breakthrough on the Color Front (Nichols), 1–2, 78, 219
Brevard, Sadie, 238n34
Brewer, John, 144
Briggs, Harry, 134
Briggs v. Elliot, 63, 111, 113, 126
Brooks, W. G., 114
Broome, Richard, 47
Brown, Edgar A., 88, 141–42
Brown, Sarah Mae (Flemming). *See* Flemming, Sarah Mae
Brownell, Herbert, 122
Brown v. Baskin, 65
Brown v. Board of Education: Civil Rights Act of 1964 and, 134; Clarendon County lawsuit and, 63; federal aid to education and, 130; South Carolina desegregation and, 118, 124–26; U.S. Supreme Court and, 2
Buchanan, George A., 28, 68, 71, 78, 88–89, 138, 145, 148, 156
"Buffalo Soldiers," 4
Bursey, Brett, 202, 204
Bussey, Charles, 234n43
Byrnes, James F., 49, 86, 142, 153

Calhoun, John, 39–40
California, 76
Campbell, L. J., 41, 47, 68, 202–3
Camp Edwards, MA, 96
Camp Gordon, GA, 59, 71–72
Camp Hancock, GA, 38
Camp Jackson, SC. *See* Fort Jackson
Camp Lejeune Marine Base, NC, 96, 128
Camp McCoy, WI, 96, 236n15
Camp Robinson, AR, 25
Camp Rucker, AL, 83
Camp Van Dorn, MS, 15
Cantey, J. Willis, 138, 146
Carmichael, Stokely, 190, 196
Carr, Terry A., 180–82
Carroll, Richard, 31
Carroll, Seymour, 31–32, 34, 41–42
Cayce, SC, 89, 144
Celebreeze, Anthony J., 131
censorship: in *Army Times*, 20; enlistments

and, 232n15; integration and, 154, 216; newspaper, 17, 49, 202; silencing subordinates, 232n20
chain of command: Army command structure and, 120–22; civilian oversight in, 137; housing survey and, 182; race relations and, 207; threats to blacks by, 18–19; "Zero Defects" program and, 185
chamber of commerce: Citizens' Design for Progress (CDP), 137, 158–59, 175–76; Columbia, 3, 28, 50, 68, 71, 138, 143; Fort Jackson relations with, 146; Greater Columbia Human Relations Council and, 4, 212–13; housing discrimination and, 181, 213; race relations and, 147; state industrial development and, 126–27; UFO Coffeehouse and, 202
chaplains, black: conflicting roles of, 23; at Fort Jackson, 14, 23, 225n72; integration and, 94; as intelligence targets, 23–24; in Spanish-American War, 31
Charleston, SC, 62, 72, 111, 128–30, 132, 209
Cheraw, SC, 128
Chester, SC, 90
churches, black: African Methodist Episcopal Church, 226n5; Baptist Church, 226n5; interdenominational relations, 56–57; Sidney Park Colored Methodist Episcopal Church, 32; USO "Pal Day" and, 113; Zion Baptist Church, 39, 193
Churchill, Winston, 12–13
Citadel military academy, 151–52
Citizens' Council, 125
Citizens' Design for Progress (CDP), 137, 158–59, 175–76
city government, Columbia: black representation in, 30; civil rights demonstrations and, 162–64; Fort Jackson relations with, 141–47; Greater Columbia Human Relations Council and, 4, 212–13; MP brutality toward blacks and, 42; school system and, 124; white majority in, 28. *See also* Columbia, SC
Civilian Conservation Corps (CCC), 5, 13, 24–26
civilian economy: Army racial policy and, 174; Fort Jackson and, 142–43; military

civilian economy (*continued*)
  impact on, 3; off-limits sanctions and,
  136–37, 155–57, 164, 167, 172, 180–81;
  on-post housing and, 176–77; post exchange (PX) and, 140–41; school desegregation and, 210
civilian labor: black women as, 11; in
  Charleston hospital strike (1969), 209;
  comparative wages for, 17, 30–32; discrimination toward blacks, 51; Fort Jackson and, 140, 150, 211–12, 218; job discrimination, 199; military use of, 10,
  18, 70. *See also* labor, wartime
civil rights: Army command structure and,
  105, 122, 135, 157; federal aid to education and, 130–35; Fort Jackson demonstrations and, 3; sit-in movement and,
  154; Truman initatives on, 64; J. Waties
  Waring and, 63–65. *See also* Commission on Civil Rights
Civil Rights Act of 1957, 137, 148–50
Civil Rights Act of 1964, 134, 159, 168, 179,
  199, 243n63
civil rights demonstrations: Army policy
  toward, 160, 164–65; Birmingham
  march (1963), 171; Greensboro sit-in
  (1960), 161; Greenville Airport (1960),
  160–61; Myrtle Beach "wade-in," 162;
  Rock Hill protest, 161; at South Carolina
  State University, 161. *See also* sit-in
  movement; student protests
civil rights movement: "Appeal for Human
  Rights," 166; armed forces and, 2, 4;
  Army relations with, 146–47, 167, 214;
  black separatism and, 190–91; bus boycotts and, 111; bus segregation and, 108,
  116–17; Fort Jackson and, 27, 147, 216–
  17; Freedom Rides of 1961, 164; "Freedom Summer" of 1964, 173; "Freedom
  Vote," 171; leadership issues within, 163;
  Lincoln Emancipation Clubs and, 55,
  57; military obligations and, 195–96,
  198; school segregation lawsuits and,
  128–29; Modjeska M. Simkins and, 52,
  163; social activism and, 54–55, 111–12,
  192–93; in South Carolina, 45, 49, 53,
  147–48; Vietnam War and, 196–97;
  Voting Rights Act of 1965 and, 172–73.
  See also desegregation; integration

Claflin College, 13
Clarendon County, 111, 113, 126, 128–29,
  134, 172
Clark, Mark, 151-52
Clark, Tom, 61
classification for military service: African
  Americans and, 190; civil rights protest
  and, 163–65; entrance examination,
  9–10; and Project 100,000, 168–70,
  187, 190
Clemson University, 128–29, 132, 134, 209,
  216–17
Clifford, Clark, 64, 213
Colclough, J. Clarence, 32, 38–39, 42
Collier's, 98
Collins, Harry, 94, 96, 101, 104
Collins, Lawton, 72
color line, 108–10, 112
Columbia, SC: as "All-American City," 127,
  154; black protest in, 198–200; bus desegregation in, 117–18; Civil Rights Act
  of 1964 and, 134, 159, 243n63; civil
  rights demonstrations, 137, 154–55, 161–
  64, 198; economic impact of military
  on, 28, 32; Fort Jackson annexation by,
  3, 146, 199; Fort Jackson closing and,
  71–73, 122, 148–49, 231n61; Fort Jackson integration and, 1, 78–80, 88; housing discrimination in, 181–86, 213; King
  assassination and, 200, 249n38; map of
  Fort Jackson and, *29;* military relations
  with, 30, 57, 154; off-post housing and,
  174–78; Project Clear investigation
  and, 97–98; race relations in, 1, 68, 95;
  school integration in, 126, 218; school
  system, 124; segregation in, 30, 67,
  107, 137; social activism and, 193; UFO
  Coffeehouse, 201–5; urban sprawl and,
  50; white fears of blacks in, 12. *See also*
  city government, Columbia; civilian
  economy; population statistics,
  Columbia
Columbia Air Base, 12, 19, 23
Columbia black community: black community leaders in, 41–42; black middle
  class in, 31; Central Committee on Civic
  Preparedness, 31; Colored Citizens'
  Committee, 39, 42, 44, 47–49, 53; Fort
  Jackson and, 147; Fort Jackson relations

with, 50–53, 57, 159; lunch counter integration and, 154; Negro Citizens' Committee and, 53, 56, 69, 110; off-post housing and, 177; relations with black soldiers, 12, 67, 95, 107; USO Senior Hosts' Committee, 112–13. *See also* organizations, black

Columbia business community: black-owned, 31–32; "Congo Square," 33; Fort Jackson relations with, 30–31, 50, 52–53, 142–47; Jim Crow racism and, 32; Lafaye-Tarrant Construction Company, 132; leadership issues and, 163; school desegregation and, 210; student protests and, 161–64; UFO Coffeehouse and, 202; Waverly District, 32–33, 112. *See also* chamber of commerce; organizations, black

Columbia Committee Against Jim Crow, 111

Columbia–Fort Jackson Community Relations Council, 144, 147

Columbia–Fort Jackson Liaison Committee, 155–56

Columbia Optimist Club, 88

Columbus, GA, 90

combat/overseas duty, black units: Korean War, 84–85; Liberia, 12; Mexican Punitive Expedition, 45; North Africa, 16; Tuskegee Airmen, 17; WACs and, 51; WWI (Europe), 6; WWII (Europe), 6, 26

combat preparedness: assembly-line concept for, 7–9, 13; black performance under fire and, 6, 12, 26, 100; integration and, 104; prejudice toward black, 151–52; training inspections for, 92–93. *See also* fighting ability

Command and General Staff College, 208

Commission on Civil Rights, 64–65

Committee on Equality of Opportunity in the Armed Forces, 136, 155

Communism/communist sympathizers, 56, 74–75, 130, 229n8

Confederacy, 82

Congress of Racial Equality (CORE), 172

Costello, N. A., 140

Cothern, Tilman C., 96

Counts, Durham, 33

county government: antipoverty program, 199; Clarendon County, 111, 113, 126, 128–29, 134; Darlington County, 209; Greenville County, 209; Horry County, 126; Lexington County, 124, 144; Newberry County, 86, 172; Richland County, 28, 124, 131–35, 144, 212–13; Sumter County, 133; Union County, 126

courts-martial. *See* Uniform Code of Military Justice (UCMJ)

Cowan, Paul, 201

Cuban Missile Crisis, 157

Dabbs, James McBride, 127

Dabney, John A., 118–20

Daniel, Charles E., 127

Darlington, SC, 28, 58

Darlington County, 209–10

Davenport, GA, 11

Davis, Benjamin O., Sr., 14, 19, 23

Davis, Henry, 195–96

Davis, Jefferson, 82

Davis, Steve, 120–21

Decker, George, 69, 168

DeLoache, William, 144

Democratic Party: Columbia city government and, 143; desegregation and, 210; "Dixiecrat" rebellion and, 64–65, 71–73; 1948 Presidential election and, 64; *Smith v. Allright* and, 54–55; SRC Voter Education Project and, 171. *See also* Mississippi Freedom Democratic Party; politics; Progressive Democratic Party

Dempsey, Col., 40–41

Denmark, SC, 209

Dent, Harry, 141, 211

Dent, John H., 240n44

Dentsville, SC, 124, 133

desegregation: 4th Infantry Training Division, 76; 5th Infantry Division, 66–69; 8th Infantry Training Division, 75; Armed Forces racial policy on, 15, 66; Civil Rights Act of 1964 and, 159; community customs and, 110, 156, 214–15; of Fort Jackson, 1, 78–79; industrial development and, 126–27; Korean War pressure on, 84–85; Little Rock Crisis, 126; National Guard policy toward, 84; Project Clear investigation and, 96–98;

272 | Index

desegregation (*continued*)
  separation of church and state and, 152–
  53; and Shaw Air Force Base, 133, 165; of
  University of Mississippi, 126. *See also*
  civil rights movement; integration;
  school desegregation
Detroit, MI, 51, 95, 190
De Weldon, Felix, 146
direct-action protest, 163. *See also* civil
  rights demonstrations; sit-in movement; student protests
discipline and punishment. *See* Fort Jackson Stockade; Uniform Code of Military
  Justice (UCMJ)
discrimination: Armed Forces racial policy
  on, 15, 66, 135; Army command structure and, 136–37; black advancement
  and, 17; toward civilian workers, 51,
  140, 150, 211–12; Elliot report on, 68;
  gender, 52, 70; housing, 173; off-limits
  sanctions and, 136–37, 155–57, 164, 167,
  172; POWs and black, 18–19
"Dixiecrat" rebellion, 64–65, 71–73, 87
"Dixie Division." *See* National Guard: 31st
  Infantry Division ("Dixie Division")
doctors, black: Columbia, 31, 33, 35;
  Joseph H. Green, 70; military, 23;
  Ernest Porter, 177, 192–93. *See also*
  health care
domestic intelligence: antiwar movement
  and, 204; black activism and, 49; on
  black newspapers, 16, 89; of bus segregation incidents, 110, 116; FBI files on,
  56, 229n8; on postwar racial violence, 2,
  58; on racial incidents, 19; racial statistics in, 223n12; stockade reports, 20,
  225n61; UFO Coffeehouse and, 201–5,
  216; U.S. Army Counter Intelligence
  Corps (CIC) and, 191–92
Dore, Henry, 35
Dorn, William Jennings Bryan, 87, 138–39,
  148–49, 155, 241n3
D'Orsa, Charles, 132, 144, 156
Dorsey, Tommy, 33
Dozier, James, 80, 145, 168
draft/draftees, military: African Americans
  and, 7; antiwar movement and, 200–
  201, 204; black mistreatment and, 50–
  51; civil rights protest and, 163–66;

Korean War reinstatement of, 75; peacetime conscription, 6; race-based quotas,
  78, 216; remedial training for, 9–10;
  segregation and, 65. *See also* induction
  and reception
Dreher, J. Clarence, 143, 145, 148
Duffie, Johnnie, 141, 180, 184, 246n27,
  246n36
Duval v. Seignous, 63

education: *Briggs v. Elliot,* 63, 111, 113, 126;
  civil rights movement and, 53, 57; discrimination toward blacks with, 18;
  Duval v. Seignous, 63; Elementary and
  Secondary Education Act of 1965, 134;
  federal aid to, 123, 129–31; freedom-of-
  choice plans, 209–10; GI bill and, 57,
  217; military dependent schools, 123–
  24; NAACP and, 90; National Defense
  Act of 1958 and, 130; off-post housing
  and, 175; Palmetto Teachers' Association and, 31; private schools, 210; Public
  Laws 815 and 874 and, 123, 131–35; segregation in, 30; white backlash toward,
  125–26, 162. *See also* intelligence testing, AGCT; school desegregation;
  schools, black
Egerton, John, 171
Eisenhower, Dwight D., 86, 116, 118, 126,
  148–49, 152–53
Elementary and Secondary Education Act
  of 1965, 134
Elko, SC, 59
Elliot, Sam, 68
Elmore, George, 55, 116
Elmore v. Rice, 55, 63, 65, 116, 128, 171
enlistment: black advancement and promotion, 17–18, 76; civil rights protesters
  and, 165; Korean War and, 81, 84; Project 100,000 and, 168–70, 187, 190;
  racial quotas, 76–77, 85, 232n15;
  Reserve Forces Act of 1955, 150–51.
  See also induction and reception
entertainment: Columbia "Burma Road,"
  32, 67; Myrtle Beach trips for, 99; prohibitions on interracial, 95; segregated
  facilities for, 13, 66. *See also* sports and
  recreation; United Services Organization (USO)

Index | 273

equal employment opportunity (EEO), 212

equality of opportunity, Army, 76, 155–59, 164, 207

equal treatment: Army regulations for, 76–77; *Duval v. Seignous* and, 63; Fort Jackson and, 166; housing and, 174, 182; Project 100,000 and, 168–70, 187, 190, 198; segregation and, 31, 45

ethnic incidents, 207–8

Ethridge, Matthew, 39

Evans, James C., 120–21

Evans, Joseph, 69

Executive Order 9981, 1, 54, 65, 74–77

Fahy, Charles, 65

Fahy Committee, 69, 76

Fair Housing Act of 1968, 213

Fancy, Henry, 194

Faubus, Orval, 126

Federal Bureau of Investigation (FBI), 56

Felder, James, 4, 165–67, 173, 211, 217–18

fighting ability: battlefield experience and, 100; black performance and, 6, 198, 234n43; as "manhood" and duty, 196, 198; patriotism and, 195–96; prejudice toward black, 12, 26, 103, 151–52; 24th Infantry Regiment, 80, 84–85, 89, 234n43. *See also* combat preparedness

Fitt, Albert, 157, 167–68

Flemming, Billie, 172, 192, 197

Flemming, Sarah Mae, 117–18

Florence, SC, 58

Fonda, Jane, 204

Fort Benning, GA, 20, 25, 45, 90, 208

Fort Bragg, NC: African Americans at, 79; basic training at, 18; integration at, 95–96, 98; physical fitness school, 102; racial incidents at, 25, 44–45, 101; Swift Strike exercise, 156

Fort Dix, NJ, 68, 73, 78, 84, 96

Fort Jackson: Armed Forces Day, 146; Army Day, 42; civilian labor relations, 51, 140, 150, 199, 211–12; civil rights movement and, 146–47, 167, 214, 216–17; closure of, 70–73, 122, 148–49, 231n61; "colored area," 5–6, 13–15, 83, 96; creation of, 6, 28, 140, 143; economic impact of, 28, 32, 87; facility expansion at, 7–9, 138–40; Billy Graham

rally at, 152–53; housing discrimination at, 174–78, 181–86, 213; integration of, 1, 78–79, 99, 105–6, 108, *139*; Korean War reactivation of, 75; map of, *8*; noncommissioned officers' housing, *178*; off-post housing survey results, 1967–68 (table of), 186; "pole orchard," *169*; postwar outprocessing, 57; Project Clear investigation at, 96–99; relocation of 12th Corps to, 154–55; as replacement training center, 66–72; school desegregation and, 123–24, 131–35; segregated facilities at, 66–67; state/local relations with, 3, 12, 52–53, 118–19, 141–47; rifle range, *170*; Station Complement, 9–10, 13, 69–70, 231n56; "struggle pit," 106; training inspections, 92–93; "Zero Defects" program, 185. *See also* Columbia, SC; population statistics, Fort Jackson; South Carolina

"Fort Jackson Eight," 204

Fort Jackson Family Housing Office, 175, 180–82

Fort Jackson Hospital, 11, 18, 138, 140, 150, 193–94, 201

Fort Jackson Induction Station, 17–18

Fort Jackson Leader, 203

Fort Jackson NCO Wives Club, 141, 187

Fort Jackson Officers Club, 144–46. *See also* service clubs/officers clubs

Fort Jackson Officer Wives Club, 218

Fort Jackson post commanders: Royden Beebe, 23, 25, 28, 45, 47–48, 50; Harry Collins, 94, 96, 101, 104; N. A. Costello, 140; John A. Dabney, 118–20; George Decker, 168; Charles D'Orsa, 132, 144, 156; James F. Hollingsworth, 208; H. D. Ives, 164–65; Frank C. McConnell, 74, 77, 78, 79, 80, 94, 104, *151*; Gines Perez, 140, 180, 182–83, 194, 199, 203; Duncan Richart, 23; Henry D. Russell, 38; Whitfield P. Shepard, 99

Fort Jackson Reception Station, 7, 21, 83, 108

Fort Jackson Stockade, 20, 58, 225n61

Fort Knox, KY, 68, 73

Fort Leavenworth, KS, 208

Fort Lewis, WA, 87, 96

Fort McPherson, GA, 120

274 | Index

Fort Myer, VA, 167
Fort Ord, CA, 76, 78, 80
Fort Sam Houston, TX, 236n27
Fort Sill, OK, 128
Fourth Service Command: Army command structure and, 9; basic training policy, 68; intelligence-gathering by, 16, 49; MP brutality investigation, 40–41, 47–48; on-post support services and, 11–12. *See also* Third Army Area
Fourth Service Corps, 227n37
France, 6, 61
Frederick, N. J., 31
freedom-of-choice plans, education and, 209–10
Freedom Rides of 1961, 164
"Freedom Summer" of 1964, 173
"Freedom Vote," 171
Friedman, Ralph, 33
Friedman, Sidney, 33, 37, 42–43, 46

Gantt, Harvey, 129, 132
Gardner, Isaac F., 35–36
GCHRC. *See* Greater Columbia Human Relations Council (GCHRC)
Geiger, Will, 38
gender discrimination, 52, 70
Geneva Convention, 10
George, Collins, 94–96, 101
Georgia: Camp Gordon, 59, 71–72; Camp Hancock, 38; Fort McPherson, 120; National Guard, 7; racial incidents in, 61; 30th Infantry Division (National Guard), 5–9, 24–26, 34, 225n75, 244n23; 12th Corps Headquarters, 154–55, 242n54
Gerig, Charles, Jr., 196
Gesell, Gerhard A., 155
Gesell Report of 1963, 137, 155–56, 167, 172, 179, 211, 215
GI bill, 57, 217
Gibson, Truman, 230n45
Gillem, Alvan C., Jr., 76, 77, 80–81, 216
Gillem, Richard Wayne, 196
Gillem Board, WWII relations and, 76, 80–81, 216
Goldwater, Barry, 140
Grace, W. P., 121
Graham, Billy, 137, 152–53

Grass Roots League, 125
Gray, Gordon, 71–72, 76–77, 81
Greater Columbia Chamber of Commerce. *See* chamber of commerce
Greater Columbia Human Relations Council (GCHRC), 4, 159, 212–13
Greater Columbia Relations Council, 159
Green, Joseph H., 70
Green Berets. *See* U.S. Army Special Forces (Green Berets)
Greenville, SC, 58, 128, 160–61
Greenville County, 209
Greenwood, SC, 89
Guthrie, Woody, 60

Haberstein, Robert, 97
Haithcock, Kie, 47
Hall, David, 37
Hamby, Dolly, 211
Hampton, George H., 31
Hampton, John, 44
Hancock, Geoffrey, 193, 195
Hannah, John A., 120
Harden, John, 145
Harlem Globetrotters, 103, 236n30
Harlem race riots, 51, 190
Harrell, Ernest D., 36
Hastie, William, 40, 44, 46, 121, 230n45
health care: black doctors and, 23, 31; black women in, 18; Charleston hospital strike (1969), 209; civil rights agenda for, 57; Green Beret training for, 193–96; Negro Health Week and, 14, 52, 200. *See also* Medical Corps; venereal disease
Hill, Lister, 121
Hinton, James, 4, 27, 38–49, 53, 55–57, 63, 69, 90, 101, 110, 116–17, 125, 127, 147, 154, 162–63, 216
Hispanic soldiers, 207–8
Hodge, John R., 78, 79
Hogan, Roy, 69
Hollings, Ernest, 125–27, 131, 140, 158, 217
Hollings, James H., 129, 240n29
Hollingsworth, James F., 208
Hopkins, Hardy, 35
housing: Army Community Services (ACS), 175, 181; Army policy and, 174, 215; Basic Allowance for Quarters (BAQ),

175–76, 245n3; discrimination, 173; Fair Housing Act of 1968, 213; Federal Housing Authority and, 176, 179, 182; Jackson Homes development, 174, 238n2; McNamara survey of, 180–88, 246nn27–28, 246n36; 1962 presidential directive on, 178–84; off-limits sanctions and, 178, 180–81, 185–86; rank-based allocations, 245n1; Vietnam escalation and, 173, 187–88. *See also* off-limits sanctions

Howard University, 128, 167, 173

Humphrey, Hubert H., 83, 122

induction and reception: entrance examination, 9–10, 17–18; integration of, 78, 222n5; segregation in, 7, 13, 107; training division, 75. *See also* enlistment; intelligence testing, AGCT

infantry divisions. *See* military units

institutional racism, 26, 147

integration: Armed Forces, 26, 75–77, 221n4; Armed Forces racial policy, 74, 78–80, 85–86; Mark Clark and, 151–52; Executive Order 9981 and, 1, 54, 65, 74–77; Gillem Board and, 76; importance of leadership in, 99–100, 104; Korean War and, 81–82, 84–85, 96–97, 100–104; NAACP and, 90; National Guard policy and, 82–84; newspaper suppression of, 78–80, 85–86, 89; Project Clear investigation on, 96–99; recruitment and enlistments and, 150–51; Truman 1948 order for, 1, 54, 64; *Utilization of Negro Manpower in the Army* (Special Reg. 600–629–1), 76–77, 84, 93, 104; Vietnam escalation and, 190; J. Waties Waring and, 63–65. *See also* civil rights movement; desegregation; military segregation; racial policy, Armed Forces

intelligence-gathering. *See* domestic intelligence

intelligence testing, AGCT, 18, 75, 93–94, 168. *See also* Project 100,000

interracial dancing, 95, 100, 192, 213

interracial marriage, 193

interracial relations: military chaplains and, 94; off-duty, 98, 108; prostitution

and, 33–34; service clubs and, 95, 100; sports competition and, 88

Ives, H. D., 164–65

Jackson, Andrew, 146

Jackson, Charley, 56

Jackson, Levi, Jr., 79, 89

Jackson, Mabel, 36–37

Jacksonville, FL, 101

James, Feltham S., 14

Javits, Jacob K., 76, 84

Jeeter, Ike, 42–43

Jenkins, D. A., 37

Jenkins, Lincoln, Jr., 4, 113, 116, 118, 128–29, 162, 217

Jim Crow racism: Anti–Jim Crow Sundays, 117; Army command structure and, 26, 135–36, 160, 205; black officers and, 207; Columbia Committee Against Jim Crow, 111; Fort Jackson and, 215; military patriotism and, 195–96; NAACP and, 111; National Guard and, 96; off-post, 32, 67, 98; public transportation and, 108–11

Johns Hopkins University, 96

Johnson, A. B. (Frank), 33, 37, 42

Johnson, C. A., 41–42

Johnson, Louis, 70, 72, 76, 80

Johnson, Lyndon, 148, 168, 179–80

Johnson, Willis C., 33, 36–38, 42, 46

Johnston, Olin, 71, 86–87, 140, 148–50, 154, 172

Jones, Dorothy Daily, 18

June's Swingmasters, 13

Kaiser, Gene, 22

Kennedy, A. G., 80, 87

Kennedy, John F., 4, 131, 155, 157, 167, 171, 178–79

Kent State Massacre, 204

Kentucky, 68, 73

Kimpson, Milton, 4, 106–8, 117, 212–13, 217

King, Lonnie, 166, 244n20

King, Martin Luther, Jr., 190, 200

Korean War: Fort Jackson role in, 74–75; integration and, 84–85, 96–97, 100–104; Project Clear investigation, 96–99; race-based assignments in, 94; 24th

276 | Index

Korean War (*continued*)
Infantry Regiment in, 80, 84–85, 89, 234n43
Krieger, Andrew, 41–43
Ku Klux Klan, 125

labor, wartime: blacks as unskilled, 5–6, 12, 17; black women and, 18; POWs as, 10; racial unrest and, 19–20. *See also* civilian labor
Laird, Melvin, 214
Lamar, SC, 210
Lander, Ernest M., Jr., 9
Lane, William T., 67
Larkin, Lt., 103
Latimer, Samuel, 78, 89, 138, 145, 148
law enforcement. *See* police, civilian; police, military (MPs)
lawlessness: alienation of black community by, 50–52; black MPs dealing with, 19; postwar racial tension and, 58–59
leadership: bureaucratic inertia and, 105; civil rights movement, 163, 198; drill sergeant academy, 170–71; increasing black, 207–8, 233n30; integration and importance of, 99–100, 104, 215–16; National Guard, 226n79; NCO academy, 75, 167, 173; "Zero Defects" program and, 185
Ledbetter, George R., 14
Leevy, Isaac Samuel, 55
Legion Lake, 25
Lehman, Herbert, 128
Lemon, Meadowlark, 103, 236n30
Levy, Howard, 190–201, 204, 247n46, 248n5
Lexington, SC, 236n30
Lexington County, 124, 144, 213
Liberia, black military units in, 12
Lincoln Emancipation Clubs, 55, 57
liquor. *See* alcohol
Little Rock, AR, 126
Long, Elliot, 59–62
Louis, Joe, 13–14, 60
Louisiana, 25, 45
loyalty investigations, 191–94
lynching/lynch mobs: Columbia Air Base (1944), 19; Elko (1945), 59; Fort Benning (1941), 25; Newberry County

attempted (1965), 172, 191; *Palmetto Leader* and, 31; Tennessee (1946), 61; white justice for, 129

Mailer, Norman, 202
Malcolm X, 191
Mance, Robert W., 33, 35, 37, 42
manpower utilization: black unskilled labor and, 5–6, 12, 17; black women and, 18; Gillem Board and, 76; integration and, 76–77, 81–82; POW labor, 5, 10; Project Clear investigation on, 96–99; segregation and, 67
Marine Corps War Memorial, 146
Marshall, Fred, 28, 47, 51
Marshall, George C., 40, 76
Marshall, Thurgood, 63, 85
Martin, J. Robert, 129
mass protest. *See* racial incidents
Mattox, Judy, 114
Maxwell, Thomas, 145
Maybank, Burnet, 49, 65, 71–72, 87, 90–91, 139–40
McAuliffe, Anthony, 152
McCarthy, Peter, 47
McConnell, Frank C., 74, 77, 78, 79, 80, 94, 104, *151*
McCray, John, 16, 45–46, 49, 51, 53, 57, 59, 68, 89–90, 101, 111, 117, 147, 154, 162–64, 216, 229n8
McDemmond, George C., 18
McFadden, Hugh, 126
McIntosh, W. Legare, 150
McKaine, Osceola, 4, 45–46, 49, 53, 55–57, 89, 229n8
McKnight, Beatrice, 193
McNair, Robert, 209
McNamara, Robert, 155–57, 167, 174, 179, 213
McVoy, John, 44
Meany, George, 130
Medal of Honor, Freddie Stowers and, 6, 222n1
Medical Corps, 11, 23, 223n19. *See also* Army Nursing Corps; health care
Merchant Marine Academy, 158
Meredith, James, 126
Mexican War, 45, 82
Militant Labor Forum, 191–92

Index | 277

military history, 2–4, 221n5. *See also* African Americans in military history

military justice. *See* Fort Jackson Stockade; Uniform Code of Military Justice (UCMJ)

military police. *See* police, military (MPs)

military segregation: black MPs and, 11; equality of opportunity and, 76–77; geographical and social isolation of, 5–6; National Guard units and, 82–84, 96–98; 1943 War Department directive, 15, 66; postwar racial violence and, 2; South Carolina and, 150–51; in sports and recreation, 13–15; 3431st Army Service Unit and, 95, 99; World War I and, 6. *See also* Fort Jackson: "colored area"; segregation

military service, classification for: African Americans and, 190; civil rights protest and, 163–65; entrance examination, 9–10; Project 100,000, 168–70, 187, 190

military units, black, combat: 9th Cavalry Regiment, 10, 23; 10th Cavalry Regiment, 4, 10, 45; 24th Infantry Regiment, 10, 76, 80, 84–85, 89, 234n43; 25th Infantry Regiment, 10; 28th Infantry Regiment ("Black Lions"), 81, 95; 92nd Infantry Division, 9, 230n45; 93rd Infantry Division, 9; 367th Infantry Battalion, 12; 371st Infantry Regiment, 6, 23; 1700th Combat Engineer Battalion, 12, 19–20, 57. *See also* combat preparedness; combat/overseas duty, black units; manpower utilization; training units

military units, black, other: 5th Composite Training Regiment, 66, 230n44; 28th Quartermaster Truck Regiment, 20, 24; 240th Quartermaster, 16; 274th Quartermaster Battalion, 14, 22–23, 225n72; 702nd Maintenance Company, 19; 710th Medical Sanitation Company, 223n19; 723rd Medical Sanitation Company, 23, 223n19; 792nd Medical Sanitation Company, 223n19; 1458th Army Service Unit, 231n56; 3431st Army Service Unit, 69–70, 74, 82, 93, 95, 99, 231n56; Colored MP Detachment, 11; "colored" quartermaster battalion, 11; medical sanitation companies, 11;

Reconstruction era, 6; Station Complement, 9–10, 13, 69–70, 231n56; WAAC Detachment Number 1, 10; WAC Detachment Number 2, 11, 18. *See also* combat preparedness; combat/overseas duty, black units; manpower utilization; training units

military units, desegregated: 4th Infantry Training Division, 76; 5th Infantry Division, 69, 74; 8th Infantry Training Division, 75, 81–82, 97, 101–2, 232n3; 9th Infantry Training Division, 78; 25th Infantry Division, 76, 80; 28th Regiment, 103, 233n25; 40th Infantry Division, 237n25; 61st Regiment, 101. *See also* training units

military units, white: 6th Infantry Division, 6, 9; 8th Infantry Division, 6, 9, 13, 34; 13th Infantry Regiment, 81–82, 95, 233n25; 36th Division, 140; 77th Infantry Division, 9, 13, 230n44; 81st Infantry Division, 6, 142; 100th Infantry Division, 9; 106th Infantry Division, 9, 57; 121st Regiment, 30th Infantry Division, 5, 24. *See also* National Guard

Minnesota, 83

Mississippi: Camp Van Dorn, 15; Freedom Rides of 1961, 164; "Freedom Summer" of 1964, 173; "Freedom Vote," 171; National Guard, 82, 96, 101–2; 1962 race riots, 126

Mississippi Freedom Democratic Party, 55

Mitchell, Clarence, 116

mobilization: Korean War, 75; National Guard, 7, 82

Monteith, Henri, 240n29

Montgomery, AL, 116, 118

Moore, John Hammond, 28

Mordecai, Ronald, 67–69

Morgan, Charles, 195, 201

Morsell, John, 96

Moss, Thomas, 211

Mount Airy, NC, 100

Mountbatten, Louis (Lord), 12–13

musicians, African American, 12–13

Musselwhite, William, 37, 43–44

Myers, Herbert, 43

Myrdal, Gunnar, 63

Myrtle Beach, SC, 58, 99, 162

278 | Index

National Association for the Advancement of Colored People (NAACP): Army relations with, 135, 147, 167–68; assistance to veterans, 57; blinding of Isaac Woodard and, 60–62; *Brown v. Baskin,* 65; civil rights movement and, 111; Columbia bus desegregation (1955), 117–18; Columbia chapter of, 31, 55; Columbia Thanksgiving incident (1953), 116–17; James Felder and, 217–18; Fort Jackson and, 147; school segregation lawsuits and, 128–29; SCOPE and, 172; South Carolina conference of, 4, 32, 49, 90; South Carolina laws against, 125, 147; student protests and, 162–63; Vietnam War and, 190. *See also* Hinton, James

National Association for the Preservation of White People, 125

National Defense Act of 1958, 130

National Guard: 26th Infantry Division ("Yankee Division"), 83; 30th Infantry Division (Georgia), 5–9, 24–26, 34, 225n75, 244n23; 31st Infantry Division ("Dixie Division"), 82–84, 96–98, 101–2; 47th Infantry Division, 83; African Americans in, 7, 82–84, 168, 190; Civil Rights Act of 1964 and, 168; desegregation of, 84, 126; Fort Jackson and, 3, 70, 74; and Kent State Massacre, 204; King assassination and, 200, 249n38; Korean War mobilization, 75; and Orangeburg Massacre, 199, 206, 209, 215; Project Clear investigation and, 96–99; race riots and, 190; South Carolina, 7, 42, 145, 199; Vietnam escalation and, 190; WWII mobilization, 7, 226n79

National Municipal League, 127, 154

National Negro Congress, 40

Neal, Talmadge, 161–62

Neeley, D. A., 114–15

Negro Business League, 31, 39

Negro Citizens' Committee, 53, 55–56, 69, 110

Negro Health Week, 14, 52, 200

Negro Tennis Championship of 1943, 14

Newberry, SC, 86, 172

Newberry County, 172, 191–92

New Jersey, 68, 73, 84

Newman, I. DeQuincey, 127, 162

New Republic, 201

news organizations, 1, 40

newspapers: antiwar movement and, 201; censorship of, 17, 49, 202, 216, 232n20; housing discrimination and, 181; integration news in, 78–80, 85–86, 89; racial depictions in, 15–16; racial incidents in, 5, 25

—black: *Army Times,* black supplement to, 15; *Atlanta Daily World,* 16; *Baltimore Afro-American,* 16; *Chicago Defender,* 16; *Detroit Free Press,* 95; *Lighthouse & Informer,* 16, 45–46, 51, 56, 89–90, 111, 117, 163, 228n55; *Militant,* 25; *Palmetto Leader,* 16, 31–32, 45–46; *Pittsburgh Courier,* 16–17, 19–20, 25–26, 32, 49, 66, 85, 90, 95, 163

—white: *Army Times,* 15–16; *Charlotte Observer,* 154; *Columbia Record,* 15, 25, 28, 78, 88–89, 111, 154–55, 202; *Fort Jackson Leader,* 184; *State,* 15, 25, 28, 52, 78, 89, 111, 154, 202

New York Post, 164

New York Times, 128, 152, 202

Nichols, David, 39

Nichols, Lee, 1–2, 74, 78, 85, 101, 110, 120, 219

Nixon, Richard, 149, 214

noncommissioned officer drill sergeant academy, 170–71, 189

noncommissioned officer leadership academy, 75, 106

noncommissioned officers, black: assignment of, 10, 108; authority of, 20–22, 70, 100–101; conflicting roles of, 23; discrimination toward, 69; NCO Wives Club, 141; off-post housing and, 177

Norfolk Naval Shipyard, 98

North Africa, black military units in, 16

North Carolina, 7, 154. *See also* Fort Bragg, NC

Nuremberg war crimes trials, 61, 195

nursing. *See* Army Nursing Corps

officer candidate school, 18

officer efficiency reports (OER), 102

officers, black: advancement and promotion of, 207–8, 233n30; assignment

limitations for, 14, 22, 66; as chaplains, 14, 23, 94; civil rights movement and, 197; Columbia black community and, 56; command assignments of, 101, 108, 208; as doctors, 23; Fort Jackson and, 51; increased presence of, 99; lack of, 82, 95, 242n32; racial incidents involving, 115–18; ROTC and, 101; women as, 51. *See also* advancement and promotion
officers, white: black unit command by, 16, 22, 66; non-prejudicial actions of, 22–23; southern stereotype of, 22, 34, 67; treatment of blacks by, 18–19, 100–104. *See also* advancement and promotion
officers clubs. *See* service clubs/officers clubs
off-limits sanctions: antiwar movement and, 202; civil rights protest and, 164; Columbia and, 48, 159; DoD policy on, 136, 214–15; Gesell Report of 1963 and, 155–57, 167, 172; housing discrimination and, 174, 178–79, 185–88; McNamara housing survey and, 179–81; MP brutality investigation and, 48; venereal disease and, 93
Olive, Graydon, 144
Operations Research Organization (ORO), 96
Orangeburg, SC, 13, 67, 161, 192
Orangeburg Massacre, 199, 206, 209, 215
organizational racism, 26
organizations, black: Colored Citizens' Committee, 39, 42, 44, 47–49, 53, 227n32; Columbia Committee Against Jim Crow, 111; Columbia Interdenominational Ministerial Alliance, 113; Lincoln Emancipation Clubs, 55, 57; Militant Labor Forum, 191–92; Ministers Interdenominational Alliance, 39; National Negro Congress, 40; Negro Business League, 31, 39; Negro Citizens' Committee, 53, 55, 69, 110; Richland County Citizens' Committee, 127, 163, 193, 198–99, 227n32; USO Senior Hosts' Committee, 112–13. *See also* National Association for the Advancement of Colored People (NAACP)
organizations, civil rights: Congress of Racial Equality (CORE), 172; Southern

Christian Leadership Conference (SCLC), 172–73; Southern Regional Council (SRC), 127, 171–73; Southern Student Organizing Committee (SSOC), 172, 202; Student Nonviolent Coordinating Committee (SNCC), 166–67, 190, 195; Summer Community Organization and Public Education (SCOPE), 172, 191–92; Voter Education Project (VEP), 171–73, 197
organizations, white: Citizens' Council, 125; Citizens' Design for Progress (CDP), 137, 158–59, 175–76; Grass Roots League, 125; Ku Klux Klan, 125; National Association for the Preservation of White People, 125; State Industrial Development Commission, 126–27, 143
Owens, Frank, 71
Owens, Lawrence B., 28, 36, 47, 231n61
Oxford, MS, 126

Page, Lewis, 22, 33–38, 40–41, 43
Pageland, SC, 149
Palmetto Teachers' Association, 31
Parker, Albert, 120–21
Parks, Rosa, 116
Parris Island Marine Base, 125–26, 170–71
Patterson, Robert, 66
Patton, Franklin W., 78
Paxton, Alexander G., 82–84
Pearl Harbor, 9
Pearson, Robert, 39
Perez, Gines, 140, 180, 182–87, 194, 199, 203
Perri, Angelo, 134, 144, 176–77, 185, 203
Perry, Bennie, 20–22, 24
Perry, Matthew, 4, 118, 128–29, 162, 172, 217
Pinckney, Frank, 168, 244n23
Pittsburgh Courier. See under newspapers, black
Plessy v. Ferguson, 63, 118
police, civilian: alienation of black community by, 50–52; black policemen for, 56; blinding of Isaac Woodard by, 59–62; Columbia Thanksgiving incident (1953), 114–17; cooperation with MPs, 34–35, 119; domestic intelligence and, 191; incidents with black soldiers, 56;

280 | Index

police, civilian (*continued*)
   joint vice operations with, 36; Krieger investigation and, 41; and Orangeburg Massacre, 199, 209, 215; State Highway Patrol, 199, 209; student protests and, 161; UFO Coffeehouse and, 202–3; voter registration and, 172
police, military (MPs): black soldiers as, 46, 48; brutality toward blacks, 21, 27, 35–48, 113, 163; civilian law enforcement by, 34–35, 202; Colored Detachment, 11, 69–70; conflicting roles of, 19, 23; as POW camp guards, 16, 18
politics: "Dixiecrat" rebellion, 64–65; domestic intelligence and, 56; Fort Jackson closing and, 71–73, 122, 148–49, 231n61; housing discrimination and, 182–84; impact of black voters on, 210–11; local and state government, 28; military desegregation and, 2–3; officer promotion lists and, 139, 156; open secrecy of integration and, 85–91, 216; Progressive Democratic Party and, 53; racial demagoguery and, 150–53, 211; South Carolina, 3; veteran activities in, 57–58. *See also* Democratic Party; Progressive Democratic Party; Republican Party
Pompey, Private, 22
population statistics, Columbia: black, in 1953, 105; military dependent schools, 124, 131–32, 134; post-WWII black, 66, 73; USO Pal Day, 113; WWII black, 30; WWII city, 28
population statistics, Fort Jackson: black, in 1953, 105; black, in 1960, 188, 214; black, in 1970, 188, 214; black, in 1980, 214; Korean War, 74–75, 81, 99; off-post housing, in 1964, 176; on-post housing, in 1964, 174; post-WWII black, 69; WWII black, 10, 20, 223n12; WWII post capacity, 7; WWII white, 223n12
population statistics, South Carolina voter registration, 210
Porter, Ernest, 177–78, 192–93
post exchange (PX), 11, 13, 66, 140–41
Powell, David, 102
Prattis, P. L., 16, 25–26
prejudice: anti-Semitism and, 37, 41, 43;

black civilian wages and, 17, 30–32; black NCOs and white soldiers, 20–21; ethnic-based, 207–8; impact of integration on, 217; military police, 34–35; newspapers as source of, 15–16; officer and command, 22–23, 67; toward black fighting ability, 6, 12, 151–52; toward black women, 11; Harry S. Truman and, 64; unwarranted statements of, 207
Pride, Hemphill P., Sr., 33, 113
Pride, Ida, 140, 144–45, 241n4
prisoners of war (POWs), 5, 10, 18–19
Progressive Democratic Party, 53, 55
Project Clear, 96–99, 236n19
Project 100,000, 168–70, 187, 190, 198, 245n28. *See also* Army General Classification Test (AGCT)
Project Transition, 245n28
promotions. *See* advancement and promotion
propaganda, 16, 49
prostitution: Columbia and, 30, 33–34; MP brutality at, 37; vice control proposal for, 36; white MPs and, 21, 35. *See also* venereal disease
publications. *See* newspapers; U.S. Department of the Army publications
public facilities: Armed Forces policy on, 153; civil rights demonstrations, 171; lunch counter integration, 137, 154–55; military and desegregation of, 152; off-limits sanctions and, 136–37, 155–57, 164, 167, 172; separation of church and state, 152–53
public transportation: bus boycotts, 111; bus segregation, 108–11, 116–17; civil rights demonstrations, 162; Columbia desegregation of, 117–18; Columbia Thanksgiving incident (1953), 112–17; Freedom Rides of 1961, 164; *Plessy v. Ferguson* and, 63, 118; racial conflict and, 19; railroad segregation, 21; segregation in, 15, 30, 95
Puerto Rican soldiers, 207–8

qualification tests. *See* advancement and promotion; classification for military service; enlistment
Quantico, VA, 98

race-based quotas: assignments and, 76–77, 94; enlistments and, 85, 232n15

race relations: Army training in, 207; black soldiers and Army, 45–46; Columbia–Fort Jackson Community Relations Council, 144, 147; Columbia–Fort Jackson Liaison Committee, 155–56; Fort Jackson integration and, 78–80, 86–87, 214–15; gender and, 52; Gillem Board and, 76; Billy Graham rally and, 153; Greater Columbia Human Relations Council and, 4, 212–13; housing discrimination and, 182–84; Korean War and, 99–100; Nichols research on, 1; sexual taboos and, 117; training in, 25–26; War Industrial Commission and, 51; WWI, 230n45. See also off-limits sanctions

race riots: Camp Robinson (1941), 25; civil rights movement and, 198; Detroit and Harlem (1943), 51, 190; Fort Benning (1951), 90; Fort Bragg (1941), 44; Fort Bragg (1969), 207; Fort Jackson (1945–46), 58, 225n61; Houston, TX (1917), 6; King assassination, 200, 249n38; Lamar bus-flipping (1971), 210; relations with black soldiers, 12; sit-in movement and, 154; University of Mississippi (1962), 126; Watts (1965), 190

racial attitudes: Army survey on, 2; civil rights movement and, 195; "Equal Opportunity Climate Survey," 157–58; impact of integration on, 217; McNamara survey of housing and, 180–88, 246nn27–28; Project Clear investigation on, 96–99

racial demagoguery, 150–53, 211

racial incidents: Army chain of command and, 120–22; blinding of Isaac Woodard (1946), 59–62; bus segregation and, 108–11; Camp Van Dorn, MS, 15; Charleston hospital strike (1969), 209; Columbia Air Base (1943), 19, 23; Columbia MP brutality (1941), 20–21, 35–48, 55, 163; Columbia Thanksgiving (1953), 105, 112–17; Craig Air Force Base (1953), 112, 116, 120; Fort Benning lynching (1941), 25; Fort Jackson (1941), 5, 24–26, 41, 225n75; Fort Jack-

son stockade (1945), 20, 225n61; Fort Jackson (1969), 249n1; Fort Jackson (1971), 207–8; march on Washington (1941), 32, 45; NAACP and, 27, 90; Orangeburg Massacre (1968), 199, 206, 209, 215; Saluda County beating (1951), 90; South Carolina civilian, 209–10; State Highway Patrol and, 199, 209; on southern buses in 1944 (table of), 110; women in, 48, 52, 56, 58–59, 105, 113–17, 213

racial policy, Armed Forces: Ailes Report and, 170–71; Army command structure and, 135, 232n20; black officer role in, 207; civil rights demonstrations, 160, 164–65, 167, 173; Mark Clark criticism of, 151–52; Collins George inspection tour on, 94–96; Columbia Thanksgiving incident (1953), 118–22; community customs and, 110, 156, 214–15, 221n4; desegregation, 153–54, 157, 214–15; equality of opportunity, 76–77, 136; Gillem Board and, 76, 80–81; housing discrimination, 174–75, 178–79, 183–84, 213; National Guard and, 82–84; Nichols research on, 98–104; 1943 War Department directive, 15, 66; off-limits sanctions, 136–37, 155–57, 167, 172, 185–86, 214; open secrecy of integration, 74, 78–80, 85–86, 216; Project Clear investigation on, 96–98; race-based ratios as, 93–94, 105–6; segregated basic training as, 66, 68. See also off-limits sanctions

racial unrest, 41

racial violence: black MPs and, 11; Camp Lejeune, NC, 206–7; Fort Jackson, 206; post-WWII, 2; school desegregation and, 124–25, 210; SCOPE workers and, 172; sit-in movement and, 154; 28th Regiment, 103

racism: Army policy and, 26, 135, 174; black MPs as tool of, 19; toward black women, 51; civil rights demonstrations and, 163; Mark Clark and, 151–52; cross-burning, 161; Fort Jackson integration and, 80, 150; housing discrimination and, 187; law enforcement and, 34–35; legal system and, 62–63; National

282 | Index

racism (*continued*)
  Guard policy and, 82–84; newspaper
  reports of, 16; separation of church
  and state and, 152–53; southern stereotype toward, 22, 67, 100–104, 222n5;
  Harry S. Truman and, 64; white supremacy and, 88
Randolph, A. Philip, 32, 45
Ray, Marcus, 66–69, 121, 230n45
Reconstruction era, 6, 156, 210–11
Red Cross, 14
Reeder, James P., 38–39, 42
regiments. *See* military units
regulations and circulars. *See* U.S. Department of the Army publications
religion, 14, 23–24. *See also* chaplains,
  black; churches, black
replacement training: centers for, 66, 75;
  combat team cohesion and, 83; soldier
  assignment from, 7–9; veteran reinduction and, 81
Republican Party: civil rights movement
  and, 171–72; 1948 presidential election
  and, 64; resistance to desegregation,
  210; South Carolina blacks and, 54–55
Reserve Forces Act of 1955, 150–51
Reserve Officer Training Corps (ROTC),
  101, 115, 208
retired military. *See* veterans/retirees
Rhodes, J. W., 111
Ribicoff, Abraham, 131–32
Rice, John I., 55, 115–16, 119, 161, 217
Richart, Duncan, 23
Richland County: educational system, 124;
  Fort Jackson relations with, 144; Greater
  Columbia Human Relations Council, 4,
  212–13; NAACP chapter, 56; off-post
  housing, 175; school desegregation,
  131–35; white influence in, 28
Richland County Citizens' Committee:
  creation of, 227n32; Howard Levy and,
  193; on-post job discrimination and,
  198–99, 211–13; Modjeska M. Simkins
  and, 127, 163
Richtel, Charles, 47–48
Riley, Corinne, 138–39, 145, 155, 171–72
Riley, John, 71, 86, 138–39, 148, 166, 176,
  234n49
Riley, Richard, 217

Rivers, L. Mendel, 3, 138–39, 146, 155, 156,
  183–84, 241n4
Robeson, Paul, 57, 60
Robinson, Carey, 34, 37
Robinson, David W., 231n61
Robinson, Jackie, 70, 161
Rock Hill, SC, 125–26, 161
Roosevelt, Franklin D., 12, 45–46
Rubin, Hyman, 142–43, 146, 148–49, 154
Russell, Henry D., 38
Russell, Richard, 72, 85
Rutte, Louis B., 121

Sapp, Claude, 61
school desegregation: Ethel Martin Bolden
  and, 4, 113; Civil Rights Act of 1964 and,
  134–35; Clarendon County and, 111, 113,
  126, 172; Columbia, 4; end of South Carolina, 209–10; enforcement of, 126; federal aid to education and, 130; federal
  facilities and, 112; Fort Jackson and, 215;
  Jackson Homes development, 238n2;
  Kennedy administration and, 131–32;
  military dependents and, 123–24, 127–
  28; private schools and, 210; Public
  Laws 815 and 874 and, 123, 131–32;
  public school, 53, 111–12; resistance to,
  124–26; Richland County, 131–35; universities and, 125–26, 128–29, 132.
  See also *Brown v. Board of Education*;
  desegregation
schools, black: Agnes Scott College, 173;
  Allen University, 13, 15, 31–32, 57, 67–
  68, 95, 226n5; Avery Institute, 45; Benedict College, 13, 31–32, 57, 67–68, 95,
  107, 226n5; Bible Teachers Training
  School, 38; Booker T. Washington High
  School, 31, 107; Clark College, 165, 173;
  Howard University, 128, 167, 173; "separate but equal" doctrine, 63; Shaw University, 166; sit-in movement and, 154,
  161–64; state retaliation toward, 125;
  Talladega College, 45; Voorhees College,
  209. *See also* education; South Carolina
  State University
schools, integrated, 125–26
Scott, Emmett, 230n45
security clearance/classification, 192
segregation: black advancement and, 17;

Briggs v. Elliot, 63, 111, 113, 126; in Columbia, 30, 67, 107; Commission on Civil Rights report on, 64–65; equal treatment under law and, 31, 45; Fort Jackson, 66; military influence on, 4; NAACP and, 32; National Guard policy and, 82–84, 168; off-post housing and, 174–77; Project Clear investigation and, 96–98; in public transportation, 15, 30; TDA positions and, 70–71; Harry S. Truman and, 1. *See also* desegregation; labor, wartime; military segregation; school desegregation

Selective Service. *See* draft/draftees, military

Sellers, Cleveland, 209

"separate but equal" doctrine, 63

separation of church and state, 152–53

service clubs/officers clubs: integration of, 95, 99, 101; local relations with, 147; off-duty entertainment at, 14; segregation in, 11, 13, 66–67, 70

Shepard, Whitfield P., 99

Sherard, Austell O., 115–16, 118, 120, 218, 237n25

Shull, Lynwood, 59–62

Simkins, Modjeska M., 42, 52, 57, 117, 127, 129, 147, 163, 172, 178, 193, 198–200, 211–13

Simmons, J. Andrew, 37–38, 42

Sims, Hugo, Jr., 86, 234n49

sit-in movement: Army policy toward, 160, 164–65; Columbia response to, 154; Greater Columbia Human Relations Council and, 4, 212; Greater Columbia Relations Council and, 159; legitimacy of, 196; soldiers in, 160. *See also* civil rights demonstrations; student protests

slavery: military service as, 200; southern stereotype toward, 22; "Uncle Tom" stereotype and, 19

Smith, Arnold M., 161

Smith, Ellison "Cotton Ed," 21, 49, 140, 222n5

Smith, Frank E., 119

Smith, R. (pseudonym), 100–104, 208–9

Smith v. Allright, 54

Solomon, James, 240n29

South Carolina: civilian racial incidents,

209–10; Civil Rights Act of 1964 and, 168; civil rights movement in, 111–12, 147–48, 215; Congressional representatives, 65, 86–87, 138–40; Fort Jackson closing and, 71–73, 122, 148–49, 231n61; impact of black voters on, 210–11; King assassination and, 200, 249n38; Ku Klux Klan violence in, 125; NAACP and, 125; National Guard, 7, 42, 145, 199; open secrecy of integration in, 85–91, 216; Project Clear investigation and, 97; school desegregation and, 124–26, 129–30; segregation and federal aid, 130–35; segregation and voting rights, 65; *Smith v. Allright* and, 54–55; voter registration, 210; voting rights, 55, 63, 65, 116, 128, 171; Voting Rights Act of 1965 and, 172–73. *See also* state government

South Carolina Council on Human Relations, 163

South Carolina Electric and Gas Company, 108–11, 117

South Carolina State Development Board, 126–27, 143

South Carolina State University: black soldiers from, 103, 107; desegregation of, 129; Orangeburg Massacre, 209; Matthew Perry at, 57, 128; Austell O. Sherard at, 115, 218; social activities for soldiers with, 67; student protests at, 161, 199

Southern Christian Leadership Conference (SCLC), 172–73

Southern Conference for Human Welfare (SCHW), 229n8

Southern Regional Council (SRC), 127, 171–73

Southern Student Organizing Committee (SSOC), 172, 202

Soviet Union, 61, 130

Spanish-American War, 31

Spartanburg, SC, 222n5

Spence, Floyd Davidson, 148–49, 240n2

Spignor, A. Fletcher, 148

sports and recreation: baseball, 23; basketball, 103; Columbia community support of, 88; Meadowlark Lemon and, 236n30; Joe Louis and, 13–14; postwar integration of, 70, 235n60; segregated

284 | Index

sports and recreation (*continued*)
  facilities for, 13; swimming facilities for,
  5, 14, 24; team competition in, 14–15.
  See also entertainment
Starks, J. J., 42
state government: "Barnwell Ring," 142;
  Brown v. Board of Education and, 124–26;
  bus segregation and, 110–11; civil rights
  demonstrations and, 162; Democratic
  control of, 55; Fort Jackson relations
  with, 141–47, 150–53; NAACP and, 125;
  open secrecy of integration and, 88,
  216; politics of, 2–3, 28; school desegregation and, 124; segregation and federal
  aid, 130–35; *Smith v. Allright* and, 54.
  See also South Carolina
states rights: community customs as, 214–
  15; desegregation on federal property
  and, 86, 141–42; Jim Crow racism and,
  135; National Guard integration and,
  84; racial demagoguery as, 150–53
States Rights Party. *See* "Dixiecrat" rebellion
Steinhart, H. W., 48–50
Stennis, John, 156
Stimson, Henry, 40
St. Matthews, SC, 107
Stone, Carl, 34, 43–44, 46–47
Stoval, Private, 22
Stowers, Freddie, 6, 222n1
Stroud, Larry, 48–50, 52
structural racism, 26
Stuck, Fred, 180–81, 246n28
Student Nonviolent Coordinating Com-
  mittee (SNCC), 166–67, 190, 195
student protests: Columbia sit-ins, 161–63;
  "Freak the Army" festival, 204; Kent
  State Massacre, 204; legal assistance to,
  163; Orangeburg Massacre, 199, 209,
  215; South Carolina State University,
  161, 209; UFO Coffeehouse and, 201–2;
  University of South Carolina, 209.
  See also antiwar movement
subversion, 23–24, 162–63
Summer Community Organization and
  Public Education (SCOPE), 172, 191–92
Sumter, SC, 156, 165
Sumter County, 133
support services: African American role

in, 9–12; Station Complement, 9–10,
  13, 69–70, 231n56; TDA positions in,
  70. *See also* Fourth Service Command;
  military units, black, other
Sutton, Carl David, 146
Swift Strike exercise, 156
Symmes, Frederic W., 16

Table of Distribution and Allowances
  (TDA), 70
Tallant, Col., 40–41
Taylor, Ann, 218
Taylor, Porcher L., 101–4, 208–9, 211–12,
  218–19
Taylor, Porcher L., III, 218
Tennessee, 7, 61, 154
Texas, 54, 88
Third Army Area, 68. *See also* Fourth Ser-
  vice Command
Third U.S. Army, 78, 120–22
Thomas, Charles, 193
Thornhill, Llewellyn T., 23, 225n72
Thurmond, J. Strom: Armed Forces racial
  policy and, 156; Civil Rights Act of 1957
  and, 137, 148–50; defection to GOP,
  171; "Dixiecrat" rebellion and, 64–65,
  71, 87; election to Senate, 140, 172,
  241n7; federal aid to education and,
  131; Fort Jackson and, 54, 71–73, 86–87,
  142; political influence of, 3, 154–55,
  183–84, 212, 217; racism of, 158, 211
Tibbs, Albert J., 94
Timmerman, George Bell, Jr., 125–26,
  137, 142, 150–53, 162
Timmerman, George Bell, Sr., 61, 118,
  161
Toal, Jean, 173, 197
Tolbert Willie Junior, 89
training: Army desegregation and, 3; Army
  inspection reports on, 92; Army Training Plan, 82; assembly-line concept for,
  7–9, 13; division combat team, 83; as
  economic opportunity, 195–96, 198;
  Korean War buildup for, 81; military
  police, 34; Project 100,000 and, 168–
  70, 187, 190; rejection of blacks for, 18;
  support services for, 9–11. *See also* basic
  training
training units: 4th Infantry Training

Index | 285

Division, 76; 5th Composite Training Regiment, 66, 230n44; 5th Infantry Division, 69; 8th Infantry Training Division, 75, 81–82, 97, 101–2, 232n3; 9th Infantry Training Division, 78, 84. *See also* military units

transportation. *See* public transportation

Travis, David J., 192–93, 196–97

Treanor, William, 172, 191–92

Truman, Harry S.: blinding of Isaac Woodard and, 61–62, 64; "Dixiecrat" rebellion and, 64, 71, 87; Executive Order 9981, 1, 54, 65, 74–77; Fahy Committee and, 76; Fort Jackson closing and, 54, 71–73; Korean War and, 74–75

Truman, Louis W., 120

Tucker, C. M., 149

Tuskegee Airmen, 14, 17

Tuskegee Army Air Field, 222n8

Tuskegee Institute, 101, 218

UFO Coffeehouse, 201–5, 216

"Uncle Tom" stereotype, MPs as, 19

Uniform Code of Military Justice (UCMJ): African Americans and, 20, 85, 102, 207; antiwar movement and, 194–96, 201, 204, 247n46; civilian police cooperation and, 119; civilian segregation ordinances and, 112, 119; disciplinary actions, 18, 92–93, 185; ethnic incidents and, 208; racial violence and, 58, 103

United Nations, Korean War and, 74–75

United Negro and Allied Veterans Association (UNAVA), 52, 57

United Press International (UPI), 1

United Services Organization (USO), 56–57; antiwar movement and, 203; Columbia community support of, 30, 67, 88, 95; desegregation of, 157; Laurel Street, 107, 112; segregated facilities, 33, 224n31; Taylor Street, 67, 69, 112–13; "Pal Day," 113, 157; Senior Hosts' Committee, 112

University of Mississippi, 126

University of South Carolina: antiwar protests, 209; black student application to, 125, 128; George A. Buchanan and, 28, 156; Columbia and, 3; Columbia housing and, 175; desegregation of,

239n29; "Freak the Army" festival, 204; student protests, 201; Porcher Taylor as Ph.D. from, 208; UFO Coffeehouse and, 201–2

University of South Carolina–Beaufort, 240n29

U.S. Air Force: Andrews Air Force Base, 180; Carswell Air Force Base, 88; Craig Air Force Base, 112, 116, 120; desegregation of, 75, 232n5; Donaldson Air Force Base, 128; Maxwell Air Force Base, 166; Myrtle Beach Air Force Base, 58, 99; Shaw Air Force Base, 133, 165

U.S. Armed Forces Commands. *See* Armed Forces; Army Ground Forces (AGF); Fourth Service Command

U.S. Army Advisory Board, 137–38

U.S. Army Counter Intelligence Corps (CIC), 191

U.S. Army Reserve: African Americans in, 190; Civil Rights Act of 1964 and, 168; 81st Regional Support Group, 243n54; Fort Jackson and, 3, 145; Korean War mobilization, 75; race riots and, 190; Reserve Forces Act of 1955, 150–51; J. Strom Thurmond and, 86, 140; 12th Corps Headquarters, 154–55, 242n54

U.S. Army Reserve Command (ARCOM), 242n54

U.S. Army Special Forces (Green Berets), 193–96

U.S. Civil Service Commission, 51

U.S. Congress: Civil Rights Act of 1957, 137, 148–50; Civil Rights Act of 1964, 134, 159, 168, 179, 243n63; Columbia Thanksgiving incident (1953) and, 116, 118–22; Elementary and Secondary Education Act of 1965, 134; Fair Housing Act of 1968, 213; House Armed Services Committee, 3, 85, 87, 138, 146, 176; House Committee on Veteran's Affairs, 138; House National Security Committee, 240n2; integration and, 76, 83–84; military dependent schools and, 123–24; National Defense Act of 1958, 130; officer promotion lists and, 139, 156; Public Laws 815 and 874, 123, 131–32; Senate Armed Services Committee, 85, 140, 156; Senate Civil Service Commit-

286 | Index

U.S. Congress (*continued*)
tee, 140; Senate Preparedness Com-
mittee, 92–93; South Carolina repre-
sentatives in, 65, 86–87, 138–40, 156;
Voting Rights Act of 1965, 172
U.S. Department of Health, Education and
Welfare, 123, 131–32
U.S. Department of the Army publications:
The Fair Housing Enforcement Program
(Army Reg. 600–4), 213; *Utilization of
Negro Manpower in the Army* (Special
Reg. 600–629–1), 76–78, 84, 93, 104;
*Utilization of Negro Manpower in the Post-
war Army* (Circular 124), 76
U.S. Executive Branch: Army command
structure and, 137; Executive Order
9981, 1, 54, 65, 74; housing discrimina-
tion and, 178–79, 213; military desegre-
gation and, 2–3; school desegregation
and, 131, 135. *See also* Kennedy, John F.;
Roosevelt, Franklin D.; Truman,
Harry S.
U.S. Fourth Circuit Court of Appeals, 129,
209, 216
U.S. Marine Corps (USMC): Charles F.
Bolden Jr. and, 158, 218; Camp Lejeune
Marine Base, 206–7; desegregation of,
232n5; Parris Island Marine Base, 125;
Quantico marine base, 98
U.S. Military Academy, 218
U.S. Military Court of Appeals, 217
U.S. military units. *See* military units;
National Guard; training units
U.S. Naval Academy, 157–58
U.S. Navy: African Americans in, 101;
Charleston Naval Yard, 72, 111, 128;
desegregation of, 75, 232n5; Norfolk
Naval Shipyard, 98; Quantico marine
base, 98
U.S. Supreme Court: *Briggs v. Elliot,* 63, 111,
113, 126; *Brown v. Board of Education,* 2,
63, 118, 124–26, 221n3; bus desegrega-
tion and, 118; *Plessy v. Ferguson,* 63, 118;
Smith v. Allright, 54

venereal disease, 14, 52, 92–93, 200. *See
also* prostitution
Veterans Administration, 57, 241n3
veterans/retirees: civil rights agenda for,

57; Columbia Chamber of Commerce
and, 143; Fort Jackson Hospital and,
138; Korean War reinduction of, 81;
NCO Wives Club, 141, 187; Project Transition, 245n28; racial violence toward,
58–62; right to vote issues, 57–58; Vietnam War support by, 201
Vietnam War: antiwar protest, 196–97,
200–201; basic training escalation for,
187; Green Beret training for, 193–95;
housing discrimination and, 173; Levy
court-martial, 195–97; 1965 U.S. troop
introduction, 189
Vinson, Carl, 85
Vinson, Fred, 221n3
violence. *See* racial violence
Virginia, 98, 167
Virginia State University, 208, 219
Voorhees College, 209
vote, right to: *Brown v. Baskin* and, 2, 63,
65; Civil Rights Act of 1957 and, 148;
civil rights movement and, 53–54, 160,
171–73; *Elmore v. Rice* and, 55, 63, 65;
Lincoln Emancipation Clubs and, 55;
Mississippi "Freedom Vote," 171; Negro
Citizens' Committee and, 55–56; *Smith
v. Allright* and, 54; South Carolina, 30;
voter registration and, 4, 192–93, 197–
98, 210–11, 248n24; white civilian
power and, 49
Voter Education Project (VEP), 171–73, 197
Voting Rights Act of 1965, 172

wages, comparative, 17, 30–32
Wallace, Geneva, 37
Wallace, Henry, 64
War Department. *See* Armed Forces; racial
policy, Armed Forces
Ware, John Robert, 196
Waring, J. Waties, 61–65
War on Poverty, 168
Warren, Earl, 221n3
Washington, D.C., 146, 167, 180
Washington Post, 249n1
Watson, Albert, 138, 140, 158, 171, 210,
240n2
Welles, Orson, 60
West, James, 191–92
West, John C., 210

West Columbia, SC, 144
Westmoreland, William, 138, 198, 201
Wheeler, Shelvie, 133
White, Raymond, 36–37, 43
White, Walter, 40, 60–61
white supremacy, 88, 119, 125
Whitmire, SC, 156, 172, 193, 243n60
Whittaker, Frank, 25, 44
Wickenberg, Charles, 145, 154
Wier, Roy, 122
Wilkins, Roy, 190
Williams, Angus, 17
Williams, Arthur W., Jr., 145
Williams, Charlie, 33
Williams, George, 33, 37
Williams, George W., 23, 225n72
Williams, Sam, 39
Wilson, Charles, 120, 122
Wilson, W. E., 22–23
Wishart, Eli, 203–4, 249n38
women: as Army officers, 51; dances and
    social activities with, 13, 57, 67, 99, 100;
    as domestic servants, 31; interracial
    dancing and, 95, 100, 192, 213; post sup-
    port services by, 5, 10–11, 18, 211–12;
    racial incidents involving, 48, 52, 56,
    58–59, 105, 113–17, 213, 238n34; racism

toward, 51; TDA positions for, 70.
    See also Army Nursing Corps
Women's Army Auxiliary Corps (WAAC),
    10, 51
Women's Army Corps (WAC), 4, 10–11, 18
Woodard, Isaac, 59–62
Works Progress Administration (WPA):
    African Americans in, 18; Civilian Con-
    servation Corps (CCC), 5, 13, 24–26;
    Defense Recreation Committee, 30, 32;
    Jackson Homes development, 174,
    238n2
World War I: African Americans in, 4,
    38, 45; Central Committee on Civic
    Preparedness, 31; race relations in, 6;
    Freddie Stowers and, 6
World War II: black frontline duty in, 6;
    black women in, 4; desegregation in, 26
Worthy, J. D., 115
Wright, E. L., 131–33, 148
Wyche, Charles C., 129

Young, C. E., 133
Young, John W., 120
Young, Nezzie, 35, 39

"Zero Defects" program, 185

THE AMERICAN SOUTH SERIES

Anne Goodwyn Jones and Susan V. Donaldson, editors
Haunted Bodies: Gender and Southern Texts

M. M. Manring
Slave in a Box: The Strange Career of Aunt Jemima

Stephen Cushman
Bloody Promenade: Reflections on a Civil War Battle

John C. Willis
Forgotten Time: The Yazoo-Mississippi Delta after the Civil War

Charlene M. Boyer Lewis
Ladies and Gentlemen on Display: Planter Society at the Virginia Springs, 1790–1860

Christopher Metress, editor
The Lynching of Emmett Till: A Documentary Narrative

Dianne Swann-Wright
A Way out of No Way: Claiming Family and Freedom in the New South

James David Miller
South by Southwest: Planter Emigration and Identity in the Slave South

Richard F. Hamm
Murder, Honor, and Law: Four Virginia Homicides from Reconstruction to the Great Depression

Andrew H. Myers
Black, White, and Olive Drab: Racial Integration at Fort Jackson, South Carolina, and the Civil Rights Movement